Customer Value, Shareholder Wealth, Community Wellbeing

Denis Kilroy • Marvin Schneider

Customer Value, Shareholder Wealth, Community Wellbeing

A Roadmap for Companies and Investors

palgrave
macmillan

Denis Kilroy
The KBA Consulting Group
Melbourne, Victoria, Australia

Marvin Schneider
The KBA Consulting Group
Melbourne, Victoria, Australia

ISBN 978-3-319-85477-9
ISBN 978-3-319-54774-9 (eBook)
DOI 10.1007/978-3-319-54774-9

Cover illustration: Alamy image HDE2MP, "Andrei Kukla / Alamy Stock Vector"

Printed on acid-free paper

This Palgrave Macmillan imprint is published by Springer Nature
The registered company is Springer International Publishing AG
The registered company address is: Gewerbestrasse 11, 6330 Cham, Switzerland

Embracing inclusive capitalism by transforming listed companies into enduring institutions that continually seek to create value for customers, build wealth for shareholders and enhance the wellbeing of the wider community

To our teachers…
…for Denis at Lambton Primary School, Newcastle Boys' High School, The Royal Australian Naval College, The University of New South Wales and the Royal Naval Engineering College;
…and for Marvin at Cooke Point Primary School, Hedland Senior High School, St Peter's Lutheran College, The University of Central Queensland and The Australian Graduate School of Management;
These teachers collectively engendered in us a love and respect for both the science of mathematics and the art of communicating with the written word.

Foreword from a Business Leader

BRIAN HARTZER
Managing Director and Chief Executive Officer
Westpac Banking Corporation

One of the most fundamental questions that confronts a new management team is 'what is our job?' Or, said another way, 'what are we here to do – on what basis should our success be measured?'

It's a critical issue to confront because management teams in our hyper-scrutinised, globally-connected world are inundated with competing priorities and challenges from a large number of stakeholder groups.

Retail shareholders, institutional investors, regulators, politicians, labour unions, social and environmental activists, management consultants, journalists, social media bloggers, governance and proxy advisors, equity and debt analysts, rating agencies, and of course customers and consumer advocates – each constituency has its own (often conflicting) views of what the management team should focus on, and how they should make their choices.

Without a clear sense of purpose, management teams risk slipping into a reactive mindset where their agenda is effectively set by others. Or, where in trying to balance the interests of multiple stakeholders, they pursue so many competing priorities that they risk achieving none of them.

In todays' market where every industry is faced with the potentially disruptive impacts of new technology and business models, the potential consequences for companies (and their leaders) of such a slip are dire. Meanwhile, many companies have learned the hard way that a single-minded focus on improving profitability and shareholder value – to the exclusion of everything else – can lead to equally dire consequences in the form of market share losses, class-action lawsuits, regulatory fines and increased oversight, or permanent reputational damage.

As a senior executive at major banks in both Australia and the UK, and before that as a consultant to financial services firms on four continents, I've watched up close as CEOs and management teams have grappled with these challenges over several decades – particularly during and after the Global Financial Crisis. As I approached becoming CEO myself, the question of 'where to focus' took on a renewed and very personal importance for me.

In my case, the challenge was even more important as, during my tenure as CEO, Westpac would celebrate its 200th anniversary. As Australia's oldest company and first bank, we have a proud history of supporting the economic growth of Australia. So, it's not surprising that 'what do you want your legacy to be?' has been one of the most frequent questions I get asked.

As the current stewards of the Westpac Group, our management team benefits from the company's long history of recognising its higher purpose of supporting Australia's economic growth, and of its broader role in the community. Indeed, we've been recognised as the world's most sustainable bank by the Dow Jones Sustainability index for the last three years. We summarise this purpose in our mission statement:

To be one of the world's great service companies, helping our customers, communities, and people to prosper and grow.

It's a statement which recognises that, in doing our job well, we have an important role to play in creating 'value' for each of these constituencies.

Nevertheless, the pressures for strong absolute and relative financial performance are relentless – as they should be, given the relative size of our market capitalisation and thus the relatively high weighting of our stock in most Australians' portfolios (whether held directly, or indirectly through their superannuation funds).

Along with our Board, we as a management team have spent many hours debating the issue of priorities, and how to reconcile stakeholders' competing demands. So, it was serendipitous that around the time of these discussions *The Legacy of Good Leadership* arrived on my desk and I had the good fortune to meet Denis Kilroy and Marvin Schneider. Their book – which has now been updated and enhanced for the purpose of worldwide release with the new title *Customer Value, Shareholder Wealth, Community Wellbeing* – gave us a framework to assess our conclusions. It also gave us the comfort of knowing that our chosen strategy – which was developed through experience, competitive and financial analysis, and debate – lined up well with the more rigorous financial and strategic models developed through their research.

For me personally, the *Economic Profit Bow Wave* framework described in this book helped provide the conceptual logic for what I had come to believe through experience: that despite what many executives and commentators believe, there is no conflict between doing the right thing by customers and doing the right thing by shareholders.

Like the authors of this book, I spent my early years in management consulting. In my case, it was at First Manhattan Consulting Group – an early pioneer in the application of economic profitability to the more systematic management of financial services firms. The logic of focusing on shareholder value and the use of economic profitability to drive strategy was compelling, and its simplicity as a framework was hugely appealing because it seemed to bring certainty and purpose to an otherwise chaotic business world.

I continue to believe that the primary goal of management is to grow shareholder value. However, over the past twenty years, three events caused me to realise that to achieve this goal management teams need to look deeper than a couple of mathematical formulas.

The first was the unwinding of Lloyd's Bank's incredible run of value creation. For years, under Brian Pitman's leadership (as described in this book) Lloyd's was the poster-child for a company that focused relentlessly on improving economic profitability. Then in the late 1990s, it all stopped – essentially their focus on short-term economic profitability led to a complete stalling in their rate of growth. For many of us shareholder-value devotees, this was a wakeup call.

The second event was the collapse in customer satisfaction among the major Australian banks in the late 1990s. Having survived a near-death experience in the recession of the early 1990s, the banks had focused on restoring their profitability through cutting costs, raising fees and shrinking or exiting low return-on-capital business activities. These were all good textbook shareholder value enhancing actions, which dramatically improved the banks' financial and stock-market performance.

Unfortunately, the consequences of these policies for customers were severe, with significant reductions in staffing levels, reduced opening hours, large numbers of branch closures, and higher fees. Complaints about service rose dramatically, customer satisfaction fell, and a negative media feeding-frenzy ensued with a litany of examples being brought forward of bad service, and of banks' putting their interests ahead of their customers' interests.

I distinctly remember John McFarlane (then the CEO of ANZ and currently Chairman of Barclays Bank) recognising how dangerous the situation had become. McFarlane told his management team: *"This. Stops. Now. We cannot build a successful and sustainable business if our customers hate us."* McFarlane subsequently kicked off an initiative known as *Restoring Customer Faith*, which led to significant improvements in customer satisfaction, market share, and staff morale – as well as in absolute and relative shareholder value.

During this same period, Westpac – under the leadership (progressively) of Bob Joss, David Morgan, and Gail Kelly – led the way in embracing sustainability as a key objective, with its famous 'squashed tomato' annual report acknowledging candidly that 'juicy profits' were insufficient if they came at the cost of stakeholder trust (a principle that continues to guide our management priorities today).

The third experience was working in the UK after the GFC had decimated the British banks. At Royal Bank of Scotland (RBS) – arguably the biggest bank failure in history – it was clear that no amount of cost cutting or pricing changes was going to restore the bank's economic profitability any time soon. In fact, I remember RBS's CEO Stephen Hester telling the market at a quarterly briefing that they shouldn't expect to see any dividends for the foreseeable future. *And the stock price went up!*

Hester's insight was that without the ability to pay dividends, the only ways to increase the value of the company were: a) to reduce the uncertainty about future losses from bad loans and investments; b) to demonstrate an improving profit trajectory; and most importantly c) to increase the long-term value of the franchise. In fact, his usual question when a business was beating its profit targets was to ask whether we were over-earning and not investing enough in the franchise!

From these examples, it became clear that focusing on the long-term health and profitability of the customer franchise was in fact the most critical driver of long-term shareholder value. Doing things that drove up short-term profit, but caused customers to leave in the longer term, was not in any company's long-term interest.

Admittedly this was not a revolutionary insight – the *Service-Profit Chain* concept popularised in the mid-1990s by James Heskett, Thomas Jones and Gary Loveman is one example of a similar understanding. But while the logic of these arguments was compelling, for me they lacked a level of financial rigour that tied them back to the fundamental insights around economic profitability.

Over the years, I tried to reconcile and explain this to my teams through the use of CAPM-driven formulae.[1] But somehow, I struggled to convince people that '*(ROE-g)/(Ke-g)*' made it all very obvious! [2]

Meanwhile, there are countless examples of stocks falling dramatically after management missed expectations, so some level of short-term performance is clearly important to maintain credibility with the market – but how much?

Customer Value, Shareholder Wealth, Community Wellbeing, and especially the *EP Bow Wave* concept, provides a framework for both understanding and explaining the answers to these questions. It provides a visual metaphor for explaining how value is created through performance, growth, returns, and the sustainability of earnings over time. In doing so it makes an important contribution to the thinking on the underpinnings of shareholder value creation.

The book also provides a number of practical tools and insights about how management teams in any industry can develop creative and impactful customer segment strategies that allow them to continue to grow the value of their company over time.

Perhaps most importantly, it provides a strong academic and ethical framework to reinforce to management teams that yes – doing the right thing by customers, by staff, and by the community, is doing the right thing by shareholders.

Given the questions that continue to get raised in the public arena about the role of business in society, this may well be Denis Kilroy's and Marvin Schneider's most important contribution. I commend this book to all business leaders, investors, and public officials who want to see our economy and the broader community continue to thrive in the years ahead.

Sydney, Australia | Brian Hartzer
January, 2017

[1] The Capital Asset Pricing Model is a widely-recognized construct through which to determine the cost of equity capital (Ke) for a listed entity.

[2] The Market to Book Formula M:B = (ROE-g) / (Ke-g), or alternatively M = B x (ROE-g) / (Ke-g), expresses the market value of a company in terms of its book value or equity capital base (B), together with its sustainable economic profitability (ROE-Ke) and the sustainable growth (g) in the capital base on which the economically profitable return is expected to be earned. It is well-known among those who have been exposed to the principles of Managing for Value (MFV) and is explored in more detail in Appendix 5. The *Bow Wave of Expected Economic Profits* introduced in Chapter 3 provides a construct that is more representative of what happens in the real world.

Foreword from a Thought Leader in Governance

FILIP GREGOR
Leader of the *Purpose of the Corporation Project*
Co-author of *Corporate Governance for a Changing World*
Head of Responsible Companies Division, *Frank Bold Lawyers*

In the wake of the Global Financial Crisis, there has been considerable debate about the role of corporations in society. It is now broadly accepted that corporations – and particularly the world's largest publicly traded corporations – need to be governed in a manner that respects both society and the environment.

However, this consensus has not yet been reflected in mainstream corporate governance models. These have been narrowing since the 1970s, in order to place the maximisation of shareholder value at the centre of corporate attention. The problem with this model is that it puts pressure on all parties involved in corporate governance, including boards and institutional investors, to focus on the short term.

There have been many negative consequences that have flowed either directly or indirectly from the adoption of a corporate governance framework for listed corporations that places the interests of shareholders above those of all other legitimate stakeholders and of the corporation itself. From the perspective of the corporations, the constant pressure for short-term capital market-oriented results created an environment that presented risks to those corporations and, paradoxically, to their shareholders. In a broader sense, it contributes to rising inequality within firms and in society at large, and to a range of negative environmental and social impacts. As a consequence, there is now mounting pressure, particularly in Europe, for listed corporations to set aside the idea that shareholder value maximisation should be regarded as a governing corporate objective, to which all other objectives must be considered subsidiary.

It was in this context that the *Purpose of the Corporation Project*, an initiative of Frank Bold with the support of the *Modern Corporation Project* at Cass Business School, launched the *Corporate Governance for a Changing World Roundtable Series*. Events were held in Breukelen, Brussels, London, New York, Oslo, Paris, and Zurich. This brought together more than 260 leaders in business management, investment, regulation and academic and civil society communities, with the aim of identifying a series of desired outcomes and principles for corporate governance, that would be fit for the challenges of the 21st century. The key questions addressed were:

- How can corporate governance contribute to robust long-term value creation for corporations?
- What is the role of stakeholders, including shareholders, in fostering a long-term focus on sustainable behaviour?
- What incentives for short-termism exist in law, corporate governance codes and business practice?

The output from the roundtables provided the building blocks for a new corporate governance framework, consistent with the belief that the goal of listed corporations should be *to create long-term sustainable value for customers and shareholders, while at the same time contributing to societal wellbeing and environmental sustainability*. It was also concluded that these objectives can and should be mutually reinforcing. There was a clear consensus supported by empirical evidence that failure to find this connection harms the economic prospects of the corporation and, in case of systemic risks, ultimately undermines its survivability. The materialisation of such adverse impacts is usually only a matter of time.

The roundtables also confirmed that corporate law across all jurisdictions offers considerable scope in terms of the goals and purpose of a corporation. The fiduciary duties of directors are typically not owed to the shareholders but rather to the corporation itself, while the interests of shareholders are satisfied as a by-product of the success of the corporation. And even in jurisdictions where directors owe duties of loyalty and care to the shareholders as well as to the corporation, the business judgment rule entitles directors to take account of a broad range of issues which they consider will further the interests of the corporation.

However, the permissive character of corporate law does not translate easily into practice. The existence of a dominant corporate governance model that gives primacy to the interests of shareholders, has tended to direct the focus of executives and boards towards the pursuit of short-term increases of market value. It is precisely in respect of this issue that the contribution of Denis and Marvin in *Customer Value, Shareholder Wealth, Community Wellbeing*, is particularly valuable.

They demonstrate that even for a corporation that must operate under a business paradigm that prioritises the interests of shareholders, its economic objective is not and has never been to maximise shareholder value or to create shareholder wealth *per se*. Instead, they argue it is to build an enduring institution that is capable of creating wealth for its shareholders on an ongoing basis, and that to meet this objective the corporation must focus primarily on its performance in the market for its products and services. This perspective elevates the importance of the questions of how wealth should be created, what is the distinction between real and artificial value, and what heed should be paid to the interests of other stakeholder groups along the way. Properly considering these issues can create the space for the inclusion of a broader purpose for the corporation in its governance structure, while at the same time providing support for a real emphasis on long-term sustainable wealth creation.

There is some common ground here with the perspective of Adam Smith which is often misunderstood when applied to the reality of the modern listed corporation. Smith argued that by pursuing his own interest as a business owner, an entrepreneur frequently promotes the interest of society more effectively than if he were to explicitly set out to serve society. As Denis and Marvin show in this book, this holds true for the relationship between corporations and shareholders as well.

Denis and Marvin highlight a significant misunderstanding in applied corporate finance and business economics that they see as an important causal factor in some of the unhelpful actions and behaviours engaged in by listed corporations. This is the belief that improving short-term financial performance (and particularly improving short-term earnings per share) will create shareholder wealth. They go on to demonstrate both analytically and empirically, that to improve capital market outcomes for shareholders over the short, the medium and the longer term; the management of listed corporations need to focus on enhancing long-term (not short-term) performance in the market for their corporation's products and services. They argue that short-termism, or the pursuit of short-term financial performance outcomes at the expense of long-term value or wealth creation, makes no sense for any of the legitimate stakeholders in a listed corporation, including its medium to longer-term shareholders. An important consequence of this understanding is that all non-shareholder stakeholders need to be regarded as allies in creating value for customers and wealth for shareholders over the long term, and not seen as adversaries in seeking to maximise profits over the short term.

This perspective would not be new to the students of the writings of the late Peter Drucker, perhaps the most influential management thinker in history.

Denis and Marvin have added a further dimension to this understanding with a new way to think about the economics of listed corporations. This is centred around their concept of the *Bow Wave of Expected Economic Profits*. They show that actions by management that enhance their corporation's *EP Bow Wave* are the same as those required to build an enduring institution. The key element is individual and organisational capability creation leading to a business that prospers well beyond the tenure of the current leadership team.

This shift in understanding may prove seminal in changing the way that investors, boards and executives think about the performance of listed corporations – and do so in a way that is beneficial to all stakeholders, including the wider community and the environment. Denis' and Marvin's work demonstrates that focusing on short-term financial performance improvement in the pursuit of short-term increases of market value is a fool's errand, that undermines the ability of listed corporations to engage in long-term sustainable value creation, and diminishes their ability to play a beneficial role in society.

The period since the Global Financial Crisis has seen the emergence of many ideas and initiatives that each seek to find a way to better align the behaviour of listed corporations with the interests of the stakeholder groups with whom they interact. Denis' and Marvin's book *Customer Value, Shareholder Wealth, Community Wellbeing* is an important contribution to this debate. This is because it provides a response to the key challenge facing listed corporations, namely the pressure to deliver improved short-term capital market performance.

Customer Value, Shareholder Wealth, Community Wellbeing provides a practical roadmap for those leaders of listed corporations that are seeking to build enduring institutions that create value for customers and wealth for shareholders on an ongoing basis, while at the same time contributing to societal wellbeing and environmental sustainability.

Brno, Czech Republic — Filip Gregor
January, 2017

Preface

In many respects, the publication of this book represents the culmination of twenty-one years' work. It is the first of a series of three books that in combination posit a new and more socially responsible business paradigm.

Much of the fundamental thinking that lies behind *Customer Value, Shareholder Wealth, Community Wellbeing* and the other two books yet to come in the series, was formed over a nine-year period from mid-1994 until late 2003. It was initially captured in a draft book that we completed in early 2004 under the working title of *Economic Equilibrium*. At the time, interest in the ideas we were putting forward was dichotomous. There was real interest in the fact that the approach we advocated seemed to produce outstanding outcomes. But at the same time there was very little interest in our idea of a more conscious approach to business.

The original draft in 2003-04 ran to nearly 900 pages and spoke to several different audiences. It outlined a systematic approach through which outstanding business performance could be achieved over the medium to long term. But it also challenged some of the fundamental building blocks of the business paradigm under which publicly listed companies operated then, and under which the majority continue to operate today.

That paradigm has come to be known as the *shareholder primacy paradigm*. It is characterised in many respects by its core belief that shareholder value maximisation should for all intents and purposes be seen as the governing corporate objective for all listed companies, and to which all other goals or objectives should be considered subsidiary. It is also characterised by an accompanying belief that this objective should be pursued with:

- A high degree of trust in the principles of *economic rationalism*,[3] including a clear commitment to the goal of economic efficiency; and
- Great faith in the wisdom of markets and the universally positive impact of competition as the means with which to both encourage economic efficiency and protect the interests of consumers.

The problem we had with the first of these accompanying beliefs was that economic efficiency was being pursed as an almost sacred goal, even though many of the social and environmental costs associated with certain business activities were not being captured in corporate accounting systems but instead were being carried by society. Our problem with the second accompanying belief was that while competition itself has many positive attributes, it is by no means the only way to protect the interests of consumers – and many consumers are often quite poorly informed about the real benefits and the true costs associated with the products and services that they choose to consume.

Ultimately, we concluded that the timing just wasn't right in 2003-04 to introduce this new thinking, so we set the book aside.

The situation changed completely in the aftermath of the Global Financial Crisis (GFC). So, in 2011 we resumed discussions with the publishing community. During these discussions, we were asked whether we would be prepared to break the original work into three books:

- One focused on demonstrating how to transform a listed company focused on either shareholder value maximisation or shareholder wealth creation *per se*, into a truly enduring institution capable of creating value for customers and wealth for shareholders *on an ongoing basis*, while at the same time enhancing the wellbeing of all other legitimate stakeholders (including the wider community and the environment);

[3] *Economic Rationalism* is a term coined in Australia to describe a market-based economic philosophy. Its key tenets share much with the economic philosophy adopted in the US under President Ronald Reagan and in Britain under Prime Minister Margaret Thatcher. It places great emphasis on the pursuit of economic efficiency through increased competition and the unlocking of market forces. The fundamental idea behind economic rationalism is that markets provide better answers to questions of choice than decisions made by politicians, bureaucrats or regulators. Two excellent definitions are provided in: Whitwell, G., "What is Economic Rationalism", *Money, Markets and the Economy*, Program 11 Transcript, Australian Broadcasting Corporation, 1998; and Stone, J., "The Future of Clear Thinking", *Quadrant*, Vol. 36, No 1-2, January and February 1992, p. 57.

- A second focused on what would be required of individual company directors and executives in order to be able to take their company on such a journey; and
- A third focused on the changes to the legal, regulatory and public policy milieu that would be required in order to encourage and support the resultant more balanced and much more socially responsible business paradigm.

We agreed and as a first step, we produced a book entitled *The Legacy of Good Leadership* which was released in Australia in late 2014. This was a limited release work that was focused entirely on the Australian business context and companies listed on the Australian Securities Exchange (ASX).

Not long after *The Legacy of Good Leadership* was released, we became aware of a number of other streams of thought that had emerged in the period following the GFC that each contained ideas that were similar or adjacent to ours. Several people we respected told us it would be helpful for the business and investment communities if we could produce a new and more comprehensive book designed for world-wide release that, in addition to articulating the core ideas that were contained in *The Legacy of Good Leadership*, would also explore:

- Where our thinking fitted in the context of other streams of thought that had emerged which were consistent with our ours, and which had been captured in books like *Firms of Endearment, Conscious Capitalism* and *The Shareholder Value Myth;*
- The differences between our approach and the less transformative though still useful shifts in thinking embedded in ideas like *Corporate Social Responsibility* and *Shared Value*;
- How our work intersected with that of groups like the *Purpose of the Corporation Project,* a European initiative that was set in train by Frank Bold (a public interest law firm with operations in the Czech Republic and Belgium); the *Modern Corporation Project* which was based at the Cass Business School in London; and similar endeavours initiated by the Aspen Institute in the US and by the Faculty of Law at the University of Oslo;
- How the book could be used as a roadmap by companies seeking to embrace the principles of *Inclusive Capitalism* and in so doing, adopt a fairer, more noble, more inclusive, more sustainable and more socially responsible approach to business; and
- Some of the potential impediments to acceptance of our ideas, as well as the practical issues that might need to be considered by those companies

considering adopting the approach to listed company performance measurement and executive reward that we advocate.

It was also suggested that we move some of the more technical corporate finance material contained in *The Legacy of Good Leadership* into the appendices; and at the same time, add something of a human dimension by including some aspects of the personal and professional journey we had been on as we first developed, and then began to apply, the thinking contained in these books.

We addressed the latter by including a prologue, together with a series of short, context-relevant vignettes that describe some of our experiences. They are written in the voice of Denis Kilroy (whereas the rest of the book is written in a joint voice) and are used solely to clarify or provide an additional perspective on situations already being described, or points already being made. No names are used for the individuals involved. Nor are companies or organisations identified. In some cases, certain details have been either suppressed or altered slightly in order to maintain confidentiality, as well as to protect the innocent (and the not so innocent in some cases).

We also took the opportunity to incorporate further breakthroughs we had made in relation to understanding the relationship between the performance produced by management in the market for their company's products and services, and the capital market outcomes experienced by shareholders; and to demonstrate how to make use of this understanding using examples from three stock markets (the Australian Securities Exchange, the New York Stock Exchange and the London Stock Exchange).

At the same time, we also incorporated new thinking in relation to why it is so clearly in the interests of all legitimate stakeholders in listed companies for their directors and executives to resist pressure to engage in practices that have come to be known collectively as short-termism, along with a comprehensive re-think on the topic of executive reward. In parallel with this, a realisation emerged that the simplistic interpretation of the fiduciary duties of directors as a requirement to maximise returns for existing shareholders that occurs in some jurisdictions, has been built on an incomplete understanding of applied corporate finance and business economics (and as a consequence, it has been contributing inadvertently to the propagation of short-termism).

We started work on *Customer Value, Shareholder Wealth, Community Wellbeing* in the second half of 2015. The other two books in the series are now planned for release in 2018 and 2019. The titles we have settled on are:

- *Noble Intent, Clear Purpose, Better Leader – A Roadmap for Company Directors and Executives.* Guiding business leaders in their most fundamental choices, both collectively and as individuals; and
- *Business Prosperity, Social Equity, Environmental Sustainability – A Roadmap for Policymakers and Regulators.* Creating the conditions for a more noble, more inclusive, more sustainable and more socially responsible approach to business.

Puting the Book in Context

In writing *Customer Value, Shareholder Wealth, Community Wellbeing*, we were particularly keen to clarify where our thinking fitted relative to the work of Raj Sisodia, John Mackey and others from the *Conscious Capitalism* movement. They had painted a picture of an end state for individual companies that was quite similar to that which we advocated, but the path they outlined in order to get there was very different.

Theirs was an approach that had four pillars (*higher purpose, stakeholder orientation, conscious leadership* and *conscious culture*), but seemed to us to be focused primarily on culture and leadership. Our approach on the other hand was grounded in a new understanding of the economics of listed companies, and focused more on the nature of the business model and the processes required to underpin it. Over the past twenty-one years, we had found that both cultural and economic aspects were important when it came to building a truly enduring institution. However, our primary expertise lay in the latter.

In parallel with the emergence of *Conscious Capitalism*, Lynn Stout had identified in *The Shareholder Value Myth* several quite serious problems that had arisen as the role of the capital markets had evolved over the years. Originally, the primary purpose of capital markets was to fund sound and sustainable economic endeavour. But over time, the capital markets had become more powerful than the companies or businesses that they were intended to fund. Many would now agree that this development has been almost entirely to the detriment of listed companies and their legitimate stakeholders.

John Mackey and Raj Sisodia had addressed what they felt needed to be done at the level of individual companies. Lynn Stout had focused on the unhelpful behaviours that both the capital markets and some listed companies engaged in under the *shareholder primacy paradigm*. We wanted to deal with both.

We felt it was particularly important to address the way the business and investment communities (as well as corporate and economic regulators), were dealing with issues such as:

- The link between product and capital market performance, and how a proper understanding of that link affects thinking in relation to matters like performance measurement and executive reward;
- The way in which an incomplete or even incorrect understanding of that linkage gives rise to a phenomenon we call *The EPS Myth* – the widely held but nonetheless misguided belief that enhancing short term financial performance will create shareholder wealth;
- The link between customer value creation and shareholder wealth creation and how a proper understanding of that linkage can have a profound effect on a whole series of corporate behaviours;
- The need to give conscious consideration to the nature of the value a company seeks to create for its customers, and how this impacts the way in which their activities affect other stakeholders – in particular the wider community and the environment;
- How best to expose and then deal with the negative consequences of certain aspects of economic rationalist thinking that many still choose to ignore, but which affect the way that the legal and regulatory regimes under which listed companies operate are evolving; and
- How to find a more appropriate way to tax the wealth created by listed companies so as to reduce the incentive for widespread and socially costly tax minimisation practices.

It is difficult if not impossible to deal comprehensively with issues of this nature from a culture-centric stance.

An Emerging Consensus

In late 2016 a conference called the *Creating Sustainable Companies Summit* was held in Brussels. One of the main objectives of the conference was to present the findings of a global consultation process conducted over a two-year period by the *Purpose of the Corporation Project* in conjunction with the *Modern Corporation Project.*

The consultation process involved some 260 leaders from business, investment, regulation, academic and civil society, who were brought together at events in Breukelen (the Netherlands), Brussels, London, New York, Oslo, Paris, and Zurich. A report entitled *Corporate Governance for a Changing World: Report of a Global Roundtable Series* which detailed these findings was also released.[4]

This report provided a particularly clear articulation of the weaknesses of the *shareholder primacy paradigm*, as well as highlighting many of the deleterious consequences that had flowed from the unquestioning way that it had been adopted. It also made a compelling case for change.

A Roadmap to More Conscious Business Leadership

Customer Value, Shareholder Wealth, Community Wellbeing provides a comprehensive roadmap for individual companies to follow in order to implement one of the key recommendations contained in *Governance for a Changing World* – namely to "create long-term sustainable value for customers and shareholders, while at the same time contributing to societal wellbeing and environmental stability". [5]

In developing this roadmap, the challenge for us over the years has been to work with publicly listed companies that were very much aligned with the *shareholder primacy paradigm*, and to gradually transition them to a more expansive view. This involved facilitating a journey of discovery that comprised six principal steps that are outlined in Chapter 6.

As this journey of discovery evolved and was subtly reshaped over the past twenty-one years, we were told many times that our ideas were ahead of their time. For example, there were many occasions when we were told that to speak in terms of *real* versus *artificial* customer value was completely inappropriate and would never be considered as acceptable language in the business community. We even coined the terms *authentic value* and *inauthentic value* to satisfy one client who was particularly uncomfortable with the terms *real* and *artificial* customer value. But in 2010, we reverted to using the words *real* and *artificial*. We did this because we held strongly to the view that if sufficient

[4] Gregor, Morrow and Veldman, Corporate Governance for a Changing World; Final Report of a Global Roundtable Series, Frank Bold and Cass Business School, Brussels and London, 2016.
[5] Ibid., p. 68.

companies elected to focus primarily on creating real or authentic value for customers (i.e. value embedded in a product or service, the consumption or use of which enhances the long-term wellbeing of the customer or end consumer), then there was every chance their actions would eventually lead to the emergence of a new and more socially responsible business paradigm.

Not many companies were up for the whole journey at the outset. So, in most cases, we just focused on helping our clients work towards building the capability to create value for customers and wealth for shareholders on an ongoing basis. We felt that once that was achieved, the chances of eventually going further would be greater – even if the additional steps occurred much further down the track when hopefully, there would be many others expressing views similar to ours.

Content and Structure of the Book

This book is laid out in four distinct parts. The first part articulates the challenge. This is to build an organisation capable of creating value for customers and wealth for shareholders on an ongoing basis; with the ability to do so in ways that either preserve or enhance the wellbeing of employees, suppliers, the wider community and the environment – should the leadership team consider this an appropriate course of action.

The second part provides the conceptual understanding required to respond effectively to that challenge. Some of the components of this are well established. Others are new. However, the way in which they are brought together is completely new.

The third part provides a roadmap for the journey. It contains a combination of process guidance and case studies drawn from work we have done with clients at various points in time between late 1994 and early 2016. We made a conscious decision to embed nearly all the illustrations, examples and case studies in this section.

Part III also includes a new way to think about executive reward that is more able to be aligned with the goal of building an enduring institution that can create value for customers and wealth for shareholders on an ongoing basis, than conventional executive incentive plan designs. (The concepts and some of the practical considerations are presented in Chapter 10. Some of the details are contained in Appendix 4.)

The fourth and last part describes the legacy that can be created by a board and executive leadership team that choose to undertake the journey described in Part III. It also positions our thinking in the context of other streams of thought that have emerged since the GFC, and sets the stage for the next two books in the series.

How to get the Most out of this Book

This book is multi-dimensional. There are elements that are philosophical. There are elements that are creative. Some parts are quite analytic in nature. And there are elements that are entirely practical.

It is designed for layered learning, so there is an element of repetition of certain key concepts. This is deliberate. It has been written in such a way that to the extent possible, each chapter stands alone. This was done to enable the reader to engage with one chapter at a time.

Customer Value, Shareholder Wealth, Community Wellbeing can be read as a text book; as a guidebook; or as inspirational work that confirms the very positive role that a more expansive, more inclusive and more conscious approach to business, can play within a capitalist society.

We trust the thinking and the arguments presented are sufficiently compelling to encourage those in positions to do so, to at least consider taking their company on the first few steps of the journey.

Melbourne, Australia
January, 2017

Denis Kilroy and Marvin Schneider

Prologue

One morning in late February 1990, I was walking along Bridge Street in Sydney with another member of the Australasian leadership team of the strategy consulting firm I was with at the time. He had recently been though a potentially life-changing personal experience. In the course of a free-ranging chat about topics like personal motivation and work-life balance, I asked him what he now thought was the true purpose of his life. Without any hesitation at all he replied "to leave behind the largest possible economic imprint on the planet for the benefit of my progeny".

That statement had quite an impact on me. At some level of my being I knew that the time had come to move on – such was the dissonance his words evoked. As each day passed after that conversation, the momentum towards my separation from the firm I was with continued to build. Eventually it became unstoppable and six months later I resigned.

My perspective in relation to that quite seminal conversation has evolved a lot over time. However, from that point on I have never once aspired to the status of being the richest man in the graveyard.

Parting company with a professional services firm can be made very difficult and my experience in September 1990 was no exception. But as I look back with the perspective and clarity that comes with the passing of more than a quarter of a century, the only emotion I now feel is one of gratitude - because that pivotal conversation back in February 1990 set me on a quest to determine the true purpose of my life.

Not long before that conversation took place, I had experienced a major inner shift. At the time, I was searching for a solution to a susceptibility I had developed to an arrhythmic heart condition known as Atrial Fibrillation (AF). I had experienced AF episodes from time to time since the early 1980s. They had first manifested when I was working around-the-clock as Catapult Officer launching aircraft on the carrier HMAS MELBOURNE in 1981.

The AF condition recurred in my consulting days in the mid-to-late 1980s – particularly when I was working long hours, jet-lagged or operating with little sleep. Unfortunately, I turned out to be allergic to one of the pharmaceuticals used to treat the condition. During the many years that it took to discover this, I suffered greatly in the days and weeks following an AF episode.

In late 1989, I experienced an AF episode that was followed by such a severe reaction to the treatment that I turned away from the medical solution entirely and chose to take the matter into my own hands. I was determined to control the condition naturally, and to that end researched and then sought out a means of learning to meditate. I found the answer in January 1990 – just a couple of weeks before the pivotal conversation took place.

As many people discover when they take up practices like meditation in pursuit of stress reduction or other health related benefits, I began to discover quite a lot about myself. My sense of what my life was about began to change and I found that I was gradually becoming a much more centred and conscious individual.

I had a month break between jobs in October 1990, and used that time to try to deepen my understanding of what was happening. I read widely in many traditions and found myself particularly attracted to an idea from one tradition that there were four primary goals of human life, namely righteousness (in thought, word and deed), wealth (in all its forms), pleasure, and spiritual growth or attainment (for those so inclined).

Over the years, it has become clear from personal observations that these goals tend to operate sequentially rather than in parallel. Consistent with this, it is only wealth acquired through righteous endeavour that leads to real and enduring pleasure or happiness. I also came to understand that while wealth has many forms, there are three key attributes that exist in relation to monetary wealth. These are the ability to earn or acquire wealth, the ability to keep or maintain wealth, and the ability to truly enjoy wealth. I have observed that in general, it is only possible to experience all three if wealth is acquired through righteous endeavour. In other words, it is not how much wealth we have that matters or that contributes to our happiness or our state of being, but the way in which we acquire it (and potentially the ends to which we apply it).

In the business world, righteous endeavour can be thought of as engaging in sound and sustainable economic endeavour in a way that enhances the wellbeing of everyone involved, as well as the wider community and the environment.

In November 1990, I moved from Sydney to Melbourne to start work with the newly established Australian practice of a US-based strategy consulting firm. The firm had an extensive base of intellectual property and a wonderful commitment to developing its staff. However, there were three events that occurred during my time there that in combination, affected me just as deeply as the conversation which had occurred at my previous firm back in February 1990.

The first was a conversation I had with a more senior partner who took issue with me using the words customer and value together in the same sentence. He made it clear that for him (and in his view for the firm), value was entirely a shareholder concept. For me, customer value creation and shareholder wealth creation constituted joint and mutually reinforcing objectives. At some level, this conversation initiated another process of disengagement for me.

The second event was a telephone conversation that I had with a client (an ex-consultant from a competitor firm) in early 1994, which I found so aggressive and so gratuitously unpleasant, that I took six weeks off to contemplate whether I wanted to leave the consulting industry completely. By that time, I had maintained a daily meditation practice for more than four years, and I knew exactly how to use that practice to contemplate a question fully. The answer that arose when I did so was that I needed to move on so that I could pursue a more conscious approach to business. However, I needed the space that the six-week break gave me in order for this idea to arise, to make a decision about it, and for that decision to then settle within me.

The third event occurred was when I returned from my six-week break and communicated an intention to move on. As an inducement to stay, I was offered the opportunity to lead my firm's largest and most important client relationship in the Asia Pacific region. But every time I so much as thought about taking up that offer, I experienced excruciating pain in the thoracic region of my spine. Yet it eased the moment that I refocused on my intention to move on and launch out on my own so that I could begin to devise a more conscious approach to business.

These events and experiences have had a significant impact in shaping the philosophy and the ideas articulated in this book – as well as the other two books that make up the trilogy.

Summary of Core Ideas

The legacy of good business leadership is an institution that not only outlives the tenure of the current board and executive team, but which prospers well into the future as a result of the decisions taken and capabilities established during their tenure.

This statement embodies a fundamental intent that is almost universally applicable within the business community. It is particularly relevant in the case of listed companies led by professional executives who are employees (rather than founders, owners or controlling shareholders) and who generally have a limited tenure as leader before passing the baton of leadership to another professional executive. The majority of listed entities and virtually all blue-chip companies would fit this description.

The most fundamental challenge facing every listed company board and executive leadership team is to build an enduring institution that prospers well into the future – delivering significant benefits to its customers and its shareholders along the way. The purpose of this book is to present a clear and compelling response to that challenge.

The response presented is both practical and actionable. Yet at the same time, it has a well-developed philosophical underpinning that has the potential to resonate with all relevant stakeholders – be they executives, institutional investors, retail shareholders, employees, customers, regulatory authorities or legislators. It is likely that it will also resonate with members of the wider community impacted by the policies, activities and operations of the company.

The first step is to be clear about the goal. Business leaders have many important responsibilities. But even under the *shareholder primacy paradigm* that is currently embraced by most within the international business and investment communities, the primary economic objective of a listed company is not to maximise shareholder value or even to create shareholder wealth *per se*. It is to build an organisation that has the capability to create wealth for its shareholders *on an ongoing basis*.

There is a great deal more to this goal than is generally understood. Its very nature means that the way a company journeys towards it is just as important as eventually getting there. In fact, if pursued with integrity, the journey and the destination can become one. This is because the way a company goes about creating wealth for its shareholders has an enormous impact on its ability to continue to do so *on an ongoing basis*.

There are two essential components to the value or wealth creation mindset that emerges from this understanding. The first is that it is important for every listed company to have a noble intent or purpose that goes well beyond seeking to maximise value for shareholders during the tenure of the current leadership team. The second is the realisation that all the legitimate stakeholders in a listed company are *allies* in creating value over the long term – not *adversaries* in the pursuit of short-term earnings or profit targets. In fact, the longer the planning horizon, the more the interests of all stakeholder groups align.

Once these ideas are understood, it is possible to embark on a transformational journey armed with both a philosophy and a toolkit that together can enable almost any company to reach the destination successfully. At each step along the way, it will be apparent just how closely the tools and the philosophy are aligned. At the same time, a number of perhaps surprising insights will become apparent.

Often the first of these insights to emerge is the realisation that the way most shareholders measure company performance from an external perspective, is both different to, and quite difficult to align with, the way management traditionally measure performance internally. Bringing these two perspectives into alignment is essential if a company is to understand the link between its strategic decisions and its financial performance; as well as how the performance management achieves in the market for the company's products and services, translates into the capital market outcomes experienced by its shareholders. Both these linkages must be understood if company directors and executives are to act in the long-term best interest of shareholders. As is often the case, there is a relatively simple answer. In this particular instance, all that is needed is to shift from accounting to economic measures of performance.

It will also be evident that in most cases, building an organisation that can create wealth for its shareholders *on an ongoing basis* requires that customer value creation and shareholder wealth creation be embraced as joint and mutually reinforcing objectives.

Most opportunities to create wealth for shareholders arise at the level of an individual needs-based customer segment – the same level at which most successful organisations seek to create value for their customers. The key to ongoing shareholder wealth creation is often the efficient delivery of incremental customer value – a reasonable proportion of which is then recaptured through price. However, to make full use of this understanding, it is necessary for a company to define its segments as *groups of customers whose needs are so similar that we can serve them in a way that is value creating for them and cost effective for us*. Once defined in this way, each segment can serve as a platform for ongoing value uplift within which it is possible to establish and maintain an enduring cycle of customer value and shareholder wealth creation.

It will also be apparent that once established, working effectively with this cycle to create customer value and build shareholder wealth *on an ongoing basis*, requires a hybrid form of thinking that draws on both creative and analytical modes of thought. This means learning how to operate in a whole brain state and deliberately make use of both the analytical left and the creative right hemispheres of the brain – not separately but at the same time. This is a deceptively easy skill to apply once developed, and the benefits that accrue from its use are simply enormous. It is the real secret to unlocking and then harnessing the creative potential of an individual or an organisation, and in so doing, making creativity a conscious rather than an unconscious process.

Having embraced customer value creation and shareholder wealth creation as joint and mutually reinforcing objectives, more forward thinking business leaders soon come to understand that they can make a conscious choice to pursue these two objectives in ways that preserve and wherever possible enhance community wellbeing – should they consider this an appropriate course of action for their company.

There is no obligation or externally imposed requirement for a leadership team to steer their company in this direction, unless the company has been set up explicitly as (or transitioned to the status of) a *benefit corporation*. However, those that do wish to move in such a direction will need to have a clear understanding of the nature of the value or benefit that they are setting out to create for their customers. Will it be real value stemming from the provision of useful, beneficial or healthy products or services, the consumption or use of which contributes to the long-term wellbeing of customers and end consumers? Or will it be artificial value arising in large part from the satisfaction of desires created by their company's own 'clever' marketing campaigns?

If sufficient companies choose to extend their journey in this way, and elect to focus mainly on the creation of real or authentic value for customers, then there is every chance that this will open up the possibility of a new and more socially responsible business paradigm. Under that paradigm, the goal of listed company leadership teams would be to seek to build organisations that prosper well into the future through serving society; by creating real or authentic value for customers, by building significant wealth for shareholders, and by doing both in ways that quite deliberately set out to enhance the wellbeing of all legitimate stakeholders (including their employees, their suppliers, the wider community and the environment). The main pillars of this new paradigm are outlined in the last few chapters.

Perhaps the most important point to appreciate at the outset is that each element of this journey is applicable to almost every listed company – from the adoption of economic performance measures, to the application of needs-based customer segmentation, to the use of *Hybrid Thinking* employing both the left and right hemispheres of the brain, and even to the possibility of embracing a new business paradigm. It is not necessary to be a participant in a new, glamorous or high growth industry to benefit from this approach. In fact, it is companies participating in lower growth and less glamorous industries that have the most to gain from the thinking presented in this book.

Contents

Part I The Challenge

1 Clarifying the Goal 3

Part II The Understanding

2 Some Important Truths 23

3 A Bow Wave of Expected Economic Profits 47

4 Two Joint and Mutually Reinforcing Objectives 71

5 Creative Thinking and the Value Creation Mindset 81

Part III The Response

6 An Overview of the Journey 99

7 Valuing the Current Strategy 109

8 The Systematic Pursuit of Higher Value Strategies 143

9 Customer Value, Shareholder Wealth and Stakeholder Wellbeing 179

10 Building an Enduring Institution 193

Part IV The Legacy

11 An Organisation that Prospers Well into the Future 225

12 Conclusion 231

Appendix 1: Exploding the EPS Myth 241

Appendix 2: Understanding TSR Alpha 245

Appendix 3: Economic Performance Scorecards 249

Appendix 4: A Holistic Re-Think of Long-Term Incentive Plan Design 261

Appendix 5: Linking Value with Sustainable Returns and Growth 265

Glossary of Terms 271

Index 277

About the Authors

Denis Kilroy has been a management consultant since 1984 when he joined the PA Consulting Group in Sydney after an initial career with the Royal Australian Navy.

Denis joined the Royal Australian Naval College in 1974, as a member of a class that produced five Admirals. He completed his Bachelor's Degree in Mechanical Engineering at the University of NSW in 1978 while a serving naval officer, and was elected President of Philip Baxter College in his final year.

After a year at sea in HMAS PERTH, he was transferred to the UK to complete postgraduate studies at the Royal Naval Engineering College at Manadon in Plymouth.

He returned to Australia in 1980 and was posted to HMAS MELBOURNE where he served as Catapult Officer – a role in which he launched the last carrierborne fixed wing aircraft in the Royal Australian Navy in October 1981 off the Queensland coast.

He completed further post graduate studies (a Master Degree in Industrial Management and Operations Research) at the University of NSW in 1983 while helping to manage the half-life refit of the guided missile destroyer HMAS BRISBANE.

Denis joined The PA Consulting Group in January 1984. In 1985, he was part of a small group from PA selected to become part of PA Strategy Partners (a London-based joint venture between PA and the then newly formed LEK Partnership). He remained with LEK when the joint venture partners decided to separate in 1987, and in 1988 became part of the team that set up LEK's operations in Australia. He played a significant role in the formative years of LEK's Australasian practice.

In late 1990, Denis left LEK to join Marakon Associates where he first became exposed to the concept of value-based management. It was as a partner with Marakon that he began to develop the idea of adopting customer value creation and shareholder wealth creation as joint and mutually reinforcing objectives, pursued in tandem at a customer segment level.

Denis left Marakon in mid-1994 to set up his own boutique firm focused on a more conscious and more socially responsible approach to business. This involved helping client companies to develop the ability to create real value for customers and significant wealth for shareholders, while at the same time seeking to enhance community and environmental wellbeing.

Throughout the mid-to-late 1990s, he was often told that the ideas that he was working with, and which now form the basis of this book and the two that will follow it, were somewhat ahead of their time.

Whether that was true or not in the past, the emergence of streams of thought like *Conscious Capitalism* in the very different business environment that emerged in the wake of the Global Financial Crisis, led him to the view that the time was now right to launch this series of books.

A keen walker and occasional cyclist and skier, Denis has a passion for philosophy and especially eastern philosophy. He practices yoga and meditation, and is widely read in many philosophical traditions.

Marvin Schneider joined Marakon in 1994 after graduating with an MBA from the Australian Graduate School of Management. Denis recruited him to Marakon, but left six months later to set up his own firm.

Marvin's first degree was in Electrical Engineering.

When Marakon decided in mid-1995 to pull back from Australia and focus its operations on North America and Europe, Marvin transferred to Marakon's London office where he was based for several years.

Marvin returned to Australia in 1999 to work with Jim McGrath (dec.) who had previously led Marakon's Melbourne office, and by then was leading AT Kearney's Asia Pacific practice. After a relatively short stint at Kearney, Marvin left to become the right-hand man to the CFO of the ANZ Banking Group. But after a few years in corporate life, he reconnected with Denis and returned to consulting in 2003.

Over the next four years, he and Denis did the development work that led to the first attempt to bring to life the *EP Bow Wave* concept. But the business and investment communities were not yet ready for such an approach.

After a hiatus of some four years and a lot more development work, during which Marvin also established a practice assisting the state and federal taxation authorities in valuation-related tax issues, he and Denis once again joined forces to develop a more formed version of the *EP Bow Wave* concept, incorporating *TSR Alpha* and the *Pair of EP Bow Waves* described in Chapter 3.

Marvin has a great love for nature and the outdoors. He will often head to the mountains either alone or with similarly inclined friends, to recharge his batteries.

Some of his most innovative models have been built while lugging a laptop around on one of his many trips to the bush.

List of Figures

Fig. 1.1	Basic components of economic performance measures	9
Fig. 1.2	The plan-based approach to managing for value	14
Fig. 1.3	TSR performance of first client versus its competitors	19
Fig. 2.1	Why earnings and EPS can be purchased at any price	25
Fig. 2.2	Linking EPS and EP per share to total shareholder return	29
Fig. 2.3	Short-termism in the ASX 300	31
Fig. 2.4	The two markets in which all listed companies participate	33
Fig. 2.5	Defining success in the product and service market	34
Fig. 2.6	Defining success in the capital market	35
Fig. 2.7	Linking cash flow, economic profit and intrinsic value	36
Fig. 2.8	Linking increase in economic profit with intrinsic value uplift	38
Fig. 3.1	The bow wave as a profile of expected economic profits	49
Fig. 3.2	Intrinsic value uplift through enhancing the EP bow wave	51
Fig. 3.3	Working with the EP bow wave to enhance value	52
Fig. 3.4	Measuring wealth creation with a pair of EP bow waves	54
Fig. 3.5	Wealth creation in banking – the internal perspective	55
Fig. 3.6	A pair of intersecting EP bow waves for CBA and Westpac	56
Fig. 3.7	Progression of EP bow waves for the Commonwealth Bank	57
Fig. 3.8	Wealth creation in banking – the external perspective	59
Fig. 3.9	Distribution of five-year TSR Alpha outcomes for ASX, NYSE, LSE	61
Fig. 3.10	The EP uplift + TSR Alpha construct	63
Fig. 3.11	Sources of wealth creation for ASX, NYSE and LSE companies – five years to 31 December 2015	64
Fig. 3.12	Sources of wealth creation for ASX, NYSE and LSE companies	65
Fig. 3.13	Movement in EP bow wave dimensions by industry sector	66
Fig. 4.1	The cycle of customer value and shareholder wealth creation	76
Fig. 5.1	Hybrid Thinking	89

Fig. 6.1	Implementation roadmap comprising three core capabilities	104
Fig. 7.1	EP expectations in the Wesfarmers share price on 31 December 2015	111
Fig. 7.2	EP expectations in the Brambles share price on 31 December 2015	113
Fig. 7.3	EP expectations in the Unilever share price on 31 December 2015	115
Fig. 7.4	EP bow wave progression for Ramsay Health Care, Home Depot and Unilever	117
Fig. 7.5	EP bow wave progression for Woolworths, Oracle and Rolls Royce	119
Fig. 7.6	Change in EP expectations for Rhipe Limited over a six-month period	120
Fig. 7.7	The product – customer matrix as a start point for needs-based customer segmentation	123
Fig. 7.8	Displaying an economic profit analysis by segment	128
Fig. 7.9	Strategic position assessment framework	129
Fig. 7.10	Linking competitive position and economic profitability	130
Fig. 7.11	Strategic position and share momentum analysis	131
Fig. 7.12	Displaying a current strategy valuation by segment	133
Fig. 7.13	Growing value creating segments	135
Fig. 7.14	Impact of investing in value creating segments	136
Fig. 7.15	EP enhancement and value uplift through resource reallocation	137
Fig. 7.16	Reducing value destruction in fire protection example	139
Fig. 7.17	Reducing value destruction in manufacturing example	140
Fig. 8.1	Electricity supply value chain	146
Fig. 8.2	Progressive competition in a value creating network	153
Fig. 8.3	Regressive competition in a traditional value chain	154
Fig. 8.4	Value-pricing versus pricing for share gain	155
Fig. 8.5	Value-pricing in electricity supply	157
Fig. 8.6	Applying Hybrid Thinking	161
Fig. 8.7	Alternative hot water system value propositions	164
Fig. 8.8	Masonry substitution solution	166
Fig. 8.9	Strategy articulation framework for a business unit	171
Fig. 8.10	Consolidated impact of higher value strategy development	174
Fig. 9.1	Incorporating community wellbeing	188
Fig. 9.2	Coverage of key topics in Books 2 and 3	190
Fig. 10.1	Economic performance measures	202
Fig. 10.2	The problem with non-economic performance metrics	208
Fig. 10.3	A pair of EP bow waves for Sonic Healthcare	210
Fig. 10.4	Potential metric combinations for executive reward	214
Fig. 11.1.	Sources of wealth creation – five years to 30 June 2015	227

Fig. A1.1	Why earnings and EPS can be purchased at any price	242
Fig. A1.2	Calculations for company B (base case)	242
Fig. A1.3	Calculations for company A	243
Fig. A1.4	Calculations for company C	243
Fig. A2.1	TSR Alpha calculation methodology	246
Fig. A2.2	Calculation of TSR Alpha for Commonwealth Bank	246
Fig. A2.3	Commonwealth Bank 5-year TSR Alpha performance	247
Fig. A3.1	Bow wave summary for the 100 largest ASX listed companies (Sorted by December 2015 market capitalisation)	254
Fig. A3.2	Bow wave summary for the 100 largest NYSE listed companies (Sorted by December 2015 market capitalisation)	256
Fig. A3.3	Bow wave summary for the 100 largest LSE listed companies (Sorted by December 2015 market capitalisation)	258
Fig. A5.1	Linking M:B Ratio with economic profitability and growth	266

Part I

The Challenge

From an economic perspective, even under a business paradigm that gives absolute primacy to the interests of shareholders, the fundamental challenge for the leadership team of a listed company is not to maximise shareholder value or to create shareholder wealth per se. It is to build an organisation that has the ability to create value for its customers and wealth for its shareholders on an ongoing basis.

1

Clarifying the Goal

The purpose of this first chapter is to set the scene with two important assertions. The first is that even under a business paradigm that gives absolute primacy to the interests of shareholders, the fundamental economic objective of a listed company is not and has never been to simply maximise shareholder value or to create shareholder wealth *per se*. It is to build an organisation that can *create wealth for shareholders on an ongoing basis*. The second assertion is that the only way to do this is to embrace customer value creation and shareholder wealth creation as joint and mutually reinforcing objectives, and to then pursue these two joint goals in tandem, in a structured and systematic manner.

The legitimacy of these two assertions will become self-evident as the book unfolds – particularly over the five chapters that comprise Parts I and II. It will become apparent in Part III that there are important choices that can be made in relation to how to go about building a value-creating organisation. These choices reveal a great deal about the principles and the values of the board and its executive leadership team.

We will begin by providing some important context.

A Short History of Managing for Value

If we could wind the clock back to the early to mid-1980s, we would find ourselves living in a period when there was no real agreement as to the fundamental economic objective of businesses in general and listed

D. Kilroy, M. Schneider, *Customer Value, Shareholder Wealth, Community Wellbeing*, DOI 10.1007/978-3-319-54774-9_1

companies in particular. Most listed companies focused on profit or earnings maximsation – both over the short term and the longer term. A few had begun to think in terms of seeking to maximise shareholder value. Some pursued the former in the belief that it would lead to the latter. But for most listed companies, shareholder value or shareholder wealth creation was just a desirable business outcome resulting from the successful pursuit of a range of other strategic and financial goals.

There were other important and thoughtful management frameworks in play at the time. They included Theodore Levitt's focus on the ability to create and keep customers as a guiding corporate objective, and R. Edward Freeman's stakeholder management framework. However, over the last two decades of the twentieth century, shareholder wealth creation evolved firstly into an explicit financial objective for every publicly listed company, and then into the governing corporate objective for many of those companies (and to which all other goals then became subordinate).

The Governing Objective Debate

The reason this occurred was that between the mid-1980s and the mid-1990s, there surfaced a notion that listed companies needed a governing corporate objective. Business leaders at the time articulated this need in simple yet compelling terms. The late Brian Pitman (who was appointed CEO of Lloyds Bank in 1983 and over the next 18 years as CEO and then Chairman, presided over a 40-fold increase in its market capitalisation) argued that without a single definition of success, there was a risk that the efforts of his management team would be diluted by the pursuit of multiple goals.

Writing in the Harvard Business Review in 2003, he explained that one of his first objectives as CEO was to get agreement within the bank as to what constituted success. He argued that if he could establish a single, well-defined measure of performance, he would be able to use it to replace the bank's existing array of metrics, which included serving shareholders, customers, employees and society in general. He felt this was necessary because "…such woolly goals get you nowhere because they aren't specific enough to have an effect on people's performance."[1]

[1] Pitman, Brian, "Leading for Value", *Harvard Business Review,* April 2003, p. 41.

Pitman's contention was in many respects a complete rejection of Freeman's more balanced stakeholder management framework. However, it resonated with many business leaders at the time.

As the debate about the need for a governing objective for business intensified during the 1980s, it became a contest between those who favoured customer value creation and believed that the purpose of a business was to create and keep customers; and those who favoured shareholder wealth creation.[2] In both cases there was a belief that if a company achieved its governing objective, its ability to meet the needs of all other stakeholders would be enhanced.

By the early 1990s, it was clear that the advocates of shareholder wealth creation had gained the ascendancy. While a survey of company directors published in the Journal of Business Ethics in 1992 indicated that board members still believed that they had very real responsibilities and obligations to a range of stakeholders other than shareholders, by the mid-1990s most listed companies had taken the view that the needs of these stakeholders could best be met by the adoption of shareholder wealth creation as a governing objective for business.[3]

The clarity of vision and unity of purpose that could be achieved in a business when the interests of shareholders are considered paramount was actually first set out some 30 years earlier, in an article entitled *The Chief Shows Them How at Indian Head* that was published in *Fortune* magazine in May 1962.

Indian Head Mills was a US textiles company that could trace its roots back to the 1820s. But between 1954 and 1962, it diversified away from textiles into a number of other unrelated businesses. In 1962 it exited the textiles industry altogether, in search of higher returns for its shareholders. The article in *Fortune* magazine provided quite an insight into the mindset of the company's management at the time that decision was made.

> The objective of our company is to increase the intrinsic value of our common stock. We are not in business to grow bigger for the sake of size, not to become more diversified, not to make the most or best of anything, not to provide jobs,

[2] One of the main advocates of customer value creation as a governing objective was Theodore Levitt (see Levitt, Theodore, *The Marketing Imagination*, Free Press, New York, 1983). The main advocates of shareholder wealth creation as a governing objective were value-based consulting firms like Marakon Associates, Stern Stewart & Co and Alcar, together with the academics that stood behind them such as Dr Bill Alberts, Joel Stern and Professor Al Rappaport.

[3] Wang, J., and Dewhirst, H.D., "Boards of Directors and Stakeholder Orientation", *Journal of Business Ethics*, Vol. 11, No. 2, 1992, pp. 115–123.

> have the most modern plants, the happiest customers, lead in new product development, or to achieve any other status which has no relation to the economic use of capital. Any or all of these may be, from time to time, a means to our objective, but means and ends must never be confused. We are in business solely to improve the inherent value of the common stockholders' equity in the company.[4]

The idea that the sole purpose of a business is to create wealth for its shareholders was no doubt quite radical in 1962. But it was not by the mid-1990s. To many business leaders, it made enormous sense to focus the entire organisation on one overriding goal. It offered a straightforward and defensible rationale for dealing with competing stakeholder interests – particularly over the short term. At the same time, the adoption of shareholder wealth creation as a governing objective began to provide a unifying theme for one side of an emerging debate between those whose primary interest was wealth creation through greater economic development, and those more concerned with environmental sustainability and social cohesion. The reason it did so is that within all economic activity, regardless of its nature, there exists the potential for conflict with social objectives along three principle dimensions – namely the impact of that activity on the long-term wellbeing of certain individuals, the wider community and the environment. Resolving these conflicts involves trade-offs and decisions that are basically ethical in nature.

A single governing objective simplifies matters for companies to a significant degree. When there is a governing objective, and particularly when the pursuit of that objective starts to become enshrined in corporate law, many of the potential dilemmas associated with these trade-offs simply do not arise. Or if they do, they can more easily be set aside.

Since the late 1990s, there has been widespread agreement that the fundamental economic objective of the board and executive leadership team of every listed company is to create shareholder wealth. However, the question of how that wealth should be created, and what heed should be paid to the interests of other stakeholder groups along the way, is still unresolved and has remained something of a conceptual frontier.

In parallel with this shift towards shareholder primacy came the development of a comprehensive management philosophy known initially as value-

[4] This quotation was drawn from the Indian Head Mills Company Manual. It was used in an article entitled "The Chief Shows Them How at Indian Head" in the May 1962 edition of Fortune Magazine, (pp. 129–130), and was used widely in training material produced by Marakon Associates in the 1980s and 1990s. It was reproduced in McTaggart, Kontes and Mankins, *The Value Imperative*, Free Press, 1994, p. 8.

based management (VBM) and later as managing for value (MFV). MFV sought to understand and explain how strategic decisions affected financial performance in the market for a company's products and services, and how product and service market performance impacted the capital market outcomes experienced by shareholders.

Ultimately, the goal was to develop a structured and replicable means by which a management team could systematically enhance the value of the business or businesses for which it was responsible, and in so doing improve the total return achieved by shareholders in the form of the combination of dividends and share price appreciation.

Three Perspectives on Value

Before we look more closely at MFV, it is important to acknowledge the different ways to think about the value of a listed company. There are three fundamental perspectives.

The first perspective is book value. Book value measures the equity capital employed in a business and recorded on the balance sheet. It captures the shareholder's funds that are physically employed in the business, and comprises mainly contributed capital and retained profits.[5]

The second perspective is market value or market capitalisation. This is the value that the capital markets have placed on the company, and which can be observed in the price of a company's shares. It is the value that investors are prepared to pay for a share in the company at a particular point in time, or the capital market's view of the value of the strategy being pursued by management.

The third perspective is intrinsic value. Intrinsic value is the underlying value of the business or businesses owned or controlled by the listed company. It is an internal view of value developed by management based on their best estimate of future financial performance – taking account of the strategy, the competitive position and the underlying economics of each business. In a sense, it is the value at which the board and executive team are seeking to sell their strategy to the capital market. Importantly, it is free from the often-capricious influence of market sentiment.

[5] Relatively recent changes to accounting standards have resulted in asset revaluations having an increasingly large impact on book value. While no doubt introduced with good intentions, these changes make it more difficult to understand the true economics of a business and serve as an impediment to the goal of building a value-creating organisation.

Not every listed company understands its intrinsic value. In fact, many boards and executive leadership teams only set out to determine the intrinsic value of their business or businesses when confronted with a takeover bid or when approached by private equity investors. However, companies that employ an MFV philosophy generally have a good understanding of the intrinsic value of each and every part of their business. We refer to these as value-managed companies.

The Metric-Based Economic Engine Approach to MFV

The idea of managing a business or a portfolio of businesses so as to systematically enhance intrinsic value emerged in the late 1970s and early 1980s when a relatively small number of prominent US corporations were just beginning to embrace shareholder wealth creation as an explicit corporate objective. Having adopted shareholder wealth creation as a high-level goal, their boards and executive leadership teams were looking for ways to align the actions of their management and staff with that goal. Until then, it was generally accepted that increasing profit or earnings meant increasing shareholder wealth. However, the early adopters of MFV quickly realised this was not necessarily the case.

Before the advent of MFV, most investors used price earnings (P/E) multiples to link market value to earnings, and those executives that were set value creation goals by their boards generally translated those goals into earnings or earnings growth targets. With the introduction of MFV came the realisation that P/E ratios were simply a way to describe the market value of a listed company, and not a way to determine value. At the same time, it became apparent that there was no real causal relationship between earnings and market value, or between earnings growth and shareholder wealth creation.

Traditional measures like earnings, earnings per share (EPS) and EPS growth were shown to have a quite poor correlation with both market capitalisation and changes in market capitalisation. This is because pure earnings-based measures are incomplete. They ignore both the amount and the cost of the capital required to achieve a given level of earnings or earnings growth – or a particular value outcome. Just how much of the economics of a business is ignored by earnings-based measures is evident in Fig. 1.1.

As a consequence of this realisation, a series of what became known as value-based performance metrics were developed. These were really just economic as distinct from accounting measures of performance, and the simplest and in many ways the most useful were the twin concepts of

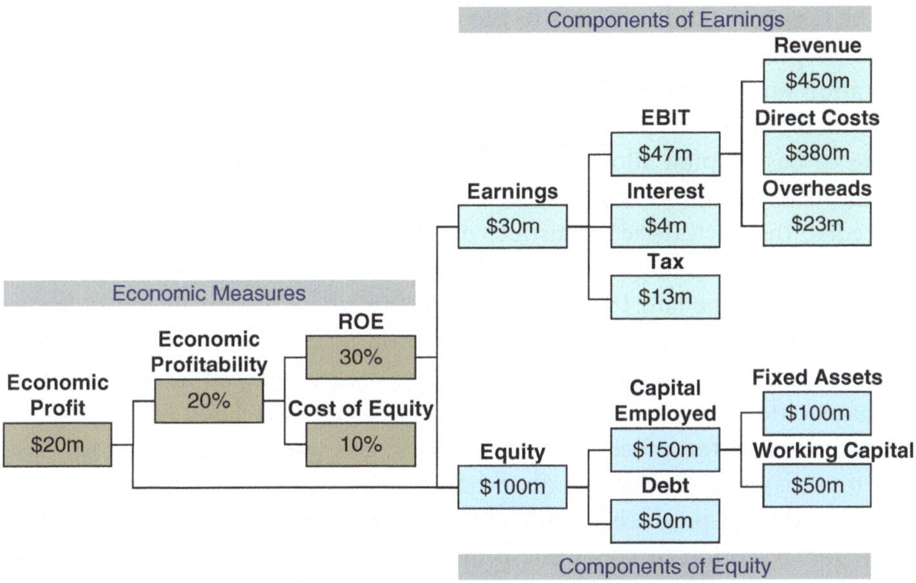

Fig. 1.1 Basic components of economic performance measures

economic profit (EP) and economic profitability (EPy). These two measures are illustrated on the left-hand side of Fig. 1.1.[6]

The 1980s and early 1990s also saw a number of proprietary variants of return on investment, economic profitability and economic profit developed by various consulting firms. The most popular of these were *economic value added* (EVA) devised by Stern Stewart & Co. and *cash flow return on investment* (CFROI), which was devised by HOLT Value Associates.

In many cases these measures introduced unnecessary complexity in the form of adjustments to financial statements and management accounts that ultimately served as impediments to their adoption. For example, CFROI proved quite effective in explaining movements in a company's share price and market capitalisation over a given measurement period. But its sophistication (and its complexity) also meant that over time, it became more popular with the professional investment community than with operating managers, who found it difficult to understand and therefore challenging to implement.[7]

---

[6] Under an equity capital construct, economic profitability is defined as return on equity (ROE) less the cost of equity (Ke). Under a total capital construct, it is defined as the return on capital (ROC) less the weighted average cost of capital (WACC).

[7] Barbera, M., and Coyte, R., *Shareholder Value Demystified: An Explanation of Methodologies and Use*, University of New South Wales Press, Sydney, 1999.

The reason that adjustments to accounts were required in order to employ these proprietary metrics was that they were being used for both capital allocation and performance measurement purposes – with a benchmark of zero often being interpreted as value preservation. It is rarely if ever appropriate to base capital allocation decisions on single period financial performance metrics – no matter how sophisticated. A multiple period perspective is needed. In effect, these sophisticated proprietary metrics were single period measures masquerading as multiple period ones.[8,9]

Throughout the late 1980s and early 1990s, there was an ongoing debate between the proponents of the various proprietary metrics. Much of this debate focused on two questions: which was the best way to measure returns to shareholders; and which metric was most closely correlated with historical stock market performance? In many respects, this was a debate about the best way to measure performance rather than the best way to create wealth. In any event, it did not produce a winner because the metrics were all proprietary. With the exception of economic profit and economic profitability, they all belonged to various consulting firms who adopted quite entrenched positions.

Throughout the 1980s and early 1990s MFV took many different forms but the differences were fairly superficial. Each approach comprised a series of business processes built around a particular performance metric. Some included an incentive scheme for senior management that was linked directly to performance measured using that metric (such as Stern Stewart's *EVA Bonus Bank*). At the core of each approach stood the idea that once the analytical mechanism that lay behind shareholder wealth creation was understood, processes and systems could be put in place that would enable management to align their entire organisation with the economic interests of shareholders.

[8] These metrics were intended for use as single period performance measures by those who devised them. But in practice, many companies used them for both performance measurement and capital allocation.

[9] Single period measures should never be used for capital allocation – no matter how sophisticated the measure. In every company that is seeking to systematically enhance the value of the capital its shareholders have invested, capital should be allocated on the basis of the expected value uplift or the shareholder wealth that is expected to be created, through the pursuit of a particular strategy. Once it has been determined which strategy represents the highest value alternative for the business, the strategy is adopted and a business plan built around it. That plan will always include a forecast income statement (or P&L), a forecast balance sheet and forecast cash flow statement for each year of the plan. From these inputs, we can determine the expected economic profitability and the expected economic profit in each forecast year. So, the business plan provides the appropriate benchmarks for each of these measures in each period – with no adjustments to management accounts required, other than to apply a charge for equity capital. Under this approach, the benchmark for economic profitability and economic profit need not be zero. In fact, they are generally not zero.

To most interested observers this seemed logical and appropriate, and there is no doubt that many companies had great success in using this metric-based "economic engine" approach to enhance business performance over the short to medium term. However, there was an underlying paradox. Focusing intensely on finding ways to improve performance as measured by management's chosen metric could help them achieve better financial outcomes under their current strategy. But at the same time, it tended to obscure the steps that needed to be taken in order to continue to enhance performance over time – and in particular to determine what needed to be done to build an organisation that could create wealth for shareholders on an ongoing basis.

Another source of concern regarding the behaviours that tended to emerge under the metric-based approach stemmed from the fact that it tended to result in non-shareholder stakeholders being considered adversaries in the pursuit of short-term financial performance improvement, rather than as allies in creating value over the longer term. This mindset manifested in many ways. One particularly insidious example was the practice of delaying payments to suppliers so as to reduce working capital requirements.

As the EVA framework in particular grew in popularity during the late 1980s and early 1990s, more and more companies began delaying payments to suppliers, and particularly to smaller suppliers who were unlikely to be able to raise their prices to recover the additional economic cost associated with slower payment.[10] This policy did enable the companies that adopted it to reduce their working capital and (at least in the short term) increase EVA at the expense of their suppliers. In some situations, this did result in an increase in share price. But such increases were often not sustained. In any event, it did nothing to help these companies to continue to create shareholder wealth beyond the initial impact of the working capital reduction initiative. It also tended to damage relationships with suppliers and in some cases caused them significant harm.

Another source of frustration with this approach stemmed from the fact that it tended to keep drawing management back to the pursuit of cost reduction and capital efficiency gains as the easiest way to improve EVA. This was particularly true in those companies that used single period EVA, or EVA over two to three years, as the basis for capital allocation. Value driver analysis could demonstrate clearly the short-term impact of a particular cost

[10] There is no intention here to "pick on" EVA. It was simply the most popular of the proprietary metrics and became the most common term used to represent economic profit, in the same way that the brand name Hoover became the way many referred to a vacuum cleaner in the 1950s and 1960s.

reduction or capital efficiency initiative. So there tended to be constant downward pressure on costs, working capital and other forms of investment.

Most business unit managers knew that they could not continue to grow EVA just by reducing costs and constraining capital investment. But in EVA-focused companies, they were often subjected to a good deal of pressure from the corporate centre to pursue such initiatives anyway. In many cases, sound investments in new and potentially higher value strategies were put off or even abandoned because to proceed would mean a lower EVA over the first year or two.

With the benefit of hindsight, it was quite naïve to think that a business could be regarded as an economic engine that just needed to be tuned to enhance its value and create shareholder wealth (by adjusting the variables that drove economic profitability and growth, and which came to be known as value drivers). Such thinking actually tended to limit management thinking to quite mechanistic responses to their performance challenges. While informed by a myriad of DuPont charts and driver trees, it produced responses that were in most cases restricted to the confines of the current strategy. It soon ran out of steam.

In 2002, I had a team working in Singapore and on one occasion, we accompanied a client to a meeting with the management of a large logistics company.

As we made our way to the meeting room, I noticed that a lot of lights were turned off on the floor. I initially thought it was an energy saving system and that the lights would come on again when movement was detected. But I then noticed that staff were working in the areas where the lights were switched off. So that was not the reason.

At the end of the meeting, I asked one of our hosts why half the lights were turned off. The response was a real surprise. I was told: "It's part of our EVA improvement program. We can improve EVA significantly by only having half the lights turned on."

The Plan-Based Approach to MFV

In the mid-1990s, a shift began to occur away from the metric-based economic engine approach, towards a somewhat more holistic perspective centred on the strategic planning process. This plan-based approach comprised an integrated approach to strategic planning, resource allocation and performance management that was centred on the identification and successful implementation of higher value strategies.

At the core of this approach was the understanding that the value of a business depended upon the strategy that its management team chose to pursue. The idea was that a management team could value its business under both the current strategy and a series of alternative strategies, and then choose between them based on value.

Importantly, the plan-based approach focused almost entirely on long term performance. The choice between alternative strategies was not based on next year's earnings or on the expected EVA outcome over the next three years. It was based on intrinsic value – capturing expectations of future financial performance over the long term.

The shift towards this approach gained momentum with the publication of *The Value Imperative* by McTaggart, Kontes and Mankins in 1994.[11] Jim McTaggart and the late Peter Kontes were two of the founders of Marakon Associates, the firm that first developed the plan-based approach.

The plan-based approach offered a more positive path forward for both management and shareholders. It dominated the development of MFV throughout the 1990s and beyond. It comprised four core elements, which are illustrated in Fig. 1.2.

The elements were: a management philosophy that embraced shareholder wealth creation as the primary economic objective; a decision-making framework that used value uplift as a basis for choosing between alternative strategies; a resource allocation mechanism or internal capital market that funded the chosen or value-maximising strategy of each business unit, providing the resources required in order to implement the strategy successfully; and a performance management system structured around ensuring the successful implementation of that strategy.

As Fig. 1.2 suggests, it was always intended that the plan-based approach incorporate an appropriately structured executive reward plan. But despite the attention that this topic has received over many years, there are still very few executive incentive plans that encourage, reinforce or reward behaviours consistent with building an organisation capable of creating wealth for shareholders on an ongoing basis. The quite fundamental shift in thinking required to design incentive plans that encourage and reward such behaviour is outlined in Chapter 10.

In July 2001, Boulos, Haspeslagh and Noda from INSEAD published the results of a two-year global study of the use of MFV. Their work showed

[11] McTaggart, Kontes and Mankins, The *Value Imperative*, Free Press, 1994.

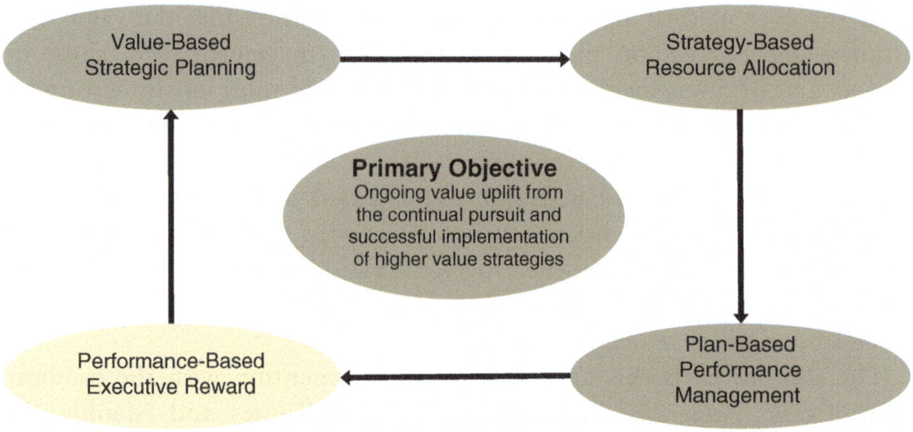

Fig. 1.2 The plan-based approach to managing for value

conclusively that the most successful value-managed companies had adopted a version of MFV that was consistent with the principles of the plan-based approach, rather than the economic engine approach. Most had sought to put in place a series of processes aimed at focusing their businesses on the identification and successful implementation of what they considered to be the value-maximising strategy for their business.[12]

Managing for Value on an Ongoing Basis

An important aspect of the plan-based approach advocated by McTaggart, Kontes and Mankins was that it incorporated a more enlightened understanding of the concept and the role of value drivers than those who advocated an entirely mechanistic approach. McTaggart et al. regarded organisational capabilities as the key determinants of a business' ability to create shareholder wealth, and saw them as the true drivers of value over the longer term.

Wealth creation occurs when there is an increase in financial performance expectations that is reflected in a new and higher share price. However, someone has to pay that higher share price. If management deliver the new and higher financial performance expectations embedded in new and higher share price, wealth will be preserved for the shareholders who invested (or

[12] Boulos, Haspeslagh and Noda, "Getting the Value Out of Value-Based Management: Findings from a Global Survey on Best Practices", *Harvard Business Review Research Report No. 7478*, July 2001, p. 12.

who chose not to sell) at that new and higher price. Wealth will only be created for that group of shareholders if the new and higher financial performance expectations are actually exceeded.

In many respects, the leadership teams of listed companies have little choice but to seek to create wealth for shareholders regardless of whether they invested three years ago, three months ago, three weeks ago or three days ago. Responding to this challenge and creating shareholder wealth on an ongoing basis is a creative endeavour on the part of a leadership team and the employees of any listed company. It almost always involves the identification, development and successful implementation of new and higher value strategies in different parts of the business at different points in time. In stark contrast to the metric-based economic engine approach, it is not just a simple analytical process devoid of the human spirit.

With that understanding in place, it is clear that in most cases, a mechanistic understanding of value drivers is only of limited use in building an organisation that can create wealth for shareholders on an ongoing basis. It can sometimes be helpful to the extent that it stimulates new ideas from which new and higher value strategies might then be developed. However there are often better, faster and more effective methods than value driver analysis to stimulate new thinking.

As will become apparent from the material contained in Part III, analysis is generally more effective when used as a proving mechanism to establish whether or not an idea will work, rather than as a discovery mechanism to generate the idea in the first place. Value driver analysis might serve as a catalyst to help stimulate the generation of ideas. But in many cases value drivers turn out to be strategy specific. So it is often better to develop the strategy first and then use tools like value drivers as part of a mechanism with which to guide and manage its implementation.

When used in this way, value drivers and other elements of the economic engine approach can turn out to be quite helpful, particularly in relation to performance measurement and management reporting. However, by the end of the 1990s it was clear to most observers that the economic engine approach was not a standalone management framework and would never become one. Unless used as part of a more holistic plan-based approach, it really only served the needs of the finance function. This was confirmed in the INSEAD study completed by Boulos, Haspeslagh and Noda. They found that "…leading edge companies adopted a holistic approach that went well beyond new measurements and incentives linked to economic profit" and included aligning planning, resource allocation and other business processes with the goal of value uplift.[13]

Over the years, MFV developed through a number of different stages and in many respects the thinking presented in this book constitutes the next stage in that development. Along the way, as more and more board members and senior executives became familiar with the principles of MFV, they came to accept that as a minimum they had an obligation to preserve shareholder wealth. This meant protecting the value of the capital entrusted to them by shareholders – which in turn meant delivering the financial performance expectations that were embedded in their company's share price.

They also came to understand that to create shareholder wealth, they needed to either deliver financial performance that exceeded market expectations, or convince the capital market that they had put in place a strategy that would enable them to do so. This was not easy. But it didn't end there. Whenever a senior executive team did succeed in creating shareholder wealth, their company's new and higher share price reflected a new and higher set of performance expectations. These needed to be met in order to preserve wealth for shareholders who had just invested, and exceeded in order to create wealth for these new shareholders. If the executive team succeeded in doing so, the process would ratchet up another level and start all over again.

By the turn of the century, to be considered truly successful by the professional investment community, a senior executive team had to be able to create wealth for shareholders not once, but on an ongoing basis. This meant being able to continually exceed financial performance expectations, which were themselves continually increasing. It was and remains an enormous challenge.

Customer Value and Shareholder Wealth

Throughout the 20-odd years from the mid-1990s to the present day, shareholder wealth creation has retained its position as the primary economic objective for listed companies. For many, it has also either become or remained the governing corporate objective. However, the way companies go about the creation of shareholder wealth has now become the subject of much greater scrutiny – primarily through the emergence of an active interest

[13] Boulos, Haspeslagh and Noda, op. cit., p. 12.

on the part of institutional investors in how companies manage their environmental, social and governance (ESG) responsibilities.

One of the most important consequences of the emergence of the ESG movement is the realisation that the way a company goes about creating wealth for its shareholders has quite an impact on its ability to continue to do so on an ongoing basis. As will become clear in Chapter 4, creating customer value in ways that deliver an appropriate return on the capital and other resources employed is fundamental to creating wealth for shareholders on an ongoing basis. In fact, in value-managed companies where ongoing shareholder wealth creation is an explicit goal, customer value creation and shareholder wealth creation serve as joint and mutually reinforcing objectives. (Although they really only become actionable as joint and mutually reinforcing objectives when pursued within the confines of a properly defined customer segment.)

It will also become apparent in Chapter 4 that most opportunities for shareholder wealth creation arise from the appropriate pricing and efficient delivery of incremental value or benefits provided to the customers that comprise one of these properly defined segments.

Synthesis and Concluding Remarks

For the past 20 to 30 years, there has been broad agreement that the primary economic objective of every listed company is to create shareholder wealth. However, it is only over the last 10 years or so that it has been recognised that the purpose of a corporation and its fundamental economic objective need not be the same; and that from a purely economic perspective, the real goal is not to maximise shareholder value or create shareholder wealth *per se*, but instead to build an enduring institution with the ability to create wealth for its shareholders on an ongoing basis. Clearly it is important to be able to create wealth for all investors, regardless of whether they invested in the company three years ago, three months ago, three weeks ago, or three days ago.

Once this is understood, there are a number of other issues that come into play. The most important of these is the realisation that the way a company goes about creating shareholder wealth has a truly enormous impact on its ability to continue to do so on an ongoing basis. The ESG community is beginning to confront this issue. So are the companies themselves, by embracing elements of the thinking of groups like Raj Sisodia's *Conscious Capitalism* movement and the less holistic but nonetheless directionally positive *Shared Value* movement.

We will examine this issue in detail in the chapters to come. However, an important factor to consider at the outset is the existence of very different time horizons among key decision makers and stakeholders – and the impact that these time horizons can have on each group's attitude and behaviour. Experienced executives know that it is entirely possible to boost earnings and cash flow over a relatively short time horizon (such as one, two or perhaps even three years), simply by taking action to minimise costs or constrain capital investment. This can be done without paying much heed at all to the needs of other stakeholder groups – as is often apparent in the actions of certain private equity groups. Often such action does translate into an immediate increase in share price and market capitalisation, although such increases are often not sustained.

It is more difficult to continually enhance both economic profit and intrinsic value every year – and particularly so once the time horizon expands to five years or more. With a longer time-horizon, the focus needs to shift to creating both customer value and shareholder wealth, and to seeing these as joint and mutually reinforcing objectives.

As the time horizon expands even further, the nature of the value a company sets out to create for its customers, as well as the way it goes about creating it, begins to become significant. This is because the longer our time horizon, the more the interests of all stakeholder groups align; so the more holistic our thinking needs to be; and the more likely we are to be prepared to put in the effort necessary to build an enduring institution organisation that can create value for customers and wealth for shareholders on an ongoing basis (as well as do so in ways that enhance the wellbeing of all stakeholders).

It is interesting to contrast this perspective with the time horizons of key decision makers and stakeholders in listed companies. Institutional investors who act as the custodians for retirement savings have long even intergenerational time horizons. But the performance of the fund managers that many institutional investors employ is measured on a quarterly basis. Employees used to have relatively long time horizons, with many working for the same organisation for much of their working life. But they are now much more mobile.[14] Senior executives and particularly CEOs have relatively short time horizons – typically less than five years in Australia. Board members tend to

[14] Job Hopping is the "New Normal" for Millennials: Three Ways to Prevent a Human Resources Nightmare, *Forbes*, 14 August 2012.

have longer tenures than CEOs, but they do have to stand for re-election every three years.

We are fast approaching a time when we will need to find a means with which to create shareholder wealth that balances and potentially even aligns the interests of all stakeholders. When this happens, listed companies will need to create the circumstances under which each of their stakeholders benefits in a fair and appropriate way from their interaction with the company. The first step towards that end is the adoption of customer value creation and shareholder wealth creation as joint and mutually reinforcing objectives.

During the first year after I stepped down as a partner with a leading international consulting firm, our team collaborated closely with another boutique firm that specialised in organisational culture and leadership development. Its core offer was a culture change program called Leading with Respect. Our program was called Managing for Value (MFV).

We worked together to help clients to develop the ability to create both customer value and shareholder wealth – and do so on an ongoing basis. The goal was not shareholder value maximisation per se.

We were involved in two client engagements together before the relationship came to an end – largely though not entirely because of the passing of the founder of the other firm in a motor vehicle accident. These engagements were very successful from the clients' perspective. The capital market performance of one is illustrated in Fig. 1.3.

There were three main reasons for this success.

Firstly, the focus was on both organisational culture and providing an economic framework built around the pursuit of customer value and shareholder wealth as joint and mutually reinforcing objectives.

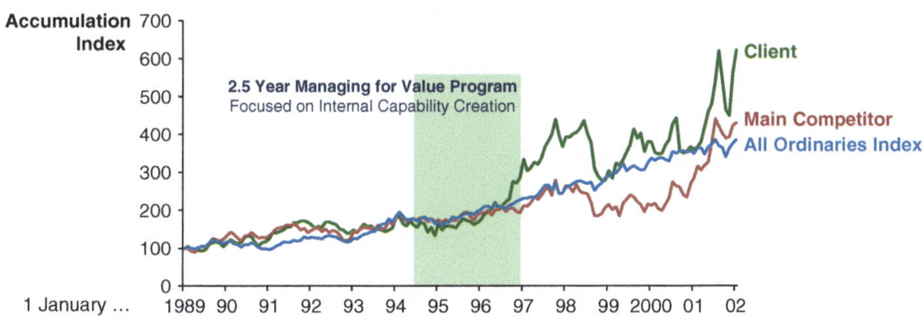

Fig. 1.3 TSR performance of first client versus its competitors

Secondly, there was a strong focus on individual and organisational capability creation, so a great deal of effort was put into creating tools, frameworks and guidebooks so the management team could do what would in the normal course of events have been done by consultants. As a result, the consulting team was a good deal smaller than it would have been had the work been undertaken as a more traditional consulting engagement.

Thirdly, we employed a powerful creative thinking process that we labelled Hybrid Thinking. This enabled managers to function in a whole brain state and in so doing, draw on both creative and analytical modes of thought. It proved hugely successful.

In both the client engagements we worked on together, there was a strong and capable CEO in place. In the larger of the two engagements, the CEO was quite committed to continually enhancing the quality of all aspects of the leadership in the business. He was also prepared to back strongly the ideas and convictions of his very capable team of general managers – many of whom over the subsequent 10 years or so went on to become very successful CEOs or senior executives of other companies, or successful entrepreneurs.

Part II

The Understanding

True commercial success for a listed company means succeeding in both the market for its products and services, and the market for shareholder capital – and doing so on an ongoing basis.

Success in the products and services market must lead to success in the capital market. But this truth is only evident through the lens provided by economic performance measures. It is obscured when using traditional internal accounting measures like earnings, EPS and EPS growth; and particularly when they are used in combination with non-economic external metrics like total shareholder return (TSR) and particularly relative TSR.

The proper use of economic performance measures gives rise to the notion of a Bow Wave of Expected Economic Profits which is embedded in the share price and market capitalisation of every listed company at every point in time. Enhancing the shape of this EP Bow Wave through success achieved in the product and services market leads inevitably to success in the capital market.

However, success in both markets can only be achieved and maintained on an ongoing basis by embracing customer value creation and shareholder wealth creation as joint and mutually reinforcing objectives – pursued in tandem using a disciplined approach to innovation.

2

Some Important Truths

The purpose of this chapter is to make explicit some important truths – particularly in relation to listed company performance measurement and how performance in the market for a company's products and services, can be aligned with the capital market outcomes experienced by shareholders.

Awareness and acceptance of these truths represents an important milestone on the journey of understanding contained in this book. They are summarised at the end of the chapter.

The Fundamental Truth of Performance Measurement

While measured in the capital market, shareholder wealth is really created in the products and services market, through the appropriate pricing and the efficient delivery of products or services that create value or benefits for customers.

Success in this endeavour is evident in the product and service market as a growing stream of economic profit (EP), and in the capital market as a total shareholder return (TSR) greater than that which shareholders require in order to preserve the value of their investment.

Another way of saying this is that true commercial success for every listed company involves succeeding in two markets – the market for its products and services and the market for shareholder capital. Success in the first leads to success in the second.

D. Kilroy, M. Schneider, *Customer Value, Shareholder Wealth, Community Wellbeing*, DOI 10.1007/978-3-319-54774-9_2

This statement constitutes a fundamental truth – a truth that is relevant to every listed company. However, it is also a truth that is only evident when viewed through the lens provided by economic performance measures. It is obscured almost entirely when performance in the product and service market is measured using accounting metrics like earnings, EPS, EPS growth and even return on equity (ROE); and when performance in the capital market is measured using non-economic metrics like TSR and relative TSR.

It is important for boards and executive leadership teams to not only understand, but also be able to demonstrate, how the performance they achieve in the market for their company's products and services (and which is captured in its income statement or P&L, balance sheet and cash flow statement) translates into the capital market outcomes experienced by shareholders. The first step towards developing this understanding is to deal with the primary impediment that stands in the way. That impediment is *The EPS Myth*.

Exploding the EPS Myth

There was a brief reference in Chapter 1 to the widespread but misguided belief that EPS and P/E ratio are the primary determinants of the share price and therefore the market capitalisation of a listed company. This belief operates in tandem with the equally widespread but misguided belief that EPS growth and P/E ratio are the primary determinants of any change in share price and market capitalisation (given a stable dividend policy and no change in the number of shares on issue).

These beliefs are not just misunderstandings or misconceptions. They are complete myths. The combination of P/E ratio and EPS is not the primary determinant of share price and market capitalisation. At the same time, the combination of P/E ratio and EPS growth is not the primary determinant of any change in share price and market capitalisation. The fact they are not, and the reasons why they are not, have been understood since the mid-1980s by many within the professional investment community and by everyone familiar with the principles of MFV.

The fundamental issue is that neither EPS nor EPS growth takes into account either the amount or the cost of the capital required in order to deliver a particular level of EPS or EPS growth. As the late Peter Kontes (a co-founder of Marakon Associates and one of the originators of the discipline of MFV) pointed out in his book *The CEO, Strategy and Shareholder Value* published in 2010, the central problem with EPS growth as standalone financial performance measure is that it can be purchased at any price. In a section entitled *Dealing with Mythology,* he makes the same telling point that Marakon partners first made with their clients in the mid-1980s, namely that if a sustainable $1.00 increase in EPS could be achieved by investing $5.00 per share, that would probably be a good thing. But if the same $1.00 increase in EPS meant investing $20.00 per share, then it would probably not be a good thing.[1]

This point is illustrated in Fig. 2.1, making use of a construct that those familiar with the principles of MFV have employed for the past 30 years to demonstrate the weaknesses inherent in earnings and EPS as performance measures. In this example, there are three companies that at the beginning of a five-year measurement period, each had equity capital of $100m and earnings of $10m. This meant that with a cost of equity capital (Ke) of 10 percent, all three companies were economically breakeven, producing an economic profit of zero.[2] The starting position for each of these companies is illustrated in the left-hand panel in Fig. 2.1.

Over the five-year measurement period, the three companies all achieved earnings growth of 15 percent per year every year. Company A achieved this by becoming more capital efficient and investing at a rate lower than the growth in earnings – growing its equity capital base at 10 percent per year. The equity capital base of Company B grew at 15 percent per year – the same as the rate of growth in earnings. Company C grew its equity capital base at 20 percent per year – five percentage points faster than its growth in earnings.

Each company doubled its earnings to $20m over the measurement period. However, because each required a different amount of capital in

	Base Year						Year 5			
	Equity Capital Employed	Earnings	Cost of Equity	Economic Profit	**Earnings Growth**	**Growth in Equity**	Equity Capital Employed	Earnings	Cost of Equity	Economic Profit
Company A	100	10	10%	0.0	15%	10%	161	20	10%	4.0
Company B	100	10	10%	0.0	15%	15%	201	20	10%	0.0
Company C	100	10	10%	0.0	15%	20%	249	20	10%	(4.8)

Fig. 2.1 Why earnings and EPS can be purchased at any price

[1] Kontes, Peter, *The CEO, Strategy and Shareholder Value,* John Wiley & Sons, NJ, 2010, p. 23.

[2] Economic Profit = Earnings of $10m less Equity Capital of $100m multiplied by the cost of equity of 10 percent.

order to achieve a 15 percent earnings growth, Company A achieved an economic profit of $4.0m in Year 5, Company B remained economically breakeven and Company C produced an economic loss of $4.8m in Year 5. More importantly, if we make some conservative assumptions about the sustainability of the performance of each company beyond Year 5, the value of the shareholders' investment in Company A would have increased at a rate of 19.2 percent per year (which is well above the cost of equity) over the five-year measurement period. In comparison, the value of the shareholders' investment in Company C would have increased by only 8.8 percent per year (which is less than the cost of equity capital, and therefore less than that required to preserve shareholder wealth).[3]

So earnings growth is clearly a poor indicator of management performance in creating shareholder wealth – because it fails to take account of the amount of capital required. But what about EPS? EPS tends not to attract the same criticism as earnings due to another widespread but nonetheless misguided belief. This is the belief that expressing earnings on a per share basis has the effect of normalising it for any additional capital requirements through the issuing of new shares. While it may seem counter intuitive to some, the normalising effect of expressing earnings on a per share basis is marginal at best. This is because new shares are issued at market value not book value. In most cases, earnings growth and EPS growth will be the same or very similar, irrespective of the number of new shares issued.

A much more detailed examination of the three companies illustrated in Fig. 2.1 is provided in Appendix 1. It reveals that EPS grows at virtually the same rate as earnings regardless of the number of new shares required to be issued. It also shows that EP does not grow at the same rate as earnings, and the value of the business is very different in each case even under the most conservative of assumptions, despite earnings, EPS and EPS growth across the three companies being virtually identical.

[3] The increase in value was estimated using the Market to Book formula M:B = (ROE-g)/(Ke-g).

For Company A in Year 5, ROE is $20m/$161m = 12.5 percent and assumed to be sustainable at this level, g is assumed to be sustainable at 5 percent, and Ke is 10 percent. This gives a M:B ratio of 1.5×. Book Equity for Company A is $161m in Year 5. So the value is 1.5 × $161m = $241m, which is a 141 percent increase over the value of $100m in the base year, and represents a 19.2 percent annual growth in value.

For Company C, in Year 5 ROE is $20m/$249m = 8.1 percent and assumed to be sustainable at this level, g is assumed to be sustainable at 5 percent and Ke is 10 percent. This gives a M:B ratio of 0.62×. Book Equity for Company C is $249m in Year 5. So the value is 0.62 × $249m = $153m. This is a 53 percent increase in value over five years, and represents an 8.8 percent annual growth in value (which is less than the 10 percent per year required to preserve shareholder wealth).

EPS and EPS growth are not incorrect measures of financial performance. They are incomplete measures. The fact that they do not take account of the amount or the cost of the capital required to deliver a particular EPS or EPS growth outcome means that as stand-alone measures, they are poor indicators of management performance in creating shareholder wealth. Yet despite this simple but compelling truth, belief in *The EPS Myth* remains strong, as evidenced by the following statement drawn from the 2013 remuneration report of a relatively new but top performing ASX-100 company.

> The board continues to believe that EPS is the most appropriate measure that best aligns the interest of shareholders with those of management.[4]

This statement might sound plausible, and many who read it in the company's annual report probably thought so as well. No doubt the company's auditors and other external professional advisors thought so too. But the fact is this statement is built on a false premise. If the company pursues its EPS goals through buying growth at any price, then it is likely that capital market performance it delivers to shareholders in the long run will be sub-optimal at best.

It is important that we explode *The EPS Myth* and do so comprehensively. To do otherwise would be dishonest and inappropriate. Perpetuation of *The EPS Myth* has a negative impact on many aspects of listed company activities. Perhaps the most deleterious of these is its encouragement of short-termism – a topic we will return to later in this chapter.

The theoretical truths illustrated in Fig. 2.1 have been known for 30 years. They should have exploded *The EPS Myth* many times over during that time. But they have not. Peter Kontes offered a humorous explanation for this – suggesting the reason smart people on Wall St and other financial centres around the world continue to believe in it has more to do with religion than business economics. But the truth is that the perpetuation of this myth is due in large part to the fact that it is not seen as myth nor portrayed as such in either undergraduate or graduate programs at business schools, or in the training programs provided by business-related professional associations. So a significant number of accountants, lawyers, sell-side securities analysts, investment bankers, proxy advisors and company directors, remain wedded to the view that a company's share price is a function of its EPS and its P/E ratio. In these circumstances, it is helpful to approach this challenge from another perspective – using a comprehensive empirical analysis.

---

[4] Carsales.com Limited 2013 Annual Report, p. 25.

An examination of the performance of S&P 500 companies over the 10 years to 31 December 2007 by Peter Kontes and his team from the Yale School of Management, and of the performance of the top 300 ASX-listed companies over the five years to 30 June 2013 by our firm, provides a clear demonstration of *The EPS Myth* at work, as well as pointing to the benefits of adopting economic performance measures.

Figure 2.2 summarises the results of that work. The research clustered the companies studied into three groups (after excluding those for which there was not a full set of data covering the entire measurement period). Focusing on the ASX 300 companies, there were:

- 84 EP dominant companies whose annualised growth in economic profit per share over five years, was at least 10 percentage points greater than their growth in EPS;
- 123 EPS dominant companies whose annualised growth in EPS over five years was at least 10 percentage points greater than their growth in economic profit per share; and
- 90 companies representing the remainder.

Over the five years to 30 June 2013, the EP-dominant companies on average delivered an annualised TSR that was 6.4 percentage points higher than the EPS-dominant companies. This is a significant margin and one that mirrored closely the outcome found by Kontes and his team for the S&P 500 over a 10-year period. In the US work, the margin was 6.6 percentage points.[5]

The margin of 6.4 percentage points in the ASX 300 study expands to 10.9 when viewed on a more meaningful risk-adjusted basis labelled *TSR Alpha* on the right-hand side of Fig. 2.2. (*TSR Alpha* is an important market-based performance metric that both adjusts for risk and strips out the impact of underlying market movements. It is discussed in detail in Chapter 3 and its method of calculation is explained in Appendix 2.)

Underpinning this unquestionably significant finding was the fact that the 84 EP-dominant companies on average grew their EPS a good deal faster than their equity capital investment per share, whereas the 123 EPS-dominant companies on average grew their equity capital investment per share much faster than their EPS. In other words, the EPS-dominant companies

[5] Kontes, Peter, op. cit., p. 4. In the US study, the criteria by which companies were defined as EPS dominant or EP dominant was based on EPS being 5 percent per annum higher than EP per share, and vice versa.

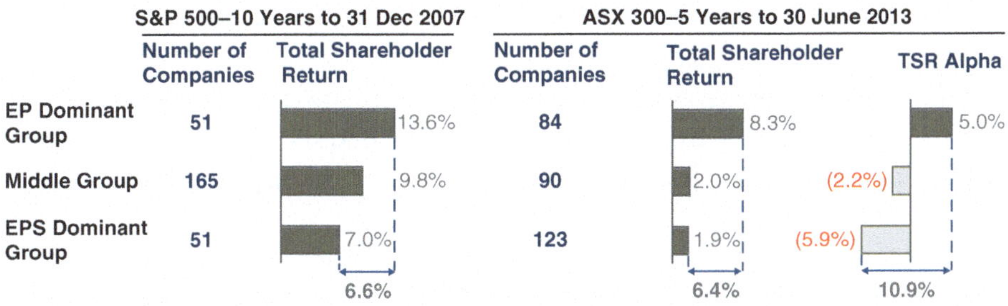

Fig. 2.2 Linking EPS and EP per share to total shareholder return

were demonstrating empirically that their management was indeed prepared to purchase EPS at any price.

Other than hopefully laying *The EPS Myth* to rest, the most important practical insight to emerge from this work is that growth in the economic profit per share achieved in the in the market for a company's products and services, is much more closely aligned with positive capital market outcomes experienced by shareholders, than growth in EPS.

The Consequences of Adhering to the EPS Myth

One of the more unfortunate consequences of adherence to *The EPS Myth* is the trashing of stock prices when a company fails to meet a short-term earnings target. The even more unfortunate corollary that sometimes goes hand in hand with this is the pursuit of short-term cost reductions in order to either meet or exceed a stated earnings target, but which can also be inconsistent with the company's long-term strategy.

Why does this occur? We believe there is more to it than the glib reference to religion that Peter Kontes used – as much out of frustration as in jest. The fact is that there is a lot of pressure on listed company boards to focus on short-term financial performance at the expense of longer-term value creation. This pressure has two primary sources.

The first is self-interest on the part of often vociferous short-term capital market players. The second is an incorrect understanding on the part of a much larger group of players and commentators, comprising virtually all the financial press, most retail investors as well as certain proxy advisors.

The self-interest of short-term capital market players is legendary, and has been the subject of a great deal of concern. BlackRock Chairman Larry Fink wrote to the Chairmen and CEOs of listed companies in 2015 asking that they not succumb to this pressure.

The incorrect understanding once again relates to the way in which the performance achieved by management in the market for their company's products and services, translates into the capital market outcomes experienced by shareholders.

The most significant issue though is not the source or even the nature of the pressure to engage in practices now referred to as short-termism; but the way that many boards choose to respond. More often than not, their response is grounded in the misunderstanding referred to above. In other words, they respond as adherents to *The EPS Myth*.

Unfortunately, the fact that there is such widespread adherence to *The EPS Myth* which is constantly being reinforced through commentary in the financial press, has effectively legitimised short-termism as a way for listed company boards to respond to pressure from external players with short-term objectives. Few if any medium to long-term shareholders benefit from short-termism, and its impact is almost universally negative for other stakeholders, who often have a much greater economic stake in the business than short-term capital market players.

We will demonstrate unequivocally in Chapter 3 that to improve short-term capital market performance for listed companies, it is necessary to improve long-term (not short-term) product and service performance. This is the absolute polar opposite of the view of those who adhere to *The EPS Myth*.

Unfortunately, short-termism is becoming institutionalised through such measures as the inclusion of stretch targets for EPS outcomes in executives' incentive plans. We will return to this topic in Chapter 10, because this practice has the potential to undermine the ability of the board of a listed company to build an organisation capable of creating wealth for shareholders on an ongoing basis – and not just because their use tends to lead to behaviours such as those just described.

Another Related Misunderstanding

There is another misunderstanding bordering on a myth that has taken root in the low interest rate environment that has prevailed since the GFC. It is the belief that shareholders place great value on achieving high levels of dividend yield.

The picture presented in Fig. 2.3 was developed by comparing the change in dividend payout ratio and change in capital growth, between the average of that which applied for the five years prior to the GFC, and the average for the five years post the GFC. It shows that roughly one third of companies in the ASX 300 were engaged in an unsustainable cycle of disinvestment – paying unsustainably high dividends in an effort to provide higher yields to shareholders in a low interest rate environment, yet destroying a great deal of shareholder wealth in the process.

Specifically, there were:

- *75 Sustainable Growers* that reduced their payout ratio and increased capital growth,
- *40 Sustainable Dividend Yield Chasers,* that increased their dividend payout ratio but also increased capital growth (slightly);
- *82 Companies that were Managing for Returns,* by decreasing (slightly) their dividend payout ratio and reducing capital growth; and
- *103 Unsustainable Dividend Yield Chasers* who increased their dividend payout ratio significantly, while decreasing capital growth.

Significantly, the *Sustainable Growers* produced a TSR outcome that was far higher than the other three groups.

The behaviour of the *Unsustainable Dividend Yield Chasers* not only constitutes a form of disinvestment (particularly when inconsistent with the strategy currently being pursued), it can lead to both the erosion of customer value and the destruction of shareholder wealth. It can also have an adverse impact on other stakeholders.

When acted upon in conjunction with *The EPS Myth*, this additional myth can lead to quite poor management practices. For example, when a cost reduction

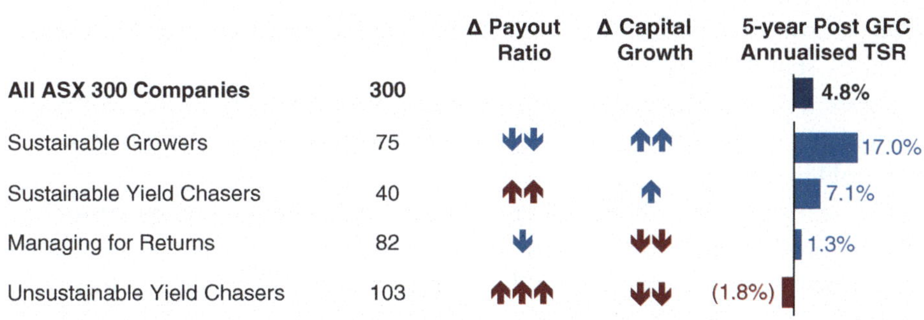

Δ Payout Ratio
Δ Capital Growth
5-year Post GFC Annualised TSR
All ASX 300 Companies
300
4.8%
Sustainable Growers
75
17.0%
Sustainable Yield Chasers
40
7.1%
Managing for Returns
82
1.3%
Unsustainable Yield Chasers
103
(1.8%)

Fig. 2.3 Short-termism in the ASX 300

initiative aimed at boosting earnings results in an earnings targets being exceeded, there can be a temptation to use the additional earnings to pay higher dividends than planned – even if the excess earnings that were achieved arose through deferring necessary expenditure. The consequence of such actions is likely to be negative for virtually all stakeholders – including most shareholders.

Linking Product and Capital Market Performance

Having delivered what should hopefully be a *coup de grâce* for *The EPS Myth*, the next step is to develop the understanding required to link the performance delivered in the product and service market with the capital market outcomes experienced by shareholders. This will be done in two ways; firstly by outlining the conceptual framework, and secondly by walking through a hypothetical situation that a board might find itself in where it needs to draw on this understanding.

We introduced this chapter with a statement to the effect that true commercial success for every listed company means succeeding in both the market for its products and services, and the market for shareholder capital. To most observers, it would seem obvious that success in the first would lead to success in the second. So it is a paradox as baffling as Olbers' was 100 years ago, that the performance measurement systems used by a majority of listed companies (as well as the myriad of analysts and commentators that observe them) actually obscures this truth.

The fact that success in the product and service market must lead to success in the capital market simply cannot be established using traditional accounting measures. It can only be observed using economic performance measures. In fact, it is only with economic measures that a listed company can establish any meaningful link at all between its strategic decisions and its financial performance in the market for its products and services, as well to observe how that performance affects the capital market outcomes experienced by shareholders.

Figure 2.4 provides an illustration of the way in which a listed company participates in the market for its products and services, and the market for shareholder capital.

The company seeks firstly to create value or benefits for it its customers with its product and service offer or offers. If it succeeds in doing so, then when priced appropriately its products and services will produce a stream of revenues commensurate with the value being created for customers. If delivered efficiently, this stream of revenues will then translate into a stream

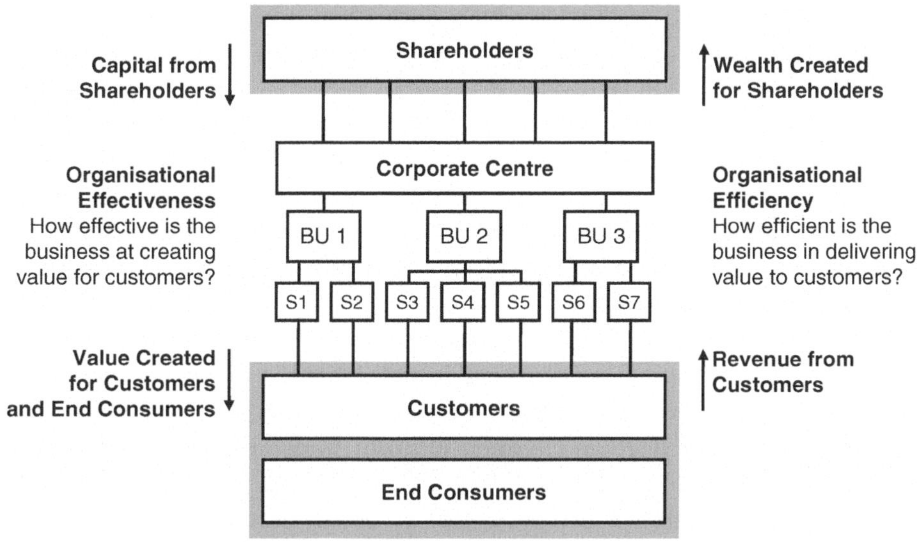

Fig. 2.4 The two markets in which all listed companies participate

of economic profits. The linkage to capital market performance stems from the way the capital market reacts to the delivery of an economic profit stream either above, below or consistent with its expectations; as well as to any change in expectations in relation to the economic profit that will be delivered in the future.

To understand this linkage properly, we need to:

- Define what we mean by success in the product and services market;
- Define what we mean by success in the capital market;
- Demonstrate the linkage between expected EP and intrinsic value;
- Demonstrate the linkage between change in expected EP and intrinsic value uplift; and
- Demonstrate the linkage between intrinsic value uplift and shareholder wealth creation as measured in capital markets.

Success in the Market for Products and Services

Success in the market for a company's products and services comes in the form of a positive and eventually a growing economic profit stream. There are two ways to think about this.

The first is as the residual profit stream after subtracting all the costs incurred in producing a revenue stream – including the opportunity cost of the equity capital employed.

The second way to think about economic profit or EP is as the product of an economically profitable return in the form of an ROE greater than Ke, and the size of the capital base on which that economically profitable return is earned. This concept is illustrated in Fig. 2.5, showing an initial focus on achieving positive economic profitability and a subsequent focus on growing the economic profit stream.

While both ways of thinking are correct, the second approach provides the more useful construct. This is because it highlights the two most important internal economic performance measures, which are economic profitability measured as a percentage and economic profit measured in dollars (or the appropriate currency).

Economic profitability (or ROE-Ke) is sometimes referred to as the economic return on the book value of equity, or the return on equity achieved over and above that required in order to preserve book value. The ROE used in the illustration in Fig. 2.5 is 30 percent and Ke is 10 percent, resulting in economic profitability of 20 percent. Economic profit is the product of economic profitability and the equity employed at the beginning of the measurement period – or $20 million in the example in Fig. 2.5.

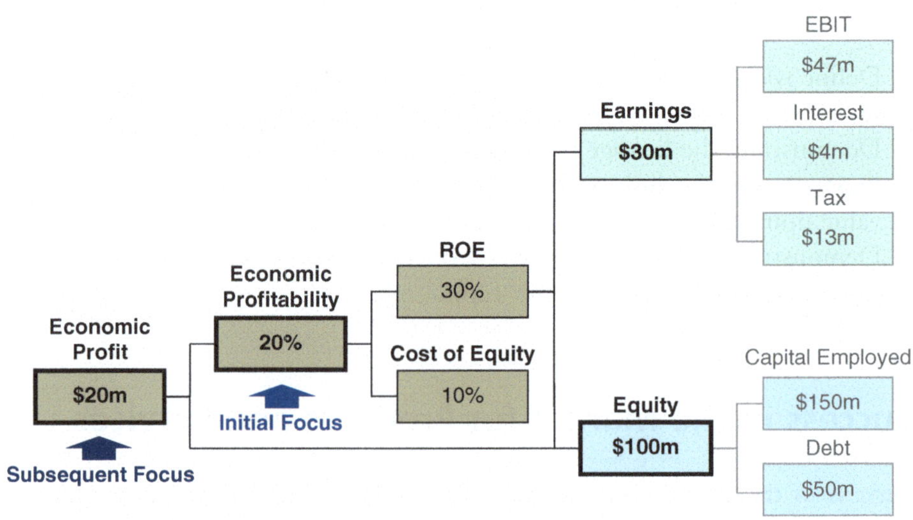

Fig. 2.5 Defining success in the product and service market

Success in the Market for Shareholder Capital

Success in the capital market means producing a TSR greater than Ke. In the product and service market, success (initially) means producing an ROE greater than Ke. In the capital markets, it means achieving a TSR greater than Ke. It's the same Ke. The point is illustrated in Fig. 2.6.

Importantly, success in the capital market has little if anything to do with achieving a TSR greater than that achieved by peer or competitor companies (which is the basis for the measure known as relative TSR). It is somewhat related to performance versus the market index, but it is not quite the same. This is because most companies don't have the same risk profile as the market as a whole. The value of higher risk companies rises faster in a rising market and falls faster in a falling one.

The challenge with TSR-Ke however is that it is a long-term measure of capital market success – not a short-term one. Over the short term, it is much easier to produce a TSR greater than Ke in a rising market, than it is in a falling one. That challenge is what led us to develop the concept of *TSR Alpha* which was touched on in Fig. 2.2 but is explained in detail in Chapter 3.

Linking Intrinsic Value to Expected Economic Profit

Whenever there is a positive economic profit stream from participation in the market for a company's products and services, the intrinsic value of the business will be greater than its book value.

Most people will be familiar with the notion of value being equal to the present value (PV) of expected future cash flows. The intrinsic value of a

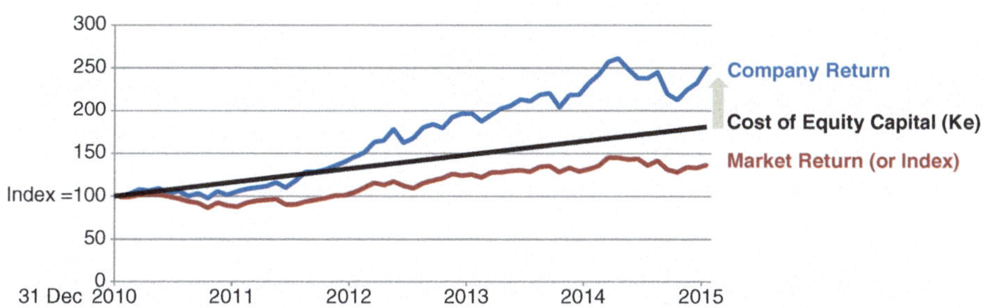

Fig. 2.6 Defining success in the capital market

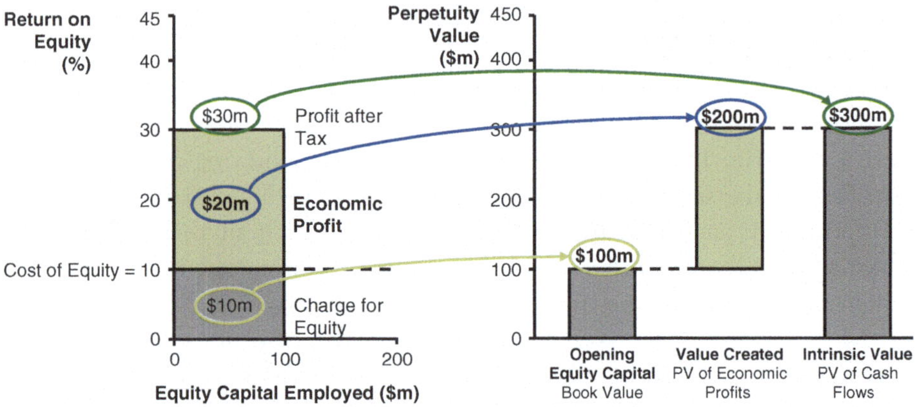

Fig. 2.7 Linking cash flow, economic profit and intrinsic value

business under any given strategy is the PV of the cash flows that are expected to be delivered under that strategy. It is also equal to the equity employed plus the PV of expected economic profit, as is illustrated in a simple, zero-growth perpetuity scenario in Fig. 2.7.

Cash flow is profit less change in investment, so in the example illustrated, earnings of $30m per year with no growth and therefore no change in capital investment, is the same as an equity cash flow of $30m per year. When capitalised in perpetuity at a Ke of 10 percent, a $30m equity cash flow stream translates into an intrinsic value of $300m. This is $200m greater than the book equity employed in the business. The difference of $200m is also equal to the PV of an economic profit stream of $20m per year capitalised in perpetuity at the same Ke.[6]

---

[6] Under the equity capital approach, we can express intrinsic value as...
Intrinsic Value = PV of [Equity Cash Flows]

= PV of [Economic Profits] + Opening Equity
= PV of [(Return on Equity − Ke) × Opening Equity] + Opening Equity

The equity capital approach can be easier to use at group level and in particular when seeking to compare performance to that of other companies. This is because the information required is generally more readily available. The equity capital approach is also more appropriate in the case of banks and other financial institutions.

Under the total capital approach, we can express intrinsic enterprise value as...
Intrinsic Value = PV of [Operating Cash Flows]

= PV of [Economic Profits] + Opening Capital
= PV of [(Return on Capital − WACC) × Opening Capital] + Opening Capital

This approach is often preferred at a business unit level since managers at that level generally find it easier to think about the economics of their business in terms of ROC rather than ROE.

While the cash flow approach and the economic profit approach are equivalent and represent two sides of exactly the same coin, the economic profit approach is the more useful construct – for two important reasons. Firstly, unlike cash flow, economic profit tends to be both relatively stable over time, and therefore much easier to incorporate into a performance management system. Secondly, unlike both cash flow and earnings, it has a base of zero at which book value is preserved and to which market forces tend to erode returns over time.[7]

The zero-growth perpetuity shown in Fig. 2.7 is a simplification used to illustrate the link between economic profit and intrinsic value. In that illustration, the intrinsic value is three times the book value. Or in other words, the market to book (M:B) ratio is 3.0×.[8]

M:B measures the extent to which the strategy being pursued by management has added value to the shareholders' equity capital invested in the business. In many respects it is like a multiple period view of economic profitability. If economic profitability had been zero rather than 20 percent, management would not have added any value to the equity capital invested and the M:B ratio would have been 1.0×.

Linking Intrinsic Value Uplift to Change in Expected EP

It is helpful to use this simplified perpetuity construct to demonstrate one further point before adopting a more sophisticated perspective that better represents what happens in the real world. Because intrinsic value can be expressed as the sum of opening equity capital employed and the PV of the expected future economic profit, intrinsic value uplift can be expressed as the PV of the increase in expected future economic profit – as illustrated in Fig. 2.8.

In Fig. 2.8, the equity cash flow stream of the simple zero-growth perpetuity introduced in Fig. 2.7 has been increased from \$30m to \$35m, and the economic profit has increased from \$20m to \$25m. When capitalised into perpetuity at a Ke of 10 percent, the \$5m increase in cash flow and economic profit in Fig. 2.8 both translate into an intrinsic value uplift of \$50m.

[7] Together, these two attributes mean it can be disaggregated meaningfully to a business unit, product or segment level – something that we will speak more about in the chapters to come.

[8] We use the term Market to Book (M:B) in this context, even though we are using intrinsic value, which is really management's view of what it thinks the market value should be, given what it knows about the likely future economic profit outcomes under the strategy currently being pursued.

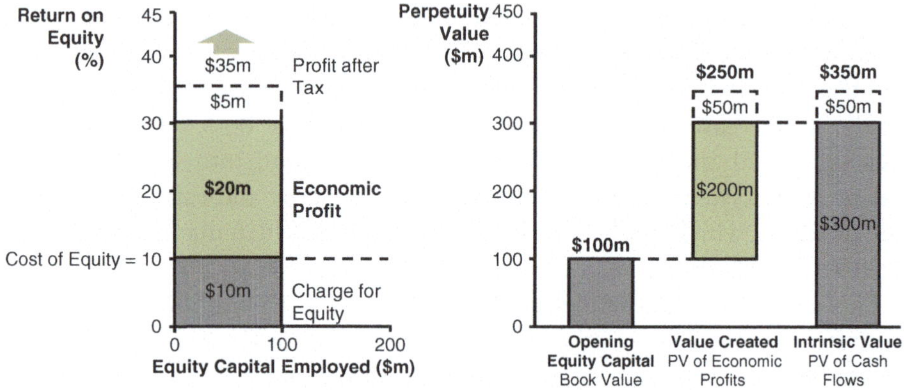

Fig. 2.8 Linking increase in economic profit with intrinsic value uplift

So, intrinsic value uplift can be expressed as the PV of the expected increase in cash flow, or the PV of the expected increase in economic profit.

Linking Shareholder Wealth Creation to Intrinsic Value Uplift

Success in the capital market arises from the way the capital market reacts to a company's success in the product and service market, and the enhanced economic profit stream which flows from that success.

We have demonstrated earlier that intrinsic value is a function of the economic profits expected to be delivered in the future, and that an uplift in intrinsic value stems from an uplift in that expected economic profit stream.

If the economic profit stream from a company's participation in the market for its products and services is consistent with the expectations the market has already embedded in its share price; then intrinsic value, market value and shareholder wealth will be preserved. When this is the case, over time the annualised TSR will be equal to the shareholders' required rate of return or cost of equity capital (Ke), and the long-term economic return on market value (TSR-Ke) will be zero.

If management adopts a strategy that is expected to result in an increase in future economic profits, then there will be an increase in intrinsic value and a commensurate increase in market value, once the capital market forms the view that the increase in expected economic profits will be delivered. Once this occurs, the share price will increase such that TSR will exceed Ke and it is at this point that shareholder wealth is created.

Applying the Truths to a Hypothetical Situation

Before we take the next step conceptually, it is useful to walk through a hypothetical situation in which we make use of the truths we have just articulated.

Let's assume for a moment that the board and senior executive team of a listed company called Example Co. are unanimous in the view that their primary economic objective is to create shareholder wealth. It seems reasonable *a priori* to also assume that they would know exactly how they would gauge their success or failure in this endeavour. It also seems reasonable to expect that if Example Co. had failed to create wealth over a particular five-year measurement period, its board would be quite clear about what it would require of the executive team during the subsequent five-year measurement period in order to achieve an acceptable outcome. Yet the fact is that some boards don't have an adequate response in either case – and to be fair to the board members, there are a number of good reasons why this is likely to be so. Let's start with the question of whether or not shareholder value or wealth was created over the five-year measurement period.

What Determines Whether Wealth Has Been Created?

For the sake of argument, let's assume that Example Co. achieved an increase in share price of 6 percent per year for each of the last five years, and didn't issue any new shares or buy back any shares. So the number of shares on issue remained exactly the same and the rate of growth in market capitalisation was the same as the rate of growth in the share price.

With a 6 percent per year increase in share price and the same number of shares on issue, did Example Co. create, preserve or destroy shareholder wealth over the five-year period? At this stage we can't answer that question because we don't have sufficient information. This is because the question of whether or not wealth was created depends on the extent to which the return shareholders achieved on the market value of their investment exceeded their required rate of return.

The return on the market value of a listed investment or TSR is defined as dividends paid plus share price appreciation achieved over a specified measurement period, divided by the share price at the beginning of that period. It is normally expressed as either an annual or an annualised figure. If we assume a dividend yield of 4 percent each year (i.e. the dividend declared each year divided by the opening share price), then the TSR outcome in the case of Example Co. would be 10 percent per year (i.e. a 6 percent annual increase in share price plus a 4 percent dividend yield).

The shareholders' required rate of return is Ke. This can be calculated a number of ways, however the most widely used approach is with the capital asset pricing model (CAPM) using a process that is contained in every corporate finance text.

The CAPM puts a price on risk, and if we assume for simplicity that Example Co. has a risk profile identical to that of the market as a whole, then we know from a great deal of historical observation that its Ke will be around 12 percent. This is made up of the return on a risk free asset such as a long-term government bond (which over the long run, has typically averaged between 5.5 and 6.0 percent in Australia, the US and the UK), plus a premium of a further 6–7 percent to capture the additional risk associated with an equity investment. For the purposes of this example, we will assume a Ke of 12 percent.

The difference between the return on market value and the shareholders' required rate of return (or TSR-Ke) is known as the economic return on market value. When it is positive, shareholder wealth is created. When it is negative, shareholder wealth is destroyed. When it is zero, shareholder wealth is preserved. In this case, Example Co. produced an economic return on market value of negative 2 percent (i.e. a TSR of 10 percent less a Ke of 12 percent). So it destroyed shareholder wealth even though its share price rose by 6 percent each year and it declared dividends commensurate with a yield of 4 percent each year.

What Must Management Do to Create Wealth?

Let's now turn to the important question of what would need to be done by the executive team in order to deliver an acceptable outcome over the next five-year period. To begin with, we need to decide what is meant by an acceptable outcome. Let's posit that preserving shareholder wealth by delivering a TSR equal to Ke constitutes an acceptable outcome. What financial performance outcome does the executive team need to achieve through its participation in the market for the company's products and services, in order to achieve this acceptable capital market outcome?

The answer to this question is that the executive team must deliver the economic profit performance expectations embedded in Example Co.'s share price at the beginning of the measurement period. If it does, then over time TSR will equal Ke. If it delivers economic profit performance in excess of expectations, then over time TSR will be greater than Ke. If it fails to meet the market's economic profit expectations, then over time TSR will be less than Ke.

Putting this another way to help ensure clarity, shareholder wealth will be preserved in the capital market when Example Co. meets the market's expectations in relation to its performance in the product and service market. Shareholder wealth will be created in the capital market when it exceeds the market's expectations in relation to its performance in the product and service market. In every case, the test as to whether shareholder wealth is created, preserved or destroyed is TSR-Ke.

This understanding gives rise to two other important streams of thought. The first is that share prices increase naturally when market expectations are met – so a rising share price alone is not enough to assert that shareholder wealth has been created. The second is that the measures used to test whether market expectations in relation to performance in the product and service markets have been met or exceeded, need to include both income statement and balance sheet components.

Share Prices Increase Naturally

The fact that share prices increase naturally is easy to demonstrate once we set aside the impact of short-term movements in price arising from shifts in overall market sentiment.

Over the medium to long term, share prices rise or fall based on whether or not investors feel they will get a return sufficient to match their required rate of return or Ke. This outcome (i.e. TSR = Ke) will be achieved if the business delivers the financial performance expectations the market has already embedded in the company's share price.

If investors believe they will get a return greater than Ke over the medium to long term (i.e. they feel the business will deliver an EP outcome greater than the expectations currently embedded in the share price), then both new and existing investors will tend to buy shares. As a result of this buying, the share price will be bid up until such time that investors believe they will get a TSR equal to Ke by investing at the new and higher share price. Similarly, if investors believe they will get a TSR less than Ke over the medium to long term (i.e. they feel the business will deliver an EP outcome less than the expectations currently embedded in the share price), they will tend to sell shares and as a consequence, the share price will fall until such time as they believe they will get a TSR equal to Ke.

To illustrate, if Ke is 12 percent, and the company pays a dividend that provides a yield of 4 percent per year, then if it delivers the financial performance that the capital market was expecting (and which was embedded in its share price at the beginning of the measurement period) its share price must rise on average by 8 percent per year.

Put another way, the value of every listed company at every point in time has embedded within it an economic profit stream that is expected to be delivered in the future. If that EP stream is delivered, TSR will equal Ke, and shareholder wealth will be preserved. If Ke is 12 percent, and the dividend yield is 4 percent, then the share price can be expected to increase by 8 percent in order to preserve shareholder wealth.

The 8 percent increase in share price highlighted in this illustration has nothing to do with shareholder wealth creation. It is simply the natural increase in share price that arises when a company preserves shareholder wealth by meeting market expectations.

Economically Meaningful Performance Measures

From the internal perspective of a board and its executive team, there are only two standalone metrics that are economically meaningful and which properly establish whether performance in the product and service markets has met or exceeded capital market expectations over a particular measurement period. The first is cash flow, or profit less change in capital employed. The second is economic profit, or profit less a charge for capital employed. Both include income statement (or P&L) and balance sheet components. The reason both components are required is that to be economically meaningful, financial performance metrics need to take into account the amount and the cost of the capital required in order to deliver a particular financial performance outcome.

Once a board accepts that it is necessary to take full account of the capital required to deliver a particular financial performance outcome, then earnings and EPS fall by the wayside as standalone performance metrics and the question shifts to whether cash flow or economic profit is the better measure. As we have already indicated, there are a number of reasons why economic profit is the better measure.

Summarising the Truths

The material covered in this chapter contains 12 fundamental truths, which are summarised below.

1. True commercial success for every listed company involves succeeding in two markets – the market for its products and services and the market for shareholder capital.
2. Success in the first leads to success in the second, but this truth can only be observed through the lens provided by economic performance measures.
3. The combination of P/E ratio and EPS is not the primary determinant of share price and market capitalisation of a listed company. The P/E ratio is an outcome, not a determinant. For the same reason, the combination of P/E ratio and EPS growth is not the primary determinant of any change in share price and market capitalisation.
4. Economically meaningful performance measures must include both income statement and balance sheet components. There are only two that do this: cash flow, or profit less change in capital employed; and economic profit, or profit less charge for capital employed.
5. Because they ignore the amount and the cost of the capital required to deliver a particular financial performance outcome, as standalone measures, both EPS and EPS growth are poor indicators of management performance in creating shareholder wealth.
6. There is a far greater alignment between growth in economic profit per share and the capital market returns achieved by shareholders, than there is between growth in EPS and the capital market returns achieved by shareholders.
7. Success in the market for a company's products and services comes in the form of a positive and ideally a growing economic profit stream.
8. Intrinsic value is a function of expected economic profit. It is also a function of expected cash flow, but economic profit is a more useful construct for management.
9. Change in intrinsic value is a function of change in expected economic profit. It is also a function of change in expected cash flow, but once again, economic profit provides a more useful construct.
10. Success in the capital market arises from the way the capital market reacts to a company's success in the product and service market (and to the enhanced economic profit stream which flows from that success).

11. Wealth is preserved over a measurement period if management deliver the EP expectations that the market had at the beginning of the measurement period, and which were embedded in the share price at that time. Wealth is created if management exceed those expectations.
12. Over the long term, share prices rise naturally by an amount equal to the shareholders' cost of equity capital less the dividend yield, so long as management deliver the EP expectations embedded in the share price at the beginning of any measurement period. This share price rise is necessary to preserve shareholder wealth. It does not represent shareholder wealth creation.

Synthesis and Concluding Remarks

Most companies communicate with their shareholders in a manner that suggests their internal management processes are structured in such a way as to encourage the ongoing creation of shareholder wealth, or even the ongoing creation of both customer value and shareholder wealth. In some cases, the words used and the content provided conveys the distinct impression that the shareholders have invested in a true, value-managed company. Yet we can demonstrate that this is often not the case simply by examining the way performance is measured.

For many and perhaps the majority of listed companies, management measures and communicates the performance it achieves in the market for its products and services using measures like earnings, EPS, EPS growth and ROE. These are also the metrics focused upon by external commentators.

In focusing on these metrics, both management and the external commentators tend to perpetuate *The EPS Myth* – albeit inadvertently.

There are three aspects to *The EPS Myth*. The first is the belief that earnings and price-earnings (P/E) ratio determine market capitalisation and that earnings growth and P/E ratio determine value uplift. But they don't. A P/E is a consequence of a value outcome, not a determinant.

The second aspect is the belief that earnings and EPS are good indicators of management's performance in the market for their company's products and services. But they are not. At best, they are incomplete measures of performance for which the only meaningful datum or benchmark is the performance achieved during a prior measurement period.

The third aspect is the belief that better short-term capital market outcomes arise from producing better short-term product and service market performance (as measured using earnings, EPS or EPS growth). However this is most certainly not true, as we will demonstrate in Chapter 3 and elsewhere, drawing on extensive research conducted with the 100 largest companies by market capitalisation listed on each of the Australian Securities Exchange (ASX), the New York Stock Exchange (NYSE) and the London Stock Exchange (LSE).

Similarly, almost all those who comment on listed company performance use TSR and relative TSR as their primary capital market performance metrics. This is despite the fact that it is difficult if not impossible to align product and service market performance measured with earnings or EPS, with capital market performance measured using TSR and relative TSR.

This disconnect between the way management measures performance internally and the way investors measure performance externally, makes it challenging for boards to set wealth creation goals that can be translated into meaningful internal performance targets for executives. It also makes it hard for executives to link what they believe are value-creating actions taken internally, with the capital market outcomes experienced by investors. It makes it extremely challenging for investors to determine how much of the change in value that occurred over a given measurement period is attributable to the decisions, initiatives and actions of the executive team.

Perhaps the biggest problem though is the way this disconnect and the combination of performance metrics that give rises to it, serve to encourage short-termism.

Fortunately, this situation can be overcome by adopting economic rather than traditional accounting measures of financial performance. The use of economic performance measures enables listed company boards and executive teams to link the performance achieved in the market for their products and services, to both the strategic decisions that gave rise to that performance, and to the capital market outcomes experienced by shareholders as a consequence of that performance.

A proper understanding of these linkages is important if business leaders are to act in the long-term best interest of shareholders. And as we will demonstrate in the chapters to come, actions that are in the long-term best interest of shareholders are often in the long-term best interest of other stakeholders as well. Such an understanding is essential if a company is to put in place processes and systems that encourage, measure and reward the ongoing pursuit of shareholder wealth. A crucial component in this understanding is the concept of *The Bow Wave of Expected Economic Profits* – which is the subject of the next chapter.

In December 2015, I was invited to give a presentation to the annual conference of the Governance Institute of Australia on the topic of "Driving Long-term Value Creation". This was the first time that I had articulated publicly the understanding that we had developed over many years as to what was driving short-termism, and how to overcome this seemingly endemic corporate malaise.

The presentation made it clear that the blame for short-termism could not be placed solely at the feet of short-term capital market players. It also challenged a lot of conventional wisdom in relation to business economics and corporate finance.

A central point in the presentation was the recognition that the key to overcoming short-termism is education. All business leaders need to understand how the performance a company produces in the market for its products and services, translates into the capital market outcomes experienced by its shareholders. Only when they have this understanding can they appreciate that short-termism makes no sense at all.

Education is also the key to enabling those in a position to do so, to develop the resolve necessary to resist calls to engage in short-termism emanating from external parties operating from narrow self-interest.

At the time of writing, the link to a video of this presentation was available at https://www.kba.com.au/publications/driving-long-term-value-creation/.

3

A Bow Wave of Expected Economic Profits

In Chapter 2, we established that the economic return on market value (TSR-Ke) is the fundamental determinant of whether or not wealth has been created for shareholders over a specified measurement period.

We also established that (all else being equal), TSR-Ke will be positive if a company takes action that the capital market expects will enable it to deliver an economic profit stream greater than it was expecting at the beginning of a measurement period.

In this chapter, we will develop these concepts a good deal further. In doing so, we will demonstrate why the use of economic performance measures is so helpful when setting out to build a truly great company with the ability to prosper well into the future. We will also demonstrate why short-termism – or the pursuit of short-term financial performance at the expense of longer-term value creation – makes no sense at all.

Managing the Link Between Product and Capital Markets

The key to establishing a meaningful link between the performance of a listed company in the market for its products and services, and the capital market performance experienced by its shareholders, lies in understanding:

- The dimensions of the economic profit stream that the capital market is expecting the company to deliver from its participation in the product and services market;

D. Kilroy, M. Schneider, *Customer Value, Shareholder Wealth, Community Wellbeing*, DOI 10.1007/978-3-319-54774-9_3

- The extent to which those economic profit expectations are delivered over a given measurement period; and
- How the actions of management during the measurement period lead to changes in expectations in relation to economic profit to be delivered beyond the measurement period.

To explore these dynamics, we need to move away from the perpetuity framework we employed in Chapter 2, and establish a construct more representative of the real world. This means relaxing the two simplifying assumptions we made, namely the zero-growth assumption and the assumption that economic profitability remains constant in perpetuity.

Preserving Value by Delivering a Bow Wave of Expected EP

If we firstly relax just the zero-growth assumption, we find that it is possible to establish a relationship between a company's sustainable economic profitability, the sustainable growth (g) in the equity capital base on which the economically profitable return is earned, and intrinsic value (and therefore the company's market to book or M:B ratio).[1] This is explored in more detail in Appendix 5. However, in the normal course of events, neither economic profitability nor growth remains constant in the real world. They build as a strategy gains traction and fall away as the effectiveness of the strategy erodes over time – in the face of technological change, innovation by competitors, changes in taste and fashion, and the impact of other market forces.

Once a strategy has played out, unless the management team devises a new strategy or finds a way to breathe new life into the existing one, then over time, these market forces will tend to erode economic profitability back to zero and growth back to average economic growth.

It is important to have a construct that incorporates these dynamics. One way to achieve this is through the use of a *Bow Wave of Expected Economic Profits* as illustrated in Fig. 3.1.

---

[1] The cash flow formulation is as follows:

M = B × (ROE-g)/(Ke-g), or M:B = (ROE-g)/(Ke-g);

where M refers to market value and B refers to book value.

This is the formula which Brian Hartzer refers to in his Foreword. It can also be expressed as:

M = B × [1 + (ROE-Ke)/(Ke-g)], or M:B = 1 + (ROE-Ke)/(Ke-g);

where M refers to market value and B refers to book value.

It is important to appreciate that it is not necessary to understand the mathematical derivation of these equations (which is provided in Appendix 5). What is important though, is to understand that M:B is a function of sustainable economic profitability (ROE-Ke) and perpetuity growth (g).

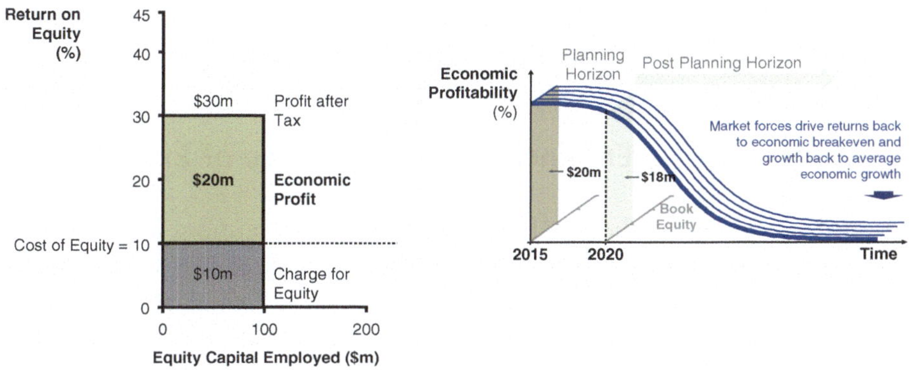

Fig. 3.1 The bow wave as a profile of expected economic profits

The *EP Bow Wave* is shaped like a child's slippery dip or slippery slide. Its dimensions are height (economic profitability), width (book equity) and length (sustainability of a positive economic profit stream). These dimensions are sometimes referred to as *returns, growth and the sustainability of both.*

A plane defined by the product of economic profitability and book equity represents the economic profit expected in any single year – as illustrated for 2015 (already achieved) and 2020 (the last year in a five-year forecast) in Fig. 3.1.

The length of the *EP Bow Wave* is both important and revealing. It represents the market's view in relation to two important characteristics of every company.

The first is the strategic position that the company has built. Strategic position is the combination of the economic attractiveness of a particular market to all participants, and the relative competitive position of an individual participant within that market. It is the primary determinant of current levels of economic profitability and growth, as well as the sustainability of these two parameters under the strategy currently being pursued.

The second characteristic is the extent to which capabilities exist within a company that will enable it to continue to refresh its strategies so as to resist market forces for longer than would otherwise be the case given its current strategic position. The existence of these capabilities confers on a company a somewhat longer *EP Bow Wave* than that related solely to the strategic position it has built under its current strategy. Where it believes they exist, the market capitalises the expected economic impact of these capabilities in the current share price.

Every listed company at every point in time has an implicit *EP Bow Wave* embedded in its share price. The market expects this to be delivered both during and beyond the current planning period in order to preserve value. When value is preserved, over time TSR will match Ke.

Creating Value by Enhancing the Bow Wave of Expected EP

The *EP Bow Wave* is the key building block in establishing a meaningful bridge between success in the product and service market, and success in the capital market. If over a given measurement period, a management team delivers an economic profit stream that is higher or wider than the *EP Bow Wave* embedded in its company's share price at the beginning of the period, or if it finds a way to make the *EP Bow Wave* longer, then it will:

- Exceed expectations in the product and services market, and therefore enhance intrinsic value; and
- Create shareholder wealth in the capital market, and over time achieve a TSR greater than Ke.

Being more specific, there are three ways that the *EP Bow Wave* can be enhanced through actions taken in the market for a company's products and services. In each case, the enhancement leads to a capital market outcome consistent with the creation of wealth for shareholders.

- The first is by improving economic profitability, (or by increasing the height of the *EP Bow Wave* relative to current expectations).
- The second is by growing the capital base on which the return is earned (or by increasing the width of the *EP Bow Wave* relative to current expectations).
- The third is by improving the ability of the company to sustain a positive economic profit stream (or by increasing the length of the *EP Bow Wave*).

Figure 3.2 illustrates what happens when a company adopts a new and higher value strategy. Its *EP Bow Wave* moves from the current profile or set of dimensions (shown in blue), to a new and an enhanced profile (shown in green).

The economic profit expectations embedded in a new and higher value strategy will incorporate an increase in returns (economic profitability), greater growth, or both. There may also be some extension in the length of the *EP Bow Wave*. It is important to appreciate however that the long-term goal is not just to enhance intrinsic value. It is to build an organisation

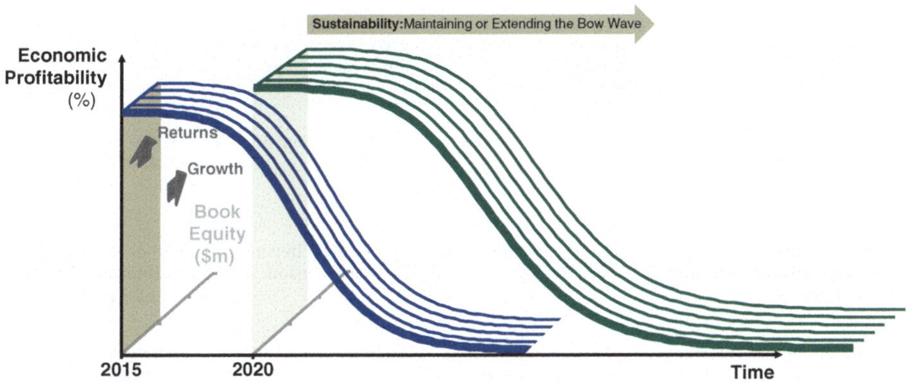

Fig. 3.2 Intrinsic value uplift through enhancing the EP bow wave

capable of continually enhancing intrinsic value. This means working with all three dimensions of the *EP Bow Wave* – not just economic profitability and growth.

In the absence of the *EP Bow Wave* construct, most value-managed companies sought to create shareholder wealth by enhancing either economic profitability or growth, or both. The *EP Bow Wave* makes it possible to think consciously and systematically about ways to create wealth by increasing the length of the bow wave as well.

Ultimately, there are only three generic types of initiative that can impact intrinsic value and therefore be used to underpin the systematic pursuit of shareholder wealth creation. They are:

1. Pursuit of initiatives aimed at improving operating performance under the current strategy,
2. Adoption and successful implementation of new and higher value strategies, and
3. A systematic effort to establish the internal capabilities necessary to continue to do both 1 and 2 on an ongoing basis.

Figure 3.3 illustrates how each type of initiative impacts the dimensions of the *EP Bow Wave* so as to enhance value and create shareholder wealth.

Undertaking a performance improvement initiative under the current strategy will generally lead to a higher level of economic profitability, and its impact will in most cases play out within one to two years. In contrast, adopting a new and higher value strategy is likely to have an impact similar to that illustrated in Fig. 3.2 – and move the company onto a new *EP Bow Wave.*

Type of Activity	Period of Primary Impact	Period of Potential Secondary Impact	Nature of Impact
Performance improvement initiative under current strategy	1-2 years	Remainder of planning horizon	Higher **economic profitability**
Adoption and successful implementation of a higher value strategy	3-5 year planning horizon	A few years beyond planning horizon	Higher **economic profitability** and / or **greater growth**
Establishment of internal capabilities necessary to continue to do both the above	Over a longer period extending well beyond the planning horizon	During the planning horizon	Extension of the **EP bow wave**

Fig. 3.3 Working with the EP bow wave to enhance value

However, the most significant potential impact stems from a systematic effort to develop the internal capabilities – both individual and organisational – required to continually improve performance under the current strategy, while at the same time developing and implementing new and higher value strategies on an ongoing basis at a disaggregated level. As we will see later, the vast majority of higher value strategies are developed at a customer segment level – with the optimum approach being to seek to develop a higher value strategy in roughly one-in-five segments each year.

A systematic effort aimed at extending the *EP Bow Wave* represents a completely new way to think about the creation of shareholder wealth. Importantly, it links the creation of shareholder wealth with the establishment of capabilities at an individual and at an organisational level. Under this construct, people within the business need to be seen as assets to be developed in the pursuit of shareholder wealth creation goals, rather than costs to be eliminated in the pursuit of short-term earnings targets.

Measuring Wealth Creation – The Internal Perspective

A particularly significant attribute of the *EP Bow Wave* is that it provides an analytical mechanism through which it is possible to align the way a board and its executive team measure product and service market performance internally, with the way its investors measure capital market performance externally.

We established in Chapter 2 that wealth will be created if a company takes action that the capital market expects will enable it to deliver an economic profit stream greater than it was expecting at the beginning of a measurement period. Now that we have introduced the *EP Bow Wave* construct, we can develop this idea further.

Over any specified measurement period, shareholder wealth is created when (all else being equal) management either delivers performance in excess of the expectations that investors had at the beginning of that measurement period, or it convinces the capital markets that it has put a strategy in place that will enable it to do so at some point in the future. When expressed in terms of a stream of economic profits, this means wealth creation can be thought of as the sum of:

- The wealth created as a consequence of the delivery of an economic profit stream over any given measurement period, in excess of the expectations that investors had at the beginning of that measurement period; and
- The wealth created as a consequence of any increase in investor expectations in relation to the economic profits to be delivered beyond the measurement period (which normally stems from the adoption of a new and higher value strategy during the measurement period).

These two components are illustrated in Fig. 3.4, for a measurement period from the end of 2010 until the end of 2015.

The X-axis in Fig. 3.4 portrays a time series starting at the end of 2010. It is the same as in Figs. 3.1 and 3.2, except that it starts five years earlier. The Y-axis is economic profit in dollars, and is equivalent to the areas of the planes illustrated in Figs. 3.1 and 3.2.

The amber line in Fig. 3.4 represents the baseline economic profit expectations in place as at the end of 2010, which is also the commencement of a five-year measurement period ended 31 December 2015. The first five years of economic profit plotted are derived from consensus analyst forecasts as at 31 December 2010. The remaining years from 2016 onwards represents the economic profit profile required to underpin the share price as at 31 December 2010.

The blue line represents actual economic profit performance over the five-year measurement period to 31 December 2015, together with the revised market expectations embedded in the share price at that time. The first five years of these new market expectations are derived from consensus analyst forecasts as at 31 December 2015. The remaining years from 2021 onwards represent the economic profit profile necessary to underpin the share price as at 31 December 2015.

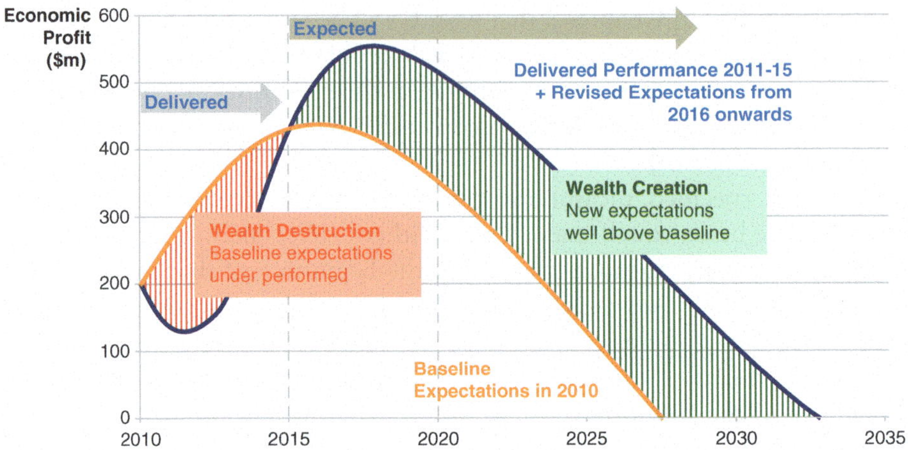

Fig. 3.4 Measuring wealth creation with a pair of EP bow waves

The red shaded area in Fig. 3.4 represents the divergence between the economic profit expectations in place at the beginning of the measurement period, and the actual economic profit performance delivered over that period. In this illustration, the company underperformed against the market's economic profit expectations over the five years to 31 December 2015. This had a negative impact on shareholder wealth.

The green area represents the extent to which strategies developed during the measurement period gave rise to an increase in expectations of future economic profit to be delivered beyond the measurement period. In this case, expectations increased resulting in a positive impact on shareholder wealth.

The sum of the present values (PVs) of the incremental economic profits represented by the red and green areas constitutes the total wealth created over the measurement period.

The tables in Fig. 3.5 show the outcome of an identical analysis completed for the participants in the Australian, the US and the UK banking sectors over the five years to 31 December 2015. These analyses constitute an internal perspective on the wealth created in the banking sector in each country, based on performance delivered and changes in performance expected, in the market for each bank's products and services.

In Fig. 3.5, Total WC means the total amount of wealth created over a five year measurement period. It is then disaggregated into two components. The first is WC Meeting Expect, which corresponds to the left-hand side of the *Pair of EP Bow Waves* in Fig. 3.4. The second is WC New Expect which corresponds to the right hand side of the *Pair of EP Bow Waves* in Fig. 3.4.

Australian Securities Exchange

Num	Name	Ticker	Total WC ($m)	WC Meeting Expect ($m)	WC New Expect ($m)	WC BW Length ($m)	WC Returns / Growth ($m)
			Results from Pair of Bow Waves				
1	Commonwealth Bank of Australia	CBA	53,185	707	52,478	34,748	17,730
2	Westpac Banking Corporation	WBC	35,354	3,157	32,198	23,034	9,164
4	ANZ Banking Group	ANZ	(337)	2,923	(3,260)	0	(3,260)
6	National Australia Bank	NAB	13,567	5,120	8,447	1,191	7,256
42	Bendigo and Adelaide Bank	BEN	(351)	(71)	(280)	(322)	42
46	Bank of Queensland	BOQ	899	(550)	1,449	400	1,049

New York Stock Exchange

Num	Name	Ticker	Total WC ($m)	WC Meeting Expect ($m)	WC New Expect ($m)	WC BW Length ($m)	WC Returns / Growth ($m)
			Results from Pair of Bow Waves				
9	Wells Fargo	WFC	29,356	(16,526)	45,881	46,759	(877)
10	JPMorgan Chase	JPM	(10,731)	(82)	(10,649)	(904)	(9,745)
17	Bank of America	BAC	(61,549)	(61,273)	(276)	5,572	(5,848)
23	Citigroup	C	(126,941)	(59,178)	(67,763)	(24,731)	(43,032)
51	U.S. Bancorp	USB	(562)	1,468	(2,030)	(1,277)	(753)
83	PNC Financial Services	PNC	(1,012)	(1,620)	608	96	512
89	Bank of New York Mellon	BK	(12,245)	(8,261)	(3,984)	256	(4,240)

London Stock Exchange

Num	Name	Ticker	Total WC (£m)	WC Meeting Expect (£m)	WC New Expect (£m)	WC BW Length (£m)	WC Returns / Growth (£m)
			Results from Pair of Bow Waves				
1	HSBC Holdings	HSBA	(57,552)	(16,655)	(40,897)	(3,307)	(37,590)
10	Lloyds Banking Group	LLOY	(28,162)	(33,280)	5,118	2,174	2,944
16	Barclays	BARC	(20,418)	(21,070)	652	2,777	(2,125)
18	Royal Bank of Scotland	RBS	(36,139)	(44,684)	8,545	8,111	434
29	Standard Chartered	STAN	(50,412)	(13,544)	(36,868)	776	(37,644)

Fig. 3.5 Wealth creation in banking – the internal perspective

This is then broken down into two further components, namely: WC BW Length which is the wealth created as a consequence of a change in the length of the *EP Bow Wave*; and WC Returns/Growth which is the wealth created as a consequence of a change in expectations in relation to future returns and/or growth.

Over the five years to 31 December 2015, three of the four major Australian banks managed to create wealth for shareholders. In those that did (Commonwealth Bank of Australia, Westpac Banking Corporation and National Australia Bank), the bulk of the wealth created arose from an increase in expectations in relation to economic profit to be delivered beyond the measurement period, but which was capitalised during the measurement period. This represented $52.5b out of a total of $53.2b in the case of the Commonwealth Bank, $32.2b out of a total of $35.4b in the case of Westpac, and $8.4b out of $13.6 in the case of the NAB.

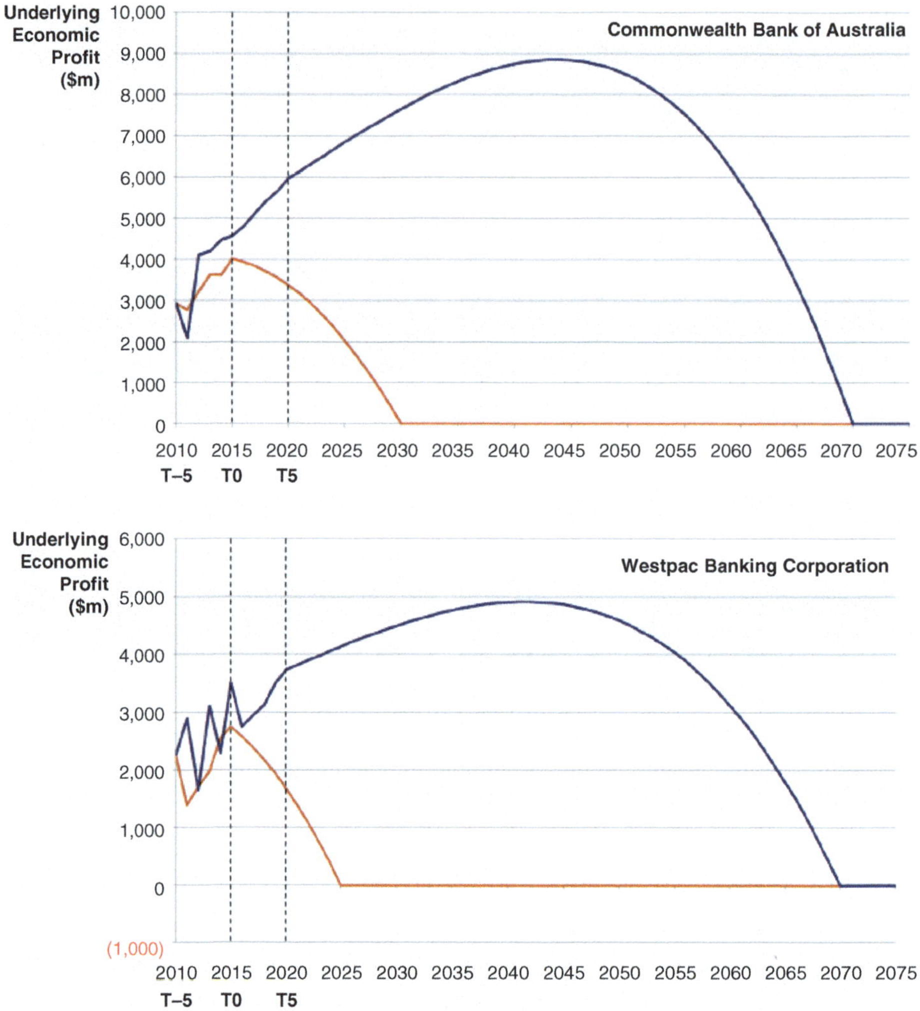

Fig. 3.6 A pair of intersecting EP bow waves for CBA and Westpac

In the US, there was one major bank that created wealth for shareholders over the measurement period. This was Wells Fargo. Its performance mirrored almost exactly the picture presented in Fig. 3.4. It failed to meet expectations over the measurement period, but more than offset this through and increase in expectations in relation to the performance to be delivered beyond the measurement period. Virtually all of this came from an increase it the length of its *EP Bow Wave*.

All five of the major UK banks destroyed shareholder wealth over the five years to 31 December 2015. For three banks, Lloyds, Barclays and Royal Bank of Scotland, this was due almost entirely to their failure to meet expectations over the measurement period. For HSBC and Standard Chartered, it was due to a combination of underperformance with respect to expectations over the measurement period, and a reduction in expectations in relation to the performance to be delivered beyond the measurement period.

The pair of intersecting, two-dimensional *EP Bow Waves* that underpin the outcomes for Australia's Commonwealth Bank and Westpac Banking Corporation are shown in Fig. 3.6.

These were Australia's two most successful banks in economic terms over the five years to 31 December 2015. In both cases, the majority of the wealth created as a consequence of the increase in expectations in relation to the economic profit to be delivered beyond the measurement period, arose from an increase in the length of the *EP Bow Wave* (as distinct from an increase in expectations in relation to future returns and growth).

This suggests that the market feels these two organisations have the processes and capabilities in place to ensure that future leadership teams will be able to deliver economically profitable performance for many years to come.

How this *EP Bow Wave* extension has manifested on a year-by-year basis is illustrated in Fig. 3.7 in the case of the Commonwealth Bank.

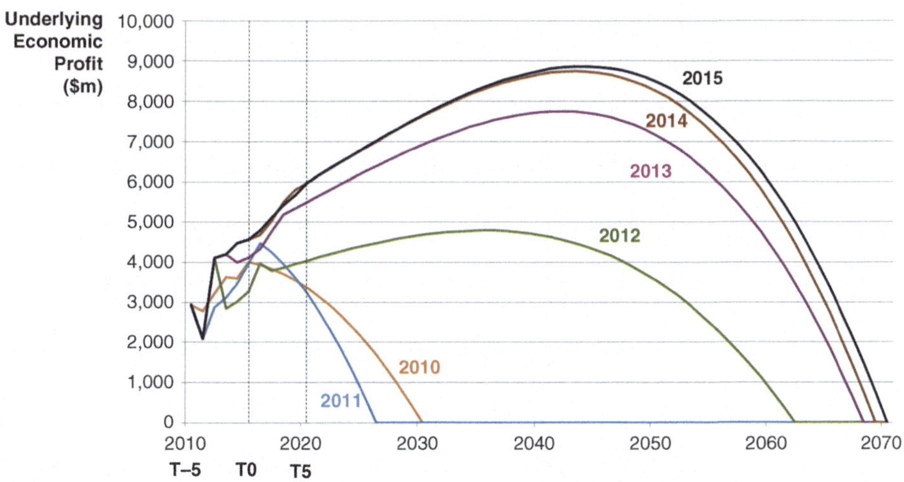

Fig. 3.7 Progression of EP bow waves for the Commonwealth Bank

The most significant shift in *EP Bow Wave* length occurred in the year to December 2012. After that, most of the change in the *EP Bow Wave* profile arose from an increase in expectations in relation to future returns and growth.

Measuring Wealth Creation – The External Perspective

The use of economic performance measures enables us to reach the same wealth creation outcome we arrived at using the *Pair of EP Bow Waves* (as summarised in Fig. 3.5) directly from capital market outcomes.

We know that shareholder wealth is preserved when the TSR delivered matches Ke, and is created when TSR exceeds Ke. We also know that over time, share prices adjust to reflect changing investor expectations and this tends to drive TSR back to Ke (or TSR-Ke to zero). However, over the short to medium term, movements in the capital market as a whole can distort the relationship between TSR and Ke – making the delivery of a TSR greater than Ke much easier to achieve in a rising market and quite difficult to achieve in a falling market.

There is a simple way to counter this. It involves separating capital market performance into two components:

- The impact on shareholder wealth arising from movements in the market as a whole (after adjusting for company-specific risk), and
- The wealth creation consequences of outperforming the market on a risk-adjusted basis, or earning what is known as a positive *TSR Alpha*.

TSR Alpha is the difference between the TSR delivered over a specified measurement period, and the TSR that would have been required by investors in order to match market performance over the same measurement period (after adjusting for company-specific risk). It is a variant of a concept known as Jensen's Alpha, which is used by investment portfolio managers. Figure 3.8 looks at shareholder wealth creation in terms of the impact of market movements and the value consequences of earning a positive *TSR Alpha* for the Australian, US and UK banking sectors.

In Fig. 3.8, TSR-Ke is the long-term economic return on market value, or the annualised difference in the return on the market value of equity (TSR) and the return that investors required in order to preserve value over the longer term (the cost of equity capital, Ke).

The total wealth created arises as a consequence of generating a positive economic return on market value, or a TSR greater than Ke, over the measurement period. The total wealth created (Total WC) numbers in Fig. 3.8 are the same as those in Fig. 3.5.

To illustrate, in the case of the Commonwealth Bank, the total wealth created is $53.2b in both Figs. 3.5 and 3.8. However, whereas this number was derived from the *Pair of EP Bow Waves* in Fig. 3.5, in Fig. 3.8 it comes from the sum of negative $24.3b (shareholder wealth destruction) arising from movements in the market as a whole, and $77.5b in shareholder wealth creation arising from outperforming the market on a risk-adjusted basis and producing a positive *TSR Alpha*.

Australian Securities Exchange

			Capital Market Outcomes			
Num	Name	Ticker	TSR-Ke (%)	Total WC ($m)	WC from MM ($m)	WC from TSRA ($m)
1	Commonwealth Bank of Australia	CBA	7.8%	53,185	(24,342)	77,527
2	Westpac Banking Corporation	WBC	6.2%	35,354	(23,300)	58,654
4	ANZ Banking Group	ANZ	(0.1%)	(337)	(21,253)	20,917
6	National Australia Bank	NAB	3.4%	13,567	(17,214)	30,781
42	Bendigo and Adelaide Bank	BEN	(1.3%)	(351)	(1,127)	777
46	Bank of Queensland	BOQ	4.7%	899	(865)	1,763

New York Stock Exchange

			Capital Market Outcomes			
Num	Name	Ticker	TSR-Ke (%)	Total WC ($m)	WC from MM ($m)	WC from TSRA ($m)
9	Wells Fargo	WFC	2.3%	29,356	35,989	(6,633)
10	JPMorgan Chase	JPM	(0.9%)	(10,731)	41,056	(51,786)
17	Bank of America	BAC	(6.4%)	(61,549)	41,039	(102,588)
23	Citigroup	C	(14.5%)	(126,941)	46,158	(173,099)
51	U.S. Bancorp	USB	(0.1%)	(562)	10,108	(10,670)
83	PNC Financial Services	PNC	(0.4%)	(1,012)	7,048	(8,060)
89	Bank of New York Mellon	BK	(4.9%)	(12,245)	7,315	(19,560)

London Stock Exchange

			Capital Market Outcomes			
Num	Name	Ticker	TSR-Ke (%)	Total WC (£m)	WC from MM (£m)	WC from TSRA (£m)
1	HSBC Holdings	HSBA	(7.9%)	(57,552)	(36,792)	(20,760)
10	Lloyds Banking Group	LLOY	(9.2%)	(28,162)	(21,304)	(6,859)
16	Barclays	BARC	(9.4%)	(20,418)	(15,165)	(5,253)
18	Royal Bank of Scotland	RBS	(14.2%)	(36,139)	(16,911)	(19,228)
29	Standard Chartered	STAN	(24.4%)	(50,412)	(17,622)	(32,790)

Fig. 3.8 Wealth creation in banking – the external perspective

Continually Producing a Positive TSR Alpha

The capital market performance of the Commonwealth Bank of Australia was so strong that it delivered a positive *TSR Alpha* in every one of the last five years.

The *TSR Alpha* performance of the CBA over that period is examined in more detail in Appendix 2. In principle, an outcome like this is very difficult to achieve. Only 24 companies in the ASX 500 achieved such an outcome over the five-years to 31 December 2015. Of these, 17 were in the ASX 100. There were 34 companies in the S&P 500 that achieved a positive *TSR Alpha* in each of the last five years, of which 11 were in the S&P 100. There were 21 in the FTSE 100.

The reason it is difficult for a company to continually deliver a positive *TSR Alpha* is that share prices adjust constantly to accommodate new or revised financial performance expectations. They move up or down in order for shareholders to achieve a TSR equal to their required rate of return. This causes TSR-Ke to tend towards zero over the long term and *TSR Alpha* to tend towards zero over the short to medium term.

If a performance improvement initiative is put in place or a new strategy is adopted that causes a company to outperform the market, it will produce a positive *TSR Alpha*. If it then delivers the new and higher performance expectations, *TSR Alpha* should revert to zero. In order to once again produce a positive *TSR Alpha*, the company must find a way to exceed these new performance expectations.

Figure 3.9 illustrates the distribution of annualised *TSR Alpha* outcomes for the ASX, NYSE and LSE companies we have analysed over the five years ended 31 December 2015. In each case, *TSR Alpha* is distributed fairly evenly around a mean of zero – and this is exactly what we would expect. But the NYSE has a narrower spread of outcomes than the LSE and a much narrower spread than the ASX. This suggests a closer relationship between underlying intrinsic value and market value in NYSE-listed companies – which is perhaps to be expected given the depth of the market and the relative size of the companies listed on the NYSE.

Delivering a positive *TSR Alpha* every year for an extended period means that, after adjusting for the value consequences of market movements, the company in question was able to continually deliver performance in excess of expectations which were themselves continually increasing. This is an enormously difficult challenge, and meeting it would normally represent quite a significant achievement.

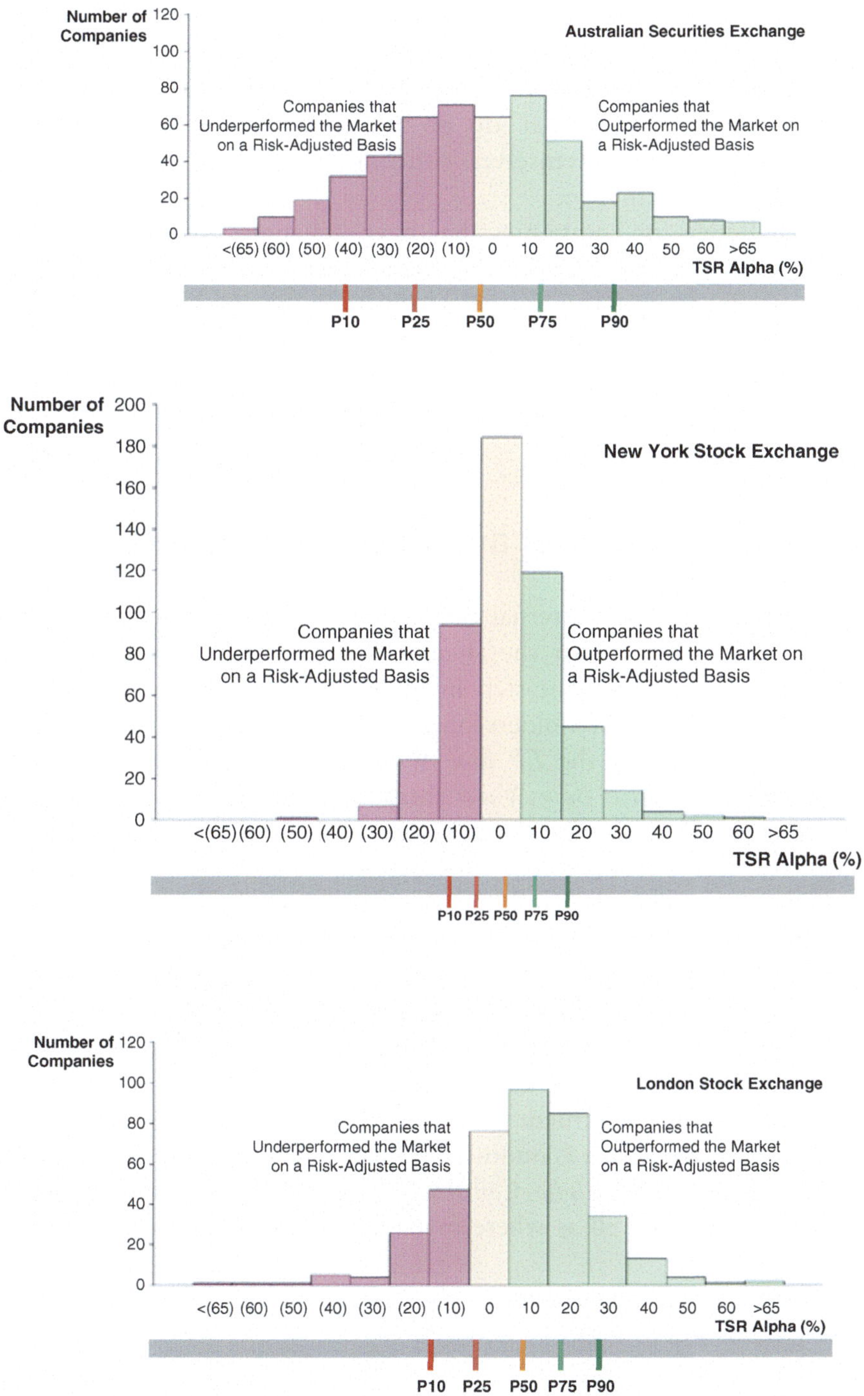

Fig. 3.9 Distribution of five-year TSR Alpha outcomes for ASX, NYSE, LSE

For exactly the same reason that it is difficult to continually deliver a positive *TSR Alpha* outcome, it is also difficult to continually deliver a negative *TSR Alpha* outcome. This is because after adjusting for market movements, companies that do so are continually failing to meet expectations that are themselves continually decreasing. It represents serious underperformance.

The challenge for companies that have delivered positive *TSR Alpha* outcomes for extended periods is that unless they have processes in place that encourage the systematic pursuit of intrinsic value uplift (primarily through the ongoing development and successful implementation of higher value strategies), it is likely to be difficult to continue to outperform the market and keep on delivering a positive *TSR Alpha*.

Aligning the Internal and External Perspectives

Aligning management's internal or product and service market perspective on performance, with the shareholders' external or capital market perspective, is an important step in building an organisation capable of creating wealth for shareholders on an ongoing basis. This can best be done with the help of the *EP Bow Wave*, and particularly by using the intersecting *Pair of EP Bow Waves* introduced in Fig. 3.4.

From a purely economic perspective, the key to ongoing shareholder wealth creation is an explicit and systematic focus on medium-term economic profit growth, while at the same time building the internal capabilities necessary to deliver longer-term economic profit growth. The success of both endeavours leads to intrinsic value uplift and the market's assessment of management's efforts in pursuing this goal is best captured in *TSR Alpha* over the short to medium term, and in TSR-Ke over the long term.

We refer to the alignment of economic performance in the product and service market, with economic performance in the capital market, as *The EP Uplift + TSR Alpha Construct*. Figure 3.10 provides a summary of how it works, as well as where management needs to focus to bring it to life.

This equivalence was evident in the case of the Australian, US and UK banking industries in Figs. 3.5 and 3.8.

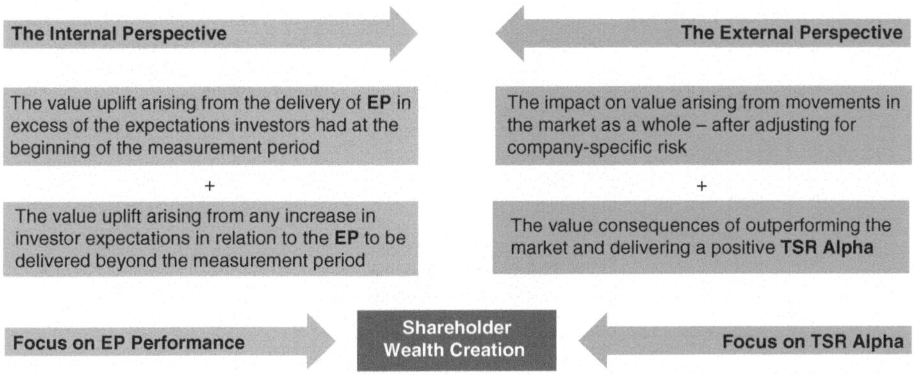

Fig. 3.10 The EP uplift + TSR Alpha construct

Economic Performance in Three Exchanges

The *EP Uplift + TSR Alpha Construct* provides a particularly powerful way to look at the performance of individual listed companies in the context of the market as a whole.

Appendix 3 contains a detailed analysis of the performance of the top 100 companies by market capitalisation listed on the ASX, NYSE and LSE over the five years to 31 December 2015 using the *EP Uplift + TSR Alpha Construct*. Central to this analysis is an examination of how the shape of the *EP Bow Wave* changed over the five-year measurement period. The analysis is most revealing.

Analytical Outcomes

Figure 3.11 summarises the outcome for all three exchanges. It shows:

- How many of the top 100 companies listed on each exchange created wealth and how many destroyed wealth over the five years to 31 December 2015;
- Of those that created wealth, how many actually met market expectations over the five years to 31 December 2015, and how many did not; and
- How much of the wealth created in each case stemmed from meeting existing expectations over the measurement period, or from creating new expectations to be delivered beyond the measurement period.

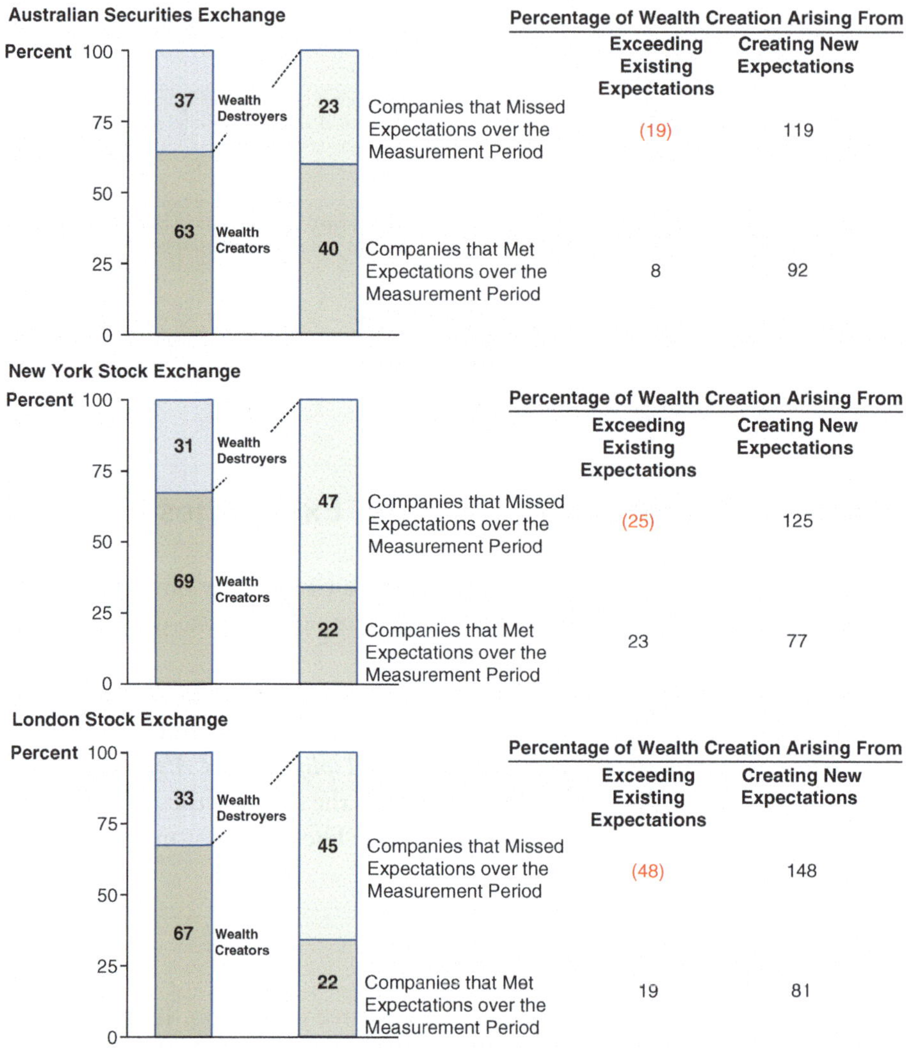

Fig. 3.11 Sources of wealth creation for ASX, NYSE and LSE companies – five years to 31 December 2015

In all three exchanges, what mattered most in terms of shareholder wealth creation amongst the top 100 listed companies, was the establishment of new EP expectations to be delivered beyond the measurement period, rather than achieving short-term performance outcomes during the measurement period.

An even more compelling picture emerges when we examine each exchange in more detail – as shown in Fig. 3.12. Once again, we have examined the 100 largest listed companies by market capitalisation in each exchange.

Australian Securities Exchange		Level of Wealth Creation Over 5 Years (TSR-Ke %)	Value Impact of Meeting EP Expectations (% Total)	Value Impact of Creating New EP Expectations (% Total)	Value Impact of Change in Bow Wave Length (% Total)	Change in Length of Bow Wave (years)
Wealth Creators	**63**	**9.4%**	**5%**	**95%**	**60%**	**20**
Met Expectations	40	10.7%	8%	92%	65%	24
Missed Expectations	23	6.4%	(19%)	119%	29%	13
Wealth Destroyers	**37**	(12.4%)	(33%)	(67%)	(1%)	(9)

New York Stock Exchange		Level of Wealth Creation Over 5 Years (TSR-Ke %)	Value Impact of Meeting EP Expectations (% Total)	Value Impact of Creating New EP Expectations (% Total)	Value Impact of Change in Bow Wave Length (% Total)	Change in Length of Bow Wave (years)
Wealth Creators	**69**	**11.8%**	**(1%)**	**101%**	**65%**	**17**
Met Expectations	22	17.8%	23%	77%	41%	10
Missed Expectations	47	8.9%	(25%)	125%	80%	21
Wealth Destroyers	**31**	(5.1%)	(23%)	(77%)	(27%)	(8)

London Stock Exchange		Level of Wealth Creation Over 5 Years (TSR-Ke %)	Value Impact of Meeting EP Expectations (% Total)	Value Impact of Creating New EP Expectations (% Total)	Value Impact of Change in Bow Wave Length (% Total)	Change in Length of Bow Wave (years)
Wealth Creators	**67**	**8.3%**	**(41%)**	**141%**	**75%**	**14**
Met Expectations	22	15.6%	19%	81%	75%	15
Missed Expectations	45	6.9%	(48%)	148%	75%	13
Wealth Destroyers	**33**	(10.9%)	(56%)	(44%)	(1%)	(4)

Fig. 3.12 Sources of wealth creation for ASX, NYSE and LSE companies

With reference to Fig. 3.11, of the 63 ASX listed companies that created shareholder wealth over the five years to 31 December 2015, 40 met expectations over the measurement period and 23 did not. Of the 69 NYSE-listed and 67 LSE-listed companies that created shareholder wealth, just 22 met expectations in each case.

With reference to Fig. 3.12, a full 95 percent of the wealth created by the 63 strong-performing ASX 100 companies, and over 100 percent of the wealth created by the 69 strong-performing NYSE listed and 67 LSE listed companies, stemmed from creating new expectations to be delivered beyond the measurement period. Most importantly of all, in all three cases the majority of this came from extending the *EP Bow Wave* – by an average of 20 years in the case of the ASX listed companies, 17 years in the case of NYSE listed companies and 14 years in the case of the LSE-listed companies.

Figure 3.13 shows how the *EP Bow Wave* changed by industry sector over the past five years for the top 100 ASX, NYSE and LSE listed companies. Some of these shifts are quite significant. They are even more significant at the level of the individual companies, and is evident from the company-level outcomes presented in Appendix 3.

One particularly interesting observation from Fig. 3.13 is that the market is expecting economic profitability (ROE-Ke) greater than 30 percent in

ASX 100 Companies	December 2010				December 2015				
	ROE-Ke (%)	Growth (%)	Bow Wave (years)	M:B Ratio	ROE-Ke (%)	Growth (%)	Bow Wave (years)	M:B Ratio	TSR-Ke (%)
Consumer Discretionary	9.7	7.8	34	4.3	13.0	8.9	45	5.4	13.2
Consumer Staples	8.8	4.5	20	2.8	8.0	4.4	47	3.4	1.1
Energy	2.5	7.3	35	2.3	(0.7)	6.0	27	1.6	(10.1)
Financials	5.2	5.0	15	1.9	5.6	4.9	34	2.2	5.2
Health Care	15.2	6.8	36	4.5	**33.8**	11.5	40	11.3	14.0
Industrials	7.4	7.4	36	3.1	8.3	8.8	40	3.1	1.1
Information Technology	22.7	9.6	50	6.9	22.5	9.9	50	7.2	3.4
Materials	14.0	12.0	44	3.7	1.6	5.4	16	1.8	(15.6)
Telecommunications	13.9	7.1	14	2.8	20.5	9.2	28	5.2	16.2
Utilities	(3.1)	1.4	5	1.1	1.0	2.4	16	1.5	5.1

NYSE 100 Companies	December 2010				December 2015				
	ROE-Ke (%)	Growth (%)	Bow Wave (years)	M:B Ratio	ROE-Ke (%)	Growth (%)	Bow Wave (years)	M:B Ratio	TSR-Ke (%)
Consumer Discretionary	32.6	20.8	27	7.3	27.4	13.1	43	11.8	13.3
Consumer Staples	22.7	6.5	31	4.3	32.1	7.7	41	8.1	6.6
Energy	11.8	4.3	45	3.1	5.4	3.0	24	1.8	(7.5)
Financials	1.6	6.4	27	1.3	0.4	4.8	31	1.2	(0.5)
Health Care	17.8	8.0	17	3.3	20.8	9.4	40	5.2	19.5
Industrials	27.7	9.4	30	5.5	33.5	10.0	43	8.4	3.1
Information Technology	23.3	16.1	33	5.9	22.2	10.7	41	5.0	5.6
Materials	14.0	11.7	39	3.9	16.6	12.1	40	4.6	(1.6)
Telecommunications	8.7	5.1	22	2.1	25.2	10.1	33	6.3	5.9
Utilities	5.1	4.7	23	1.7	5.7	5.0	38	2.1	8.0

LSE 100 Companies	December 2010				December 2015				
	ROE-Ke (%)	Growth (%)	Bow Wave (years)	M:B Ratio	ROE-Ke (%)	Growth (%)	Bow Wave (years)	M:B Ratio	TSR-Ke (%)
Consumer Discretionary	22.1	13.5	26	6.7	26.7	12.4	40	8.4	9.6
Consumer Staples	23.3	6.7	36	4.3	36.9	7.3	47	7.2	4.9
Energy	7.8	2.7	5	1.4	(1.3)	1.3	12	0.9	(9.3)
Financials	2.4	6.5	27	1.4	2.0	6.2	29	1.5	(3.7)
Health Care	32.6	9.2	22	5.1	38.7	11.4	33	7.9	5.6
Industrials	17.5	14.8	16	4.0	19.0	13.2	33	5.0	7.9
Information Technology	12.5	12.1	27	4.3	16.6	14.0	45	6.7	6.5
Materials	17.1	13.6	45	3.4	2.5	6.4	27	1.7	(17.9)
Telecommunications	53.0	20.5	14	19.0	53.0	23.1	15	19.0	7.6
Utilities	18.5	8.6	26	3.9	16.1	11.6	37	4.0	2.9

Fig. 3.13 Movement in EP bow wave dimensions by industry sector

some sectors. This is so high that it calls into question whether the companies in these sectors are treating their stakeholders as allies in the creation of value over the long term – or seeing them as adversaries in the pursuit of short-term financial performance outcomes (and exploiting them in some way in order to achieve those outcomes).

Why Short-Termism Makes No Sense

This analysis provides compelling support for the proposition that short-termism – or the pursuit of short-term financial performance outcomes at the expense of longer-term value creation – makes no sense at all.

Two of the most significant insights to emerge from this work were:

- The extent to which the wealth created for shareholders over the past five years arose from creating new EP expectations to be delivered in the future, rather than from meeting existing EP expectations over the five-year measurement period; and
- How much of the wealth creation associated with these new expectations stemmed from an increase in the length of the *EP Bow Wave* – or in other words from making the business more sustainable.

Overall, only a tiny proportion of the wealth created for shareholders arose from companies exceeding short-term expectations over the measurement period. So why are market commentators, proxy advisors, retail investors and the financial press so fixated on short-term performance? What this analysis demonstrates once again is that to improve performance in the capital market over the short, the medium and the longer-term, listed company leadership teams need to focus on improving performance in the product and services market over the long term (not the short term). The pursuit of short-term financial performance outcomes at the expense of longer-term value creation really makes no sense. It is just another unfortunate manifestation of *The EPS Myth* which we exploded in Chapter 2.

Once again, it is difficult to escape the conclusion that there is a very real and indeed a pressing need to improve the understanding of business leaders in relation to these matters. Only through a proper understanding will it be possible to strengthen their resolve in resisting calls from self-interested capital market players with short-term agendas, and who want companies to put short-term financial performance outcomes ahead of longer-term value creation. As we said at the outset, the real challenge for the leaders of a listed company is not to create shareholder wealth *per se*, but to build an enduring institution that can create value for customers and wealth for shareholders *on an ongoing basis*, and wherever possible to do so in ways that enhance the wellbeing of other stakeholders as well.

We will return to this topic later. But for now, it is sufficient to point out that to move forward in this way, it is important to have:

- A proper understanding of how product and service market performance translates into capital market performance – by understanding the change in the shape of the *EP Bow Wave*;
- A noble intent that goes well beyond simply trying to maximise share price during the tenure of the current leadership team; and
- A win-win mindset in which all stakeholders are seen as allies in the pursuit of value uplift over the long term, rather than adversaries in the pursuit of short-term profit targets.

Being conscious of these three attributes is essential for those leaders of listed companies that are intent on building an enduring institution. At the same time, the changing shape of the *EP Bow Wave* can provide some interesting insights into an individual company's progress on this journey.

Synthesis and Concluding Remarks

The way most shareholders measure the performance of their investment in a listed company is both different to and quite difficult to align with the way the management team has traditionally measured its performance in the market for its company's products and services. Bringing these two perspectives into alignment is essential if a company is to understand the link between its strategic decisions and its financial performance; as well as how the performance achieved by management in the market for the company's products and services, translates into the capital market outcomes experienced by shareholders.

The key to aligning these two perspectives is to use economic performance measures in conjunction with the concept of the *EP Bow Wave* and the *Pair of EP Bow Waves* constructed at the beginning and the end of a measurement period. The *EP Bow Wave* also provides a valuable mechanism through which to focus management attention on the three primary drivers of value for every listed company. These are returns, growth and the sustainability of both – or the height, the width and the length of the *EP Bow Wave*.

The *Pair of Intersecting EP Bow Wave*s enables us to think in terms of the two fundamental components of shareholder wealth creation that a management team can give effect to, namely:

- The delivery of an economic profit stream in excess of the expectations that investors had at the beginning of a given measurement period; and
- The development and successful implementation of one or a number of higher value strategies, leading to an increase in market expectations in relation to the economic profit to be delivered beyond the measurement period.

It also enables us to put a value on the benefit of investing in a medium to long-term initiative aimed at extending the *EP Bow Wave* through the development of the individual and organisational capabilities necessary to continually deliver a positive economic profit stream – through the ongoing pursuit and successful implementation of higher value strategies.

In addition, the *EP Uplift + TSR Alpha Construct* enables us to align the way shareholder wealth is created by management in the product and services market, with the way wealth creation is experienced by shareholders in the capital market.

Perhaps most importantly of all, an examination of the change in shape of the *EP Bow Wave* over a particular measurement period, such the five years to 31 December 2015 we have used throughout this chapter, provides compelling support for the proposition that short-termism – or the pursuit of short-term financial performance outcomes at the expense of longer-term value creation – makes absolutely no sense at all.

We can extend this line of thinking somewhat further by focusing on the fact that in certain jurisdictions, the fiduciary duty of directors of listed companies is sometimes boiled down to a requirement to simply maximise returns for existing shareholders. This could be better expressed as a duty to seek to continually enhance the shape of the company's *EP Bow Wave*. This will drive ongoing value uplift and over time, the wealth created is likely to be much greater than that achieved by seeking to maximise earnings or EPS.

As will become clear in the chapters to come, the management actions required to continually enhance the shape of a company's *EP Bow Wave* are the same as those needed to build an enduring institution that can create value for its customer and wealth for its shareholders on an ongoing basis. So, it could also be argued that the duty of a director might be even better expressed as a requirement to encourage the building of such an institution. Importantly, the *EP Uplift + TSR Alpha Construct* means that management's success in such an endeavour can be measured in the product and services market through the improvement in the shape of the *EP Bow Wave*, and in the capital market by the extent to which TSR exceeds Ke over the long term, or by the *TSR Alpha* outcome over the short-to-medium term.

4

Two Joint and Mutually Reinforcing Objectives

In Chapter 3, we introduced three new concepts that in combination constitute what we call *The EP Uplift + TSR Alpha Construct*. The first was the notion of a *Bow Wave of Expected Economic Profit* that underpins the share price and market capitalisation of every listed company at every point in time. The second was the idea of a *Pair of Economic Profit Bow Waves* that could be used to quantify the extent to which a company had created shareholder wealth by either exceeding market expectations over a given measurement period, or by convincing the capital market that it had developed the ability to do so at some point beyond the measurement period. The third was the concept of *TSR Alpha*, which in combination with the *Pair of EP Bow Waves,* enabled us to link performance either delivered or expected in the market for a company's products and services, with the capital market outcomes experienced by shareholders.

In this chapter, we will take the thinking one step further. But before we take that next step, there is an important conceptual point that needs to be made in relation to capital market performance and the metrics based on TSR that are used to measure it.

The Three Drivers of TSR

TSR is a well-understood measure of listed company performance. It is also an essential element in both the metrics we use to measure the economic return on market value; namely TSR-Ke and *TSR Alpha*.

TSR is defined as dividends plus change in share price over a given measurement period, divided by the share price at the beginning of the

D. Kilroy, M. Schneider, *Customer Value, Shareholder Wealth, Community Wellbeing*, DOI 10.1007/978-3-319-54774-9_4

measurement period. However, there is another way to think about TSR. That is in terms of the components or factors that drive it up or down.

On both a standalone basis, and as a component of TSR-Ke and *TSR Alpha*, TSR is driven by three distinct factors: changes in the underlying intrinsic value of a business; shifts in company-specific sentiment; and shifts in sentiment affecting the market as a whole.

Shifts in sentiment affecting the whole market are a given. There is little if anything that the board or its executive team can do about the impact of this on their company's share price.

Material shifts in company-specific sentiment do occur. But in a well-governed company operating in a fully informed and well-attended market, they should not occur very often – at least in theory. When they do, it is generally associated with the existence of a material gap between intrinsic value and market value. The shift in sentiment causes the gap to emerge, to widen or to narrow. Ultimately, it is only share traders and other short-term capital market players that benefit from the existence of and movements in company-specific sentiment. The interests of long-term investors (many of whom are continually investing in the companies in their portfolio) are best served by neutral sentiment where market value is in line with intrinsic value. Companies should seek to achieve this alignment wherever possible.

That leaves changes in intrinsic value, and this is the component of TSR that executives can and should seek to influence. From an economic perspective, their primary focus should be on trying to find ways to enhance the intrinsic value of the business, by either:

- Delivering an economic profit stream in excess of market expectations; or by
- Developing and implementing new and higher value strategies that will enhance market expectations in relation to the economic profit to be delivered in the future.

In the long run, these are the only ways that a management team can go about the systematic pursuit of shareholder wealth creation, and particularly when seeking to do so on an ongoing basis.

Higher Value Strategy Development

While both these building blocks are important, the second is more important. As was demonstrated empirically in Chapter 3, for most companies, a good deal more wealth can be created though the development and successful implementation of higher value strategies, than through delivering better than expected financial performance under the current strategy. This is because there are generally many more courses of action available for higher value strategy development than there are for operational performance improvement under an existing strategy.

In fact, if the market is properly informed, and good management practice is not corrupted by the introduction of the notion of stretch targets that encourage executives to try to extract earnings or even economic profit outcomes beyond that which the approved strategy is capable of delivering, then the potential to safely exceed expectations through operational performance improvement under the current strategy is generally quite limited.

Value-managed companies that have a systematic approach to ongoing shareholder wealth creation, make greater use of this understanding than other companies. Their shareholders benefit accordingly. It is important to understand how and why this happens.

It is often argued that opportunities for higher value strategy development arise infrequently, and that in between those infrequent but potentially pivotal points in time, operational performance improvement should be the primary focus of the management team. However, this has not been our experience in working with companies in many industries in many different countries over the past 20 years. On the contrary, we have seen many companies manage to deliver continual value uplift – using an approach we will introduce in the next few pages and describe in detail in the chapters to come.

Nevertheless, the argument that opportunities for value uplift through higher value strategy development arise infrequently, is one of the driving forces behind the relentless push for greater and greater levels of economic efficiency we see in many companies. This push for greater efficiency can certainly deliver financial performance improvement over the short to medium term. But it can also block the path to larger (and sometimes much larger) medium to long-term wealth creation opportunities.

Successful value-managed companies don't get stuck in this argument. They move beyond it because they know either explicitly or implicitly, that higher value strategy development is best pursued at a disaggregated level – sometimes at a business unit level but much more frequently at a customer segment level. When pursued at a customer segment level, the search for higher value strategies can become systematic and continuous, rather than opportunistic and infrequent.

As a simple illustration, let's consider a listed company that has an intention to double its intrinsic value over a five-year period. It is possible (but probably quite unlikely) that this goal will be achieved through the adoption of one new all-encompassing corporate strategy. At the same time, there is very little chance that it could be achieved by trying to add 15 to 20 percent to the value of each and every part of the business every year (and no chance whatsoever that this outcome could be achieved solely through cost reduction). There is however a good chance that the goal could be met by setting out to double the value of one-in-five segments each year. The key to this is a systematic approach to higher value strategy development pursued at the level of a properly defined customer segment – focused in the first instance on finding ways to enhance value for customers.

We will discuss the application of this process in some detail in Part III. At this point, our objective is to demonstrate the link that exists between customer value creation and shareholder wealth creation in a listed company, and highlight its role and significance in a value-managed company.

The fact is there is an explicit relationship linking customer value creation and shareholder wealth creation that exists in virtually all listed companies. However, in many cases it is dormant or latent rather than active in an operational sense.

While this relationship exists conceptually at group, divisional and business unit levels, it functions most effectively at the level of an individual customer segment. It is fundamental to the ability of most value-managed companies to continually build shareholder wealth through the ongoing development and successful implementation of higher value strategies.

Linking Customer Value and Shareholder Wealth

Figure 2.4 illustrated how a listed company participates in the market for its products and services and the market for shareholder capital.

Shareholders firstly provide capital to the corporate centre. The corporate centre then deploys the funds at its disposal in its various business units, which use it to fund both the development and the provision of products and services that create value for customers.

Customer value represents a benefit or a combination of benefits for which a customer is prepared to pay. So if priced appropriately, a product or service that creates value for customers will generate a revenue stream commensurate with the value created for customers. If the products or services from which customers derive value can be produced and delivered for an economic cost that is less than the price customers are prepared to pay, then there will be a residual economic profit stream available to the providers of capital.

Whenever there is a positive economic profit stream from participation in the market for the company's products and services, the intrinsic value and ultimately the market value of the business will be greater than its book value. In other words, it will have a M:B greater than 1.0×.

If the economic profit stream delivered is consistent with market expectations, shareholder wealth will be preserved. If the economic profit stream delivered is greater than market expectations, or if the capital market forms the view that it will exceed current market expectations at some point in the future, then shareholder wealth will be created.

There are three primary factors that determine how well a company is able to operate simultaneously in both the market for its products and services, and the market for shareholder capital. They are:

- How effective it is in using its capital and other resources to create value for customers;
- How much of the value created for customers is recaptured in the revenue stream and particularly in price; and
- How efficient it is at delivering value to customers and therefore the extent to which its revenue stream exceeds the economic cost of generating that revenue stream.

Needs-Based Customer Segmentation

One of the most important pillars of the MFV philosophy is the realisation that success along all three dimensions is most likely to occur within what is known as a needs-based customer segment. This is a segment defined by a company as *a group of customers whose needs are so similar that we can serve them in a way that is value creating for them, and cost effective for us.*

Within every needs-based customer segment, it is possible to establish an enduring cycle of customer value and shareholder wealth creation. This cycle is the primary driver of ongoing shareholder wealth creation in every value-managed company. It is illustrated in Fig. 4.1 and operates in two ways.

Firstly, it provides a framework for management to think about the relationships linking:

- The value derived from the company's products and services by the customers that comprise the segment;

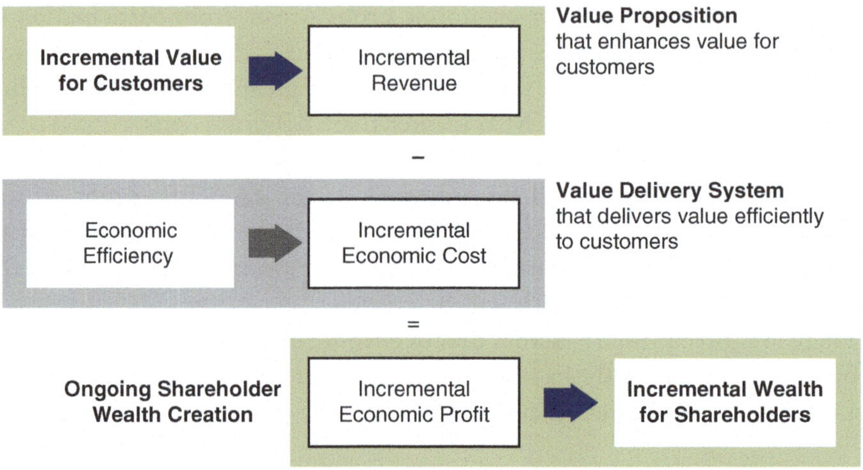

Fig. 4.1 The cycle of customer value and shareholder wealth creation

- The pricing of those products and services;
- The economic cost (i.e. the operating cost plus the capital cost) incurred in serving the customers in the segment; and
- The economic profitability achieved and the economic profit generated as a consequence.

Secondly and more importantly, it provides a mechanism through which to create value for customers and build wealth for shareholders *on an ongoing basis*. It does this by translating incremental customer value provided to customers in a particular needs-based segment, into incremental intrinsic value and ultimately incremental shareholder wealth.[1] There are five steps involved, which we will outline here and cover in more detail in Part III.

Step 1. Firstly, it is important to understand the needs of the customers in the segment and how they derive value from both the current offer and ideally from potential enhancements to that offer. There are many ways to approach this and not all are analytical in nature. However conjoint analysis and discrete choice modelling are particularly powerful analytical techniques.[2]

[1] If priced appropriately, the delivery of incremental customer value will result in additional revenues. If delivered efficiently, the incremental revenues will translate into incremental economic profit, the PV of which is incremental intrinsic value. When recognised by the capital markets, this will translate into incremental shareholder wealth.

[2] See Orme, Bryan K., *Getting Started with Conjoint Analysis – Strategies for Product Design and Pricing Research*, Research Publishers LLC, Madison, 2010.

Step 2. Based on that understanding, a decision can then be taken to augment or enhance the current offer by adding a series of additional features that create additional value or benefit for the customers in the segment (or potentially to eliminate certain features whose value to customers is less than their cost).

Step 3. Techniques such as micro-economic analysis and discrete choice modelling can then be used to quantify the change in value derived by customers in the segment, and how that translates into price or a willingness to pay.

Step 4. A decision then needs to be taken as to whether or not the incremental value delivered to customers will be recaptured through price or through additional volume. In most but not all cases, the best economic outcome for shareholders and most other stakeholders is to seek to recapture incremental customer value primarily through price. This is often referred to as value pricing, or pricing on the basis of benefits delivered rather than cost to serve. It will be explored in more detail in Part III.

Step 5. So long as pricing is appropriate, and the incremental revenues exceed the incremental economic costs involved in creating and delivering the incremental value to customers, the cycle will produce an incremental economic profit stream. The PV of the incremental economic profit stream is the change in the intrinsic value of the segment. In the normal course of events, this eventually translates into incremental shareholder wealth.

A significant point to appreciate here is that, while made up of discrete steps aimed firstly at finding ways to enhance customer value and then recapture it as incremental shareholder wealth, this process is essentially a continuous one. Over time, a company's understanding of the customers within a particular segment, how best to create value for them and how to do so in ways that are economically profitable, will continue to improve over time.

The Role of Innovation

An important aspect of this process is the way it places innovation in an absolutely seminal role. We will discuss both the creative process and the disciplined approach to innovation required in a value-managed company in some detail later. However, it is important to acknowledge the significance of the role played by innovative thinking in every cycle of customer value and shareholder wealth creation. Once we appreciate how this cycle works, it also becomes clear that the real key to wealth creation is innovation. Ultimately, most of the wealth created for shareholders in a value-managed company stems from the successful implementation of higher value strategies developed from new ideas. This is because shareholder wealth creation really is a creative act on the part of the executives and the employees of every listed company. It has its genesis in customer value creation because while measured in the capital markets, shareholder wealth is created in the product and services markets by using innovation or creative thinking to develop products or devise services that deliver greater value to customers. While cost management is important, it is rare to find a situation in which standalone cost reduction is the only course of action available to create wealth for shareholders. It is equally rare to find a situation in which a lower cost structure leading to lower prices is the only way to enhance value for customers.

In every value-managed company, customer value creation and shareholder wealth creation serve as joint and mutually reinforcing objectives – and they reinforce each other most strongly at the level of an individual needs-based customer segment. Economic efficiency provides the link between these two joint goals. But it is only on rare occasions that it should be pursued as an objective in its own right.

One of the first engagements we took on in late 1994 arose when the most profitable part of our client's business came under "attack" from a competitor. We were asked to help devise a pricing strategy to minimise the expected loss of market share.

This offered a wonderful opportunity to use a more innovative approach. Instead of helping them to wage war over market share in a particularly profitable segment, my team chose to use a technique we had developed called Hybrid Thinking, which will be described in the next chapter.

We convened a workshop attended by the key decision-makers, and began the workshop by posing a paradigm shifting question. That question was: "how do we make the market for our product so big, that the actions of our competitor will not matter". The result was utterly transformative.

The outcome of that workshop put the company on a completely different value growth trajectory for the next five years. The focus was almost entirely on customer value creation through a series of segment specific value propositions. But the consequences for shareholder wealth creation were simply extraordinary.

Synthesis and Concluding Remarks

The real key to ongoing shareholder wealth creation is the continual pursuit and successful implementation of higher value strategies – developed mainly at the level of an individual needs-based customer segment. In most cases this approach generates a good deal more wealth for shareholders than the pursuit of improved operational performance under the current strategy.

The adoption of customer value creation and shareholder wealth creation as joint and mutually reinforcing objectives, pursued at the level of a properly defined needs-based customer segment, provides the main engine for higher value strategy development, intrinsic value uplift and ultimately the ongoing creation of shareholder wealth.

Many executives who have been down this path find that this understanding (applied to both segmentation and the ongoing process of segment-level strategy development) is the most important shift in thinking required to set their organisation on a completely different and more sustainable value growth trajectory.

5

Creative Thinking and the Value Creation Mindset

This chapter describes the type of mindset required in order to succeed in creating value for customers and wealth for shareholders on an ongoing basis, and in building an organisation with the capability to do so. Some examples of the very positive outcomes that stem from the establishment and application of such a mindset are provided in Part III.

There are two aspects to a value creation mindset. The first is an understanding and acceptance of the fundamental relationship that exists between customer value creation and shareholder wealth creation. The second is the ability and the willingness to use creative thinking and logical analysis in combination rather than in isolation.

The fundamental relationship that exists linking customer value creation and shareholder wealth creation was described in Chapter 4. Once this relationship is recognised and understood, it does not take long for a management team to come to the conclusion that they will find it difficult to create wealth for shareholders on an ongoing basis unless they continually look for ways to enhance the value that their business delivers to both its direct customers and the end-consumers of its products or services. The importance of including a focus on end-consumer value creation is discussed in some detail in Chapter 9.

At least in theory, there is no limit to the revenue growth that can flow from the creation of additional value for customers and end-consumers (particularly given the access to capital to fund growth that is available to a successful listed company). The possibilities are constrained only by the imagination, the creativity and the capability of the management team.

D. Kilroy, M. Schneider, *Customer Value, Shareholder Wealth, Community Wellbeing*, DOI 10.1007/978-3-319-54774-9_5

There are also relatively few constraints on the resultant economic profit that can flow from the appropriate pricing and efficient delivery of value created for customers in this way. The same applies to shareholder wealth creation. Ultimately, this is also constrained only by the imagination, the creativity and the capability of the management team.

It is the imagination, the creativity and the capability of the management and employees of a value-managed company that fuels the ongoing creation of both customer value and shareholder wealth. But the engine that converts this energy into a growing stream of economic profits is the cycle of customer value and shareholder wealth that was introduced in Chapter 4.

Avoiding a Cost Reduction Mindset

One of the most effective ways to grow economic profits in relatively mature markets is to re-segment so as to identify new segments or sub-segments for which it is possible to create additional customer value, and then try to recapture a proportion of that value through an appropriate pricing policy. How much of the resultant incremental revenue stream is converted into additional economic profit depends entirely on the efficiency of the organisation. But ultimately, economic efficiency only provides the linkage between customer value creation and shareholder wealth creation. As we have already pointed out, it is rare to find a situation in which it should be considered an objective in its own right – and particularly so over the long term.

Improving economic efficiency can enhance short-term economic profit. But it is can never be a driver of long-term economic profit growth or the ongoing creation of shareholder wealth. Despite this, some management teams work tirelessly to reduce operating costs and to improve capital efficiency in an effort to increase both earnings and economic profit. In most cases, they do achieve short-term performance improvement. But over the longer term, the results of their efforts can often be disappointing – for customers as well as for shareholders. They can sometimes be disastrous for other stakeholders.

Often, such thinking leads to commoditisation, where higher quality ingredients, components or elements are stripped out of products and services in an effort to reduce price in the often-mistaken belief that this is what customers want. There is no doubt that many customers welcome lower prices. But many also value non-price benefits and are often prepared to pay for them.

In the case of the food industry for example, consumers are usually not told when a natural ingredient is replaced with a cheaper synthetic alternative to reduce the cost of manufacture. Nor do they know when an additional preservative is added to increase shelf life. There are instances in which the inclusion of a synthetic ingredient or a certain preservative results in adverse health outcomes – and the inclusion of calcium propionate in factory made bread may well be an example of this. Calcium propionate is a mould retarding preservative that improves manufacturing efficiencies for manufacturers of factory made sliced bread. But its presence in food has been linked to the incidence of *Attention Deficit and Hyperactivity Disorder* in children.[1,2]

In situations such as this, the additional health related cost for the consumer almost certainly outweighs the savings achieved by the manufacturer and far outweighs the small proportion of those savings passed on to consumers through lower prices.

We will look more closely at issues of this nature in Part III. At this stage, we simply want to make the point that a cost reduction mindset can lead to quite narrow thinking, as well as a number of unintended consequences. With a relatively slight shift in management thinking, a great deal more can be achieved for customers, for end-consumers, for employees and for shareholders; and also for other stakeholders including the wider community in many cases.

Disciplined Innovation and the Creative Process

Business thinking is dominated by logical fact-based analysis. This is entirely understandable. But it does tend to limit management's thinking to logical and generally only incremental extensions to what is already being done. In contrast, when creative thinking is used to generate new ideas and logical analysis is employed to determine or prove whether or not they will work, management thinking becomes much more powerful. At the same time, if good logical analysis demonstrates that a new idea is unlikely to work at this point in time, then management's energy can be redirected towards developing other ideas that might come to fruition more easily or earlier. This hybrid form of thinking involving both creative and analytical modes of

[1] Dengate, S., *Fed Up: Understanding How Food Affects Your Child and What You Can Do About It*, Random House, Sydney, 1998.

[2] Dengate, S., and Ruben, A., "Controlled Trial of Cumulative Behavioural Effects of a Common Bread Preservative", *Journal of Paediatrics and Child Health*, Vol. 38, No. 4, pp. 373–376.

thought is fundamental to the establishment of both a disciplined approach to innovation and the ability to create value for customers and wealth for shareholders on an ongoing basis. Its effective use relies on a proper understanding of the creative process.

Understanding the Creative Process

Much has been written about the importance of creativity and innovation in business. But what about the creative process itself? What does it involve and how does it work? Unless the creative process is understood, it is difficult to unlock it and harness it in an organisation.

It is important to appreciate that while creativity begins with an idea, it is really an act – the act of bringing something into being. It is far more than simply the generation of one or more ideas. Ideas are in the domain of thinking, feeling or knowing. Creativity is about doing or acting.

In contrast to what many believe, successful pursuit of the creative process is not about physical or mental effort. More important is the degree of absorption or the degree of intensity with which an individual engages with a problem or a challenge.[3]

At the same time, ideas for new products, services, or even scientific breakthroughs, tend to arrive fully formed in the mind. But they only arrive in the mind of a person who is intensely or passionately engaged with the issue at hand. Often, the idea will break through in opposition to the beliefs to which an individual is clinging. Frequently, this will occur just as they detach from conscious effort or let go, such as at a point of transition between work and relaxation.

With this understanding in mind, creativity can be viewed as the outcome of an encounter between an intensely or passionately engaged individual (or group) with a particular challenge or particular set of information.[4]

To stimulate organisational creativity, we need to understand the types of encounter that need to occur and then create the conditions under which such encounters can occur.[5]

Experience has demonstrated time and time again that by focusing in the first instance on the objective of customer and end-consumer value creation, it is possible to tap into a desire or an enthusiasm to create value for (or

[3] May, Rollo, *The Courage to Create*, W.W. Norton, New York, 1994, pp. 39–40.
[4] ibid, pp. 38–63.
[5] May, op. cit., p. 77.

deliver benefits to) others that is present within all of us, but which often lies dormant in the workplace due to organisationally imposed conditions or constraints. By setting *up intense encounters with immediately relevant information* – particularly in a workshop environment – it is possible to unlock and then tap into this creative potential. When this happens, ideas can be generated for new or enhanced value propositions that when priced appropriately and delivered efficiently, can lead to significant increases in economic profit, intrinsic value and shareholder wealth.

One of our early clients was involved in the manufacture of bathroom products as well as the materials used to construct bathrooms in both new and renovated homes.

A creative thinking workshop was convened to come up with a wet area lining system that would have greater integrity that those generally used by the residential building industry.

After orchestrating an intense encounter with immediately relevant information (provided by builders, home owners, architects and materials scientists) the group was taken through an idea generation process and then split into four groups to work with these ideas.

A brilliant breakthrough idea did emerge. In fact, the identical idea emerged from two separate breakout groups. In one group, the source was a man who had been in the industry all his life and was approaching retirement. In the other, the source was a graduate trainee who had only been with the business for a few months.

Imagination and Belief

The creative process by which breakthrough ideas emerge and take form almost always has at its centre an intense or passionate encounter with information. It has two other essential ingredients. The first is our imagination, which we use to shape the kernel of the idea into a concept from which to begin to develop a new or enhanced value proposition. The second is our belief in the idea or the concept, and in our ability to bring it to life. It is important to recognise that creativity is as much about believing in our ideas and bringing them into form, as it is about generating the ideas in the first place.

Most companies acknowledge the importance of new ideas, but many (often quite inadvertently) impose conditions that can make it difficult for such ideas to be developed. The logical fact-based thinking processes they employ rely almost entirely on data, analysis, argument, debate and criticism.

They honour scepticism and demand proof before there is belief; using phrases like *seeing is believing* or *I'll believe it when I see it.*

The fact is though, if you demand proof before being prepared to believe in something you will never create anything. You must be prepared to believe before you will see, not the other way around.

If you can imagine something, then in a sense it already exists, albeit in a diffuse or subtle form. Ideas are like new products or services in a very diffuse state. It is belief, which is often most evident in the form of an emotional commitment, that carries an idea from the mind of an inventor or an entrepreneur, to success in the market place. It can also lead to a strong conviction within a team combined with an unequivocal commitment to succeed.

When backed by a strong belief, an idea gradually becomes less diffuse, gaining in density as it moves firstly to the drawing board, then into a prototype, and ultimately into a commercially viable product or service. Every product or service begins life as a new idea, just as every city building begins life as a concept in the mind of an architect. Ultimately, all customer value creation and most shareholder wealth creation stem from such ideas.

Nevertheless, before a new idea can be incorporated into a company's strategy development process, it must be given form – in the same way that an architect must express an idea for a new building as a design concept before a detailed design can be completed and the development process can move forward. Once again, a key ingredient during this conceptual or formative stage is a strong belief in the new idea on the part of those responsible for it, as well as an equally strong belief in their own ability to bring it into form. Once the idea has been formed into a testable proposition, it can be exposed to sound logical analysis to help prove to others that it has merit. With each step forward, the number of people who believe in the idea and are prepared to support it increases.

Integrating Creative Thinking with Logical Analysis

Successful businesses make use of both creative thinking and logical analysis. If they did not, they would not be successful. But in many cases they are used in isolation, with logical analysis playing the dominant role. This is not surprising, given the status that logical or rational thinking has been accorded within our society. But at the same time it is unfortunate, because when properly integrated they can be much more powerful. This is particularly true when applied to strategy development.

Like scientific thinking, most business thinking is based on a blend of rationalism and empiricism. Empiricism teaches that the senses are the only reliable bases for knowing. It demands empirical evidence. The phrase "seeing is believing" constitutes the classic empirical maxim. Rationalism contends that logic or reasoning is the only legitimate path to the truth. When used together, hypotheses developed from empirical observations are tested with rigorous logical analysis.

However, philosophers and scientists from many cultures have often pointed to intuitive knowledge that is in some way beyond reason and information collected via the senses. This instinctive knowledge, perception or insight is not gained by reasoning. But in the West, and particularly in the business world, it has been largely dismissed due to the importance that we have placed on logical or rational analysis.[6]

In his book *The Intuitive Edge* published in 1983, Philip Goldberg offers the view that the way we are taught to use our minds in school and university, is so skewed towards what he describes as "the rational-empirical ideal" that there is little if any discussion of the existence, the nature or the use of intuition, and even less encouragement for its use. He argues that in the West, we are taught to rely on rationalism and empiricism in our thinking, in our problem solving and in our decision-making. As a direct result, "intuition is subject to various forms of censure and constraint."[7]

Albert Einstein held a similar view, arguing that the intuitive mind was a sacred gift while the rational mind was its faithful servant. But rather than recognising this, instead we "created a society that honours the servant and has forgotten the gift."[8]

Logical analysis has an extremely important role to play in any business and particularly in the strategy development process. However on its own, it is not sufficient. It is really a proving mechanism, not a discovery mechanism. To create something new, or even to discover something new, we must employ creative thinking. Intuition often has a big role to play in this. But intuition alone is also inadequate for the business world. Few would be prepared to invest in a business proposition based solely on intuition. While a brilliant creative idea may have been accessed through an intuitive insight, a solid proof based on sound logical analysis will be required before a

[6] Goldberg, P., *The Intuitive Edge – Understanding Intuition and Applying It in Every Day Life*, Putnam, New York, 1983, p. 19.

[7] Ibid.

[8] Calaprice, A. (ed.), *The Expanded Quotable Einstein*, Princeton University Press, 2000.

board will fund, or a team will follow, a strategy developed from such an insight.

It is when we learn to use creative thinking and logical analysis in combination, that we develop the ability to bring new things into being. Mintzberg seemed to appreciate this when he pointed out that most successful business leaders are holistic thinkers who rely constantly on their feelings or hunches in order to cope with a constant stream of challenges or problems that individually are too complex for rational analysis, and collectively are potentially overwhelming.

He concluded that: "…organisational effectiveness does not lie in that narrow-minded concept called 'rationality' [but in] a blend of clear-headed logic and powerful intuition."[9]

The insights from which all successful strategies evolve are arrived at mainly through a creative process, not an analytical one. That is the very nature of an insight. In fact, it can even be argued that nothing is ever discovered through logical analysis alone. As we reflect on our experiences working with these processes over the last 20 years, we have formed the view that even when we think we have discovered something analytically, what has really happened is that the mind has "created an understanding" and we have simply used the process of analysis to prove to ourselves what we may have already known or sensed intuitively.[10]

Hybrid Thinking

Disciplined innovation in an organisational context requires a hybrid form of thinking that draws on both creative and analytical modes of thought, while at the same time engaging the feelings and the emotions of those involved.

Throughout history, many great visionaries have employed hybrid forms of thinking. The physical sciences provide a number of excellent examples:

- In commenting on the discovery of natural laws, Einstein offered the view that there were no logical paths to these laws "…only intuition resting on sympathetic understanding of experience can reach them."

[9] Mintzberg, Henry quoted in Goldberg, op. cit., p. 23.

[10] There is an important symbiosis here, because the process of completing the analysis can help stimulate the mind to create the understanding.

- Commenting on Isaac Newton, John Maynard Keynes offered the view that what set Newton apart was the power of his intuition. Keynes observed that Newton seemed to know far more than he could hope to prove. "The proofs were…dressed up afterwards; they were not the instrument of discovery."
- Mendeleev's articulation of the periodic table of elements, Kekule's discovery of the benzene rings, Faraday's development of the first dynamo and Tesla's conviction about the superiority of alternating current over direct current, all had their genesis in intuitive insights.[11]

To harness this thinking process for use in business strategy development, it is necessary to give it form, just like any new idea to which it would be applied. The form we devised in 1996 and refined in 1998–1999 is illustrated in Fig. 5.1. The name *Hybrid Thinking* was adopted in 1996.[12] *Hybrid Thinking* is the key to unlocking and harnessing creativity within any organisation.

The words *Hybrid Thinking* were later appropriated by another organisation to describe a somewhat different process. We believe it remains the most appropriate label for the process we are describing – although in recent years the name *Design Thinking* has been adopted for a process that shares a number of aspects with the process we first described in the mid-1990s.

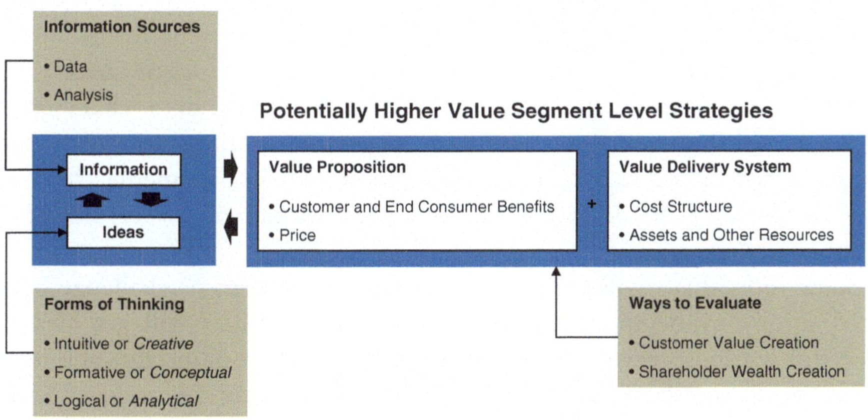

Fig. 5.1 Hybrid thinking

[11] Goleman, D., *Emotional Intelligence*, Bantam, New York, 1995, pp. 21, 77.

[12] Kilroy, D., "Creating the Future: How Creativity and Innovation Drive Shareholder Wealth", *Management Decision*, Vol. 37, No. 4, 1999, MCB University Press, pp. 363–371.

Hybrid Thinking is the process by which an idea, accessed through an intuitive insight, is firstly given form as a potential customer value proposition, then tested in terms of customer value creation potential, and finally developed into a potentially higher value strategy and evaluated in terms of shareholder wealth creation potential. It is a higher order thinking process that incorporates both creative and analytical modes of thought. It involves three distinct stages of thinking: intuitive thinking; formative thinking; and analytical thinking.

The Intuitive or Creative Thinking Stage

The first or creative stage is where the ideas are generated. This requires the intense engagement or encounter with data or information described earlier – leading either to insights into a challenge or a problem being faced, or to ideas or possibilities as to how to respond and move forward.

When applying *Hybrid Thinking* systematically, as part of an ongoing business process, one of the most effective ways to create such an encounter is to structure a workshop on completion of a current strategy valuation, at the start point of the search for higher value strategies.

During such workshops, we find that insights and ideas arise either purely intuitively, or through a blend of intuition combined with the use of the intellect. But they always arise as a result of an intense encounter with data or information. The actual encounter can take many different forms, any of which can stimulate the mind to produce an idea or a series of ideas.

The stimulus for new ideas might take the form of a challenge, a paradigm-shifting question, a lecture, a debate, a discussion or a contemplation – or perhaps some combination of these elements. It could also be in the form of raw data, or a presentation of the results of an analysis of that data.

Some individuals will gain an insight into a problem or challenge being faced simply by being exposed to this stimulus. Others will get ideas. A powerful symbiosis exists between information, intuition, insights and ideas. Information stimulates the mind to produce ideas. Some are intuitive. Some, when processed systematically, cause important insights to emerge.

In a workshop environment, one person's insight can stimulate another person to generate an idea. In other cases, ideas lead to insights that lead to further ideas. What is possible is imagined and then expressed as an idea. Original thought needs to be encouraged and expressed. Intuition must be welcomed. If the right environment is created, some people may even choose to download thoughts, feelings or ideas that they have not previously been comfortable sharing with their colleagues, and which they have kept to themselves for years.

Regardless of whether it is a workshop environment, a small group working together in an office, or an individual working alone, one of the keys to successful creative thinking is to be completely centred – or to be in what is sometimes referred to as a whole brain state with both the left (analytical) and the right (creative) sides of the brain engaged. There are a number of ways to achieve this and our firm has a variety of approaches.

The power of the whole brain state is that when in this state, we are far more able to deal with large and potentially overwhelming volumes of data, difficult information or stressful situations. Our experience is that an intense encounter with information in a workshop environment will be orders of magnitude more productive if participants are in a whole brain state and not stuck in rational, analytical left-brained mode. Keen insights will arise and good ideas for forward movement will emerge – often quite rapidly.

In the mid-1990s, a regional bank asked us to assist them deal with the rapid loss in market share that they were experiencing in the residential mortgage segment.

To chart a path forward, a Hybrid Thinking workshop was convened and a paradigm-shifting question posed to shift the focus of the relevant managers away from how to defend their market share, to how to create value for customers in the segment. The question used was simply: If interest rates didn't matter, what would drive value for customers in the mortgage segment?

It soon became clear within the group that a holistic perspective was needed and that it was important to examine the whole-of-life cost of housing for families. An intuitive understanding soon emerged that suggested most of the avoidable cost associated with purchasing housing in Australia arose from the cost of transactions, in particular real estate agent fees, relocation costs and government transaction charges. The reason for this high cost seemed to be the number of houses many people puchased on the way to getting the home that they wanted. It was felt that this behaviour in turn arose (at least in part) from the so-called deposit gap, which was the gap between the funds required to purchase a house and the amount that banks were prepared to lend. It was also felt that the existence of the deposit gap caused people to buy the house that they could afford and then continually upgrade until they eventually acquired the house that they needed or wanted.

The team also felt that this uneconomical behaviour could be eliminated if it were possible to offer a different form of financing, without the deposit gap. Zero deposit mortgages would be one possibility. Shared equity mortgages would be another. But the best option appeared to be a lease with a 100 percent residual or balloon payment. Under this approach, the entire value of the house could potentially be saved in tax-sheltered retirement savings accounts if the residual payment were timed for payment just after retirement.

It took just a few hours for the combination of intuitive insight (as to how value could be created for home purchasers) and creative ideas (for new financing products) to be tabled. It then took two weeks of research and analysis for the team to prove to itself that their ideas had real merit. This analysis demonstrated that the lease concept could potentially reduce the total whole-of-life cost of home ownership by 30-40 percent for a large proportion of the Australian population. At the same time, it had the potential to accelerate the government's retirement savings objectives. It was even suggested that the idea had the potential to encourage higher quality housing stock by reducing the demand for cheaper, lower quality housing built for first homebuyers.

For the retail banks, it offered the potential to re-establish a leadership position in the housing mortgage related market. The nature of the relationship that a financier would require with the homeowner under this approach was likely to disadvantage if not preclude participation by the commodity mortgage originators. They would be lending on the whole-of-life earnings potential of the borrower, not just against the value of the property, so a credit assessment potentially involving an actuarial analysis of their lifetime earnings would be required and the facility itself could become central to a multi-faceted long-term customer relationship.

Ultimately, the senior management team chose not to proceed because of a reluctance to confront potential resistance from regulatory authorities. Interestingly, about five years after this work was done, the team involved in the project became aware that a similar concept had recently been implemented in Scandinavia.

The Formative or Conceptual Thinking Stage

The second or formative stage is where ideas are formulated into testable propositions. This is sometimes referred to as the conceptual stage or the conceptual thinking stage.

As the idea moves to this formative or conceptual stage, the imagination is used to mould or shape the idea into a concept that can be both communicated to others and evaluated analytically.

Usually, the concept that is developed takes the form of a new or enhanced customer value proposition, which is a deliberate combination of customer or end-consumer benefits, and price.

The Logical or Analytical Thinking Stage

The final stage employs logical analysis to establish whether the idea that arose at the first stage, and which was given form at the second stage, will actually work. Beyond basic technical feasibility, this analysis falls into two distinct categories. The first is a form of analysis used to assess customer value creation potential. The second form of analysis is that used to assess shareholder wealth creation potential.

Customer value analysis is used to test the concept in terms of the benefits that customers or end-consumers will derive. This enables the nature and the strength of the demand for the underlying value proposition to be assessed, leading to an understanding of its price realisation and revenue generation potential. This often involves either understanding whole of life cost for the customer and the end-consumer, or using some form of conjoint analysis or choice modelling.

Once demand and revenue generation potential are understood, the strategy's shareholder wealth creation potential can be determined by modelling the value delivery system, which comprises the physical or other type of infrastructure required to deliver the value proposition to customers, along with its associated costs and capital requirements. This enables management to forecast future economic profit and thereby establish shareholder wealth creation potential.

It is important to appreciate that all three forms of thinking – creative or intuitive, formative or conceptual, and logical or analytical – are both complementary and inter-dependent. Goldberg argued that rational thinking and intuition work in tandem in creative thinkers, with rational thinking both preceding and following intuition. Often we begin with analysis or reasoning. Then we get an idea or an intuitive breakthrough emerges. Then we return to reasoning and analysis in order to confirm or elaborate on our thinking – or to prove to ourselves whether or not our idea or our ideas will work. In the words of Goldberg:

> ...rationality and intuition are...symbiotic...they work not only in tandem but together, like two separate pipes feeding the same fawcett.[13]

[13] Goldberg, op. cit., p. 33.

Establishing a Mindset for Success

In conjunction with the use of *Hybrid Thinking*, it is important to establish a mindset for success. This means having a clear conscious intent to succeed with a chosen strategy. It also means having a series of beliefs or intentions embedded in the subconscious mind that are entirely consistent with that conscious intent.

If we use the analogy of a motor vehicle, the conscious mind plays the roles of starter motor and steering wheel. It gets us started and points us in the right direction. But to actually create something new, it is the subconscious mind that is the real engine that does all the work.

Professional sportsmen and women understand this very well. They appreciate that while we set our intentions with our conscious mind, it is the subconscious that controls our instinctive reactions and responses on a month-by-month, week-by-week, day-by-day, minute-by-minute and second-by-second basis. If it is not in alignment with our conscious intent, we tend to trip ourselves up. At best, we achieve suboptimal outcomes.

There are a number of psychological techniques available through which to either achieve or enhance this alignment that can be used effectively in a workshop environment. A number involve firstly being in a whole brain state. Recent research suggests this is because we exhibit a greater degree of neuroplasticity when in that state, and so are more able to embrace new thinking, adopt new beliefs and discard self-limiting ones.[14]

Techniques to achieve this alignment are touched on in Part III and covered in more detail in the second book in this series.

Synthesis and Concluding Remarks

Both customer value creation and shareholder wealth creation are creative endeavours.

Shareholder wealth creation in particular is not just a simple analytical process devoid of the human spirit, as some would have us believe. Most shareholder wealth creation stems from the successful implementation of higher value strategies developed from new ideas – not just from the

[14] Askensy, J., and Lehmann, J., "Consciousness, Brain, Neuroplasticity", *Frontiers in Psychology*, Vol. 4, 2013.

adoption of value-based performance measurement systems or executive incentive plans.

To create wealth for shareholders on an ongoing basis, management must continually exceed expectations that are themselves continually increasing. This is an enormous challenge that can only be met with a response that uses creative thinking and logical analysis in combination rather than in isolation, together with an ability to make effective use of the relationship that exists between customer value creation and shareholder wealth creation.

The response to this challenge is best focussed at a customer segment level. This is the level at which it is possible to establish a cycle of customer value and shareholder wealth creation. That cycle is sustained with *Hybrid Thinking*.

When applied to business strategy development, *Hybrid Thinking* involves three principle steps:

- Generating ideas or concepts from which to develop new or enhanced value propositions appropriate for a particular target segment;
- Formulating those ideas into testable value propositions, and evaluating them in terms of customer value creation potential; and
- Developing the enhanced value propositions into potentially higher value alternative strategies, and evaluating them on the basis of shareholder wealth creation potential.

When a *Hybrid Thinking* capability is fully established in an organisation, it has the potential to enable a management team to continually create the future for their business. Trying to do this while relying solely on logical analysis is a little like driving down a freeway with your eyes glued to the rear vision mirror. You will only reach your destination safely if there are no bends in the road and you don't have to share the road with any other traffic. The business world is more like a winding road that is shared with lots of other traffic – and on which there is always the possibility that we will encounter something quite unexpected around the next corner.

Part III

The Response

It is possible to build an organisation that can create value for customers and wealth for shareholders on an ongoing basis. In fact, there is a well-developed and clearly defined path to follow in order to do so.

Once established on this path, a board and its executive leadership team can make a conscious choice to pursue the joint goals of customer value and shareholder wealth creation in ways that preserve and wherever possible enhance the wellbeing of all stakeholders. However, this does still constitute a choice. There is no externally imposed requirement to move in this direction – at least not yet.

Whether the goal is the ongoing creation of customer value and shareholder wealth, or the pursuit of these two joint goals while also seeking to enhance stakeholder wellbeing, there is one essential ingredient required for success. That ingredient is people at all levels of the organisation with the right mindset as well as the right skillsets.

The next five chapters describe a systematic approach to the development of both.

6

An Overview of the Journey

The journey that will be outlined in this chapter and then developed further in Chapters 7, 8, 9 and 10, is focused on the development of a series of capabilities underpinned by a philosophy that sees business as an opportunity to serve society, rather than an opportunity to exploit it.

From a philosophical perspective, there are six main steps to the journey.

- *Step One* involves coming to the understanding that even under a business paradigm that gives absolute primacy to the interests of shareholders, the primary economic objective is not to create shareholder wealth *per se*, but to build an organisation with the capability to create wealth for its shareholders *on an ongoing basis*.
- *Step Two* involves understanding that *the way* a listed company and each of its business units go about creating wealth for shareholders has an enormous impact on their ability to continue to do so on an ongoing basis.
- *Step Three* involves understanding that the key to ongoing shareholder wealth creation lies in embracing customer value creation and shareholder wealth creation as joint and mutually reinforcing objectives.[1]

[1] As a corollary, it also becomes apparent at this stage that the continual pursuit of economic efficiency through ongoing cost reductions and capital efficiency gains is unlikely to ever enable a listed company to realise the goal of ongoing shareholder wealth creation. Economic efficiency is really just a link between customer value creation and shareholder wealth creation. There are few situations where it should be considered an objective in its own right.

D. Kilroy, M. Schneider, *Customer Value, Shareholder Wealth, Community Wellbeing*, DOI 10.1007/978-3-319-54774-9_6

- *Step Four* involves understanding that, having embraced customer value creation and shareholder wealth creation as joint and mutually reinforcing objectives, business leaders can then make a conscious choice about the type of value that their organisation will seek to create for customers, as well as the way that they would go about creating it. This choice has enormous implications for stakeholder and ultimately societal wellbeing.
- *Step Five* involves understanding that, in confronting the question of the type of value that they will create for customers, an issue arises that touches on personal and organisational ethics. That question really goes to the heart of a more fundamental question – namely whether the leadership team considers being in business an opportunity to serve society, or an opportunity to exploit it.
- *Step Six* involves the leadership team examining its true intentions. It also means accepting that, while the outcomes arising from any chosen course of action can be positive or negative for different stakeholders to varying degrees, this is never true with intentions. When clear, intentions must either be black or white. There are no shades of grey. Either the intention is to serve, or it is to exploit. It is a binary choice rather than a continuum.

In a practical sense, the journey involves firstly establishing the necessary mindset, and then building the required skillset.

Establishing the Necessary Mindset

There are two aspects to the mindset required in order to build an organisation that can create value for its customers and wealth for its shareholders on an ongoing basis, and where considered appropriate, to do both in ways that also enhance community wellbeing. The first aspect is economic. The second is philosophical.

The Economic Aspect

The economic aspect of the mindset needed is centred on the establishment of a proper understanding of how the performance achieved in the market for a company's products and services, translates into the capital market outcomes experienced by shareholders. This was presented in Part II. Perhaps the most important consequence of this understanding is the realisation that the best way for a company to continually produce good capital market outcomes over the short, the medium and the longer term, is to focus on improving long-term (not short-term) outcomes in the market for its products and services.

This realisation also constitutes something of an antidote to the malaise of short-termism which leads companies to try to maximise their share price today by focusing on short-term earnings outcomes. Such actions tend to compromise future wealth creation for shareholders, and harm the interests of other stakeholders along the way.

Another important realisation that emerges from this understanding is the need to focus the strategy development effort at a customer segment level, i.e. the level at which customer value creation and shareholder wealth creation function as joint and mutually reinforcing objectives.

Once a listed company leadership team understands properly the performance expectations embedded in its share price, and therefore what it must deliver in order to preserve shareholder wealth (and exceed so as to create wealth), it is generally faced with one of two situations. It will either discover that it has a strategy in place that can deliver the expectations already embedded in its share price, but it still needs a higher value strategy in order to exceed those expectations and in so doing create shareholder wealth. Or it will find that its current strategy does not have the capacity to meet the expectations built into its share price, and that it needs to develop a higher value strategy simply to justify or underpin the current share price. Either way, the most effective path forward involves focusing the strategy development effort primarily at a customer segment level. This will become evident in a series of examples in Chapters 7 and 8.

The Philosophical Aspect

Once they understand how the performance achieved in the market for their company's products and services, translates into the capital market outcome experienced by shareholders, the leaders of listed companies face a simple yet fundamental choice. They can choose to run their companies as *long-term value creators*. Or they can choose to run them as *short-term share price managers*.

Long-term value creators are companies whose leaders seek to build enduring institutions. Their primary focus in an economic sense is on seeking to continually enhance the intrinsic value of their business by making their *EP Bow Wave* higher, wider and longer. They go about this by embracing customer value creation and shareholder wealth creation as joint and mutually reinforcing objectives – and pursuing them in tandem at the level of an individual needs-based customer segment. They also tend to put the needs to their company, its medium to long-term shareholders, and its other legitimate stakeholders, ahead of the often quite vocal demands of short-term capital market players. Their understanding of the concepts outlined in Part II (whether explicit or intuitive) serves to strengthen their resolve in resisting demands from such players to put short-term financial performance outcomes ahead of actions that will create value for customers and wealth for shareholders over the longer term.

Short-term share price managers are very different. They are companies whose leaders seek to maximise share price over the relatively short term, and particularly during their own tenure as leaders. Their focus is more on short-term market value uplift than on long-term intrinsic value uplift. They have a strong almost myopic focus on short-term earnings and EPS outcomes because of their adherence to *The EPS Myth*. But this leaves them quite vulnerable to the demands of short-term capital market players.

It is important from both a social and an economic perspective, for the leaders of listed companies to make an explicit choice to be *long-term value creators* rather than *short-term share price managers*. This is because it is the only way for listed companies to play their optimum role in both the economy and society — which ultimately must be to enhance the wellbeing of all who interact legitimately with the company.

However, to make this choice with conviction, business leaders must accept the economic truths presented in Parts I and II. They must also have:

- *A noble intent* for the business that goes well beyond simply trying to maximise the company's share price during the tenure of the current leadership team; and
- *A win-win mindset* in which all stakeholders are seen as allies it the pursuit of value uplift over the long term, rather than as adversaries in the pursuit of short-term earnings targets.

A Noble Intent

It is virtually impossible for the leadership of a listed company to build an enduring institution that can create wealth for its shareholders on an ongoing basis without having a noble intent that goes well beyond simply seeking to maximise share price or market value. This is because with a noble intent, the journey and the destination become one. In other words, the way a listed company goes about creating shareholder wealth determines its ability to continue to do so on an ongoing basis.

The key to ongoing shareholder wealth creation lies in embracing customer value creation and shareholder wealth creation as joint and mutually reinforcing objectives. Once this is understood, forward thinking business leaders quickly come to understand that it is possible to make a conscious choice to pursue these two joint goals in ways that preserve and wherever possible enhance the wellbeing of all stakeholders — be they customers, shareholders, suppliers, employees or even the wider community and the environment.

There is no obligation or externally imposed requirement to steer a listed company in this direction (although *benefit corporations* are moving that way). But those that do choose to do so will need to have a clear understanding right from the outset as to the nature of the value that are seeking to create for their customers. At one end of the spectrum is real or authentic customer value, stemming from the provision of useful, beneficial or healthy products and services, the consumption or use of which enhances long-term wellbeing. At the other end is artificial value, created in large part through the satisfaction of desires created through sophisticated marketing campaigns — with little consideration given to long-term wellbeing. Businesses that set out with the clear intention to enhance wellbeing will by definition lean towards creating real rather than artificial value for their customers.

A Win-Win Mindset

Many business leaders operate with a win-lose mindset. It's all about winning against the competition. But once we understand how wealth is really created – by working with the *Pair of EP Bow Waves* and recognising that the key is almost always to focus on the longer term – a different mindset can begin to develop.

The three-dimensional *EP Bow Wave* construct encourages a switch in focus from short-term earnings growth to long-term intrinsic value uplift. If we are to make the *EP Bow Wave* longer, we need a mind-set that regards the stakeholders in a business as allies in the pursuit of long-term value uplift. No longer can they be thought of as adversaries in the pursuit of short-term earnings growth. A short-term earnings focus might make the *EP Bow Wave* higher for a year or two, but it will almost certainly shorten it as well — and destroy shareholder wealth in the process. This win-win mindset can then begin to affect many other aspects of a company's activities. They include:

- Focusing on true wealth creation rather than trying to appropriate wealth from competitors, from suppliers, from customers or even from tax authorities;
- Recognising that there are two very different forms of competition — regressive competition in which we seek to win against the competition, and progressive competition where the primary focus is on making an offer more worthy; and
- Resisting the temptation to externalise costs — such as passing the consequences of the consumption of fast foods onto the healthcare system.

A long-term focus changes everything. This is because the longer a company's planning horizon, the more the interests of all its stakeholders align.

Establishing the Necessary Skillset

There are three fundamental organisational capabilities that a leadership team must establish if it is to create wealth for its shareholders on an ongoing basis by systematically enhancing the shape of its *EP Bow Wave*. Each of these three capabilities can be broken down into five individual steps or processes. They are illustrated in the form of an implementation roadmap in Fig. 6.1.

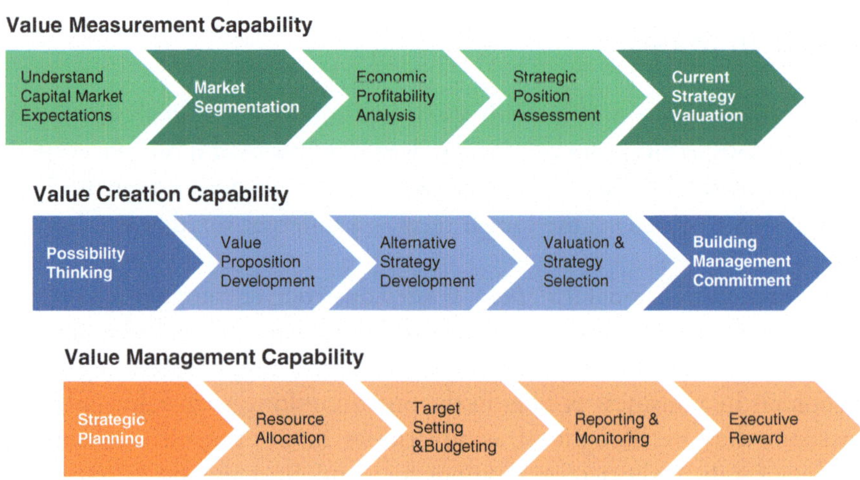

Fig. 6.1 Implementation roadmap comprising three core capabilities

Establishing a *Value Measurement Capability* means developing the ability to determine where value is being created, where it is being destroyed, and why, under the strategy currently being pursued.

Establishing a *Value Creation Capability* means putting in place the ability to continually develop and implement new and higher value strategies at a disaggregated level that enhance value for customers and create wealth for shareholders. The majority of these strategies are developed and implemented at a customer segment level.

Establishing a *Value Management Capability* involves putting in place (or refining existing) business processes and systems so as to encourage the ongoing pursuit and successful implementation of higher value strategies over time.

The power of the implementation roadmap depicted in Fig. 6.1 is that it allows a company to start anywhere it likes. Most companies choose to start at the beginning of the green ribbon. But some start with *Executive Reward.* Others start with *Possibility Thinking* leading to higher value strategy development. It just doesn't matter.

Both while being implemented and when fully operational, the process is "bookended" with a series of important workshops where the thinking of the leadership team is stimulated, expressed, coalesced and aligned. These are shown in bold white font in Fig. 6.1.

The first of these workshops is focused on *Market Segmentation.* Here, the initial objective is to disaggregate the business to unlock strategic insight. But the ultimate goal is to break the business down into a series of needs-based customer segments – using an approach described in Chapter 7. It is difficult to overstate the truly remarkable transformation in thinking that can occur once this new segmentation scheme has taken form.

The second workshop is where the *Current Strategy Valuation* is presented and examined. The current strategy valuation not only establishes where value is being created, where it is being destroyed, and why under the strategy currently being pursued, it also provides both a platform from which to develop, and a datum or benchmark against which to compare, potentially higher value alternative strategies.

The third workshop focuses on *Possibility Thinking* to come up with ideas for enhanced segment-specific customer value propositions. These are high energy events that represent the first step in a *Hybrid Thinking* process aimed at identifying and then developing higher value segment-level strategies.

The fourth workshop focuses on strategy selection and *Building Management Commitment* to the strategy or strategies selected. This is the final and very important step in the *Hybrid Thinking* process. Its goal is to ensure that both the conscious intent and the unconscious beliefs of the management team are aligned with the goal of successfully implementing the chosen strategy.

The fifth workshop focuses on *Strategic Planning*. Here, the strategy is formed into the elements of a prospectus-quality business plan in which the management team commits to a particular value outcome (underpinned by a promised economic profit stream), in return for the capital and other resources that they are seeking in order to implement their strategy successfully.

Current Strategy Valuation

Once the segmentation scheme has been agreed, the process of completing a current strategy valuation involves:

- Attributing revenues and direct costs, and allocating fixed costs and capital, to each segment to determine economic profitability and economic profit by segment;
- Assessing the strategic position of the business in each segment, as an input to forecasting expected future economic profits and cash flows; and
- Forecasting expected economic profits and cash flows to determine value at a segment level.

The *Value Measurement* process is described in detail in Chapter 7.

Higher Value Strategy Development

Higher value strategy development mainly involves the application of *Hybrid Thinking* at a customer segment level. It involves:

- Using a creative or possibility thinking process to generate ideas or concepts from which new or enhanced customer value propositions might be developed (often stimulated by the use of a paradigm shifting question);
- Developing some of those ideas into testable propositions, and using customer value analysis to measure customer value creation and then assess revenue generation potential;
- Further developing attractive value propositions into potentially higher value alternative strategies by taking into account the cost and capital required in order to deliver the proposed value proposition to customers;

- Forecasting the expected economic profit and cash flow streams from each alternative strategy, using that forecast to determine the value of each strategy, and then selecting the strategy with which to move forward (which in the majority of cases should be the value-maximising strategy); and finally
- Building management commitment to the chosen strategy.

The *Value Creation* process is described in detail in Chapters 8 and 9.

Delivering Planned Performance

The core business processes in a value-managed company are centred on an integrated approach to business planning, resource allocation and performance management that ensures the delivery of the performance promised in a business plan built around a chosen (and generally value-maximising) strategy, while at the same time encouraging the pursuit of even higher value strategies over time.

The strategic planning process sets out to develop higher value alternative strategies, value each alternative, select a strategy (which is generally the value-maximising alternative) and then build a prospectus-quality business plan around that chosen strategy. This plan acts as both a roadmap for the business, and a prospectus for capital and other resources.

The resource allocation mechanism operates like an internal capital market. It funds approved strategies and in so doing, sets up an interlocking commitment between the corporate centre and each business unit management team. Business units commit to delivering a value outcome in the form an economic profit stream. In return, the corporate centre commits the human, capital and other resources required by the business unit in order to implement its strategy and deliver its promised value outcome.

The performance management system aims to ensure that the economic profit performance promised in the plan built around the value maximising strategy, is actually delivered; and therefore that the business unit's promised value outcome is achieved.

Any executive reward mechanism must encourage not only the delivery of planned performance, but also the pursuit of even higher value strategies over time. We will return to the topic of executive reward in Chapter 10.

Synthesis and Concluding Remarks

Succeeding in the journey involved in building an enduring institution that can create value for customers and wealth for shareholders on an ongoing basis, requires the combination of the right mindset and the right skillset.

Establishing the right mindset begins with a proper understanding of the linkage between product and capital market performance. With this as a start point, the business leaders then need to decide whether their company will be a *long-term value creator* or a *short-term share price manager*. If they choose the former, they must then embrace a noble intent for their business, and adopt a win-win approach to their relationships with stakeholders.

Establishing the necessary skillset involves putting in place three core organisational capabilities which underpin a series of essential business processes.

The journey is described in detail over the next few chapters.

7

Valuing the Current Strategy

The primary purpose of a current strategy valuation is to determine where a business is creating value, where it is destroying value, and why, under the strategy currently being pursued. It is completed at a disaggregated level, and when done at a customer segment level, provides both a starting point from which to pursue, and a datum or benchmark against which to compare, potentially higher value alternative strategies.

There are five process steps involved, as was illustrated in Fig. 6.1. They are:

- Understanding the capital market expectations embedded in the current share price and market capitalisation;
- Developing a needs-based customer segmentation scheme;
- Determining economic profit and economic profitability by segment;
- Completing a strategic position assessment for each segment; and
- Valuing each segment under the current strategy before consolidating to determine the value of the current strategy for the business as a whole.

Understanding Embedded Expectations

While the primary purpose of the current strategy valuation is to understand where a business is creating value, where it is destroying value, and why (as a start point for a systematic approach to ongoing value uplift) there is another reason for completing it. This is to determine whether or not the strategy

D. Kilroy, M. Schneider, *Customer Value, Shareholder Wealth, Community Wellbeing*, DOI 10.1007/978-3-319-54774-9_7

currently being employed has the ability to meet the economic profit expectations embedded in the current share price and market capitalisation. This is an understanding that every board and executive leadership team needs to have. So it makes sense to determine those expectations before completing the current strategy valuation.

In assessing the capital market expectations embedded in a company's share price and market capitalisation, we are really setting out to answer two questions.

- Is the expected level of economic profitability over the next five years too high, too low or about right; given management's own internal perspective? And are the growth expectations over the next five years consistent with management's internal views?
- Is the length of the *EP Bow Wave* appropriate? A long *EP Bow Wave* and the high share price that results from it, might give comfort to some directors and executives. However, it can be due to positive market sentiment which can disappear quite rapidly, with negative consequences for executives, for the board and for shareholders.

It is difficult if not impossible to pose these questions in a meaningful way when relying on the earnings forecasts that most commentators use when talking about market expectations. Why this is the case was explained in the discussion on *The EPS Myth* in Chapter 2.

What Must be Delivered over the Next Five Years

When looking at the economic profit expectations embedded in a company's share price, there are really three periods over which the three fundamental drivers of intrinsic value need to be considered:

- The typical three to five-year planning period over which the current strategy will play out, and during which economic profitability and growth will be determined by the attractiveness of the markets in which the business competes, its competitive position relative to its competitors and the effectiveness of the strategy itself;
- The much longer erosion period (or convergence horizon) during which market forces and competitive pressures drive returns back to the cost of capital and growth back to average economic growth – forming the remainder of the *EP Bow Wave*; and

- The sustainable period, which commences once economic profitability has eroded to zero, and growth has settled back to average economic growth.

However, in the majority of cases, most of the variability in economic profitability and growth that we need to consider explicitly will play out in the first five years.

Illustration – Wesfarmers Limited

Figure 7.1 presents the characteristics of the *EP Bow Wave* for the ASX-listed Wesfarmers Limited as at 31 December 2015. It illustrates the *Pair of EP Bow Waves* for Wesfarmers over the five years to 31 December 2015, and highlights the explicit economic profitability and growth expectations for the

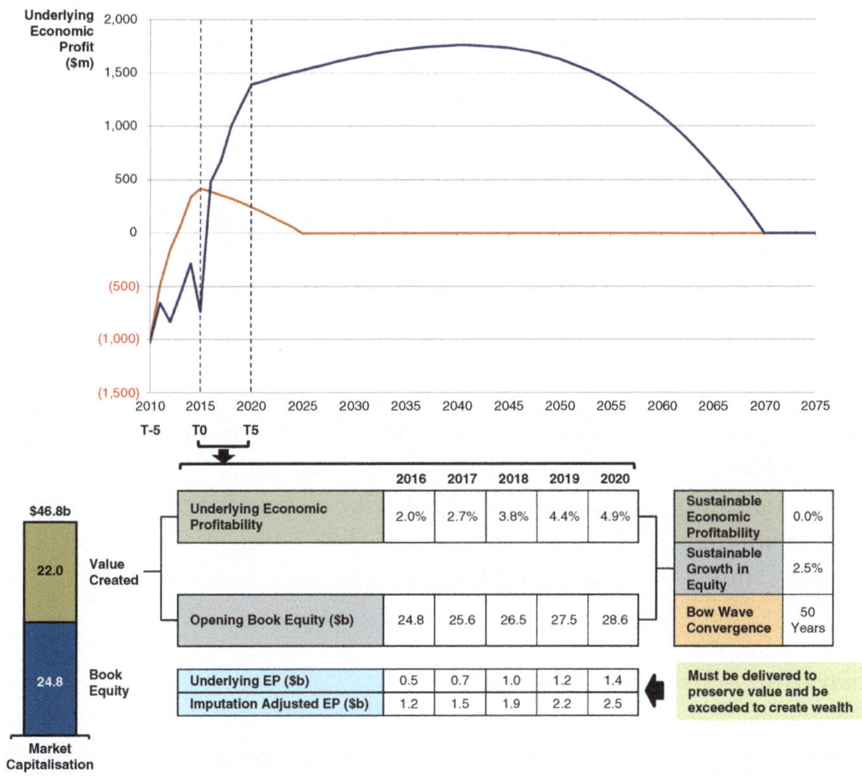

Fig. 7.1 EP expectations in the Wesfarmers share price on 31 December 2015

next five years that were embedded in Wesfarmers' share price and market capitalisation at that time.

The dimensions of the company's *EP Bow Wave* as at 31 December 2015 were:

- An expected economic profitability of 2.0% in 2016 which was expected to grow to 4.9% by 2020;
- A capital base of $24.8b on which that return would be earned, and which was expected to grow by 3.8% per annum over the five years to 2020
- A convergence period of a full 50 years beyond the explicit forecast period to 2020.

It is unlikely that one particular strategy would enable any company to sustain economically profitable returns for 50 years (the length of Wesfarmers' *EP Bow Wave*). Strategies need to be constantly refreshed in order to resist the erosion of economic profit back to zero.

What the long *EP Bow Wave* illustrated in Fig. 7.1 does suggest however is that investors appear to be confident in the ability of the Wesfarmers leadership team to continually refresh the company's corporate and business unit strategies so as to avoid erosion of economic profits, as well as in their ability to develop new generations of managers with the ability to continue to do so on an ongoing basis.

At a business unit level, the shape of the *EP Bow Wave* is determined by the economics of the business, which is in turn driven by the attractiveness of the markets in which it competes, its competitive position in each of those markets, and the effectiveness of its strategy. However at a group level, the length of the *EP Bow Wave* can be enhanced if the market believes the company has institutionalised the individual and organisational capabilities necessary in order to continue to develop and successfully implement new and higher values strategies over time. In effect, the capital market "capitalises" expectations associated with future higher value strategy development efforts within the current share price, because of the capabilities that it believes exist within the company.

There are two other examples we would like to examine to illustrate some further points about this type of analysis. The companies are ASX-listed Brambles Limited and LSE-listed Unilever plc.

Illustration – Brambles Limited

Brambles is a respected player in the international logistics business. As at 31 December 2015, it had a book value or shareholders' funds employed of $3.4b, and a market capitalisation of $18.2b. The difference of $14.8b represents the present value of a stream of imputation adjusted economic profits (EP) that was expected to be delivered in the future. The situation is depicted in Fig. 7.2, along with the *Pair of EP Bow Waves* for Brambles over the five years to 31 December 2015.

There are two particularly interesting aspects to the *EP Bow Wave* in Fig. 7.2.

The first is the growth in economic profit expected over the five years to 31 December 2020. The three-dimensional *EP Bow Wave* construct enables us to establish that this change in expected economic profit is driven by a combination of an expectation of greater economic profitability and an expectation of growth (in the capital base on which returns are earned) that is well above average economic growth. It is not just about higher returns. In fact, the average level of economic profitability and growth expected of Brambles over the five years to 31 December 2020, are both higher than that which was expected of and delivered by Brambles over the five years to 31 December 2015. This is evident in part from the *Pair of EP*

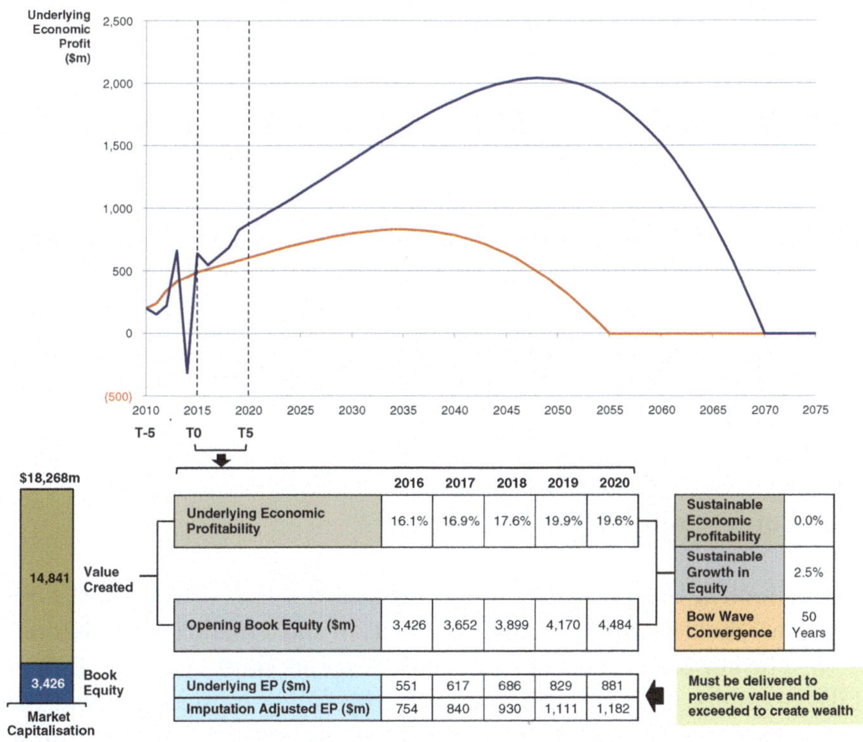

Fig. 7.2 EP expectations in the Brambles share price on 31 December 2015

Bow Waves shown in the top half of Fig. 7.2, and more fully from the detailed *Economic Performance Scorecards* contained in Appendix 3.

The second interesting aspect of the Brambles *EP Bow Wave* is its change in shape between 31 December 2010 and 31 December 2015.

Details related to Brambles' *Pair of EP Bow Waves* contained in the *Economic Performance Scorecard* in Appendix 3, reveal that Brambles destroyed $0.8b in shareholder wealth by failing to meet the expectations in place as at 31 December 2010. But it also added $5.8b by creating new EP expectations to be delivered beyond 31 December 2015. So the net position was an increase in shareholder wealth of $5.0b.

Of the $5.8b in wealth created from new and higher EP expectations, $2.2b came from an increase in the length of the *EP Bow Wave*, and $3.6b arose from an increase in expectations in relation to returns and growth. Its *EP Bow Wave* increased in length from 40 years as at 31 December 2010 to 50 years as at 31 December 2015.

To get an improvement in all three dimensions of the *EP Bow Wave* is quite an achievement. As a result, the M:B ratio increased from a high figure of 4.9x as at 31 December 2010 (high for an industrial company) to an even higher 5.3x as at 31 December 2015.

However, having delivered this quite outstanding capital market outcome for shareholders over the five years to 31 December 2015, Brambles now faces the challenge of having to deliver the product and service market performance that underpins it. If its current strategy has the capability to deliver such performance, then shareholder wealth will be preserved. But in order to create shareholder wealth, a higher value strategy will be required so as to outperform the expectations in place as at 31 December 2015.

If Brambles' current strategy is not capable of delivering the performance already embedded in its share price, then a higher value strategy will be needed at the outset to underpin the 31 December 2015 share price and market capitalisation.

Illustration – Unilever Plc

Let's now look at Unilever Plc. As at 31 December 2015, Unilever had a book value or shareholders' funds employed of £11.4b and a market capitalisation of £83.1b. The key dimensions of its *EP Bow Wave* are illustrated in Fig. 7.3.

Like Brambles, Unilever destroyed value by failing to meet market expectations over the measurement period. In this case, the value destruction was negative £11.6b10.9b. Again like Brambles, this was more than offset by the

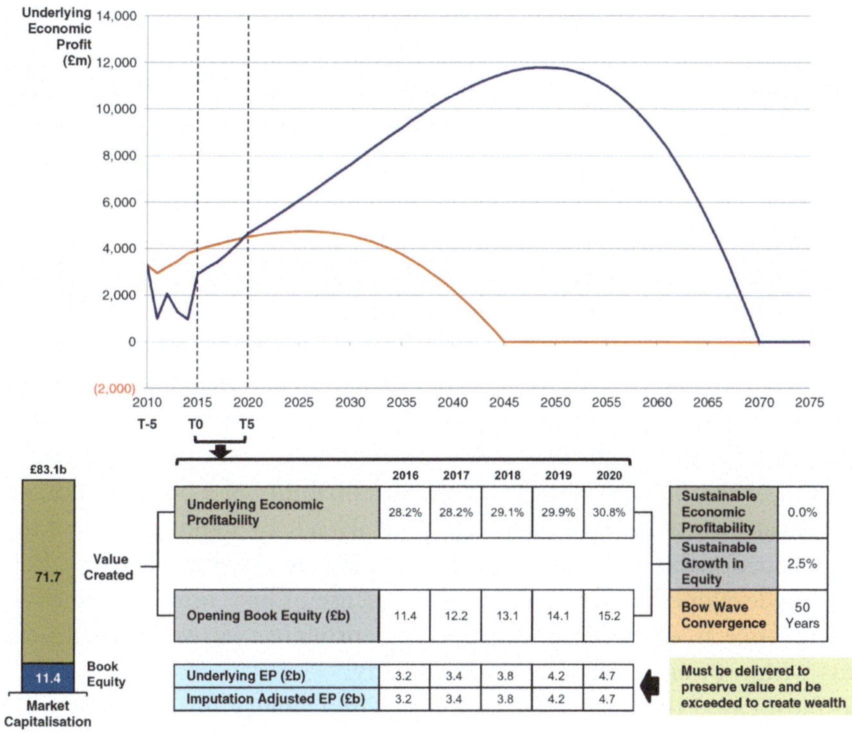

Fig. 7.3 EP expectations in the Unilever share price on 31 December 2015

establishment of a set of new EP expectations. These added £28.0b 27.3b– giving a net position of £16.4b in shareholder wealth creation.

However nearly all the £28.0b27.3b stemmed from an increase in expectations in relation to future economic profitability and growth (rather than from an increase in the length of the *EP Bow Wave*). Most of it came from an increase in expected economic profitability.

Economic profitability for Unilever is expected to be 28.2 percent for the year to 31 December 2016 and rise to even higher figure of 30.8 percent by 2020. These are very high return expectations, given that market forces are constantly operating to drive economic profitability to zero over time.

Dealing with the Impact of Sentiment

Market sentiment can at times play a significant role in determining a company's share price. It can be either positive or negative, and its existence can have a material effect on the ability of a company to meet or exceed embedded economic profit expectations. But it is inherently unstable. So its effect on share price changes over time – and sometimes over relatively short periods of time.

A positive shift in sentiment can benefit existing shareholders. But its unstable nature means that any benefit is unlikely to be sustained. At the same time, newer shareholders can incur significant losses if sentiment then shifts back in the opposite direction. In addition, if positive sentiment embeds a set of expectations that are beyond the ability of an executive team to deliver, it can pose some real problems.

The three-dimensional *EP Bow Wave* construct can be used to deconstruct a company's changing share price into changes in the market's expectations in relation to the three fundamental drivers of intrinsic value; economic profitability (or the height of the *EP Bow Wave*), growth (which determines the width of the *EP Bow Wave*) and the sustainability of a positive economic profit stream (or the length of the *EP Bow Wave*). By looking at these three drivers at reasonably short intervals, it is possible to observe how the *EP Bow Wave* has developed, and in so doing get a sense of how much of the change in share price is attributable to shifts in sentiment, versus actual developments within or announced by the company.

In most cases, the impact on share price of a change in sentiment will be evident in a significant change in the shape (and particularly the length) of a company's *EP Bow Wave* over a relatively short period.

Figure 7.4 illustrates the progression of *EP Bow Waves* over the past five years for three companies that *do not appear* to have suffered from the often capricious impact of changes in market sentiment. The companies are (from top to bottom) the ASX-listed Ramsay Health Care, the NYSE-listed Home Depot Inc. and the LSE-listed Unilever Plc. All of these companies have enjoyed a steady progression in the enhancement of the shape of their *EP Bow Waves* – although it could be argued that the 2015 *EP Bow Wave* for Home Depot may have over-reached to some extent.

It is useful to look a little more closely at the example of Unilever in Fig. 7.4.

Unilever is often held up as an exemplar when it comes to focusing on the long term rather than the short term. Consistent with this, it enhanced the shape of its *EP Bow Wave* over each of the past five years and in doing so, delivered a steady increase in shareholder wealth. But at the same time, it generally failed to meet the market's short-term EP expectations.

In contrast to what tends to occur with other companies, sentiment did not move against Unilever when short-term expectations were missed – perhaps

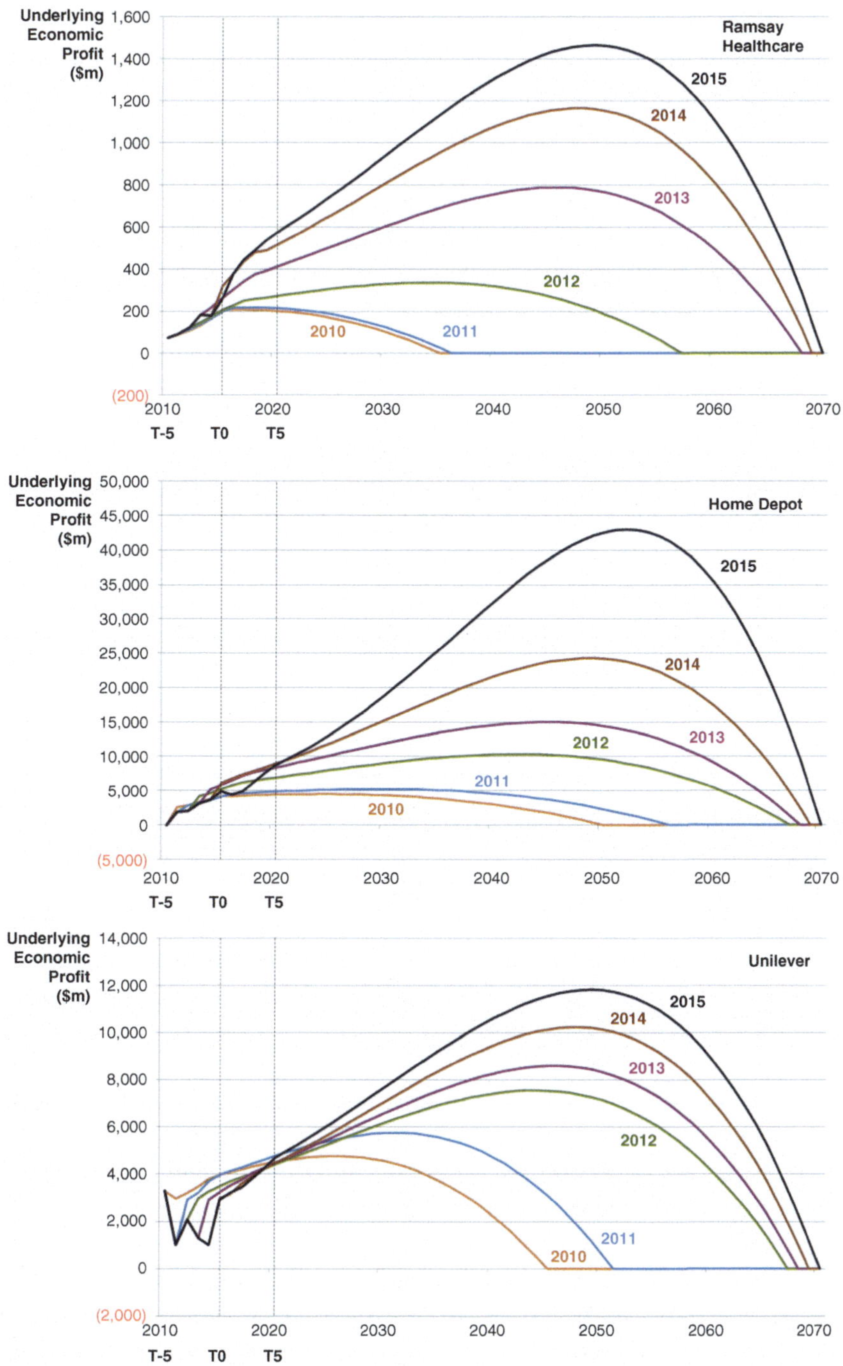

Fig. 7.4 EP bow wave progression for Ramsay Health Care, Home Depot and Unilever

because shareholders understand that the company is focused primarily on long-term value creation. This may have served as a means of insulating the company from swings in sentiment.

Figure 7.5 illustrates the progression of *EP Bow Waves* over the past five years for three companies that *do appear* to have suffered from the impact of sentiment. The companies are (from top to bottom) the ASX-listed Woolworths Limited, the NYSE-listed Oracle Inc. and the LSE-listed Rolls Royce Plc. Their *EP Bow Waves* have expanded and contracted quite significantly at different points in time.

There is one further illustration of the impact of sentiment that we would like to look at before moving on to the actual process of completing a current strategy valuation at a customer segment level. This illustration relates to an ASX-listed cloud technology company called Rhipe Limited.

Rhipe was listed on the ASX in early 2014. As at 31 December 2015, it had a book value or shareholders' funds employed of $38m and a market capitalisation of $202m, giving it a M:B ratio of 5.3x. The difference of $164m between market value and book value, represented the present value of a stream of imputation adjusted economic profits (EP) that were expected to be delivered into the future.

The dimensions of its *EP Bow Wave* at that point in time were:

- An expected economic profitability of negative 9.8% in 2016, which was expected to improve dramatically to positive 16.8% by 2020;
- A capital base of $38.0m on which that return would be earned, which was expected to grow by 11.3% per annum over the five years to 2020 (with a resultant underlying EP stream that was expected to grow from negative $4m to positive $10m over the five years to 31 December 2020); and
- A convergence period or *EP Bow Wave* length of a full 50 years, which is long for a recently listed company.

An *EP Bow Wave* with these dimensions (and particularly with a length of 50-years) tends to indicate the existence of positive sentiment.

Six months later, the company's market capitalisation had fallen to $116m and its *EP Bow Wave* had contracted to a more conservative 20 years – as is evident in Fig. 7.6.

This situation is an excellent example of the power of the *EP Bow Wave* as a means with which to deconstruct a share price into the product and service market performance that management must deliver in order to justify its share price and market capitalisation. When examined through the lens of the *EP Bow Wave* construct, the EP

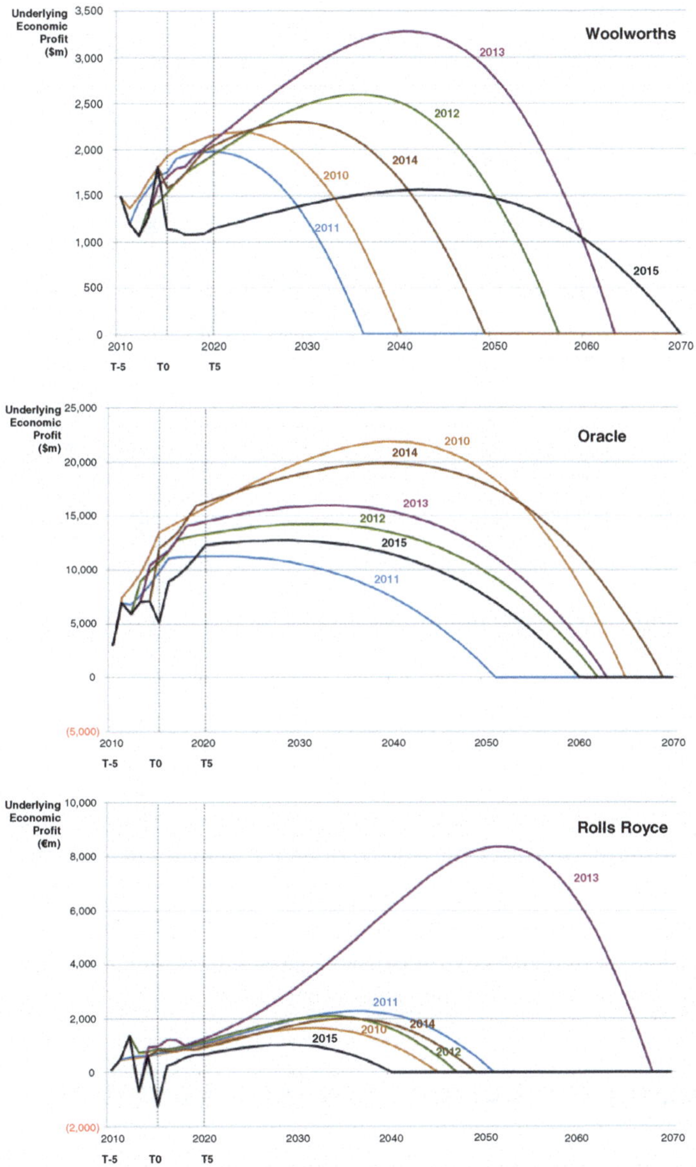

Fig. 7.5 EP bow wave progression for Woolworths, Oracle and Rolls Royce

expectations embedded in the market capitalisation on 31 December 2015 looked challenging.

We identified more than 20 other ASX 300 companies in a similar situation when this analysis was undertaken.

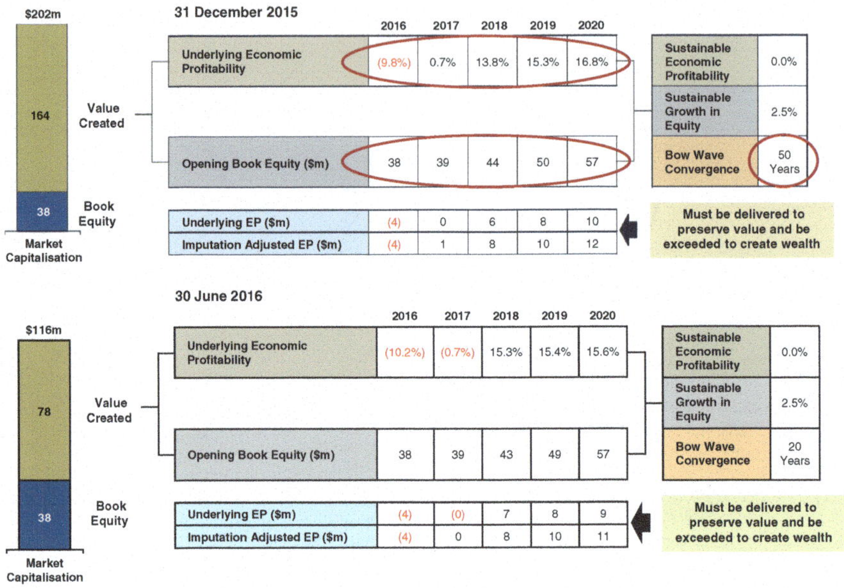

Fig. 7.6 Change in EP expectations for Rhipe Limited over a six-month period

As a general rule, it is better for a company's market capitalisation to reflect closely its intrinsic value – with no sentiment to artificially inflate or deflate the share price.

However, regardless of whether a company's share price is benefiting from positive sentiment or suffering under negative sentiment, the management team must still seek to identify and implement higher value strategies. Where positive sentiment exists, a higher value strategy may be necessary to justify the share price. When negative sentiment exists, a higher value strategy may be necessary to overcome the negative sentiment.

Completing the Current Strategy Valuation

Once embedded economic profit expectations are understood, the focus turns to the four process steps necessary to complete the current strategy valuation at a disaggregated level – ideally at the level of a needs-based customer segment. These steps are:

- Agreeing on an appropriate segmentation scheme;
- Establishing the financial measurement principles upon which both the economic profitability analysis and the strategy valuation will be based,

and then allocating revenues, costs and capital to segments to determine economic profit by segment for either the last full year or the first forecast year;

- Completing a segment-level strategic analysis to assess the likely levels of future economic profitability, growth and *EP Bow Wave* length; and
- Using the outputs of the two previous steps to forecast both an expected economic profit stream and an expected cash flow stream for each segment (effectively imputing the shape of the *EP Bow Wave* in each case), as a basis for determining the value of each segment under the current strategy.

There are a number of quite technical aspects to these four steps. However, it is important to appreciate that it is not necessary for every reader to become skilled in all of them. Market segmentation and strategic positon analysis are typically part of the skillset of strategic marketing professionals. Economic profitability analysis and segment level valuations are typically part of the skillset of finance professionals. What is necessary however for any reader that wants to make use of the thinking contained in this chapter, is an understanding of what each step involves, together with a familiarity with the outputs and an understanding of how to interpret them.

In many respects, the power of the process described in the remainder of this chapter is the way that it brings strategic marketing and finance skills together – in many cases within a multi-disciplinary strategic planning team.

Market Segmentation

Market segmentation is a particularly important step – not just in valuing the current strategy, but also in setting up the process of ongoing higher value strategy development. It is crucial to adopt the correct approach, but also to accept that there is no one right answer. With the right approach and the right mindset, the segmentation scheme can evolve over time.

There are many ways to define a customer segment. But it is important to come up with a segmentation scheme that will not only help unlock strategic insight, but also provide an effective platform for the pursuit of higher value strategies.

Business planners often think in terms of demographic segments because they find it easier to forecast along demographic lines. Some choose to segment by region, by industry or even by industry classification code. But such groupings are really just classification mechanisms. In many cases, customers within them are not bound together by a common set of needs that are relevant to the products or services that a company might offer to them.

Strategy consultants have traditionally regarded segments as product-market units that act as arenas in which it is possible to establish and maintain a source of competitive advantage. This can be a useful way to think about segments, but it is not appropriate for our purposes here.

The advertising industry often thinks in terms of psychographic segmentation. This means grouping customers according to their social values or sense of social identity, rather than their specific needs. Psychographic segmentation can be very helpful in targeting an advertising or public relations campaign, but once again it is not appropriate for our purposes here.

Strategic marketing professionals tend to think in terms of needs-based customer groupings. This is the approach that needs to be taken in a value-managed company.

With this goal in mind, one of the best ways to start the process is to lay out a product-customer matrix such as those illustrated in the examples shown in Fig. 7.7. In each of the three examples shown, the Y-axis contains groups of customers with either similar needs or similar costs to serve. The X-axis captures either products or services, or the application for which those products and services are used.

There is no one right needs-based customer segmentation scheme for a business, and there can also be different versions of the product-customer matrix. What is most important is to use the concept of the product-customer matrix to facilitate a discussion and reach agreement within the management team as to the most appropriate segmentation scheme to adopt – while recognising that it can evolve over time.

This discussion can prove most enlightening. It is not unusual for it to result in a completely new way to look at the business – particularly when the discussion occurs in a workshop environment in which the participants are operating in a *whole-brain state* (This is touched on in Chapters 5 and 9 and will be discussed in more detail in the second book in this series).

However, it is not always as revolutionary as that. As a first step, it can sometimes be sufficient simply to find a way to segment that unlocks some strategic insight. Fig. 7.7 provides some examples. The first relates to an agricultural equipment manufacturer.

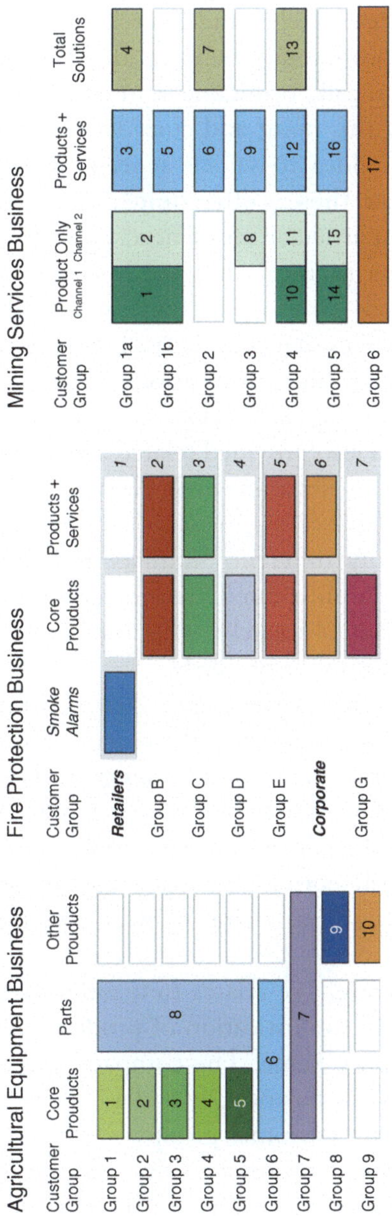

Fig. 7.7 The product – customer matrix as a start point for needs-based customer segmentation

In this particular business, there was a strong alignment between products and segments. Products were essentially segment specific. So in this case, the insight came more from an understanding of economic profit by product and segment, than from a different segmentation scheme. There was a significant difference in economic profitability between the most economically profitable and the least economically profitable segment.

It is useful to pause at this point and consider the fact that most start-up businesses begin with an idea to satisfy a need for a particular group of customers. So at the outset, there is often quite a clear alignment between the customer group with its particular set of needs, and the product or services that a company provides to meet that need. However over time, things become more complicated. To move forward successfully, we need (at least to some degree) to get back to that simplicity of needs-based customer groups with clear, segment specific value propositions.

The second example in Fig. 7.7 relates to a business that produced fire protection equipment and also provided related services. It will be used again throughout this chapter to illustrate each element of the current strategy valuation process.

This business had many different products and services, ranging from simple hoses and reels, to sophisticated fire protection systems with attaching maintenance contracts. But ultimately, what bound the customers together in each group was a common set of needs.

The types of products and services required by customers in each segment were relatively similar. Two segments (Retailers and Corporate) have been highlighted because it was changes to the strategy in these two segments that formed the basis of a significantly higher value strategy for the business. One related almost entirely to the sale of domestic smoke alarms through the retail channel. The other was the corporate client segment for which the primary offer was the installation and servicing of fire protection systems in office buildings

The third example in Fig. 7.7 relates to a somewhat different situation, where the different level of sophistication of products and services was a key factor in the segmentation scheme. The company was a division of a large international mining services business. It had 17 segments and three fundamental offers to six primary customer groups.

The offer with the lowest customer value was the supply of products. Next was products plus services. The most value adding offer was the provision of total solutions where customers paid for a specific and clearly identified outcome, not for the products and services used to deliver that outcome.

Different customers within each of the primary groups tended to focus their purchasing on products, products plus services, or total solutions. Their different purchasing behaviour was a clear indication of their different underlying needs. It proved to be very meaningful to analyse economic profitability according to the columns and rows, as well as the shaded cells in the product-customer matrix. There was as much variation in economic profitability between the columns as there was between rows.

Once a management team has agreed on an initial segmentation scheme, it is useful to test the integrity of the scheme. There are a couple of quite simple ways to do this. One is to attempt to analyse each segment using the strategic position assessment framework described later in this chapter. If a group of customers is not really a segment, then it will often prove difficult to analyse using this framework. Another way involves testing adjacent segments and asking the question: *can we be in one segment and not the other*? If the answer is no, then it is likely that the two segments are actually just one.

Once the management team is happy with the segmentation scheme, they can move forward with the three remaining analytical steps to determine value by segment under the current strategy.

Economic Profitability Analysis

It is important that financial performance is measured using economic profit to capture single period performance and intrinsic value to understand the longer-term economics of the business at a segment, business unit or group level.

In essence, economic profitability analysis is all about allocating business unit revenues, costs and capital to the newly defined customer segments – as the data will generally not exist at this level.

There will always be a series of decisions that need to be made at the outset in order to customise the process to suit a particular business. They are generally made at the corporate centre, not at the level of a business unit, because it is important to have a consistent approach across the group. These decisions comprise:

- Deciding whether to analyse and value the business on an equity capital basis or on a total capital (debt plus equity) basis;
- Deciding on the cost of capital to be employed, and whether one cost of capital will be used across the group, or a different one will be used for each business unit;

- Defining the level of detail required to allocate historical data so as to determine economic profitability and economic profit by segment for the last full year or the first forecast year; and
- Defining the level of detail appropriate for forecasting financial performance so as to value the business at a segment level under both its current strategy and potentially higher value alternative strategies.

The equity capital approach is a way of analysing and valuing a business under a given strategy on an ROE-Ke basis. The outcome is the intrinsic value of the shareholders' equity. The total capital approach is a way of analysing and valuing a business under a given strategy based on a ROC-WACC basis. The outcome is intrinsic enterprise value. When done correctly, both approaches will yield a consistent outcome.

In general, the equity approach is preferred for banks and other financial institutions, whereas for other businesses the total capital approach is preferred. The equity approach is used throughout this book for the simple reason that it is easier to analyse companies this way when relying on external information.

The question of whether to use one cost of capital right across the group, or a different one for each business unit, is a matter of preference for the company involved but it is usually resolved on a cost-benefit basis. Although the use of business unit specific costs of capital is the more technically correct approach, most companies choose to employ just one cost of capital. Even those that ultimately choose to use different costs of capital, tend to employ just one during their first few years as a value-managed company.

Determining the level of detail required to allocate historical data so as to determine segment economic profitability is something that must generally be resolved on a case-by-case basis. However, it is useful to approach this calculation with a flexible mindset, and if possible with a model that enables the outcome to be tested under a range of allocation methodologies. In most cases, once a meaningful allocation methodology has been agreed, refining the allocation methodology will tend to change the numbers but not the underlying shape of the segment economic profitability profile.

The level of detail required in forecasting economic profit and cash flow streams under both the current strategy and any potential alternative strategies is generally a lot less than that required to calculate historical economic profit and economic profitability. It is important to come up with a series of drivers that are meaningful for those involved in the process, and which enable the impact of the pursuit of different strategies on revenues, costs and capital to be captured.

Once the measurement principles have been agreed, determining economic profitability (and economic profit) by segment becomes a relatively straightforward revenue, cost and capital allocation process. The first step is to allocate revenues and direct costs to segments. In most cases, neither the business nor its financial systems will be structured around the new segmentation scheme. So it is often necessary to assign customers to segments before revenues and direct costs can even be determined.

Once this is done and gross margin by segment has been established, indirect costs can be allocated to each segment using the best information available. It is important to use flexible allocation rules to enable sensitivity to different allocation assumptions to be tested. Balance sheet items are also allocated and the capital employed in each segment is charged at the appropriate cost of capital.

The output of an economic profitability analysis is usually presented using one of the three types of chart illustrated in Fig. 7.8. The business to which these charts refer is the fire protection business that was referred to in Fig. 7.7.

The first chart type plots return on capital against the proportion of capital employed, and shows economic profit as the area above the cost of capital line. The second does the same thing in a slightly different way. Both displays provide clear ways to summarise the single period financial performance of a business unit by segment.

Another way to present the same information is to plot economic profit margin or economic profit as a percent of sales on the Y-axis, against proportion of sales on the X-axis. This approach, which is shown in the third display in Fig. 7.8, can be particularly useful in businesses for which capital employed is relatively low – such as professional services firms, high volume retailers and some contracting businesses. In some of these businesses, working capital can be negative as a result of suppliers being paid well after the goods they supply have either been sold in the case of a retailer, or covered by pre-payments in the case of a building contractor.

When completing an economic profitability analysis by segment for the first time, there can often be a good deal of debate about how costs and capital are allocated. This is particularly true if the analysis produces outcomes that surprise some members of the management team. Such debate is healthy and useful, and it can be particularly useful if the analysis has been completed with the help of a flexible allocation model. It is important for the analysts to be able to quickly define new allocation rules, or change existing

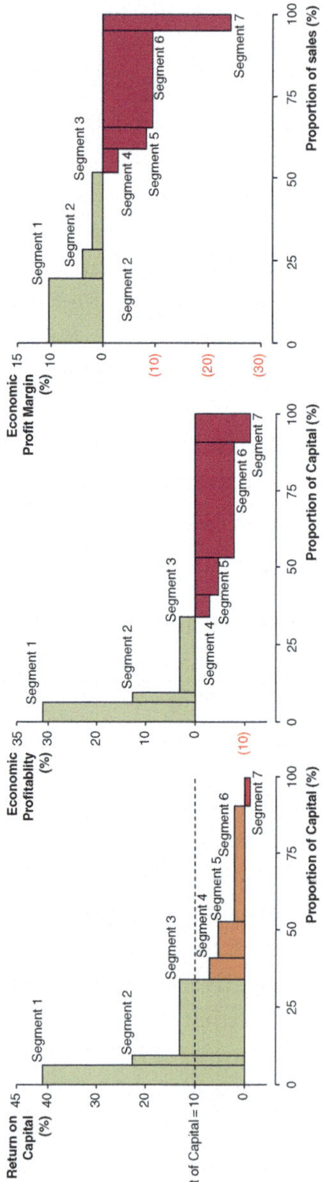

Fig. 7.8 Displaying an economic profit analysis by segment

ones, with just a few keystrokes. The impact of a change on the shape of the charts shown in Fig. 7.8 can then be seen immediately.

Another issue that emerges after a management team has had some experience with this approach is they tend to come to the realisation that the greater the divergence in return between the most economically profitable segment and the least economically profitable segment, the "better" the segmentation scheme. Divergent outcomes certainly lead to more actionable insights.

Strategic Position Assessment

Once economic profitability by segment has been determined, the next step is to assess the sustainability of that performance as a basis for forecasting future financial performance. The sustainability of current levels of returns and growth can be assessed in a systematic fashion using the Strategic Position Assessment (SPA) framework illustrated in Fig. 7.9, using the same business for which economic profitability was presented in Fig. 7.8.

This framework provides a mechanism by which the management team can firstly assess the economic attractiveness of each segment, and then determine the nature and strength of its competitive position. The SPA provides a strategic characterisation of the business by segment that can be used as a basis for assessing the sustainability of current levels of both returns and growth.

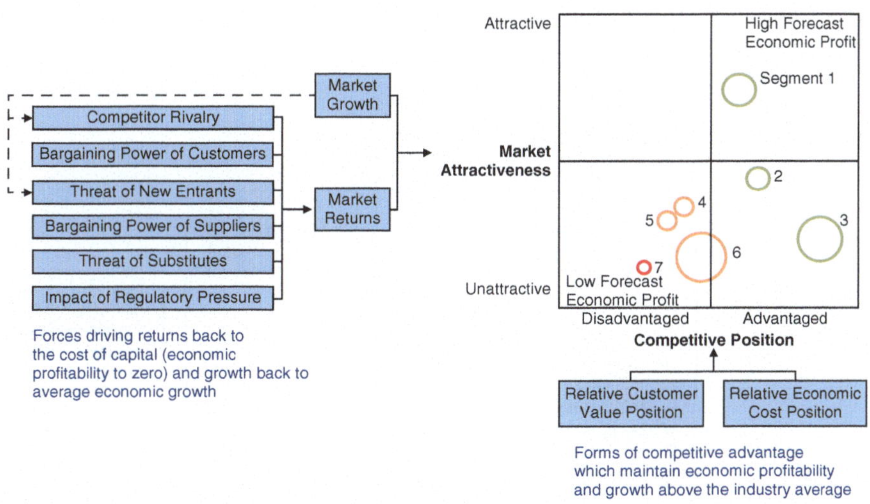

Fig. 7.9 Strategic position assessment framework

The vertical axis of the SPA chart is an assessment of the economic attractiveness of a particular market segment. This assessment is derived by assessing each of the forces (first described by Michael Porter) that determine the economic attractiveness of a market. Being above the horizontal axis implies that the economics of the segment as a whole (made up of all businesses participating in the segment) are more favourable than for the economy generally. When this is the case, the economic profitability for the segment as a whole is likely to be positive. Growth is also likely to be greater than average economic growth.

The horizontal axis of the SPA chart is an assessment of an individual company's competitive position in each segment – relative to that of its competitors. Being to the right of the vertical axis is an indication that economic profitability for a particular company can be expected to be better than the average for the segment as a whole.

There are two forms of competitive advantage. The first is a relative customer value advantage, which confers a right to charge a price premium. The second is a relative economic cost advantage. They work in combination to determine a company's overall competitive position in a given segment. As is illustrated in Fig. 7.10, there is a direct relationship between competitive position and economic profitability.

A company that has a customer value advantage can choose to charge a price premium. It can also choose to adopt a more aggressive stance and match the competition on price, using its customer value advantage to gain market share. The combination of its chosen price and the resultant volume will determine its revenues.

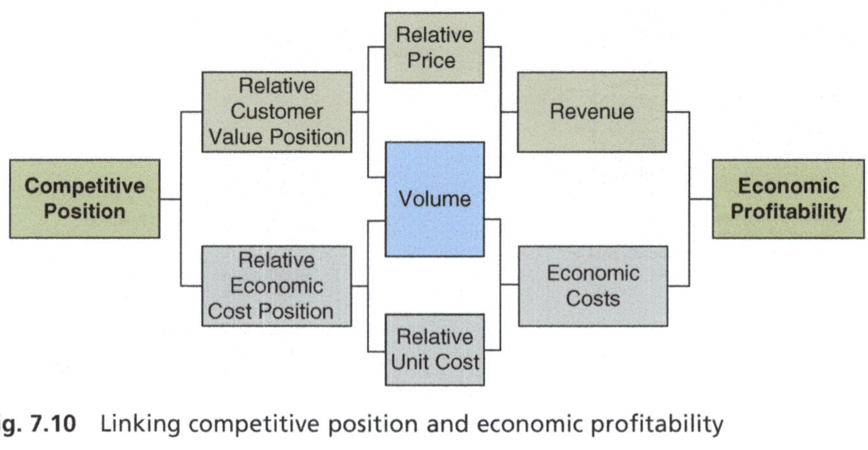

Fig. 7.10 Linking competitive position and economic profitability

A company that has a significant cost advantage can match the competition on price and maintain a higher margin than the competition. In this case it is likely to maintain its market share. However, it can also adopt a more aggressive stance and drop price to match the competition on margin, but grow volume including taking share from the competition.

In the company to which Figs. 7.8 and 7.9 relate, only Segment 1 was operating in an economically attractive market, and the company was competitively advantaged in just three segments (Segments 1, 2 and 3).

Another important perspective that emerges from the SPA framework is a share momentum analysis. This indicates where the company is gaining share and where it is losing share, and can be used to help assess likely future growth rates over the short to medium term.

The share momentum analysis on the right-hand side of Fig. 7.11 displays market share by segment, and identifies which segments were gaining and which were losing market share versus the competition. In this case, the company is gaining or holding share in the three segments in which it has a competitive advantage.

If a company is gaining share in a segment in which its current share is relatively low, then it is likely that a growth rate higher than market growth could be maintained for the short to medium term. On the other hand, if it has been gaining share but holds a dominant position, it is likely that future growth will be capped at the market growth rate.

The analyses in Fig. 7.11 suggests that the economic profitability by segment illustrated in Fig. 7.8 was likely to be maintained, and that Segment 1 in particular was likely to experience significant growth, at least in the short term. The market was growing rapidly and the business

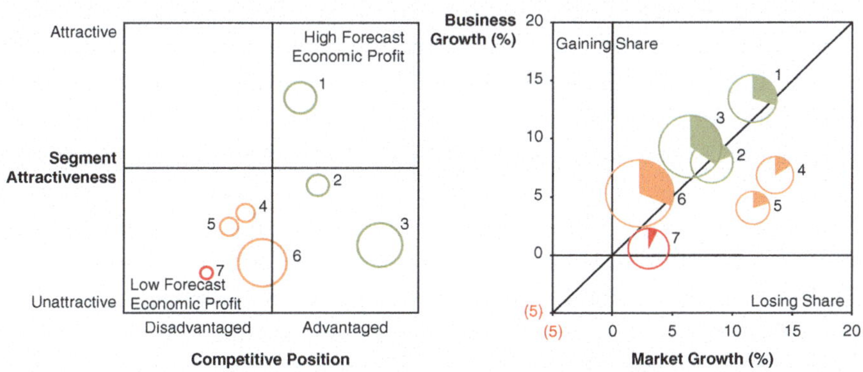

Fig. 7.11 Strategic position and share momentum analysis

was gaining share. Because of the share it was starting with, it had the potential to continue to gain share and grow faster than the market as a whole.

Strategy Valuation

The final step in the process of determining the value of the business by segment under the current strategy involves using segment economic profitability, strategic position assessment, and any other relevant information, to forecast and then value the expected future economic profit stream for each segment and for the business as a whole. The economic profit forecasts are grounded by the understanding of the sustainability or otherwise of current levels of economic profitability and growth provided by the strategic position assessment and the share momentum analysis.

The current strategy valuation represents the leadership team's view of the value of their business if they continue to pursue that strategy. It also represents their current view as to where the business is creating value and where it is destroying value relative to the underlying capital employed. If the analysis that underpins the current strategy valuation is thorough and there is a real belief in the veracity of the conclusions, then it can provide a powerful stimulus for the generation of ideas from which potentially higher value strategies might be developed. In that respect, it can form the basis for (or provide an important element in) the intense encounter with directly relevant information referred to in Chapter 5.

The output is generally presented using the two formats illustrated in Fig. 7.12.

The current strategy valuation captured in Fig. 7.12 once again relates to the fire protection business. This business served seven primary customer segments. Both the displays in Fig. 7.12 show which segments had an intrinsic value greater than book value (the capital invested in them under the strategy being pursued) and which had an intrinsic value less than book value.

Businesses or segments for which the intrinsic value is greater than the capital invested in them are normally termed value creating. Those that are worth less than the capital invested are labelled value destroying.

The value creating segments each have a M:B greater than 1.0x. As was pointed out in Chapter 3, this means that they are expected to be able to sustain economically profitable returns for a reasonably long period of time.

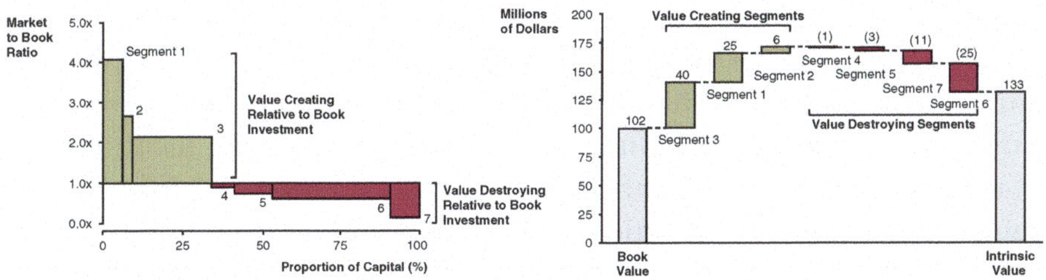

Fig. 7.12 Displaying a current strategy valuation by segment

A M:B less than 1.0x means that the business is value destroying and is expected to be economically unprofitable.

The X-axis in the display on the left-hand side of Fig. 7.12 is the proportion of book equity or equity capital employed in each segment. It is normally shown in percentage rather than absolute terms for ease of interpretation. When presented in this way, the area of each of the rectangles is proportional to the value that has been added to the capital employed in each segment by pursuing the current strategy.

The same information is presented in a slightly different form on the right-hand side of Fig. 7.12. The total book value of $102 million is shown in the first column. The next seven columns show the value that has been added to or subtracted from the underlying capital employed in each segment by pursuing the current strategy (i.e. the intrinsic value less the book value for each segment). The height of each of these shaded bars corresponds to the areas of the rectangles in the display on the left-hand side of Fig. 7.12. They also represent the PV of the future economic profit stream expected from each segment under the current strategy. The final column is the sum of all the other columns, and represents the intrinsic value of the business unit under the current strategy.

There are three quite common issues that can emerge during the process of completing a current strategy valuation – particularly when it is done for the first time. These are important to acknowledge, but they should not be allowed to become impediments to forward movement.

The first is that some organisations find it difficult to move from their current segmentation scheme to one composed entirely of needs-based customer groups. This is not a major problem. The goal is to move in that direction and get there over time. This may take a couple of planning cycles for some businesses. The key point the first time around is to ensure that the segmentation scheme disaggregates the business in a way that helps unlock strategic insight.

The second issue is that there will often be a vigorous debate in relation to the way in which fixed costs, and both fixed assets and working capital, are allocated to segments. While this debate can be informed and resolved by testing the sensitivity of outcomes to different allocation rules, the issue tends to recede once the focus switches from single period economic profitability to multiple period strategy valuation. The single period analysis resulting from the allocation process is just the start point for the valuation. What happens to economic profitability and growth both during and beyond the planning period is generally more important in determining the value of the segment under a particular strategy. It is certainly more important when it comes to assessing the difference in value for a particular segment under a range of alternative strategies.

The third issue is that there will sometimes be a misalignment between the strategic position of a segment and its economic profitability. This is because an economic profitability analysis is a static, single period picture whereas both a SPA and a strategy valuation are forward looking and multiple-period in nature.

Identifying Opportunities for Immediate Value Uplift

The current strategy valuation provides a strategic value map of a business. The most important application of the output of a current strategy valuation process (and the understanding that underpins it) is to provide a start point from which to pursue, and a datum or benchmark against which to compare, potentially higher value alternative strategies.

The systematic and ongoing pursuit of higher value strategies will be the focus of the next chapter. However, the current strategy valuation can also be used in a somewhat mechanistic sense to guide either the allocation or the re-allocation of capital and other resources, in ways that lead to a higher economic profit stream and therefore a higher intrinsic value outcome under the current strategy.

While initiatives of this type can often lead to significant and sometimes quite rapid uplift in economic profit, they tend to be one-off rather than ongoing in nature. We generally refer to them *as opportunities for immediate or short-term value uplift*.

Opportunities of this nature that arise directly from the current strategy valuation tend to occur along three principal dimensions:

- Investing in and growing economically profitable segments while understanding the trade-off between economic profitability and growth;
- Reallocating resources from economically unprofitable segments to economically profitable ones; or
- Reducing and where possible eliminating value destruction.

Investing in Economically Profitable Segments

The relationship between economic profitability, growth and intrinsic value was discussed in Chapter 3. For economically profitable businesses, growth tends to amplify intrinsic value uplift. In other words, in an economically profitable segment, it is often more value creating to invest so as to grow the segment, than it is to try to make the segment more profitable.

Illustration – Fire Protection Business

The management team of the fire protection business shown in Figs. 7.8, 7.9, 7.11 and 7.12 was able to use their understanding of economic profit and intrinsic value by segment to come up with two segment-level strategic initiatives that when implemented, more than doubled the value of their business. The impact of these two initiatives is illustrated in Fig. 7.13.

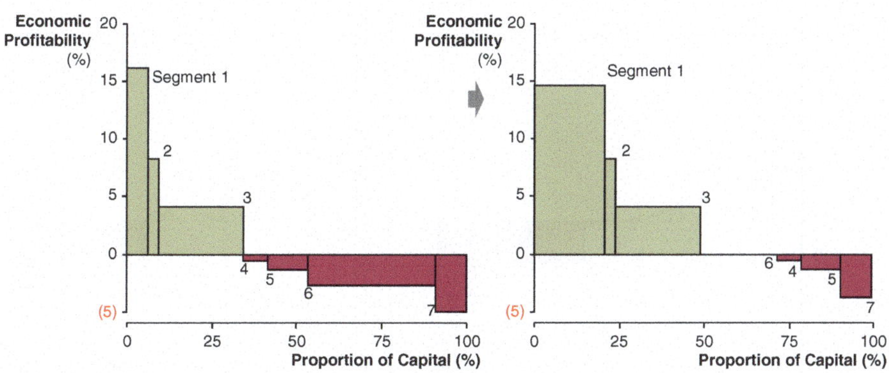

Fig. 7.13 Growing value creating segments

The most significant of the two initiatives in terms of value uplift involved investing to grow the new and highly economically profitable Segment 1. This segment consisted of retailers who stocked the company's domestic smoke alarms for sale to homeowners. Because of the way in which performance had been measured before this analysis was completed, the attractive economics, high profitability and significant growth potential of this segment had not been evident. Consequently, it had not received much attention from management. Once its economics and its potential were revealed, the management team resolved to invest in the segment and grow it strongly.

The additional investment in Segment 1 did reduce economic profitability slightly, but this was more than offset by additional growth. So economic profit grew substantially and so did intrinsic value.

Illustration – Capital Intensive Manufacturing Business

Figure 7.14 relates to a manufacturing business that participated in 10 value creating segments serving different elements of one industry, and four value destroying segments serving different elements of another. The value creation profile of the business under the current strategy is shown on the left-hand side.

The profile on the right-hand side illustrates the impact on value of two segment level strategic initiatives (in the darker-shaded segments) together with an investment to build capacity to service profitable growth opportunities in almost all of the value creating segments. These initiatives

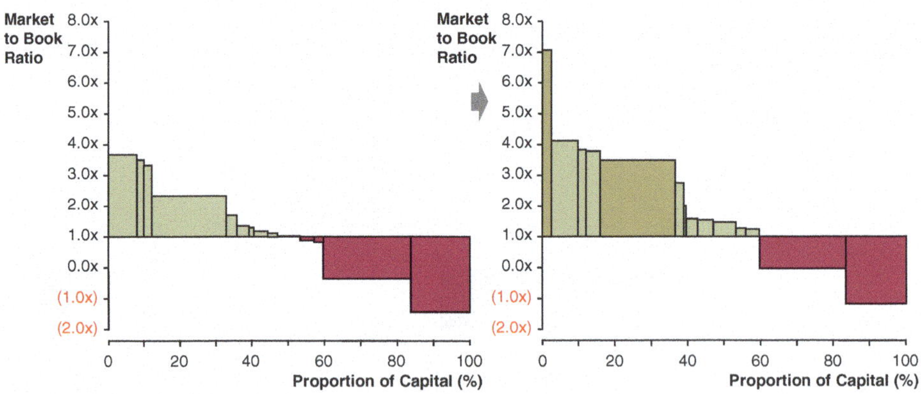

Fig. 7.14 Impact of investing in value creating segments

in combination added slightly more than 50 percent to the value of the business under its current strategy.

Reallocating Resources

While not possible in every industry, there are sometimes opportunities to reallocate resources away from less economically profitable segments or activities, and invest some or all of those resources in segments with higher levels of current and expected economic profitability – as is evident in the example shown in Fig. 7.15.

Illustration – Wine Producer

The business illustrated in Fig. 7.15 was a fully integrated wine producer. It had a large number of individual labels or brands. Fig. 7.15 shows an analysis of economic profit at a disaggregated level, together with an illustrative representation of a major strategic initiative that arose from the current strategy valuation.

This was an interesting case for two quite different reasons.

The first reason was that it involved a current strategy valuation conducted by label (or brand) since in this business, the customer value proposition was closely linked to the label. The economic profit analysis was also completed by category, such as premium red wine, premium white wine, fortified wine,

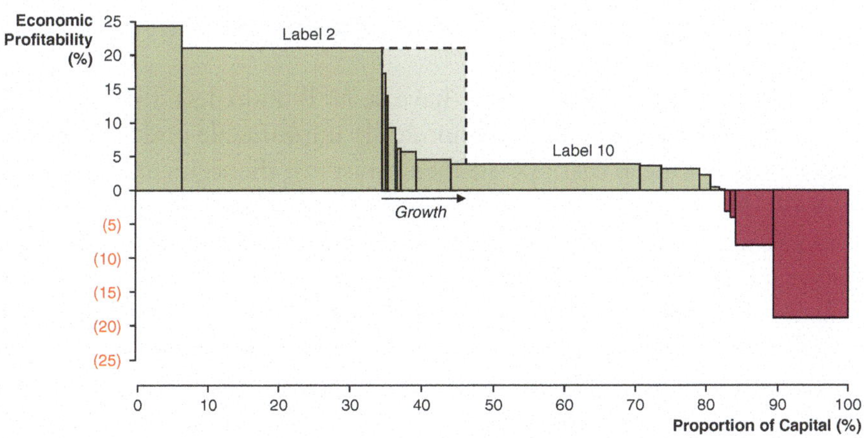

Fig. 7.15 EP enhancement and value uplift through resource reallocation

sparkling wine and so on. So management knew the economic profitability of each category within each label. This led to an insight that resulted in a significant opportunity for immediate value uplift (although it did take some time to implement).

A number of the smaller labels as well as Label 10 required quite high quality fruit for certain elements of their range. Management was able to rationalise labels and in so doing, redirect these high quality grapes to one of the more economically profitable and higher value labels (mainly Label 2). The impact of this initiative on the intrinsic value of the business as a whole was significant.

The second reason this case proved particularly interesting related to the reaction of senior executives at the corporate centre when first presented with the current strategy valuation by label. Some thought the analysis was intended to communicate the need to exit the red-shaded value destroying parts of the business. However, the purpose of the analysis was simply to show where value was being created and where it was being destroyed (and why).

Reallocating resources away from less economically profitable labels to those with a greater economic profitability (so as to grow economic profit for the business as a whole) was just one idea that emerged from the current strategy valuation. In this case, the economic losses from the value-destroying labels were necessary for the success of the overall strategy. This is because the value-destroying labels were mainly generic products that played an important role securing access to retail distribution for the higher value labels in certain countries.

Managers who are not familiar with this type of analysis will often focus on the value destroying segments as the best way to improve performance. But it is rare for the elimination of value destroying segments or activities to be the only way to enhance value.

The fact that a segment might have a M:B ratio less than one, and therefore be expected to remain economically unprofitable under the current strategy, does not mean that management must exit the segment. They might choose to, but the underlying goal should always be to seek to either find a way to enhance economic profitability under the current strategy, or develop a higher value alternative strategy. Withdrawing from a segment is one alternative strategy that might be higher in value. But there are likely to be fixed costs and capital that will need to be carried elsewhere under an exit plan. Whether or not pursuing an exit will create wealth depends upon whether or not an exit will cause the value of the business as a whole to increase – not just the value of one segment.

This takes us to the third type of initiative.

Reducing Value Destruction

The third type of initiative that can flow directly from a current strategy valuation is to seek to reduce value destruction.

It is important to understand that in the first instance, the focus should normally be on reducing the level of value destruction, not on eliminating or exiting these segments. Reducing the amount of value destruction, or the size of the red-shaded area in any economic profit or M:B chart, will result in value uplift in the same way that occurs when the size of the gold-shaded area increases.

Illustration – Fire Protection Business

Returning to the fire protection business example illustrated in Fig. 7.13, the second segment-level strategic initiative pursed by management involved reducing value destruction.

Segment 6 was the corporate customer segment, in which the company installed, serviced and maintained fire protection systems in office buildings. It was a resource intensive segment in which the company was market leader. However, it was economically unprofitable, and the principle reason for this performance was that it was discounting price to try to increase its already substantial market share.

On the basis of this analysis, the business unit general manager took a decision to lift price to the level required to achieve slightly better than economic breakeven at current volumes. Initially, the business lost a significant amount of market share, and this is reflected in the illustration in Fig. 7.16. But

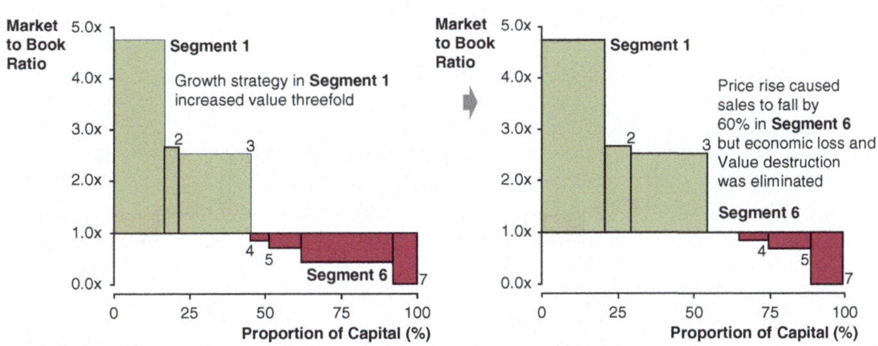

Fig. 7.16 Reducing value destruction in fire protection example

within a year or two, they had won back much of the lost share as their competitors also raised price.

Illustration – Capital Intensive Manufacturing Business

Figure 7.17 shows another example of reducing value destruction, in this case relating to the same manufacturing business shown in Fig. 7.14 (The left-hand panel in Fig. 7.17 is the same as the right in Fig. 7.14).

Two initiatives were proposed that were able to reduce value destruction. One involved changes to the process used to produce the products sold in the most economically unprofitable and value-destroying segment. The other involved a marketing initiative to migrate customers from that segment to a better performing but still economically unprofitable segment, by creating incentives for them to purchase a slightly different type of product.

Together, the impact of these two initiatives amounted to less than 10 percent of the value uplift produced by the initiatives illustrated in Fig. 7.14. But the key message here is the importance of the continual pursuit of opportunities for value uplift. Sometimes they will be significant. At other times they will be much smaller. But they all add up.

In some cases, it is possible to reduce value destruction by completely eliminating value-destroying activities. However, this generally requires an understanding of strategy valuation at a plant or site level as well as at a segment level. This is because plants or sites can be closed or reassigned whereas a decision to exit a segment requires shared costs to be borne by other segments.

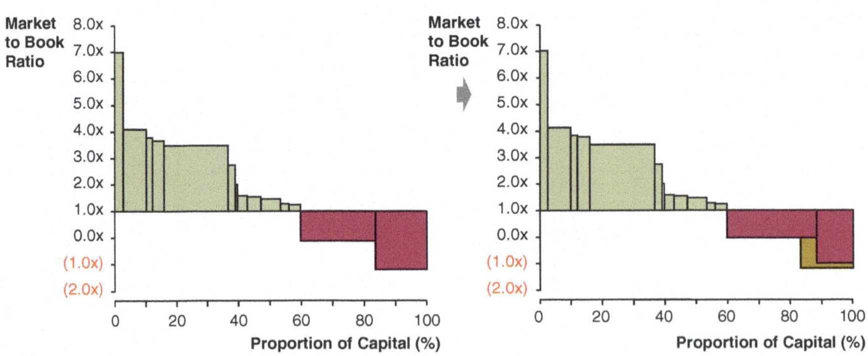

Fig. 7.17 Reducing value destruction in manufacturing example

Synthesis and Concluding Remarks

The current strategy valuation provides both the start point from which to pursue, and a datum or benchmark against which to compare, potentially higher value alternative strategies. It generally provides enormous insight for a management team – both during its development and when the final outcome of the strategy valuation process is available.

The fact that each element of the analysis can be presented with meaningful graphical displays makes the process of completing a current strategy valuation a particularly useful learning experience for managers whose background is not in strategic planning, corporate finance or management accounting. In fact, it is very important in a value-managed company for all executives to understand and feel comfortable working with the economic framework outlined in Chapters 1, 2 and 3, and used in this chapter. The best way to develop that understanding is to complete a current strategy valuation.

Completing the current strategy valuation at a customer segment level enables a link to be established between segment level economic performance and the strategic position that a company has established in each case. It also leads naturally to the identification of one off opportunities for economic profit enhancement leading to immediate value uplift under the current strategy (which was discussed in this chapter), and to higher value strategy development at a customer segment level which is discussed in Chapter 8.

8

The Systematic Pursuit of Higher Value Strategies

A higher value strategy is a strategy that, if implemented successfully, will create shareholder wealth by producing a higher intrinsic value outcome for a business than if it continued to pursue its current strategy. By definition, such a strategy will have a higher expected economic profit stream than the current strategy.

The existence of a *Bow Wave of Expected Economic Profit* points to three possible ways to enhance economic profit and if sustained, increase intrinsic value and create shareholder wealth. They are to increase economic profitability (increase the height of the *EP Bow Wave*), to grow the capital base on which economically profitable returns are earned (increasing the width of the *EP Bow Wave*), and to increase the sustainability of the economic profit stream (which means increasing the length of the *EP Bow Wave*).

It is important to appreciate that actions intended to enhance one dimension of the *EP Bow Wave* can often bring with them a material risk of a deterioration in one or both of the other dimensions. Raising price without a commensurate enhancement to customer value, aggressive cost reductions that undermine organisational capabilities, or price reductions aimed solely at volume growth, are all examples of such actions.

Where an action enhances one dimension of the *EP Bow Wave* at the expense of another, the chances are relatively slim that any resultant improvement in short-term economic profit, will translate into a sustainable value uplift and therefore into an ability to outperform the expectations embedded in the *EP Bow Wave* so as to create shareholder wealth.

A more fruitful course of action is to make the *EP Bow Wave* higher, wider and potentially slightly longer, through the development and successful

D. Kilroy, M. Schneider, *Customer Value, Shareholder Wealth, Community Wellbeing*, DOI 10.1007/978-3-319-54774-9_8

implementation of a higher value strategy. If successful, this course of action will produce a good outcome for existing shareholders. But what about the new shareholders who paid the new and higher share price that gave rise to the shape of the new *EP Bow Wave?* The company must deliver the expectations embedded in the new *EP Bow Wave* simply to preserve wealth for new shareholders. It must then exceed those new expectations in order to create wealth for them. So in responding to one challenge, another is created.

In Chapter 7, we introduced three ways to enhance an economic profit stream so as to achieve immediate value uplift under the current strategy. While these opportunities can have a significant positive impact on value, they tend to be one off in nature. In this chapter, we will demonstrate how to create wealth for shareholders *on an ongoing basis*. It involves a systematic effort to continually create both customer value and shareholder wealth at the level of an individual needs-based customer segment.

While having the necessary skillset and applying it with the right mindset are important in all aspects of the journey being described throughout Part III, nowhere are they more important than when setting out to create customer value and build shareholder wealth on an ongoing basis within a properly defined, needs-based customer segment. When approached with the right mindset, needs-based customer segments can serve as enduring platforms for ongoing value uplift.

There are four key aspects to the approach required to underpin the ongoing creation of both customer value and shareholder wealth through the application of *Hybrid Thinking* within a needs-based customer segment.

1. *A focus on end-consumer needs.* This means taking account of the needs of end consumers when setting out to generate ideas for new or enhanced value propositions, and not just focussing on the needs of direct customers.
2. *A preparedness to form value creating networks.* A value creating network involves companies working together in collaboration within a value chain so as to enhance the value or benefit delivered to the ultimate customer or end-consumer, in a way that creates wealth for all participants.
3. *A bias towards value pricing.* This means setting prices wherever possible on the basis of the benefits delivered to or derived by customers and end-consumers, rather than just the underlying cost to serve them.
4. *A willingness to back new ideas.* Generally speaking, this means regarding analysis as more a proving mechanism than a discovery mechanism. It often means using analysis primarily as a means of proving whether or not an idea will work by assessing its customer value and shareholder wealth creation potential, rather than as a means of coming up with new ideas in the first place.

A Focus on End-Consumer Needs

When thinking about new value propositions and when looking for ways with which to enhance existing ones, it is important that the needs of end-consumers as well as direct customers are taken into account. In some cases, it can even be appropriate to allow the needs of end-consumers to completely dominate those of direct customers. The electricity industry in Australia provides an interesting illustration of how the absence of a clear focus on end-consumer needs can compromise the ability of a company to create value for customer and wealth for shareholders on an ongoing basis.

Illustration – Electricity Supply

Structural changes to the electricity industry introduced to comply with the prevailing economic policies in most Australian states during the mid-to-late 1990s tended to reduce the focus of many industry participants on the real needs of end-consumers.

Until the emergence in recent years of solar panels and other decentralised generation mechanisms, the value chain that delivered most electricity to residential customers began with either a hydrocarbon fuel source or a dam in the case of hydro-electric power. The energy source was then converted into high voltage supply by a power station turbo-generator. Electricity was fed to cities via a network of high voltage transmission cables. When it reached the city, the high voltage supply was transformed down in a number of stages until it reached the level required for household supply. It was then delivered to each household via a local supply network that used either an underground or an overhead cabling infrastructure. In Australia, most electricity is still supplied in this way.

Transmission from the generator to the city, and distribution within the city, were both natural monopolies subject to regulation. However, generation, trading and retailing were competitive markets. Between the generators and retailers, a wholesale energy market emerged. This eventually led to the integration of generators and retailers into what became known as *gentailers* – as is illustrated in Fig. 8.1.

At the interface with the end-user, there was a competitive retail electricity market. Electricity retailers competed with each other to supply energy to households. But in many respects this was a somewhat artificial market. While competing retailers sold the energy, they did not own or operate the physical network that distributed the energy – and the physical nature and

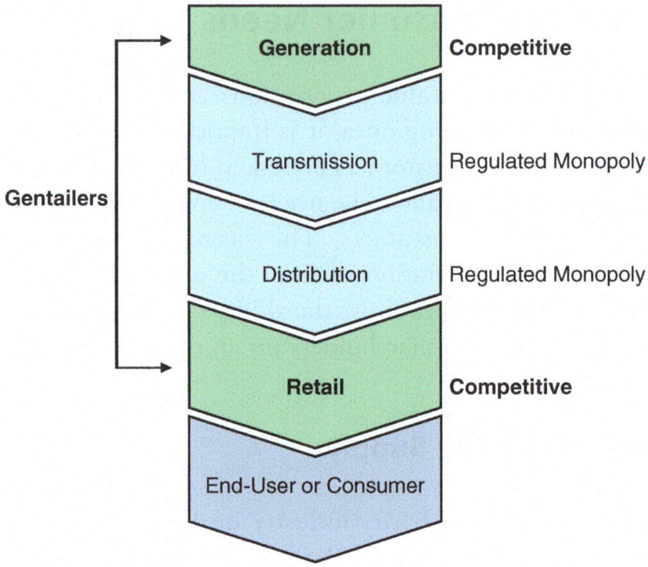

Fig. 8.1 Electricity supply value chain

condition of this network was a major determinant of the quality of the supply that the end-consumer purchased from the retailer that they chose.

This "deconstruction" of the industry value chain had a quite interesting impact. If the position of a retailer were adopted, its goal was to win in those elements of the value chain in which it competed. This might include:

- Seeking to win in the wholesale energy market by pursuing an energy sourcing strategy that delivered it a lower overall energy cost than its competitors;
- Manoeuvring itself into a position from which it could ensure that the distributors who actually delivered the energy sold to end-users by the retailer would be fully accountable for reliability and quality of supply;
- Keeping their operating costs as low as possible;
- Building market share in the end-consumer market by being responsive to customers and by managing customer relationships as effectively as possible;
- Locking large customers into contracts that enabled the retailer to recover high spot electricity prices incurred during periods of peak demand; and
- Making use of its residential customer base to build its "share of wallet" by selling other products and services to customers.

If the perspective of a residential electricity consumer were adopted, a somewhat different picture emerges.

The needs of consumers included a low whole-of-life cost associated with the use of electrical appliances, together with adequate levels of reliability, quality and safety of supply. An increasing number of customers also had needs or desires in relation to environmental factors including reducing greenhouse gas emissions through the type of generator used to produce the electricity, the efficient use of power within their home, and effective use of thermal insulation. Some may also have been concerned about the aesthetics of a distribution network based around poles and wires.

But the retailer was not in a position to do anything about many of the aspects of electricity supply that impacted value for the end-consumer.

Three Issues to Consider

There are three important issues to consider here.

The first relates to the fact that the motives of direct customers in a channel can be different to those of the originator of the product or service, and when acting as intermediaries, their utility function can sometimes be very different to that of end-consumers. When their motives are not properly aligned, strong intermediaries can damage the value proposition a supplier is seeking to provide to an end consumer.

The second relates to the problems that can occur when the lines of communication between the originator of a product or service and its ultimate customer or end consumer, become too stretched.

The third relates to commoditisation. Unless a company's products or services are aligned with the current and emerging needs of end-consumers, they can become disconnected from the true drivers of value for customers in their industry, and risk becoming commoditised.

Different Motives

When acting as intermediaries, the motives of direct customers can sometimes be quite different to those of end-consumers. When their behaviour is not fully aligned with the goal of delivering value or benefit to end-consumers, intermediaries can inhibit the operation of the cycle of customer value and shareholder wealth creation. We can illustrate this with a case study from the building products industry.

Illustration – Building Products

In the early to mid-1990s, fibre-reinforced cement siding was introduced by a number of companies to the residential construction market in the United States. When compared to the engineered wood products for which it was a substitute, fibre cement offered significant benefits to homeowners (who were the end-consumers in this case).

The most notable of these were a longer life due to a greater resistance to degradation from moisture, together with lower maintenance costs due to a longer interval between installation and re-painting. One company's fibre cement offer even included a 50-year limited guarantee, which was very important in the more extreme climatic zones such as Florida, the Gulf of Mexico and the Pacific North West.

But despite all of the advantages that fibre cement offered to homeowners, builders (who were the direct customers of the fibre cement manufacturers) were initially slow to embrace it. They were aware of the benefits it offered homeowners, but they were resistant because it was heavier and therefore more difficult and more costly to install than traditional siding products. In contrast, homeowners were almost completely unaware of the benefits or advantages offered by fibre cement siding. In fact, most had no idea that it even existed.

This type of situation generally translates into two quite different utility functions for customers and end-consumers. In this case the customer was a builder and the end-consumer was a home owner.

The challenge for the fibre cement manufacturers was to set up a cycle of customer value and shareholder wealth creation in which the builders' motivations were in alignment with the manufacturers' value proposition as well as with the long-term best interests of homeowners. Ultimately, this did occur by marketing directly to homeowners as well as working with builders to provide them with purpose-built equipment that made installation easier. Within a period of five years, fibre cement became the building material of choice in framed residential construction in many regions in the USA – almost from a standing start.

Lack of Direct Communication

In some industries, strong intermediaries can so distort the communication between product or service originators and end-consumers, that they prevent the establishment of a value creation cycle. This is most likely in those industries in which suppliers of products and services have ceded sufficient economic power to intermediaries that the wealth creation cycle can be distorted by their demands. It can also occur when end-consumers are fragmented or poorly informed. We can illustrate this with a case study from the financial planning industry.

Illustration – Financial Planning

In Australia in the 1980s and 1990s, many financial planners and life insurance agents were able to act in a manner that served their own interest, but which was detrimental to the interest of both their suppliers (life insurance companies and in some cases investment fund managers), and end-consumers (individual investors and insurance policy holders).

The behaviour of many financial planners was driven by their desire to maximise commissions, rather than to act in the long-term best interest of their clients. Using techniques that became known as "twisting", they encouraged policyholders out of one life insurance product or other form of investment and into another, and in so doing created churn, leading to significant additional commission payments. This was only possible because the financial planners and life insurance agents (rather than the product manufacturers) owned the end-consumer relationship.

This situation benefited the financial planners and life insurance agents to a significant degree. Initially this benefit came at the expense of the life insurance companies. The commissions paid to agents and financial planners created what was and still is known in that industry as "new business strain". The cash impact of writing the new business created through churning customers put pressure on the life insurance company's balance sheet.

In some cases, the growth ambitions of certain life insurance companies contributed to this new business strain as a result of them offering incentives to agents in the form of large, interest free agency development loans in an effort to get agents to change allegiance and bring their clients with them.

But ultimately, end-consumers funded the additional commissions. They experienced either lower investment returns or lower policy surrender values, or both.

A similar situation emerged again 20 years later in the Australian financial planning industry, where planners working for large banks once again put their own interests well ahead of those of their clients – to the detriment of both the bank and their clients.

Helping to Avert Commoditisation

Companies often specialise in specific elements of their industry value chain, and compete with other players who are similarly specialised. However when they do, their strategic objectives can quite easily become disconnected from the fundamental objective of their industry, which in the case of electricity generation and distribution for example, is to serve the needs of the ultimate consumers of electricity.

It is important to appreciate that the ability of an organisation to create customer value and build shareholder wealth on an ongoing basis is closely linked with the extent to which its products or its services are aligned with the current or emerging needs of end-consumers.

If this is not the case, then they can quickly become disconnected from the real underlying drivers of customer value in their industry. When this happens, they risk being commoditised – or being consigned to supplying low value elements of a customer value proposition, rather than supplying the core value proposition itself.

Once this occurs, the primary means at their disposal to deliver greater value to customers is to reduce price, and then the only way to create wealth for shareholders will be to reduce costs. Without a major change in strategy, they will find it difficult to escape the cost reduction trap, and may lose any chance they had to establish a business and a culture focused on customer value and shareholder wealth creation.

The packaging industry provides a good example of how to manage the threat of commoditisation.

Illustration – Packaging Industry

Packaging companies that provide packaging to both the fresh and the processed food industries are always at risk of being commoditised by their large food manufacturer and retailer customers. This is particularly true for those packaging companies that build their customer value propositions around an efficient response to a specification issued by a retailer or food manufacturer.

On the other hand, it is possible to resist commoditisation by innovating and introducing products like micro-perforated modified-atmosphere (MPMA) packaging. MPMA packaging extends the shelf life of fresh-cut produce for both retailers and end-consumers. It can also enable a crisp crust to be maintained on factory-made bread. These outcomes are beneficial to both the customers of the packaging company, and the end-consumers of the products being packaged. If the associated intellectual property can be protected, then it could be possible to stave off commoditisation for some time.

At the same time, when a packaging company focuses specifically on trying to meet a specific unmet end-consumer need, such as a packaging format that prevents cheese from sweating, or enables food to be micro-waved and come out crisp, it is more likely to innovate in a way that makes its technology crucial or at least important to its customers' own value proposition, and thereby avert the threat of commoditisation.

Illustration – Steel Industry

Companies that fail to avert the threat of commoditisation eventually experience a fall in returns as the forces of competition drive economic profitability and economic profit back to zero. This fate is generally evident in the length of a company's *EP Bow Wave*.

The Australian steel industry provided a good example of this. In 2006 there were three main steel companies operating in Australia – namely BlueScope Steel, OneSteel and Smorgon Steel. In June 2006, BlueScope had an *EP Bow Wave* 50 years in length, OneSteel had an *EP Bow Wave* of 30 years and Smorgon had an *EP Bow Wave* of 15 years.

Smorgon's product mix was the most commoditised of the three competitors, with significant volumes of its steel production being channelled into low value products like concrete reinforcing mesh. On the other hand, BlueScope had a significant proportion of value-added products in its mix, including a number of innovative architectural products that provided clear benefits to architects, builders and home owners.

A Preparedness to Build Value Creating Networks

The second aspect of the mindset required for disciplined innovation based on *Hybrid Thinking* is a preparedness to build value creating networks.

Companies that continually seek to meet current and emerging end-consumer needs are in a good position to hold back the forces of commoditisation. This does not mean that they must vertically integrate and participate in every element of the value chain. But it can mean working with a group of companies that seek to align their interests with the objective of creating value for end-consumers.

Becoming part of such a group forces companies that participate at the upper end of the value chain to specifically consider the needs of end-consumer at the lower end of the chain, and take care to avoid the emergence of industry structures that tend to make this difficult.

Many industries are now structured in a way that sees businesses operating in relatively small and sometimes quite isolated components of their industry value chain, where they are neither in touch with end-consumers, nor seeking to co-operate with other participants in the value chain for the benefit of end-consumers. A lot of their energy and resources are expended in competing with their direct rivals in their element of the industry value chain, or in "value-grabbing" manoeuvres with adjacent upstream and downstream participants in the chain. In the process, meeting the needs of end-consumers becomes secondary to winning in their part of the value chain, or capturing value that was previously generated in the value chain element immediately above or below them. In some cases, true end-consumer needs are not even clearly apparent to those players whose focus is solely within one element of the value chain.

One particularly effective way to align value chain participants' interests with those of end-consumers, and in so doing hold back the forces of commoditisation, involves the formation of value-creating networks. The idea of the network is for companies to work together across all elements of the value chain to co-create value for end-users or consumers in a way that creates wealth for all participants in the value chain.

Progressive Competition

Companies working together in such a network effectively engage in what might be considered a more progressive form of competition. They seek to do the best they can for end-consumers, by efficiently delivering additional value or benefit. The focus of the network is on end-consumer value creation and the main focal point of competition is in the end-consumer market or interface. The concept is illustrated in Fig. 8.2.

Progressive competition emerges from a progressive management consciousness where the goal is to make a product, service or customer value proposition *more worthy* in the eyes of customers or end-consumers.

(There is some alignment between the concept of progressive competition and the ideas behind the *Shared Value* movement.)

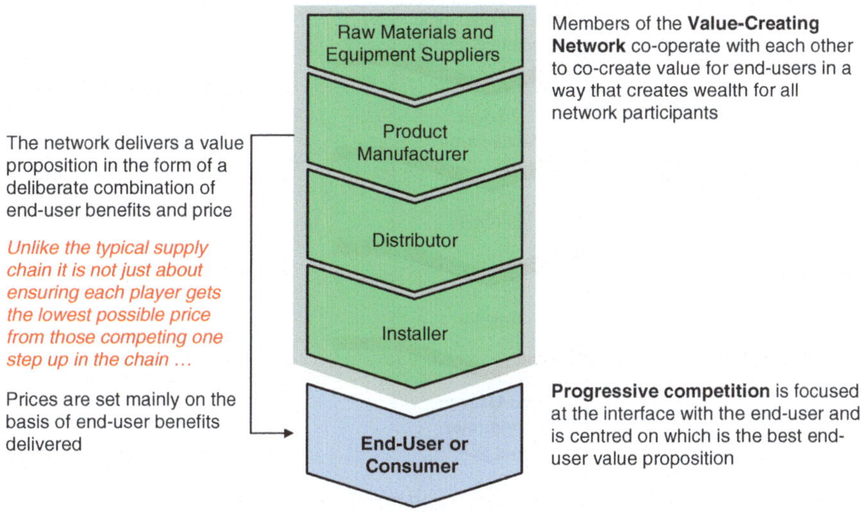
Raw Materials and Equipment Suppliers
Product Manufacturer
Distributor
Installer
End-User or Consumer
Members of the Value-Creating Network co-operate with each other to co-create value for end-users in a way that creates wealth for all network participants
The network delivers a value proposition in the form of a deliberate combination of end-user benefits and price
Unlike the typical supply chain it is not just about ensuring each player gets the lowest possible price from those competing one step up in the chain ...
Prices are set mainly on the basis of end-user benefits delivered
Progressive competition is focused at the interface with the end-user and is centred on which is the best end-user value proposition

Fig. 8.2 Progressive competition in a value creating network

Regressive Competition

The situation portrayed in Fig. 8.2 is quite different from the somewhat regressive price-based competition that occurs between participants in upstream elements of the traditional value chain. In this more regressive form of competition, there is intense competition at the interface between each value chain element that tends to force down prices and encourages commoditisation – by stripping out customer value.

Regressive competition stems from regressive management consciousness where the goal is simply to win. This more traditional situation is illustrated in Fig. 8.3.

It is important to appreciate that, contrary to the dogma occasionally espoused by some business economists, it is not competition *per se* that drives innovation leading to greater choice for end-consumers. The true underlying driver of greater choice for end-consumers is individual and organisational creativity – often underpinned by a desire to serve or help customers and end-consumers. Progressive competition based on the quality of competing value propositions offered at the end-consumer interface, does a great deal to encourage innovation, while at the same time serving the long-term best interests of end-consumers.

On the other hand, regressive competition in each of the intermediate markets within the traditional value chain, tends to be less conductive to creativity and

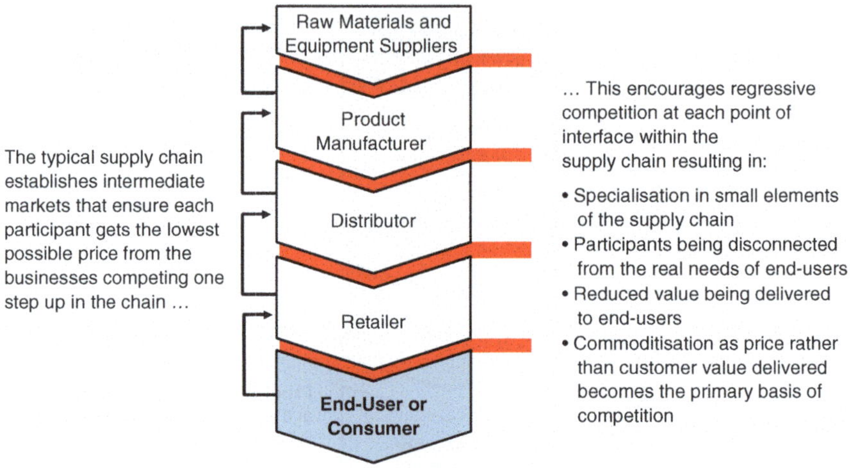

Fig. 8.3 Regressive competition in a traditional value chain

innovation – particularly creativity and innovation aimed at enhancing customer value and feeding the cycle of customer value and shareholder wealth creation.

A Bias Towards Value Pricing

The third aspect of the mindset required for disciplined innovation based on *Hybrid Thinking* is a bias towards value pricing.

If a company succeeds in creating additional value for customers in a particular segment, then it can either capture that value in a higher price, or it can seek to gain market share – as indicated by the green and red arrows linking the simulated demand curves shown in Fig. 8.4.

These curves relate to an existing and an enhanced end-consumer value proposition. They were developed in the course of an actual client engagement using a form of conjoint analysis.

By definition, additional customer value means an additional benefit for which the customer is prepared to pay. Obviously there must be some flexibility and it is entirely appropriate for a company to choose not to recapture all of the additional value created for customers through price. In doing so, a company can build goodwill with their customer base or even accelerate the rate at which their product replaces an older technology.

It has been our experience that better outcomes are achieved for all stakeholders when management does everything that it can to ensure prices

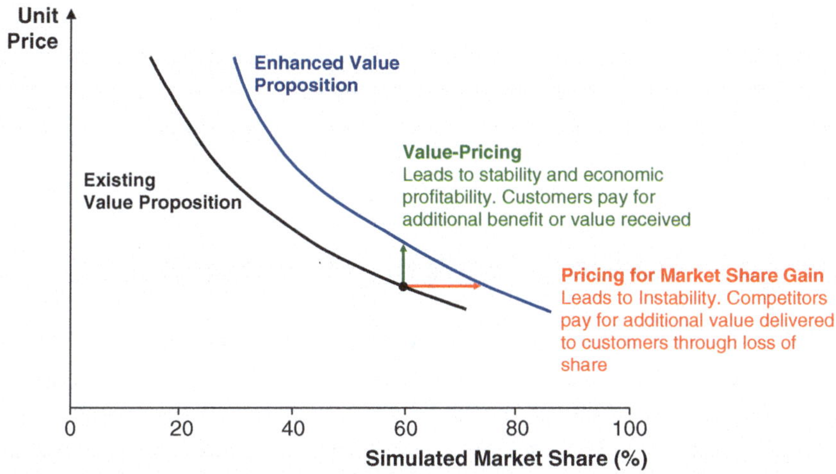

Fig. 8.4 Value-pricing versus pricing for share gain

are set primarily on the basis of benefits delivered to or received by customers or end-consumers; and not just on the basis of cost to serve, what the most aggressive competitor is prepared to accept, or what will cause the most difficulty for the competition.

Unless prices are set on the basis of the benefits the customer receives, it will not be possible to sustain a cycle of customer value and shareholder wealth creation over any length of time. Eventually, all market participants will suffer.

If a company introduces a significantly enhanced value proposition, and then tries to recapture all of the additional value created for its customers in the form of a market share gain rather than a price rise, then it is in effect attempting to give something to its customers while forcing its competitors to meet much of the cost. If the competitors choose to match the offer to protect market share, industry profitability will fall. As a result, fewer resources will be available to invest in the development of new products or services that would have enhanced the value delivered to customers over time.

Value pricing is more likely to lead to market stability and create a more balanced outcome. In so doing, the long-term wellbeing of all market participants is generally enhanced – including customers and end-consumers.

Unfortunately, there is an implicit belief among some business economists that the best way to create value for customers is to reduce the price that they are asked to pay for a particular product or service – or alternatively to offer them additional value for the same price. In parallel with this, there is an explicit belief that competition, and particularly price-based competition, is the best form of "protection" for consumers. This thinking is quite entrenched in some industry regulatory frameworks, government competition policies, and the pricing policies of many corporations. This way of thinking needs to be challenged.

Illustration – Electricity Distribution Infrastructure

In 1998 and 1999, in an effort to understand the willingness of residential consumers to pay for enhanced levels of service in their electricity supply, a total of four studies were undertaken by our firm in the metropolitan and surrounding areas of Sydney and Melbourne. In each case, the research technique employed a combination of discrete choice modelling and conjoint analysis.

The results of only two of these studies were made public – one relating to Sydney and its surrounding areas, and one relating to Melbourne.[1] In all four studies, three alternative electricity supply infrastructures were tested: *overhead bare wire, aerial bundled conductor* and *underground cable.*

Overhead bare wire was the low cost alternative and was the most common existing infrastructure. However, it was considered by many to be quite ugly. Where trees existed in a street to camouflage the wires, they needed to be cut back heavily. There was also a perception of a significant risk associated with fallen wires arising from storm damage or motor vehicle accidents, or accidental contact being made with wires such as with the mast of a sailing boat. In addition, the supply to those areas served with overhead bare wire infrastructure was somewhat less reliable than in those suburbs served by underground supply, with a higher risk of an interruption to supply.

Aerial bundled conductor is a thick insulated cable that is suspended on poles like overhead bare wire. It is more expensive than overhead bare wire, but it also delivers greater benefits. Because it is insulated, trees can camouflage it

[1] The results of the Sydney study, which involved approximately a 1,000 respondent, face-to-face, PC-administered survey of residential electricity consumers from 155 postcode locations in Sydney and surrounding areas, were released in January 1999 by Energy Australia in an appendix to a Discussion Paper entitled *Meeting Customer Requirements under the Regulatory Framework*. This paper was available from www.ipart.nsw.gov. The results of the Melbourne study, which involved 400 respondents from different parts of the state of Victoria in 1998–1999, were quoted in the South Australian Independent Industry Regulator's *Information Paper on Electricity Tariffs and Security of Supply* issued in June 2000. A detailed description of the methodology developed to complete both studies was presented and reviewed in Williams, P. and Kilroy, D., "Calibrating Price in ACA: The ACA Price Effect and How to Manage It", *Proceedings of the 2000 Sawtooth Software Annual Conference*, September 2000.

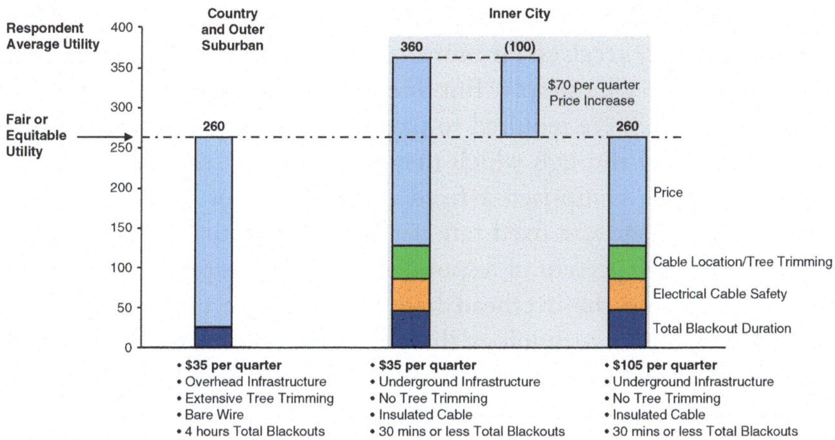

Fig. 8.5 Value-pricing in electricity supply

without the need for trimming. It also exhibits a higher level of reliability and the studies showed that it was perceived by customers to be safer. While costing more than overhead bare wire, it is lower cost than an underground supply infrastructure.

Underground supply is the high cost, high value distribution alternative. Its use eliminates the need for poles and wires. It also offers the highest level of reliability and respondents in the studies perceived it to be the safest alternative. However, a switch to an underground supply could have caused significant inconvenience as trenches were dug in streets and through properties.

The research revealed that the utility or value derived by customers from each of the three alternative supply infrastructures differed significantly.

Figure. 8.5 compares the utility that respondents in one city derived from a low cost overhead bare wire supply infrastructure, to that which they derived from an underground supply.

The height of the first stacked bar represents the utility that respondents derived from the overhead bare wire alternative. Most of their utility was derived from its low price. The second stacked bar represents the value or utility that respondents derived from an underground infrastructure provided at the same regulated price as overhead bare wire. The third stacked bar represents the outcome if the fixed component of the price for underground supply were increased by $70 per quarter so as to make the overall utility from underground supply match the overall utility derived from overhead bare wire.

Consumers supplied via the more reliable and more aesthetically pleasing underground supply received far more value or benefit than those connected to an overhead bare wire supply. But due to the regulatory regime in place at the time, customers were required to pay the same regulated price regardless of the infrastructure through which they received their electricity supply. At the time, this price comprised a fixed quarterly fee of $35 and a variable charge based on usage at a fixed rate per Kilowatt-Hour.

Approximately 30 percent of respondents indicated a preparedness to meet the cost of replacing the overhead bare wire with an underground supply using cable installation technology that existed at the time of the study. This meant paying a fixed fee of $105 per quarter rather than the existing fee of $35 on the fixed component of their electricity bill.

A further 50 percent indicated that, if given a choice, they would opt for aerial bundled conductor at a higher price than overhead bare wire. But if the fixed price of an underground supply had been somewhat lower than $105 per quarter, they would have opted for underground.

Twenty percent of customers were not interested in paying for an enhanced supply and opted for overhead bare wire.

A value-pricing strategy developed using this understanding of customer value creation was shown to have the potential to add significantly to the value of the distribution network operators, while at the same time better meeting the needs of end-consumers. Under this strategy, customers connected to an underground supply would have paid a higher price, and those supplied via overhead bare wire would have received a discount.

Ultimately, these research outcomes were rejected by the various regulatory bodies. This was despite the fact that the quite innovative approach adopted received an excellent reception and peer review when presented at an international conjoint analysis and choice modelling conference in the US in May 2000. Despite being seen as controversial at the time, the research results did demonstrate that while all consumers welcomed the idea of lower prices, most also valued other aspects of their electricity supply and the majority of those who did were prepared to pay for them.[2]

In the late 1990s, our focus on customer value and shareholder wealth creation as joint and mutually reinforcing objectives led to an interesting brush with the economic rationalist community. The results of four separate studies we had undertaken for different electricity utilities had indicated that consumers of electricity were

[2] Williams, P. and Kilroy, D., "Calibrating Price in ACA: The ACA Price Effect and How to Manage It", *Proceedings of the 2000 Sawtooth Software Annual Conference*, September 2000, pp. 81–95.

prepared to pay higher prices for certain aspects of the way in which they received their electricity supply – from an industry that was then a regulated monopoly.

Of particular interest was the fact that the studies all showed that roughly 30 percent of consumers in urban areas were prepared to pay a much higher price in order to have their electricity supply relocated underground. This finding was at odds with the views of the regulator, whom we understood was of the opinion that the best way to provide greater value to consumers was to offer them lower prices – and that the electricity utilities needed to improve their efficiency in order to fund those price reductions.

Ultimately, the findings of our work were set aside because of doubts being raised about the methodology we employed. Since our findings were so counter to the current paradigm, the regulator decided that our work needed to be subjected to a peer review. The academic who conducted the review met with us for only an hour or so to discuss the approach we had employed, before submitting a somewhat negative review a few weeks later. While he made some valid although perhaps somewhat impractical suggestions as to how the sampling method might have been improved, he had simply not understood the technique we employed.

Ironically, roughly two years later we presented our approach at an international market research conference in Hilton Head, South Carolina. Our work was subjected to a thorough peer review, and was particularly well received. In fact, for several years after that (until an important breakthrough in discrete choice modelling emerged) it was regarded as one of the better approaches available for the type of research challenge we were seeking to address.[3,4,5]

Backing New Ideas with Analysis as a Proving Mechanism

The fourth aspect to the mindset required for disciplined innovation based on *Hybrid Thinking* is a preparedness to back new ideas and to use logical analysis primarily as a proving mechanism as distinct from a discovery mechanism.

---

[3] Williams, P. and Kilroy, D., op. cit.

[4] McCullough, D., "Comment on Williams and Kilroy", *Proceedings of the 2000 Sawtooth Software Annual Conference*, September 2000, pp. 97–100.

[5] Orme, Bryan K., *Getting Started with Conjoint Analysis*, Research Publishers, Maddison Wisconsin, Second Edition, 2010, p. 42.

Far more insight is generally gained by developing ideas for potential customer value propositions and then testing them through research and analysis, than by trying to use research and analysis as the primary source of new ideas. It is also more efficient. There is little point in boiling the ocean just to find out what lies on the bottom – even in today's world where data processing power enables you to do so. It is more effective to integrate this powerful analytical capacity with an even more powerful creative process.

Hybrid Thinking requires two primary forms of research and analysis:

- Customer value analysis, leading to an understanding of customer value creation potential; and
- Economic profitability analysis leading to an assessment of intrinsic value uplift and shareholder wealth creation potential.

Customer value analysis seeks to understand the value or utility associated with the elements of a particular value proposition, and use this as a basis for refining the value proposition and then determining price and forecasting demand. Its primary outputs are a refined value proposition and an understanding of customer benefit or utility sufficient to develop an optimal pricing strategy, so as to forecast volume demand and revenue under that pricing strategy.

An assessment of shareholder wealth creation potential involves assessing the costs that will be incurred and the capital that will be required in order to deliver the value proposition, and then calculating the present value of the associated economic profit and cash flow streams.

The primary role of research and analysis when using the *Hybrid Thinking* framework is to prove to the team responsible for the idea (and those who must either approve it or implement it) that the idea will either:

- Work and lead to the creation of both customer value and shareholder wealth; or
- Not work at this point in time, in which case the team should look elsewhere for opportunities to create customer value and shareholder wealth.

Disciplined Innovation using Hybrid Thinking

Once the required mindset has been established, with its four characteristics of a focus on end-user needs, a preparedness build value creating networks, a

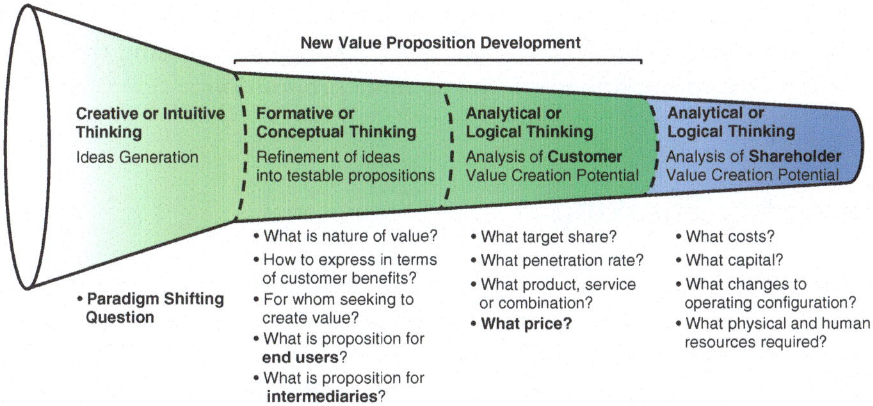

Fig. 8.6 Applying hybrid thinking

bias towards value pricing, and a willingness to back new ideas while using analysis more as a proving mechanism than a discovery mechanism; it becomes possible to continually generate new ideas with the potential to be developed into enhanced value propositions for customers in a specific needs-based customer segment.

These can then be refined systematically, and processed into potentially new and higher value strategies.

In fact, this is how the cycle of customer value and shareholder wealth creation operates in practice. It is a process that has major implications for both strategy development and for business planning.

Hybrid Thinking can form the core of a business planning process that operates as a systematic ideas capturing mechanism. The way that ideas are captured and processed is illustrated in Fig. 8.6.

How the *Hybrid Thinking* process fits within the overall series of business processes was illustrated in Fig. 6.1. There are five process steps:

- Possibility thinking,
- Value proposition development;
- Alternative strategy development;
- Valuation and strategy selection; and
- Building management commitment.

It begins with a workshop designed to come up with potential value propositions in the manner described in Chapter 5 and for which some examples are provided below. It ends with another workshop in which the management team commit to a higher value strategy built around the new or enhanced value proposition or series of value propositions.

Possibility Thinking

In a practical sense, developing higher value strategies begins with possibility thinking, which incorporates the creative and conceptual thinking stages of the *Hybrid Thinking* process.

Higher value strategies identified at a segment level will generally involve either the enhancement of an existing value proposition or the development of a new one. This is because over the longer term, the most fruitful place to focus possibility thinking is on the pursuit of ideas or concepts that lead to the creation of additional value for customers and end-consumers.

In focusing its thinking in this way, management lays the groundwork for the establishment of a cycle of customer value and shareholder wealth creation in each segment.

The first step is to capture ideas or concepts for solutions to unmet needs. Often this is best done in a workshop environment. In most businesses, there are ideas for enhanced value propositions already partly or even fully formed in the minds of people within the organisation. However, it is usually necessary to create the right environment for these ideas to emerge.

This is why a workshop is so valuable. Within such a workshop, one of the best ways to both draw out these ideas and at the same time generate new ones is to pose a paradigm-shifting question.

A paradigm-shifting question is a question that changes the frame of reference of the participants in a workshop and in so doing creates the intense encounter with information that was described in Chapter 5.

Often it enables or even forces workshop participants to look at a customer or end-consumer need, or a series of needs, in a broader context or from a completely different perspective.

This process is best described with some examples. There are many we could draw upon, but there are two from the late 1990s that are particularly instructive.

Illustration – Electricity Retailing

One of the consequences of the separation of electricity distribution from electricity retailing that occurred in Australia in the late 1990s was that retailers initially began to look at ways of stimulating demand as well as fighting for market share.

There was some irony in this, because at the same time that retailers were seeking to stimulate demand, the social imperative to reduce energy consumption and associated greenhouse gas emissions was beginning to emerge.

A number of electricity utilities were faced with the problem of potentially significant losses of market share through the introduction of contestability in retail markets that had previously been regulated monopolies.

In a workshop conducted for one Sydney-based retailer to address this issue in early 1997, the following question was used to shift the frame of reference for the participants: "If we were new to this market, how would we create significant additional value for customers and then recapture it in our revenue stream?"

The main idea that arose in response to this paradigm-shifting question was for the retailer to redefine itself as an organisation that both supplied electricity to customers and at the same time helped its customers to become efficient users of that electricity.

These two goals could have been seen as conflicting since increasing the efficiency with which households consume electricity could potentially reduce demand. However, they could also be perfectly complementary. One way to make them complementary was to help customers take advantage of the lower whole-of-life cost associated with different ways of using electricity. Hot water supply provided one quite compelling example, but there were many other forms of domestic electricity consumption to which this thinking could be applied. Induction cooking appliances were another example examined.

In those parts of Australia that were not supplied by natural gas, electricity was the main means of heating water. At the time, water heaters that used resistance elements cost less than $1,000 to purchase, but well over $8,000 to run (in present value terms) for the average home over a typical 15-year life.

A more energy efficient water heater based on a heat pump cost nearly $3,000 to buy but used only 40 percent of the energy to produce the same amount of hot water over the same 15-year life. As a result, the heat pump

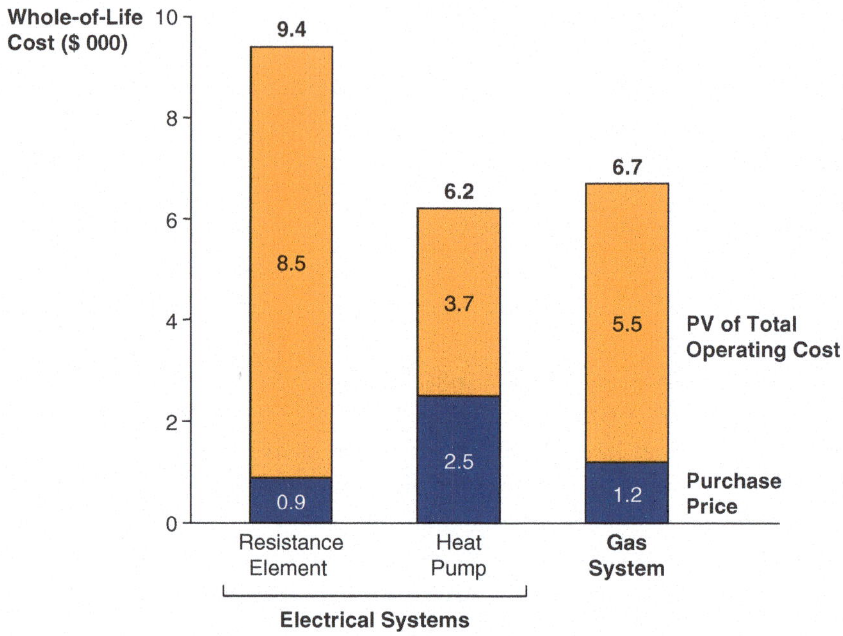

Fig. 8.7 Alternative hot water system value propositions

provided the more economical solution with a whole-of-life cost of approximately $6,000 over a 15-year life, versus more than $9,000 for the more common resistance element alternative.

The economics of the alternative systems based on a 15-year life are illustrated in Fig. 8.7.

If offered by an electricity retailer on a whole-of-life cost basis combined with a leasing package that spread the purchase cost over the life of the unit, the system based on a heat pump would be the best long-term solution for the customer, the community and for the company. The cost to customers would be up to 30 percent lower. The community would benefit because electricity consumption would be reduced by more than 50 percent.

From the company's perspective, the difference in whole-of-life cost of more than $3,000 between the two offers represented a loss of revenue from energy consumption. But the saving to the customer also provided plenty of scope for a reasonably priced household energy efficiency audit. The fees from that audit, together with the sale of products designed to improve the energy efficiency of a house or an apartment, had the potential to generate far more economic profit than that foregone as a result of lost revenue on very low margin electricity supply. Again, the customer, the community and the company would be all have been winners.

It proved to be quite some years before this thinking filtered through to actual market behaviours. One of the reasons it took so long was that it ran counter to the nature of the regulatory framework and the economic philosophy that underpinned it. This is one of the issues that will be explored in some detail in the third book in this series.

Illustration – Building Products Manufacturing

In 1995, a major Australian building products manufacturer was for the first time facing the prospect of real competition from another powerful building products player in the domestic fibre cement market.

The company involved had enjoyed a virtual monopoly for many years and the immediate reaction of some members of the management team to the impending loss of this strong market position was to propose a price cut to defend market share. Others were not sure. Ultimately, a successful path forward emerged from thinking stimulated by the following paradigm shifting question. "How can we make the market for fibre cement so big that the competitor's entry will not stop us continuing to grow our economic profit stream for the next 10 to 15 years?"

Many ideas emerged for potential paths forward. They included expansion into other geographic regions as well as a number of responses specific to the Australian domestic market. Ultimately, the ideas for the domestic market were distilled into a series of concepts for new value propositions. One of the more interesting was an innovative alternative to the use of brick veneer in residential construction.

Australia was primarily a framed construction market, with most houses in the mid-1990s still being built using brick veneer – a building technique that almost certainly served the needs of builders more than it did those of householders.

Several ideas for new value propositions emerged around the concept of "masonry substitution". Each involved the use of fibre cement board as a substitute for rendered brick veneer.

What was eventually developed was a series of offers including a new walling system that comprised a timber frame with an outer skin of fibre cement sheet, an inner skin of either fibre cement or plasterboard, and lightweight concrete filler plus a layer of insulating material in between. Although more expensive than basic brick veneer, it was competitive in price with rendered brick and

Fig. 8.8 Masonry substitution solution

from the end-users' perspective, the new value proposition outperformed traditional brick veneer in many ways. Particularly important was the fact that the frame was inside the wall rather than adjacent to it as was the case with brick veneer. Because of this, an average-sized single family dwelling gained an extra 10 square metres of living space on the inside with the same external dimensions.

The system developed is illustrated in Fig. 8.8. It won an industry award in 1999 for the most innovative new building product in Australia.

Value Proposition Development

Once a series of ideas are on the table, and the management team has agreed that they should be developed further; the ideas can begin to be formulated into potential value propositions. An important element at this stage of the process is to express the value proposition in terms of the benefits that it delivers to customer and end-consumers, and then analyse it in terms of the actual value that customers and end-consumers derive from each individual attribute, as well as from the value proposition as a whole.

Properly defined, a value proposition is a deliberate combination of customer or end-consumer benefits and price that a business offers to a particular needs-based customer segment.

The Mindset Required in New Value Proposition Development

Formulating a new or enhanced value proposition involves taking an idea for a means of meeting a particular customer need, and structuring it into a product or service offer that incorporates a series of clear benefits for customers or end-consumers. Again, it is helpful to illustrate how this is done using examples, because the original idea is often just the catalyst for the thinking that produces the value proposition that is ultimately developed and commercialised.

In the case of the building materials manufacturer mentioned in the previous section, 12 concepts for potential new value propositions based on fibre cement emerged from a distillation of nearly two hundred ideas put forward by the management team in the course of a three-day workshop. The idea that eventually evolved into the masonary substitution system illustrated in Fig. 8.8, actually began life as an idea to use fibre cement as a means with which to provide first home buyers with a two storey home for the price of a single story brick veneer dwelling.

When the economics were understood fully, it became clear that it would not be possible to deliver on the original idea. But a new walling system was born out of the process of seeking to develop a masonry substitution offer that would outperform brick veneer.

Something similar happened with another idea. This was to develop a building system that would enable landscaping before (rather than after) building on sloping sites. This idea emerged from a perceived need to replace the expensive and environmentally damaging "cut and fill" construction technique used to build brick homes on sloping sites.

What eventually emerged was a framed construction technique that employed screw-in steel pylons supporting a compressed fibre cement deck. The remainder of the house could be built with fibre cement cladding or even the new walling system already described. While landscaping still happened after the building was completed, the environmental impact was far less and in most cases the entire property was more stable as a result.

In both cases, the original ideas caused the management team to think more broadly than they had in the past, and to be open to new (and sometimes even radical) concepts. In a sense, the final value proposition developed in each case only delivered part of what was envisaged in the original idea. But they were both successful in their own right and provided platforms from which to pursue the original ideas more fully at a later date if desired. More importantly, the final outcome created more value for individual customers, and offered that value to many more customers, than the original idea. In a sense, the idea was like a lead or a hint at where to look further.

This type of flexibility when following an idea that captures a team's collective imagination is fundamental to the creative process. It is a natural and an essential part of a well-structured value proposition development process.

Assessing Customer Value Creation

Once a potential value proposition has been formulated in response to a perceived need, the next step is to employ customer value analysis to measure the value or benefit that it will create for customers in a given segment.

It is important that this analysis is structured in such a way that management is able to quantify the value that customers derive from each attribute of the products and services that make up the potential value proposition. This enables them to determine the price that customers would be willing to pay for the overall value proposition, as well as how much each attribute of the value proposition contributes to that price. More importantly, it provides an analytical basis for refining the product or service to better meet customer needs, for adjusting the value proposition to meet the needs of a particular sub-segment, and also for optimising price.

The most basic form of customer value analysis involves modelling the economic cost to the customer, and particularly whole-of-life economic cost, as a proxy for customer utility or value. In many situations, whole-of-life cost can be a good indicator of likely customer behaviour. The hot water system example discussed earlier in this chapter is a good example. But it does not work in those segments in which fashion, image or brand name are determinants of customer behaviour rather than just tangible economic benefits.

Techniques like discrete choice modelling and conjoint analysis provide a more direct way to understand the value created for customers by a particular product or service.[6]

---

[6] These techniques rely on management being able to express each attribute in terms of the benefits that it delivers to customers. For example, in the electricity supply illustration shown in Figure 8.5, the

Choice modelling and conjoint analysis typically involve interviewing current or potential customers and determining how and why they would choose between different products or services. Respondents are asked to choose between different offers with different attribute combinations to enable the researcher to understand the utility associated with each level of each attribute – such as underground electricity supply with greater perceived safety and better reliability at a higher price, versus overhead bare wire with lower perceived safety and less reliability at a lower price.

The understanding of utility that emerges from an analysis of survey responses can be used to refine the value proposition, inform the pricing decision and also to segment the sample into groups with different preferences.

There is an excellent discussion of these techniques in Bryan Orme's book entitled *Getting Started with Conjoint Analysis – Strategies for Product Design and Pricing Research.* Used properly, they can be very powerful. Perhaps more importantly, familiarity with these techniques and exposure to their output can help embed the type of thinking required to continue to refine customer value propositions over time.

Determining "Value Price"

One particularly important piece of information provided from utility data is an understanding of value price. Price is nearly always included as an attribute in a conjoint or choice modelling study, and if approached in the right way, it is possible to assign an incremental "value price" to each level of each attribute. This means, for example, that the incremental price a group of customers might be prepared to pay for a two-year warranty rather than a one-year warranty can be predicted.

The value price associated with a particular attribute, or attribute level, is simply the price that a customer is willing to pay for that attribute or attribute level to be included in a product or service. It can also be thought of as the reduction in price for which a customer would be willing to accept the removal of the attribute from the product or service.

---

attributes used to differentiate between each of the three alternative supply infrastructures were price, nature of infrastructure (overhead or underground), the need for tree trimming, whether the cable was insulated or not, and the level of supply reliability. To define each offer in terms of these attributes required distinct levels to be defined that related to each offer (or potential offer). For example, underground supply had outages from blackouts totalling a fraction of that experienced with overhead bare wire.

In developing a value proposition, a management team must both design the product or service offer and set an appropriate price. Both involve choice. In designing a product or service offer, management can choose to include many benefits and charge a high price, or provide few benefits for a relatively low price. The idea is to get the right mix of customer benefits, price, and cost to deliver to suit the needs of a particular needs-based customer group. In simple terms, the aim is to include features or attributes on which customers place more value than the cost of providing those features or attributes.

At the same time, it is important to avoid additional features or benefits that are more costly to provide than the amount that customers are willing to pay. This may seem obvious, but it is important to maintain this discipline. Conjoint analysis and choice modelling provide the analytical tools necessary to underpin these decisions.

When it comes to setting pricing policy, management can choose to set prices so as to fully recapture all of the value created for customers, or at a lower level in order to gain market share. Which path is more appropriate in the short term will depend upon the economics associated with producing and delivering the value proposition. But in the long term, as has already been discussed, continually adding value to a product or service and then attempting to recapture that value in the form of market share gains, is an aggressive approach that can ultimately lead to a reduction in long-term profitability for the segment as a whole.

Alternative Strategy Development

As is illustrated in Fig. 8.9, a business unit strategy comprises a decision as to the segments in which the business will participate, and a decision as to how it will participate in each segment it has chosen to serve.

The strategy for each segment comprises an articulation of the value proposition that will be offered to the customers in that segment, and a value delivery system which ensures the efficient delivery of the value proposition – often to a number of segments.

When using the *Hybrid Thinking* framework, the primary focus is generally on value proposition enhancement. Virtually all of the creative effort is focused on customer or end-consumer value enhancement and much of the analytical effort goes into customer value analysis.

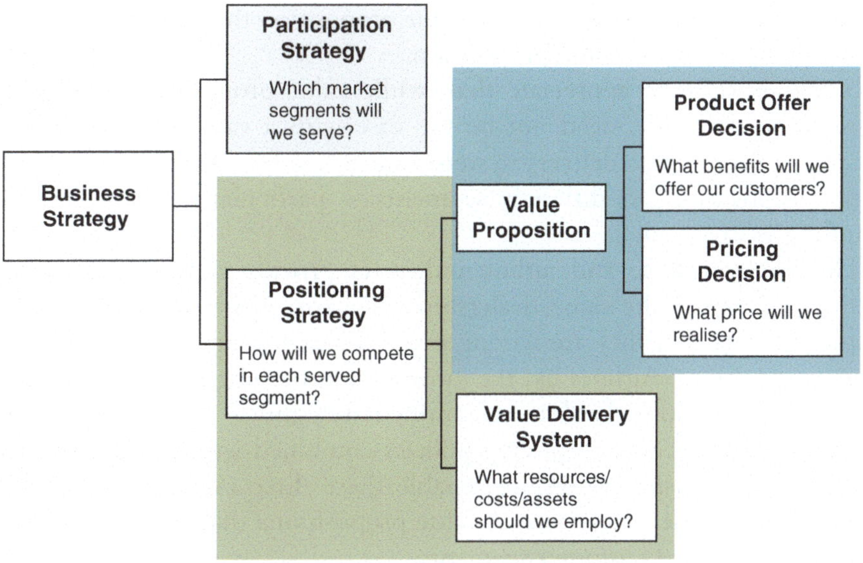

Fig. 8.9 Strategy articulation framework for a business unit

Once a value proposition has been identified, its ability to provide enhanced value for customers has been established, and a decision has been taken as to how much of the value created for customers will be recaptured through price, most of the hard work has been done.

To develop a new or enhanced value proposition into a new strategy, there are two questions that must be answered.

- How will the value proposition be communicated and then delivered to customers in the target segment? In other words, what form will the value delivery system take?
- If the business forms part of a value-creating alliance or network of businesses, what role will it play in that system?

The Value Delivery System

A value delivery system is a physical, on-line or hybrid business system designed to deliver a value proposition to customers. It can be thought of as simply the physical configuration of assets and resources that are required to deliver a value proposition. However, in many cases the value delivery system is so closely aligned with the value proposition that customers see it as an integral part of the value proposition.

It is important to appreciate that, while value propositions tend to be segment specific, this need not be the case with a value delivery system. Often the same value delivery system can be used to deliver a number of value propositions to different segments – particularly when umbrella branding is involved.

The motor vehicle and airline industries provide good examples. Car manufacturers use the same dealership system to distribute their vehicles, despite the fact that they are serving many different segments with different value propositions. Airlines use the same aircraft to deliver three broad value propositions on long haul inter-continental flights – first, business and economy classes. Targeted pricing policies combined with purchasing, cancellation and transfer conditions, enable these three categories to be subdivided into a much larger set of value propositions that serve much more specific needs-based customer segments.

The main function of the value delivery system is to deliver the value proposition intact to the customer in a manner consistent with its nature and intent – regardless of whether it is delivering one or a number of value propositions.

The Value Delivery System in a Value Creating Network

The nature and the efficiency of a value delivery system are important drivers of economic cost for any business. But this cost must be viewed in the context of the value delivered to customers, and not in isolation.

Structuring a value delivery system today is a very different exercise than was the case in the 1980s when the value chain concept provided most if not all of the building blocks.

We defined a value creating network earlier as a group of companies that work together in a way that enables them to co-create value for customers and particularly end-consumers, in a way that enables wealth to be created for all members of the network. This is very different from the concept of one company owning the end-consumer relationship, and all other participants being seen as members of its supply chain (and continually being subjected to price pressure to ensure that the company that has the relationship with the end-consumer captures most of the economic profit available in the market).

Whether delivered by one company acting alone, or through an alliance or value-creating network, customer expectations must be met with a value proposition that is both priced appropriately and delivered reasonably efficiently. In this context, reasonably efficient delivery means that the incremental revenues arising from the appropriate pricing of incremental customer value, translate into incremental economic profit and ultimately, intrinsic value uplift and shareholder wealth creation. At the same time, the value delivery system must ensure that the value proposition is delivered in a manner that does not undermine or diminish the value or utility it is intended to provide to the customer.

The fibre cement walling system discussed earlier in this chapter provides an excellent example of the importance of alignment between the value proposition and its delivery system. The residential construction business is conservative and slow to adopt new materials and techniques. So a crucial element in the strategy was for the manufacturer to put in place a value delivery system that required it to be involved directly in the product's installation in the early years. This represented a significant step for a building products manufacturing company, but it was necessary to gain acceptance and build penetration until such time as the new product began to be pulled through by end-users, and the industry was able to accommodate the new installation methods.

When formulating a higher value strategy based on a new or enhanced value proposition, or a new and better value delivery system, there are generally two cases that arise in relation to the delivery of value to customers. The first is where the value proposition can be produced and delivered at marginal additional cost using existing infrastructure. The second is where new infrastructure is required. The first case is more common, but both can be modelled relatively easily.

Valuation and Strategy Selection

The key question that must be answered at the point of segment-level strategy selection is…

Will the incremental revenues generated by the new value proposition exceed the incremental costs and capital required to deliver it, and in doing so, result in an enhanced EP stream and an uplift in intrinsic value for the segment?

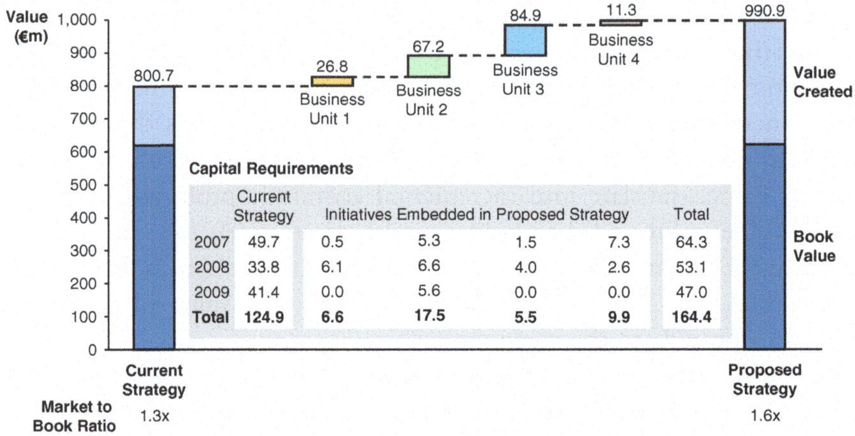

	Current Strategy	Initiatives Embedded in Proposed Strategy				Total
2007	49.7	0.5	5.3	1.5	7.3	64.3
2008	33.8	6.1	6.6	4.0	2.6	53.1
2009	41.4	0.0	5.6	0.0	0.0	47.0
Total	**124.9**	**6.6**	**17.5**	**5.5**	**9.9**	**164.4**

Fig. 8.10 Consolidated impact of higher value strategy development

Once the value proposition has been formulated, and an understanding of customer value creation has been used to set an appropriate pricing policy, revenues can be forecast with a reasonable degree of accuracy. Once it has been decided how the value proposition will be delivered, which parts of the delivery system will be owned, and which could be outsourced to business partners in a value creating network, it is possible to model the associated cost and capital requirements. This enables the strategy to be valued to determine its potential to create wealth for shareholders.

Figure. 8.10 illustrates a group level summary of the intrinsic value uplift expected at the end of one company's strategic planning process. There were a number of new segment-level value propositions embedded in the strategies of each business unit. There was also a major plant rationalisation proposal embedded in the strategy for one of the business units. But when presented in this decision-ready form, the task for the decision-making authority (usually the board) is made much simpler. In the case illustrated, the board was being asked to approve a strategy that management believed would require the investment of an additional €40 million over three years to deliver a €190 million uplift in intrinsic value.

Building Management Commitment

A strategy development process based on disciplined innovation and centred on the *Hybrid Thinking* process almost always involves the entire management team at the start and at the end, but passes the ball to a smaller working group to shape the strategy in the middle.

Commitment is essential both at the point that responsibility is handed to the smaller group, and also once the decision to move forward is made by the full management team at the end of the process.

It was mentioned earlier that the reason for valuing strategies is to enable the highest value alternative to be identified and adopted. But that selection process is only valid if the management team responsible for the implementation of the chosen strategy is fully committed to delivering the economic profit stream and the intrinsic value outcome that caused them to select this strategy from among the other alternatives that were considered and discarded during the planning process.

The quality and the rigor of the analysis completed along the way is an important part of this. But once a decision to proceed is made, it is absolutely essential that there is full commitment to that decision.

The full commitment required to ensure success is only really possible with the right mindset – and once again there are two aspects of this to consider. These are our conscious intent and our subconscious beliefs. Both are important.

Our conscious intent is important because often, our decisions are only right in retrospect rather than in prospect. In other words, we don't so much make right decisions. More often than not, we make our decisions right. We do this in part through the strength and the clarity of our conscious intent, in part through the extent to which that intent is underpinned by a set of consistent beliefs embedded in the subconscious mind, and in part by the way we speak, the way we act, and the way we react, after having made our decision.

The subconscious controls the way we act and react instinctively on a day-to-day basis. Alignment between our conscious intent and our subconscious beliefs ensures that the way we act, and particularly the way we react, will always be consistent with our conscious intent. This is how we make our decisions right.

There are a number of techniques that can be used to align our beliefs with our conscious intent. Each makes use of the neuroplasticity that exists when we are in a whole brain state. Sports psychologists are particularly adept at the use of such techniques. Our firm has adapted them successfully to the business environment with a series of simple protocols that can only be taught properly in a workshop context. Once learned, managers can use them continually to enhance their own performance as well as that of the teams that they lead.

Synthesis and Concluding Remarks

The engine room for long-term wealth creation will always be the identification and successful implementation of higher value strategies.

While this is fundamentally a creative endeavour, it does not need to be completely free form. In fact, experience suggests that giving it some structure increases the chances of the process being embedded successfully in an organisation.

The first step in structuring the creative process is to focus on needs-based customer segments. The second is to apply *Hybrid Thinking* – or the use of creative thinking and logical analysis in combination in the pursuit of segment-level strategies that enhance value for customers and create wealth for shareholders. The third step is to adopt the four-dimensional mindset described at the beginning of this chapter, incorporating a focus on end-consumer needs, a preparedness to build value creating networks, a bias towards value pricing, and a willingness to back new ideas by using analysis more as a proving mechanism than a discovery mechanism.

Giving any more structure to an innovative process would almost certainly not be appropriate.

Creativity is a uniquely human skill. However, it is difficult for creativity to flourish in an environment of fear or uncertainty. If an organisation is to institutionalise disciplined innovation as we have described, it needs to give creativity and innovation pivotal roles. This is only possible when people know that they are valued as assets to be developed and not seen costs that might need to be eliminated. Creativity is also far more likely to flourish if the consciousness of the organisation is more progressive than regressive. This means the focus is primarily on making an offer more worthy in the eyes of customers and end-consumers, rather than on trying to defeat or even smash the competition.

Building an organisation capable of creating value for customers and wealth for shareholders on an ongoing basis also carries with it the implicit requirement that other stakeholder groups derive a fair or appropriate amount of value or benefit from their interaction with the company. Ultimately, all stakeholders (including employees) need to be allies in the pursuit of both customer value and shareholder wealth, rather than adversaries in the pursuit of short-term earnings outcomes (which can often represent the creation of an economic benefit for one group of stakeholders at the expense of other stakeholder groups).

One way to begin to do this is to make a conscious decision to create value for customers and wealth for shareholders in ways that at minimum preserve and wherever possible enhance, societal wellbeing (and environmental sustainability). This is the focus of Chapter 9.

9

Customer Value, Shareholder Wealth and Stakeholder Wellbeing

Chapter 8 demonstrated how with the right mindset, a disciplined approach to innovation can underpin the ongoing creation of both customer value and shareholder wealth for a listed company. However just below the surface of this thinking is another important consideration. Once customer value creation and shareholder wealth creation are embraced as joint and mutually reinforcing objectives, business leaders can (if they want) make a conscious choice to pursue these two joint goals in ways that either preserve or enhance the wellbeing of all legitimate stakeholders. These include employees, suppliers, the wider community and the environment. Choosing to act in this way is somewhat analogous to an institutional investor choosing to invest in socially responsible companies.

The purpose of this chapter is twofold. The first is to demonstrate that a conscious decision to create customer value and build shareholder wealth in ways that at minimum preserve and wherever possible enhance the wellbeing of all other legitimate stakeholders, is both a logical and an appropriate next step for visionary business leaders. The second is to point to some of the elements of a new business paradigm that would emerge around this thinking if sufficient business leaders were to decide to move in this direction. These will be developed further in the other two books in the series.

D. Kilroy, M. Schneider, *Customer Value, Shareholder Wealth, Community Wellbeing*, DOI 10.1007/978-3-319-54774-9_9

A Shift in Thinking

Since the turn of the century, there has been an emerging interest in the notion of responsible investment, together with a greatly increased focus by the investment community on environmental, social and corporate governance (ESG) issues. The latter arose in large part from a UN sponsored study by Freshfields Bruckhaus Deringer in 2005, which concluded that consideration of ESG issues in investment analysis was arguably part of the fiduciary duty of all institutional investors.[1] Institutional investors now accept that such considerations are an important element in the evaluation of potential investment opportunities, and in their engagement with the companies in which they are invested. Their fiduciary duties require it, and the evidence suggests such consideration has a material positive impact on investment returns. However, the real momentum for this shift in thinking came in the wake of the GFC in 2008–2009.[2]

In the aftermath of the GFC, there have been many calls for an end to the notion of shareholder primacy. The *Shareholder Primacy Paradigm,* which had its genesis in the mid-1980s and which was almost universally accepted by the mid to late-1990s, held that the fundamental economic objective of businesses in general and listed companies in particular, was to maximise shareholder value. However, what was never properly resolved as this approach grew to dominate management thinking in the last two decades of the twentieth century, was the question of how that wealth should be created, and what heed should be paid to the interests of other stakeholder groups along the way.

The now quite widespread questioning of the *Shareholder Primacy Paradigm* began in Europe in the wake of the GFC. Today, there is mounting pressure in Europe and elsewhere for listed companies to set aside the idea that shareholder value maximisation (SVM) should be seen as a governing corporate objective to which all other objectives must by definition be considered subsidiary. Some of the main contributors to this thinking are groups like:

[1] Freshfields Bruckhaus Deringer, *A Legal Framework for the Integration of Environmental, Social and Governance Issues into Institutional Investment: A report produced for the asset management working group of the UNEP FI.* (http://www.unepfi.org/fileadmin/documents/freshfields_legal_resp_20051123.pdf, 2005).

[2] Barnett, Michael and Salomon, Robert, "Beyond Dichotomy: The Curvilinear Relationship between Social Responsibility and Financial Performance", *Strategic Management Journal,* Vol. 27, 2006.

- The *Purpose of the Corporation Project,* an initiative set up by Frank Bold Lawyers, a public interest law firm with operations in the Czech Republic and in Belgium;
- The *Modern Corporation Project* at the Cass Business School in London;
- The Oslo-based *Sustainable Companies Project*;
- The US-based Aspen Institute's *Business in Society Program*; together with the work of
- Professor Roger Martin of the Rotman School of Management at the University of Toronto; and
- Professor Lynn Stout of Cornell Law School, whose book *The Shareholder Value Myth* caused many to pause and think more carefully about the direction in which business and particularly the capital markets were heading.

The Governance Institute of Australia is now involved as well, with a very well-written discussion paper entitled "Shareholder primacy: Is there a need for change?" that was released in late 2014.

Much (but by no means all) of the work being done by these and other similarly motivated groups has a legal, regulatory or governance focus. This "outside in" approach looks closely at the rules, regulations and requirements that govern the behaviour of listed companies. It has also tended to view short-term earnings maximisation as either being synonymous with or else a path to shareholder value maximisation – which it is not. It was made clear in Part I that the stand-alone pursuit of short-term earnings maximisation is rarely if ever in the long-term best interest of shareholders, or any of the many other legitimate stakeholders in a listed company.

In aggregate, the work of these groups clearly articulates the nature of the problem being addressed and in doing so, makes a compelling case for change. However, we need more than a clear articulation of the problem. We need a robust and practical path forward.

If we approach the issue from the "inside out" rather than from the "outside in", we can develop a meaningful response and chart a path forward that is both realistic and practical. However in doing so, we need to be prepared to retain that which is correct and valuable about the current business paradigm – and not just focus on its shortcomings.

The key is to make the seemingly subtle but actually quite profound change to the fundamental economic objective for all listed companies that we spoke about in Part I. We need to let go of the idea that businesses in general and listed companies in particular should be seeking to create shareholder wealth *per se*. Instead, we need to recognise that the real goal is to build an enduring institution that can create wealth for shareholders *on an ongoing basis.* When we do, something quite profound occurs. It becomes apparent that the journey and the destination have become one. As we asserted in the *Summary of Core Ideas* at the beginning of this book, this is because the way a company goes about creating shareholder wealth has an enormous impact on its ability to continue to do so *on an ongoing basis.*

The existence of a link between the way a company sets out to create shareholder wealth, and both its success in doing so and its ability to continue to do so on an ongoing basis, is something that has been suggested by others – most notably Raj Sisodia and the *Conscious Capitalism* movement. Sisodia *et al.* observed empirically that companies which his team judged to be conscious businesses or *Firms of Endearment* performed better than other companies. But it is only with the *EP Bow Wave* construct and the *Enduring Cycle of Customer Value and Shareholder Wealth Creation* supported by *Hybrid Thinking*, that we can underpin this observed link both conceptually and analytically.

It's not all about corporate culture and leadership. These things are extremely important. But there is more to the story than that. We need a more expansive or enlightened approach to corporate finance and business economics. We also need to be able to unlock and harness individual and organisational creativity. But most important of all, we need an approach to business that seeks to enhance the wellbeing of all. This means finding a way of doing business such that everyone who interacts legitimately with a company, benefits in some way from that interaction.

An Explicit Focus on Societal Wellbeing

It is not only possible to make a conscious decision to create customer value and build shareholder wealth in ways that at minimum preserve and wherever possible enhance the wellbeing of all legitimate stakeholders. It is actually desirable, and companies that choose to do so can enjoy great success – as evidenced by the work of Sisodia et al in *Firms of Endearment* and *Conscious Capitalism.* In fact, having embraced customer value and shareholder wealth as joint and mutually reinforcing objectives, seeking to do so in ways that enhance the wellbeing of all is both a logical and an appropriate next step for business leaders

It is important to point out though, that there is absolutely no externally imposed requirement for business leaders to even give consideration to the ideas we are putting forward here, let alone to move in the direction we are advocating. In fact, it is entirely a decision for the board of each company as to whether it will move in the direction we are advocating and become a *Long-Term Value Creator*, or turn away and simply operate as a *Short-Term Share Price Manager*. However, it is important and arguably imperative that each and every director understand the difference between these two alternative paths, so that this choice (which all listed company boards do make either explicitly or implicitly) can become a conscious choice rather than an unconscious one.

Those that chose to become *Long-Term Value Creators* must confront a series of decisions that we have already spoken about.

- Firstly, they need to accept that the goal is not to create shareholder wealth *per se*, but to build an enduring institution that can create wealth for shareholders on an ongoing basis.
- Secondly, they need to embrace customer value and shareholder wealth creation as joint and mutually reinforcing objectives.
- Thirdly they need to have a noble purpose for the business that goes well beyond just seeking to create shareholder wealth (which is actually more an outcome than an objective), or seeking to maximise the market value of their company during the tenure of the current leadership team.
- Fourthly, they need to regard other stakeholders as allies in the creation of customer value and shareholder wealth over the long term, rather than adversaries in achieving short-term earnings growth.

Beyond this, there are two further steps that need to be taken if a company is to incorporate an intention to enhance the wellbeing of all.

The first is to adopt a truly long-term perspective. This can be challenging given the short CEO tenure in many western economies (currently 4.2 years in Australia) and the fact that executive reward plans tend to be structured around a three-year cycle.[3] However, adopting a long-term perspective is crucial. Ideally that means adopting a ten, 15 or even 20-year time horizon.

The second is to make a conscious decision in relation to the nature of the value that will be created for customers and end-consumers.

[3] Tucker, R., *Executive Salary, Incentives and Tenure – How Much is Too Much*, S. G. Hiscock and Company, Melbourne, 2013, p. 15.

Adopting a Long-Term Perspective

The reason it is so important to adopt a long-term perspective was touched on earlier. The longer the time horizon, the more the interests of customers, shareholders and the wider community begin to align.

In some situations, it is possible to create shareholder wealth by acting solely in the perceived short-term interests of existing shareholders – such as with an aggressive cost reduction program or a freeze on capital expenditure. Such action will generally lead to a short-term improvement in earnings, cash flow and economic profit, and in some cases, deliver a short-term increase in market capitalisation. This can be done without giving any thought whatsoever to the creation of customer value; or to the short, medium or long-term wellbeing other legitimate stakeholders. However, such measures generally don't lead to a sustainable improvement in economic profit, intrinsic value or market capitalisation, because they don't enhance the overall shape of the *EP Bow Wave*.

If we adopt a slightly longer perspective, and set out to continually create shareholder wealth over the typical three to five-year tenure of a CEO and his or her leadership team, then it cannot be done just by seeking to improve performance under the current strategy as a result of a series of initiatives aimed at elimination of under-performing products or services, cost reduction or capital efficiency gains. In almost all situations, continually creating wealth for shareholders over a period of three to five years, requires initiatives that involve a focus on the dual objectives of customer value creation and shareholder wealth creation.

If we take an even longer-term perspective, an interesting picture begins to emerge. It is difficult to focus on the joint objectives of customer value creation and shareholder wealth creation over a lengthy period without extending the field of view to consider the end-consumer interface. This is because many of the primary factors that drive new developments in any industry are the emerging needs or indeed demands of end-consumers.

End-consumers are part of the wider community – or society at large. So, by adopting a long-term perspective, a company implicitly begins to take account of the interests of society more broadly. But this is really only true if we understand properly the true nature of the demands coming from end-consumers. This in turn requires and understanding of the nature of the value that they derive from various products and services.

The Nature of the Value Created for Customers and End-Consumers

The most important decision a company must make if it is to institutionalise socially responsible behaviour and succeed in creating customer value, building shareholder wealth and enhancing societal wellbeing, is to clarify the nature of the value or benefit that it is setting out to create for its customers and for end-consumers.

Will it seek to create real or authentic value – from the provision of useful, beneficial or healthy products or services, the consumption or use of which contributes to the long-term wellbeing of either customers or end-consumers? Or will it settle for simply creating artificial value, which is value derived by customers from the satisfaction of a desire created by the company's own consumer marketing campaigns? This is a fundamental question for every company and it has a significant ethical dimension.

If a company sets out to create real or authentic value for customers and particularly for end-consumers, and the market it is serving is properly informed, then in creating something that customers will value, it is also contributing to the wellbeing of society.

It is useful to think in terms of some examples to explain this point. Tobacco is perhaps the clearest example of a product for which the value derived by customers is entirely artificial. Fresh fruit and vegetables delivered in good condition and free of pesticide residues are examples of products whose value to customers is entirely authentic or real – assuming the price is reasonable. However, there are many products and services that provide customers and end-consumers with a combination of real and artificial value – branded bottled water being a case in point. The water itself provides real value (so long as the price is fair). So does the fact that it is bottled in the case of customers for whom portability is important, or for whom other sources of water are contaminated (except to the extent that the container itself creates environmental problems upon disposal). But any price premium achieved through branding of a product like water is almost certainly the result of the creation of artificial customer value.

It is important to appreciate that there need not be anything inherently wrong with providing artificial value, and customers are perfectly entitled to pay for that value should they choose to do so. However, having worked with this concept for some time, we have found it to be a powerful device through which to encourage paradigm-shifting thinking – and in so doing, to help business leaders get their teams to adopt a fresh perspective on their business.

Those that do confront this question openly, soon find that there are two other companion questions that they must also address in order to formulate a meaningful position and chart a path forward.

The first companion question involves asking whether there are any material economic or social costs that arise from the production, the distribution or the consumption (or use) of the product or service, that are not clear to customers or end-consumers at the outset. Again, it is useful to illustrate with an example.

In 2001, a book by Eric Schlosser entitled *Fast Food Nation* was published. Scholsser's contention was that the low price of many fast foods did not reflect their true cost. He argued that the profits earned by fast food chains were only possible because of "*losses imposed on the rest of society*". He also pointed out that the annual cost of obesity in the US at the time of writing, was twice the revenues of the entire fast food industry.[4] Most observers would agree that since Schlosser's book was published, there have been some positive developments in the menus of fast food chains.

The second question is more confronting. It involves a board and its executive leadership team asking themselves in a very open and honest fashion, whether they regard their business as an opportunity to serve society, or an opportunity to exploit it. Or put another way, is it their intention to serve their customers and the wider community, or is it their intention to exploit them?

The reason this question is so confronting is that there is an important difference between an intention and an outcome. The decision to act with the intention to serve, or to act with an intention to exploit, represents a conscious choice between two mutually exclusive alternatives. Outcomes arising from actions might be positive or negative to varying degrees. But that can never be the case with intentions. With intentions, the choice is black or white. There are no shades of grey. Again, it is useful to illustrate with an example.

Between 1982 and 1986, at a time of very high domestic interest rates, Australia's banks began promoting low interest rate foreign currency denominated loans to farmers through their rural branch networks. In promoting these loans, bank managers failed to explain to farmers the nature and extent of the associated exchange rate risk.

---

[4] Schlosser, E., *Fast Food Nation: What the All American Meal is Doing to the World*, Penguin, London 2001, pp. 261–262.

It is possible that many of the staff in the banks' rural branch networks may not have even understood these risks themselves. But ultimately, many famers suffered huge losses when in 1985, the Australian dollar depreciated against the currencies in which these loans were written. Many were forced to sell farms that had been in their families for generations.

Investigations initiated in 1995 by three Members of Australia's Federal Parliament revealed that at least one of the banks might have adopted a policy under which their most trusting customers were exploited.[5] Evidence presented to a Parliamentary inquiry in December 1995 indicated that officers of one bank had added loadings to the exchange rates that they applied, based on the nature of their relationship with each customer. Customers were classified as either captive or competitive. Captive customers were those considered unsophisticated in foreign exchange matters, or so loyal as to be unlikely to seek a quote from a competitor.[6]

As an example for the purpose of illustration, the foreign exchange loans case is quite revealing. Over the last few pages, we identified three questions that needed to be confronted consciously if a company is to create the conditions under which it can create customer value, build shareholder wealth and the same time seek to enhance the wellbeing of all stakeholders (which we tend to shorten with the expression *enhance community wellbeing*). They are:

- Will we set out to create a predominance of real (as distinct from artificial) value for our customers and for end-consumers?
- Do we believe that there are no material economic or social costs that arise from the production, distribution or consumption of our products and services that are not clear to our customers and to end-consumers at the outset?
- Do we regard our business as an opportunity to serve society, rather than an opportunity to exploit it?

If the answer to all three of the questions posed is *yes*, it points to an organisation that should be able to create customer value, build shareholder wealth and at the same time enhance societal wellbeing.

[5] The three parliamentarians were Ken Aldred, Ray Braithwaite and Bob Katter. All were members of Australia's conservative Federal Opposition in 1995.

[6] Griffiths, C., "Opposition Calls for Banking Royal Commission", The Courier-Mail, 2 December, 1995.

However, in the case of the foreign currency loans saga, the bank's fundamental intention appeared to be to exploit its customers. In addition, there were potential material costs that were not clear at the outset. It would also appear that, because the risks were not properly explained, the type of value that they were setting out to create for their customers was not consistent with their long-term wellbeing.

A high-level framework for thinking along these lines is presented in Fig. 9.1.

The first step is to set out to create real value for customers – either entirely or predominantly.

If those customers are end-consumers (or if the company is part of a value-creating network that is seeking to enhance value for end-consumers) then there will always be a good chance that in seeking to create real value for its customers, the company will be acting in a manner consistent with enhancing the wellbeing of the wider community or society as a whole.

If the production and distribution of the product or service is effected in a manner that is consistent with the long-term best interest of the wider community and the environment, then the company will have established a business model that incorporates a cycle of customer value and shareholder wealth creation that will at minimum preserve but more likely enhance, community wellbeing.

The question of serving society rather than exploiting it, and indeed the decision (whether conscious or unconscious) that every company makes in relation to this issue, will be explored in detail in the second book in this series.

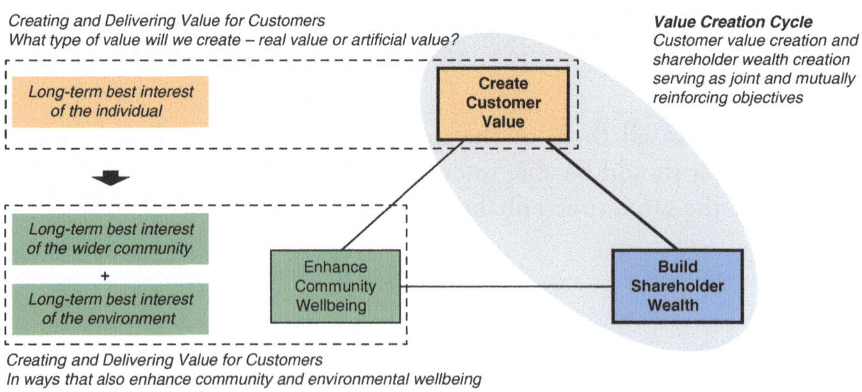

Fig. 9.1 Incorporating community wellbeing

Elements of a New Business Paradigm

The thinking we have presented in this chapter constitutes a platform upon which it may be possible to begin to construct a new and more socially responsible business paradigm.

The current business paradigm considers shareholder value maximisation to be the primary economic objective for all listed companies. Some companies choose to make it their governing objective. It considers other objectives like customer value creation and socially responsible behaviour as potential means through which individual companies might achieve the end goal of shareholder value maximisation. However, some of the thinking we have presented opens the door to the possibility of an alternative paradigm, in which the objective is not to create shareholder wealth *per se*, but to build an organisation that serves society over the long term by continually creating value for customers, building wealth for shareholders and enhancing the wellbeing of all other stakeholders, including the wider community and the environment.

Many of the building blocks that underpin this construct have been put in place over the last few chapters, but there are some more ideas that need to be put into play. These additional ideas can be clustered into eight main groups which are listed in Fig. 9.2.

We will explore one of these topics briefly now, simply to give a sense of a completely different way of thinking. It will be developed fully in the second book in the series, along with other ideas listed in Fig. 9.2 – some of which will be covered in Book 2 and some in Book 3.

Wealth Creation versus Wealth Appropriation

Under the current business paradigm, much of the business community is focused on winning against the competition – reflecting a mindset borne of a more regressive form of consciousness.

When working from this type of consciousness, it is often the case that wealth generated for shareholders is wealth that has not actually been created *per se*, but instead has been appropriated from other stakeholders, be they competitors, suppliers, customers, the wider community (including the wider community as represented by taxation authorities) and the environment.

In one sense, understanding the distinction between wealth creation and wealth appropriation is as simple as recognising the difference between creating something and taking something. But because under the current

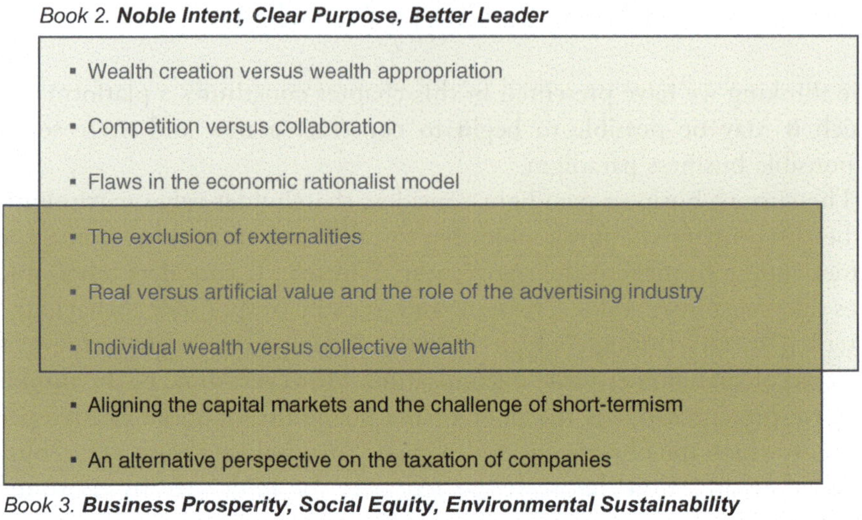

Book 2. Noble Intent, Clear Purpose, Better Leader
Wealth creation versus wealth appropriation
Competition versus collaboration
Flaws in the economic rationalist model
The exclusion of externalities
Real versus artificial value and the role of the advertising industry
Individual wealth versus collective wealth
Aligning the capital markets and the challenge of short-termism
An alternative perspective on the taxation of companies
Book 3. Business Prosperity, Social Equity, Environmental Sustainability

Fig. 9.2 Coverage of key topics in Books 2 and 3

business paradigm, it is considered entirely acceptable to "take" market share from a competitor in order to enhance economic profits and "create" shareholder wealth, it is necessary to build our understanding in a series of incremental steps.

When we create something, we do just that. The meaning of this statement is essentially unchanged if we add the word "new". So when we create something, "we create something new".

In most cases, we would be able to qualify this statement further. So when we create something new, "we create something new and different that did not exist before".

Ideally, we would be able to qualify it even further, in the following way. When we create something new, we create something new and different that did not exist before, "that delivers benefits to the economy and to society as a whole."

Wealth created from a creative endeavour of this nature constitutes true and beneficial wealth creation. Importantly, it does not arise at the expense of anyone else. Unfortunately, under the current business paradigm, much of what is considered wealth creation does not arise in this way. It is garnered at the expense of someone else. No wealth is actually created. It is simply transferred or appropriated by one entity at the expense of another, or at the expense of a series of individuals. It is wealth appropriation – not wealth creation.

Once we are aware of the distinction between wealth creation and wealth appropriation, it is instructive to consider the nature of the mindset that lies behind these two quite different behaviours and outcomes. Genuine wealth creation arises from value created for customers out of an equally genuine desire to enhance the wellbeing of others. This constitutes a truly noble purpose. In contrast, wealth appropriation arises from a desire to dominate or win, or to obtain something at the expense of others. Importantly, with a wealth creation mindset, there is room to give proper consideration to the wellbeing of all. This means the focus need not just be the wellbeing of customers (although that is almost certainly the original motive). The wellbeing of all stakeholders can be enhanced. This type of thinking is completely absent with a wealth appropriation mindset.

For decades, the business world has been obsessed with winning against the competition. But once the distinction between wealth creation and wealth appropriation is understood, it is apparent that there is also room for collaboration. Win-win is vastly superior to win-lose. It's not really about winning. It's about making our offer more worthy.

In the late 1990s, I spent a good deal of time studying various philosophies to help me give form to the ideas I was developing in relation to the need for a different and more socially responsible business paradigm.

Several writers and thinkers proved to be influential, and this aspect of my journey will be elaborated upon in the second book in this series. However, there is one philosophy that I feel warrants mention at this point – primarily because it deals so comprehensively with the need to embrace long-term thinking.

The philosophy I am referring to is that of the Native American Haudenosuanee or Iroquois Confederacy.

Haudenosuanee philosophy is thought to have influenced the thinking of several the founding fathers of the United States of America, particularly in the framing of the United States Constitution – something that was acknowledged by the US Congress in 1988.[7]

The Haudensuanee were masters of long-term thinking. They saw themselves as custodians of the earth for future generations and consequently, their decision-making processes were characterised by two key attributes.

---

[7] H. Con. Res. 331 (100th Congress): A concurrent resolution to acknowledge the contribution of the Iroquois Confederacy of Nations to the development of the United States Constitution and to reaffirm the continuing government-to-government relationship between Indian tribes and the United States established in the Constitution, October 21, 1988.

Their criterion for all decisions was "what is in the best interests of all of our people for the next seven generations", and they only made decisions when their leaders had reached a point of consensus or even unanimity on a path forward.

Unlike what we see today, they did not employ mechanisms that suppressed a minority view – in the way that voting is sometimes used. Yet at the same time, they were not paralysed by indecision though the adoption of this approach – perhaps because of their noble intent and the absence of individual self-interest in their decision making-process.

10

Building an Enduring Institution

With a clear intention and real commitment, it is entirely feasible to build an enduring institution that can create value for customers and wealth for shareholders on an ongoing basis.

It is also possible that if desired, a similar outcome can be achieved in a way that also enhances the wellbeing of all legitimate stakeholders including the wider community and the environment. Many of the companies that Raj Sisodia and his co-authors have referred to as *Firms of Endearment* would fit this description. Again, a clear intention and a strong commitment are required.

However, widespread propagation of this approach to business requires the right understanding and a clear roadmap to follow. Along the way, it is necessary to establish the required capabilities at both an individual and an organisational level; align business processes with this approach; put in place the right performance measures; and ensure that any executive reward plan is consistent with the underlying intent.

Establising the Right Understanding

The technical understanding required to succeed in building an organisation that can create value for customers and build wealth for shareholders on an ongoing basis was introduced in Chapters 1, 2 and 3; and developed further in subsequent chapters.

D. Kilroy, M. Schneider, *Customer Value, Shareholder Wealth, Community Wellbeing*, DOI 10.1007/978-3-319-54774-9_10

Establishing this understanding is not just an intellectual exercise. It certainly requires an intellectual understanding. But it also requires practical engagement together with a willingness to let go of traditional thinking in those areas where it no longer serves us.

The right understanding can only be established and embedded through a combination of exposure to the concepts and principles we have presented, and practical experience developed through applying them. That means being part of an organisation that chooses to undertake the journey.

It is useful however to summarise the 12 main concepts and principles we have outlined that need to be embraced to establish what we have termed the right understanding. They are listed below.

The 12 Key Principles

1. Even under a business paradigm that gives absolute primacy to the interests of shareholders, the principal economic objective of the leadership of a listed company is not to maximise shareholder value or even create shareholder wealth *per se*. It is to build an enduring institution that can create wealth for its shareholders *on an ongoing basis*.
2. Success in this endeavour will be apparent in two markets: the market for the company's products and services; and the market for shareholder capital. Success in the product and service market is initially evident in the form of an economically profitable return, or an ROE greater than the cost of equity capital (Ke). Once economic profitability has been achieved, success takes the form of a growing economic profit stream. Success in the capital market means producing a TSR greater than Ke over the long term, or a positive *TSR Alpha* over the short-to-medium term.
3. We can link success in the product and service market with success in the capital market. Wealth will be created for shareholders in the capital market, if the management team succeed in making the company's *EP Bow Wave* higher, wider or longer through the way that they choose to participate in the product and service market.
4. One of the consequences of this understanding is the very important realisation that to improve capital market outcomes for shareholders over the short, the medium or the longer term, management must focus on enhancing long-term (not short-term) product and service market performance.

5. Over any given measurement period, intrinsic value can be enhanced and shareholder wealth can be created, by either delivering an economic profit stream greater than that which the market was expecting at the commencement of the measurement period, or by developing one or more higher value strategies during the measurement period that result in a series of new and higher economic profit expectations to be delivered beyond the measurement period. These two sources of value uplift can be quantified using a *Pair of EP Bow Waves* constructed at the beginning and at the end of the measurement period.
6. Over the longer term, the primary focus should be on establishing and maintaining the capabilities required to continue to improve economic profit outcomes by enhancing the shape of the *EP Bow Wave*. Individual and organisational capability creation are value-creating endeavours in their own right. In most cases, investment in such capability creation will tend to increase in the length of the *EP Bow Wave*.
7. Most opportunities to enhance intrinsic value through the systematic pursuit of higher value strategies arise at the level of properly defined needs-based customer segments.
8. It is difficult to create wealth for shareholders *on an ongoing basis* unless customer value creation and shareholder wealth creation are embraced as joint and mutually reinforcing objectives – and pursued in tandem within each needs-based customer segment.
9. The key to the ongoing identification and successful implementation of strategies that enhance both customer value and shareholder wealth is a disciplined approach to innovation centred on *Hybrid Thinking*. *Hybrid Thinking* is a higher order thinking process that relies on both creative and analytical modes of thought. It not only helps unlock ideas for potentially higher value strategies, it helps establish the mindset required to bring those strategies to life successfully.
10. There are four important aspects to the mindset required for the successful application of disciplined innovation using *Hybrid Thinking*. They are: a focus on end-consumer needs; a preparedness to form value creating networks; a bias towards value pricing; and a willingness to back new ideas (particularly those that arise through either intuition or insight) while using analysis more as a proving mechanism than as a discovery mechanism.
11. Once customer value creation and shareholder wealth creation have been embraced as joint objectives, it is possible for the board and its executive leadership team to make a conscious choice to use disciplined innovation to pursue these two joint goals in ways that either

preserve or enhance the wellbeing of all stakeholders. A decision to move in this direction will tend to be evident in two ways. Firstly, the company will be able to point to a noble purpose that goes well beyond simply seeking to maximise its market value during the tenure of the current leadership team. Secondly, it will tend to think of its stakeholders as allies in the creation of customer value and shareholder wealth over the long term, rather than as adversaries in the pursuit of earnings growth over the short term.

12. In making this choice, the most fundamental issue that a leadership team must confront relates to the nature of the value that they set out to create for customers. Will it be real value – meaning that the consumption or use of its products or services contributes to the long-term wellbeing of customers and end-consumers? Or will it be artificial value arising largely from the satisfaction of desires created through clever marketing, with no real concern for the long-term wellbeing of customers and end-consumers?

Establishing the Right Capabilities

Building an enduring institution that can create value for customers and wealth for shareholders on an ongoing basis is an exercise in capability creation. The way a company goes about this is particularly important.

There are three fundamental organisational capabilities that must be developed. They were introduced in Chapter 6 and were illustrated in Fig. 6.1. They are a *Value Measurement Capability*, a *Value Creation Capability* and a *Value Management Capability*.

A *Value Measurement Capability* is the ability to determine where value is being created, where it is being destroyed, and why, under the strategy currently being pursued. A *Value Creation Capability* is the ability to continually develop and implement new and higher value strategies that enhance value for customers and create wealth for shareholders – primarily at a customer segment level. A *Value Management Capability* is the ability to focus the bulk of an organisation's energy on the second capability. It involves either establishing or refining existing business processes and systems to encourage the ongoing pursuit and successful implementation of higher value strategies over time.

Each of these three capabilities can be broken down into five individual steps or processes, and in each of these steps or processes there are a series of individual and organisational capabilities required.

The key elements involved in the establishment of a *Value Measurement Capability* were presented in Chapter 7, and the principal steps involved in establishing a *Value Creation Capability* were covered in Chapters 8 and 9. That understanding needs to be brought to life with experience. But what holds all this together and ensures the first two capabilities are properly embedded, is the establishment of the third or *Value Management Capability*. Establishing this capability means putting in place the right business processes.

Establishing the Right Business Processes

The *Value Management Capability* is structured around an integrated series of business processes comprising strategic planning, resource allocation and performance management. In combination, these processes focus management attention on the ongoing development and successful implementation of higher value strategies. The way they operate was illustrated in Fig. 1.2 in Chapter 1.

In a mechanistic sense, this integrated series of business processes seeks to ensure delivery of the performance promised in a business plan built around a higher value strategy, while at the same time encouraging the pursuit of even higher value strategies over time. At its core is a strategic planning process that provides the mechanism through which new ideas and innovative thinking are captured by the organisation – mainly at a needs-based customer segment level.

The integrated planning, resource allocation and performance management system has four main elements:

- *A value-based business planning process* that not only acts as an idea capturing mechanism, but produces a prospectus quality business plan that acts as both a roadmap for the business and a prospectus for capital and other resources;
- *A strategy-based resource allocation mechanism* that operates like an internal capital market; allocating human, capital and other resources to strategies (as distinct from projects) based on their potential to enhance intrinsic value and create shareholder wealth;

- *A plan-based performance management system* incorporating both a target setting and a budgeting process that sets targets for financial and other performance indicators for the first year of the plan, and a reporting and monitoring mechanism that monitors performance in relation to the agreed indicators and their targets (so that being on track with the budget means being on track with the plan); and
- *A performance-based executive reward plan* that links executive remuneration to the goal of enhancing the shape of the *EP Bow Wave* or the returns, growth and the sustainability of both expected through the company's participation in the market for its products and services, and potentially to the consequences of this as reflected in capital market performance (namely a TSR greater than Ke over the long term, or a positive *TSR Alpha* over the short-to-medium term).

The Business Planning Process

For this integrated series of business processes to perform its function properly, business plans must be prospectus quality. They must be sufficiently robust to act as both a roadmap for the business and a prospectus for capital and other resources.

The management team responsible for the business unit strategic plan must be absolutely committed to delivering the performance promised in that plan, which in most cases will be an amalgam of segment-level strategies.

Commitment is essential. The chosen strategy was selected because it was the highest value alternative. However, the valuation that caused it to be selected is only real if management is fully committed to delivering the associated economic profit stream.

The Resource Allocation Mechanism

The business planning process is linked to the performance management system through a disciplined resource allocation mechanism that operates via an interlocking commitment between the corporate centre and each business unit management team.

In submitting its plan, a business unit management team commits to a value outcome (in the form of a planned and promised economic profit stream) in return for the resources that it requires to deliver that outcome.

In approving the plan, the corporate centre commits the human, capital and other resources required by the business unit, in return for the economic profit stream and value outcome promised by the business unit management team. At the same time, an agreement is reached as to how the corporate centre will determine whether the business unit is on track in delivering the performance that it promised in its plan. That agreement establishes the outcomes that will be tracked by the performance management system.

The Performance Management System

If management succeeds in implementing a higher value strategy, then the promised increase in the intrinsic value of the business will be secure. So, the primary role of the performance management system is to ensure that the business is on track with the implementation of its proposed strategy and is delivering the performance that it promised in its plan.

The performance management system is generally designed to also monitor operational performance outcomes that are not strategy dependent. But this function is secondary to the primary requirement that the business be on track with its chosen strategy.

The Executive Reward Plan

The executive reward plan should firstly encourage and reward the delivery of the performance promised in the plan built around the chosen strategy, and secondly it should encourage and reward the pursuit and successful implementation of higher value strategies over time.

In terms of the *Pair of EP Bow Waves* introduced in Chapter 3 and illustrated in Fig. 3.4, this means seeking to ensure that promised performance is delivered over a three to five-year measurement period (so the area shaded in red in an illustrative sense on the left hand side of Fig. 3.4 is actually "green" but probably quite small), and that the green-shaded area on the right hand side of Fig. 3.4 is not only "green" but also the primary source of wealth creation over the measurement period.

It is important that executive reward plans do not inadvertently encourage short-termism, which unfortunately is the case with many reward plan designs currently in use.

Integrating the Processes

This integrated approach to business planning, resource allocation and performance management offers several important benefits.

When implemented properly, it encourages integrity in business planning. In putting forward a business plan, a business unit management team is asking the corporate centre to invest in its strategy. In the same way that the board would make a performance commitment in any prospectus they might offer to the external capital market, the business unit management team is making a commitment to deliver a value outcome in the form of a promised economic profit stream, in return for the capital and other resources required to deliver that performance.

If it proposes soft targets, it risks not getting the resources it needs. If it over-commits, it risks under-performance.

By investing in strategies developed by business unit management teams, and for which those teams are fully responsible, the corporate centre is investing in the ideas of its people. In so doing, it is encouraging innovation. But it is also ensuring accountability.

Many organisations base their investment decisions on projects rather than strategies. This usually leads to an intense focus on the new investment associated with a particular project. Much less attention is paid to how well the remaining 80 or 90 percent of resources are deployed in the ongoing pursuit of an agreed strategy. This can lead to opportunities for performance improvement being missed.

But the real problem with project-based resource allocation processes in most organisations arises from the lack of clear ongoing accountability. Once a project is complete, it can be difficult to know whether the benefits promised when it was approved were eventually delivered. While the promised benefits might take many forms, most can ultimately be expressed in terms of incremental revenues, incremental cost savings and /or incremental capital efficiency gains. It can be difficult to measure these gains when the project has been completed because they just tend to get lost in the amorphous mass of revenues, costs and capital movements in the business. Consequently, it is difficult to hold anyone accountable for delivering them.

However, if the resource allocation process focuses on investing in business plans built around chosen strategies, and a particular project must be undertaken as part of that strategy, then there is clear accountability in place.

This does not mean that companies should cease evaluating capital projects. But it does mean that on a standalone basis, a project-based assessment can be insufficient to underpin a well-informed resource allocation process.

Establishing the Right Performance Measures

It is important to employ economic as distinct from traditional accounting measures of performance. As was discussed earlier, it is only with economic performance measures that a company can:

- Align its performance in the markets for its products and services, with the strategic position it has built in those markets; and
- Align the performance it achieves through its participation in the products and services market, with the economic outcomes experienced by shareholders in the external capital market.

It is also important to be able to understand how the performance achieved in the market for a company's products and services, translates into the creation, preservation or destruction of wealth for shareholders. This is only possible through the lens provided by economic performance measures. The building blocks of these economic measures are presented in Fig. 10.1.

Figure 10.1 shows the two alternative ways to approach economic performance measurement. While we recommend using an approach based around equity capital for the external capital market, it is possible to use either the equity approach (EPy = ROE-Ke) or the total capital approach (EPy = ROC-WACC) internally to measure performance in the product and services market. Further details in relation to the external capital market measure (and particularly *TSR Alpha*) are provided in Appendix 2.

Establishing the link between internally measured performance in the product and service market, and externally measured performance in the capital market, requires the *Pair of EP Bow Waves* introduced in Fig. 3.4. The form this link takes is the *EP Uplift + TSR Alpha Construct* which was introduced in Chapter 3 and illustrated in Fig. 3.10.

There is however one very important proviso. It is important to avoid falling into the trap of imposing one or both of the flawed target setting mechanisms that some companies use, and which many commentators seem to think are beneficial. These mechanisms undermine the entire business

	Internal Measure used by Management	External Measures used by Investors	
Equity Approach	Book Value of Equity	Market Value of Equity	Market Value of Equity
Return Delivered	ROE%	TSR%	TSR%
Return Required	Ke%	Ke%	TSRr%
Economic Return	**ROE–Ke**	**TSR–Ke**	**TSR Alpha** = TSR –TSRr

Total Capital Approach	Book Value of Capital	Market Value of Equity	Market Value of Equity
Return Delivered	ROC%	TSR%	TSR%
Return Required	WACC%	Ke%	TSRr%
Economic Return	**ROC–WACC**	**TSR–Ke**	**TSR Alpha** = TSR–TSRr
	Economic Return on Book Value	**Economic Return on Market Value** (long term)	**Economic Return on Market Value** (short to medium term)

Fig. 10.1 Economic performance measures

Note: The derivation of TSR Alpha is contained in Appendix 2

planning, resource allocation and performance management process. They are:

- Top down targets that are not the result of a bottom up strategy development process; and
- Stretch targets that encourage management to outperform that which they believe is possible under their chosen strategy, and often compromise the implementation of the strategy in the process.

Top down targets set goals for which there is no real commitment and no real belief on the part of the people who must deliver them. They serve little purpose other than perhaps to define a range of outcomes that the board or senior executive team would like to see achieved. In contrast, bottom up targets built around the outcomes associated with higher value strategies developed at segment and business unit levels, generally have at least one and sometimes two or more layers of management commitment behind them.

Stretch targets also serve little if any useful purpose. They lead to situations where the approved strategy can be undermined by a desire to extract more from the business than is possible under that strategy. And they encourage behaviours in which long-term value creation potential is sacrificed in the pursuit of short-term profit growth.

The pursuit of both top down targets and stretch targets tend to undermine the integrity of the integrated business planning, resource allocation and performance management process. In addition, they can at times lead to ill-considered short-term actions. These can erode organisational capabilities and even put at risk the ability of a business to either continue to pursue its current strategy or develop higher value strategies over time.

Ultimately, if strategies have been developed with the right intent, and approved with sound processes, then the performance management system only needs to answer two fundamental questions.

- Is the business on track with its chosen strategy?
- Is it delivering good operational performance regardless of the strategy being pursued?

If the answer to both is yes, then the business is performing properly – so long as it is also continuing to employ a disciplined approach to innovation to continually look for higher value strategies over time.

Ensuring the Right Executive Reward Plan Design

Just like top down goals and stretch targets, incentive plans that use inappropriate metrics, or are constructed without a proper understanding of how product and services market performance translates into capital market outcomes, can undermine the whole business planning, resource allocation and performance management system. This then undermines the entire business transformation initiative.

At the end of Chapter 1, we described some of the defining characteristics of one of our firm's early business transformation engagements undertaken using the thinking that now forms the basis of this book.

Towards the end of our involvement with the company in question, it chose to implement an executive reward plan based around meeting stretch EP targets. While later discarded, one of the consequences of the adoption of this scheme was that the focus of management attention shifted away from the pursuit of customer value and shareholder wealth as joint and mutually reinforcing objectives, towards a singular focus on short-term EP growth.

In many respects this constituted a reversion to the economic engine approach to Managing for Value – leaving little room for customer value creation as an explicit corporate objective, let alone any concern for community wellbeing.

A few years later, the company lost its way in a governance sense under a new leadership team. While it is difficult to establish causality between the adoption of the executive reward plan and subsequent governance failures, what occurred within the company at that time was completely incongruous with the positive culture and the strong capabilities that had been put in place under the previous leadership team. Under the previous leadership team, the company had a clear focus on the ongoing creation of both customer value and shareholder wealth, together with a leadership philosophy centred on respect for all. In fact, towards the end of our involvement, I had several discussions with executives about how to incorporate the pursuit of community wellbeing into the customer value and shareholder wealth creation framework that we had developed together.

It is also worth noting that the governance failures that occurred within this company took place during a period in which the shareholder primacy paradigm was approaching its zenith in Australia and elsewhere in the world. This was evidenced quite spectacularly at the time by the views expressed by a leading sector analyst with a respected broking firm when commenting on the actions of the company in 2004. He observed that: "Ultimately, questions of negligence or other misconduct by company executives are only of interest to the extent that they affect shareholder value".[1]

The content of this statement says a lot about how disconnected the capital markets had become from the underlying social responsibilities of business in the years leading up to the GFC.

Understanding Current Practice in Executive Reward

It is useful to begin with a simple description of current practices in executive reward plan design, which at least in Australia are grounded almost entirely in the principles of the *shareholder primacy paradigm*.

Most listed companies in Australia employ executive reward plans that incorporate a short-term incentive (STI) and a long-term incentive (LTI). Both are designed with the mindset that STIs should encourage behaviours that lead to shareholder wealth creation, and LTIs should reward wealth creation once it has occurred.

There are many different measures and metrics employed in STI design. While from a purely economic perspective, the objective of the STI under the *shareholder primacy paradigm* is to encourage behaviours that should lead to shareholder wealth creation, in recent times there has been a move to

[1] Quoted in Combet, Greg, "The Sickening Silence of Business", The Age, 5 August 2004.

incorporate other metrics that relate to meeting customer and other stakeholder needs, and to maintaining certain cultural norms. This has occurred in an effort to both encourage sound corporate behaviour, and also to discourage situations where generous reward plan outcomes arise at the expense of other stakeholders.

While there is a wide range of structures and an even wider range of metrics employed in STI plan design, the opposite is true with LTIs. Almost all LTI plans involve an award or allocation of rights to shares (or in some cases options) at the beginning of a measurement period, which then vest over time based on the performance achieved.

The process of determining the number of rights awarded is not straightforward. The number of rights awarded at the beginning of a measurement period is determined by three factors: the target LTI payment, the value of each right and the planned level of vesting at targeted performance. So, if the target LTI payment is one million dollars, and rights to shares are valued at one dollar, then the number of rights awarded would be one million if the intention were that full vesting should occur at targeted performance.

Vesting of rights once awarded almost always occurs based on two performance metrics; 50 percent of shares vest based on product and service market performance and the other 50 percent vest based on capital market outcomes. Most listed companies in Australia and the UK use relative TSR as the capital market metric, and a non-economic accounting metric like Earnings, EPS, EPS growth, ROC or ROE as the product and service market metric.

A Critique of Current Practice

There is lot that is less than ideal about the current approach to executive reward – at least the variant used in most listed companies in Australia (which is similar to that used in the UK). There are problems with both the structure and the metrics used in the design of the plans. In some cases, there are problems with the quantum of the reward as well – with reward plans producing outcomes that are inconsistent with both shareholder and community expectations.

The problems related to quantum are often an unintended consequence of the use of a complex and open-ended structure, in combination with inappropriate performance metrics.

Focusing firstly on the structure, we have already noted that there is some disagreement between experts (including remuneration consultants, governance experts and proxy advisors) as to how the number of rights to be awarded should be calculated. At the same time, with any mechanism that awards rights to shares which then vest over time, it will be difficult if not impossible to determine in advance what the payment to an individual executive will be at the end of the measurement period. It depends on what happens to the share price. Because the structure is completely open-ended, in some cases payments to executives can be well out of line with shareholder and community expectations. There can also be complex tax considerations that arise from this type of structure.

The bottom line is that a structure based on awarding shares which then vest over time is probably always going to be complex. Both shareholders and external commentators find such structures difficult to understand.

While there are concerns about the structure, it is arguably the metrics used that constitute the greatest cause for concern. To begin with, the fundamental notion that STIs are meant to encourage wealth creation, while LTIs should reward wealth creation once it has occurred, is fine in principle for listed companies operating under the *shareholder primacy paradigm*. But the metrics used simply don't achieve this. In fact, the metrics used in most executive reward plans can obscure (and ultimately even undermine) the relationship between the product and service market performance produced by management and the capital market outcomes experienced by shareholders.

The metrics used for the financial performance component the STI, and as the vesting criterion for those shares awarded under the LTI plan that are intended to encourage and reward improved product and service market performance, are almost always non-economic financial measures like EBIT, EBIT growth, Earnings, EPS, EPS growth, ROC or ROE. As was explained in Chapter 2, thcsc arc incomplete measures of financial performance.

The metric used to assess capital market performance is almost always relative TSR. Relative TSR is a measure of TSR performance relative to a basket of "peer" companies (or in some cases an index). It is expressed as a percentile outcome – indicating where the company's TSR sits within the distribution of outcomes achieved by its peer set (or chosen index) over the measurement period. As a stand-alone capital market performance measure, it has many flaws. Three of these are listed below.

- Peer group selection is more an art than a science. Unless all companies in the peer group are similar in many ways, including operating in similar industries with similar capital structures and similar risk profiles, and are not the focus of acquisition activity, the relative TSR outcome can often say little about the performance of the management team.

- Higher risk companies (i.e. companies with a higher *Beta*) tend to win by achieving a higher TSR in a rising market and lose by producing a lower TSR in a falling market – irrespective of the performance of management.
- Companies in the peer set will all be at different points in their strategy development cycle. Those that are implementing a strategy for which the performance expectations were captured in the share price some years back, will tend to have a lower TSR than those who have just come up with a new strategy that has been well received by the market. (This is a shortcoming that can be overcome to some extent by using a longer measurement period than the typical three to five years employed in most executive reward plan designs.)

Relative TSR has one other potentially fatal flaw that is less well-known but which was explored in Chapter 2. It is not possible to build a meaningful bridge between the product and service market performance produced by management, and the capital market outcomes experienced by shareholders, when using non-economic financial metrics to measure product and service market performance, and relative TSR to assess capital market outcomes.

The problem with metrics does not end there. The behaviours that the use of relative TSR in combination with non-economic financial performance metrics tends to encourage, is at least as big a problem as the inherent weaknesses of the metrics themselves.

Relative TSR is essentially a lottery (or a *crap-shoot* in the words of one American-born CEO of an ASX-listed company). Many senior executives treat it as such. So, their focus shifts naturally to trying to improve product and service market performance – something over which they can exercise some control.

This would not really be such a problem if the measure used to gauge product and service market success were economic profitability or ROE-Ke in the first instance, and then EP growth over the medium to longer term. But most reward plan designs use EPS or EPS growth. The use of these incomplete measures leaves the company vulnerable to the *EPS Myth* and tends to encourage behaviours that have come to be known as short-termism.

Many boards are aware of this issue and in an effort to overcome it, have adopted ROC or ROE as the product and service market performance metric, since these measures do take capital utilisation into account. But as is apparent from the picture portrayed in Fig. 10.2, ROE and ROC are no better than earnings, EPS or EPS growth as product and service market performance metrics to be used in tandem with *relative TSR*.

We showed in Chapter 2 that earnings is an incomplete measure of financial performance. Fig. 10.2 demonstrates this once again, showing that the charge for equity capital needs to be subtracted to get to the true economic outcome, namely EP. In the same way, ROE is an incomplete measure of return. The cost of equity needs to be subtracted to get to the economic return on equity or ROE-Ke.

At the same time, earnings can be thought of as the product of ROE and equity capital employed (or book equity). This is represented by the area shaded with red cross-hatching in Fig. 10.2. ROE is simply one of the two dimensions that make up this area (or one of the two factors that combine to produce earnings).

What this means is that neither earnings nor ROE is complete as a product and service market metric that can be linked to capital market performance using the *EP Bow Wave* construct. To align product and capital market performance with capital market outcomes, we need to measure product and service market performance in a manner consistent with the way it impacts capital market outcomes. We need to use EP and then think in terms of either changes in the height (ROE-Ke), the width (equity capital employed

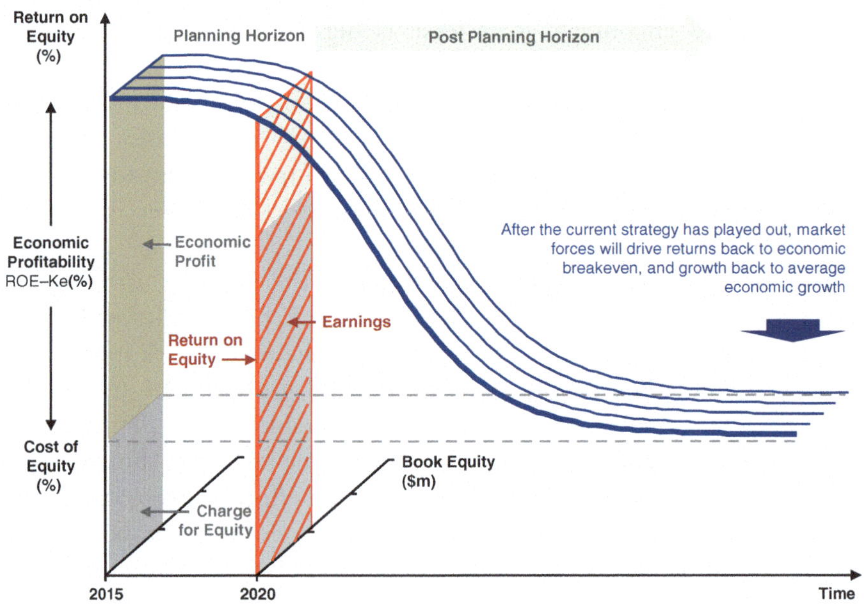

Fig. 10.2 The problem with non-economic performance metrics

or book equity) and the length of the *EP Bow Wave*; or in terms of changes to the volume under the *EP Bow Wave.*

Non-economic financial performance measures like EBIT, Earnings, EPS, EPS growth, ROE and ROC are all incomplete measures of management performance in the market for their company's products and services. But they have quite a following with the financial press, among retail investment advisors and in some cases within the companies themselves. This is particularly true of EPS and EPS growth. There is a great reluctance to discard them in favour of more meaningful measures.

The net result of all this is that we now have a situation in which the combination of metrics embedded in the executive reward plans of most listed companies neither encourage the creation of shareholder wealth *per se*, nor the building of an enduring institution that can create value for customers and wealth for shareholders on an ongoing basis. Worse than that, the use of these metrics encourages short-termism – albeit inadvertently.

The combination of metrics currently in use is simply not up to the task.

Illustration – ASX-listed Sonic Healthcare Limited

Sonic Healthcare had a long-term incentive (LTI) plan that included a series of options and rights designed to vest over a five-year measurement period from 1 July 2011 to 30 June 2016.

Vesting of this series of rights and options was based on both product and service market performance and capital market performance – with 50 percent awarded for each.

The product and service market performance metric was the compound annual rate of growth in return on capital (ROC).

The capital market metric was TSR relative to a selected subset of ASX 100 peer companies. Vesting occurred on a sliding scale, with 50 percent vesting if the company's TSR outcome was at the 51st percentile of the peer set, to full vesting above the 75th percentile.

The compound annual growth in ROC achieved by the company over the measurement period was below the minimum target threshold. This meant that none of the rights or options vested based on product and service market performance.

The TSR outcome for the company put it between the 55th and 60th percentile relative to the TSR performance of the other companies in the designated peer set, depending on whether measured on a point in time or volume weighted average price (VWAP) basis. This translated into a vesting outcome of 70 percent.

In aggregate, 35 percent (70 percent of 50 percent) of the rights and options awarded under the LTI plan vested based on performance achieved over the five years to 30 June 2016.

While we make no comment whatsoever as to the quantum of the payments made, the vesting outcomes from this reward plan were materially at odds with both the product and service market performance produced by the company, and the capital market outcomes experienced by shareholders, over the five years to 30 June 2016.

When viewed through the lens of the *EP Uplift + TSR Alpha Construct*, it becomes apparent that the company created $2.9b in shareholder wealth over a five-year period, starting from a market capitalisation of $5.0b. As can be seen from the *Pair of EP Bow Waves* illustrated in Fig. 10.3:

- $171m in shareholder wealth was created over the measurement period through the delivery of an EP stream that exceeded the expectations that investors had on 1 July 2011 (and which were embedded in the share price at that point in time); and
- A further $2,717m in shareholder wealth was created through the establishment of a series of new and higher EP expectations to be delivered beyond 1 July 2016.

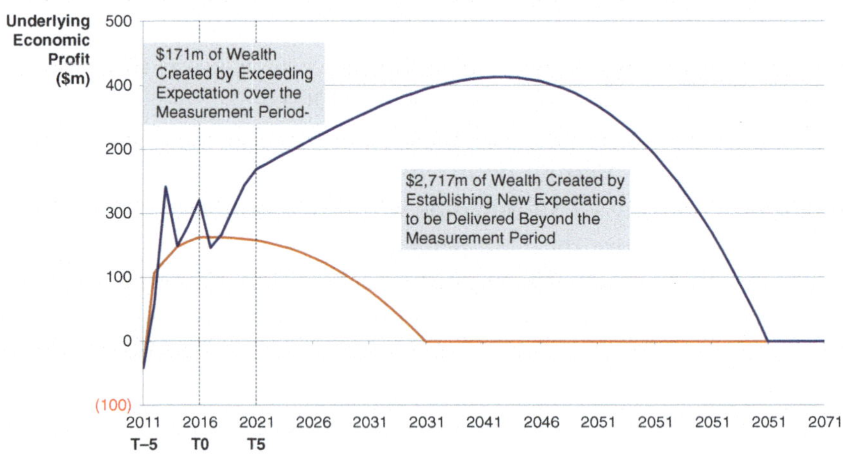

Fig. 10.3 A pair of EP bow waves for Sonic Healthcare

While the latter figure can at times be distorted by positive or negative market sentiment, in most cases the bulk of it will have arisen through management identifying, developing and then successfully implementing one or more new and higher value strategies in different parts of the business. Consequently, both elements are either largely or entirely due to management decisions, management actions, or the capital market's reaction to those decisions and actions. Clearly the market's reaction was positive in this case.

To summarise, this company's LTI plan set out to measure and reward product and service market performance using a variant of an accounting metric (growth in ROC), and capital market performance using a non-economic capital market metric (relative TSR). Although used widely, there are three fundamental weaknesses in this type of LTI plan design.

- Both ROC and growth in ROC (as well as EPS and growth in EPS) are incomplete measures of success in relation to the performance achieved by management in the market for a listed company's products and services.
- *Relative TSR* is a poor proxy for the capital market performance experienced by shareholders.
- There is no meaningful or causal relationship between product and service market "success" measured in terms of ROC, growth in ROC (or any other purely accounting metric) and capital market "success" measured in terms of *relative TSR*. So, there is no conceptual or empirical reason to expect that "success" in the former will lead to "success" in the latter.

The consequence of adopting this approach was that even though the company produced outstanding performance in both the market for its products and services and in the market for shareholder capital, the vesting outcome under the LTI Plan would suggest that overall performance was mediocre.

A more meaningful way to assess product and service market performance would have been to determine whether the company delivered an EP stream that met, exceeded or underperformed investor expectations over the measurement period. All else being equal, meeting those expectations would mean preserving shareholder wealth. Over the five years to 30 June 2016, the company delivered an EP stream somewhat higher than investor expectations.

A more meaningful way to assess capital market performance would have been to use the economic return on market value. This means TSR-Ke over the long term, or *TSR Alpha* over the short-to-medium term. For both metrics, the benchmark performance is zero, at which point shareholder wealth is preserved. The company produced an annualised TSR-Ke of 7.2 percent and an annualised *TSR Alpha* of 9.4 percent over the five years to 30 June 2016. The difference of 2.2 percent represents the shareholder wealth destroyed over the period because of movements in the equity market as a whole – something that was outside the control of management.

Achieving an annualised TSR-Ke of 7.2 percent and an annualised *TSR Alpha* of 9.4 percent over the five years to 30 June 2015 constituted strong performance by the company and its leadership team.

Aligning Reward with the Building of an Enduring Institution

A *Pair of EP Bow Waves* constructed at the beginning and at the end of a measurement period provides a more meaningful basis for listed company performance measurement and executive reward plan design.

The *EP Bow Wave* construct provides the understanding required for executives to systematically and consciously enhance capital market outcomes, through the way they participate in the market for their company's products and services. The *Pair of EP Bow Waves* provides the most accurate means by which their success in this endeavour can be measured.

The question of how to align executive reward with the goal of building of an enduring institution that can create value for customers and wealth for shareholders on an ongoing basis, is quite fundamental.

If we focus in the first instance on the LTI component of executive reward, one way to improve LTI design significantly would be to replace the combination of *relative TSR* and a *non-economic financial performance metric*, with the combination of *TSR Alpha* and *EP performance versus expectations over the measurement period.*

In completing the research that sits behind this book, we investigated what was likely to happen if the top 100 companies in the ASX, the NYSE and the LSE all adopted this approach. Two things became clear. Firstly, perverse outcomes such as that which arose in the case of Sonic Healthcare would not occur. Secondly, there were some additional refinements that could be made that would bring reward plan design even more into alignment with the goal of building an enduring intuition that would create value for customers and wealth for shareholders on an ongoing basis.

Before we explore these refinements, there are four principles that were established earlier that it is useful to revisit.

1. From both a conceptual and an empirical perspective, the key to creating wealth for shareholders on an ongoing basis is to focus on the long-term rather than the short-term.[2] This was evident from the research findings documented at the end of Chapter 3.
2. It is important to focus management attention on the right-hand side of the *Pair of EP Bow Waves* shown in Fig. 3.4. This means establishing new and higher EP expectations by identifying new and higher value strategies. Most of these strategies will be identified, developed and implemented at a disaggregated level – mostly at an individual customer segment level. This should be the primary source of the wealth created over the measurement period.
3. It is important to meet EP expectations over the measurement period, but not to try to exceed them to any significant degree – and particularly through the pursuit of short-term initiatives that might undermine longer-term wealth creation. This means that the area on the left-hand side of the *Pair of EP Bow Waves* in Fig. 3.4 should ideally be positive but generally quite small.
4. The use of stretch targets needs to be avoided, as this tends to encourage short-termism. The goal is to continually come up with new and higher value strategies at a disaggregated level, capture and communicate the revised expectations associated with this, and then deliver those expectations. In terms of the shape of the *Pair of EP Bow Waves* in Fig. 3.4, this means capturing new and higher expectations in the green area on the right-hand side, and delivering them on the left-hand side in subsequent periods.

In summary, the LTI plan should seek to:

- Reward management for meeting expectations over the measurement period (but with no incentive to exceed expectations to any great degree), while at the same time not penalising them for any slight underperformance;
- Reward the creation of wealth through the ongoing development and successful implementation of higher value strategies, mainly at a disaggregated level; and

[2] Unilever Plc is an excellent example of this phenomenon – as was evident in Figs. 7.3 and 7.4 in Chapter 7. It has often failed to meet the market's EP expectations over the short term. But at the same time, it has been able to steadily enhance the shape of its EP Bow Wave by establishing new EP expectation to be delivered beyond the measurement period.

- Discourage behaviour aimed at managing the share price over the short-term, but which is not consistent with long-term value creation.

Achieving this outcome requires changes to metrics and to structure. It may also require some way of ensuring that the quantum of reward is consistent with shareholder and community expectations.

One solution to the question of metrics is illustrated in Fig. 10.4.

In terms of capital market performance, TSR-Ke is ideal as a longer-term metric. It is the long-term economic return on the market value of a listed company. However, over the typical tenure of a CEO or the length of most LTI plans, it is important to be able to separate the effect of market movements from the underlying capital market performance of the company. This is captured in *TSR Alpha*.

In terms of product and service market performance, the left-hand side of the *Pair of EP Bow Waves* illustrated in Fig. 3.4 is a very important indicator of management performance. This represents the extent to which a company met the EP expectations embedded in its share price and market capitalisation at the beginning of the measurement period. But even more important is the right-hand side of the *Pair of EP Bow Waves.* This captures management's success in the ongoing creation of customer value and shareholder wealth.

Potential Refinements to Executive Reward Plan Design

It is useful to consider refinements to LTI plan design in two ways:

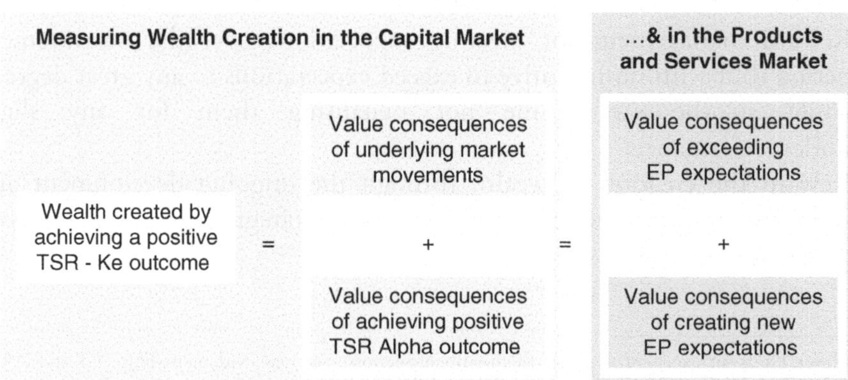

Fig. 10.4 Potential metric combinations for executive reward

- By simply changing the metrics used to determine LTI vesting, while retaining the same fundamental reward plan structure currently used in most listed companies; and
- By contemplating a quite different approach by means of a more holistic rethink.

Simply Changing the Vesting Metric

Referring to the *Pair of EP Bow Waves* illustrated in Fig. 3.4, and thinking in terms of vesting outcomes for executives over three rolling three-year measurement periods that in combination span a total of five years; one approach that would accord with the principles we have established involves awarding rights to shares that would vest in the following manner.

There must firstly be a positive *TSR Alpha* outcome. If the *TSR Alpha* outcome for the period is not positive, there would be no LTI award. If *TSR Alpha* is positive, then the available options or rights to shares would vest in two tranches.

- *Tranche 1.* A small proportion would vest based on the wealth creation consequences of meeting or exceeding EP expectations over the measurement period. This corresponds to the left-hand side of the *Pair of EP Bow Waves* in Fig. 3.4. There would need to be some tolerance of under-performance, and full vesting would occur if expectations were met.
- *Tranche 2.* The majority would vest based on the wealth creation consequences of the *TSR Alpha* outcome, less that already accounted for in the first tranche – a difference that we will refer to as *Residual TSR Alpha.* This difference corresponds to the right-hand side of the *Pair of EP Bow Waves* in Fig. 3.4. Full vesting would occur at a *Residual TSR Alpha* outcome of 10 percent per year, with a sliding scale down to zero vesting at a *Residual TSR Alpha* of zero percent.

This approach would retain the current structure of LTI plan design, but change the metrics to focus management attention primarily on the right-hand side of *Pair of EP Bow Waves* in Fig. 3.4. It would also strip out the impact of market movements, which have nothing to do with the efforts of management.

The primary intention would be to encourage continual value uplift, through the ongoing pursuit, development and successful implementation of higher value strategies – mainly at a disaggregated level. A secondary intention would be to discourage short-termism and "bet the farm" behaviour.

Ideally, management would meet (or slightly exceed) EP expectations during the measurement period. If expectations were met, then all else being else being equal, wealth would be preserved and the entire *TSR Alpha* outcome would stem from the establishment of new EP expectations to be delivered beyond the measurement period (i.e. the right-hand side of Fig. 3.4, after adjusting for market movements). When this is the case, *Residual TSR Alpha* would be equal to *TSR Alpha*.

We know from our research that delivering an annualised *TSR Alpha* of 10 percent per year over three consecutive three-year periods constitutes excellent performance in any stock market. We can use this to set the performance required for full vesting.

Applying the Principles in a More Wholistic Way

The thinking already presented provides an opportunity to properly align executive reward plan design with the goal of building an enduring institution that can create value for customers and wealth for shareholders on an ongoing basis. The further refinements proposed below also impact the structure of the incentive plan and the quantum of reward. In doing so they can achieve two further important outcomes. They can simplify executive reward plan design; and they can make the entire plan much more transparent, both at the beginning when it is adopted and at the end when its outcome becomes apparent.

The proposed approach would avoid open-ended arrangements by approaching quantum and structure as separate considerations. It would have three distinct components.

- There would be a small STI paid annually and based on performance achieved in relation to a series of non-financial outcomes related to culture and the type of organisation that the board was seeking to build.
- There would be a larger medium-term incentive (MTI) that would pay out based on the financial performance achieved in the product and service market over a three-to-five-year period. This relates to

the left-hand side of the *Pair of EP Bow Waves*. The objective would be to encourage EP expectations to be met over the medium term.
- There would be an even larger LTI that would be truly long-term in nature and focus on the right-hand side of the *Pair of EP Bow Waves*. The objective of this component would be to encourage the ongoing creation of customer value and shareholder wealth, as well as the building of an enduring institution with the ability to continue to do so well into the future.

There would be 11 steps involved in the design process, which are detailed in Appendix 4.

A crucial first step would be to approach the questions of design (including structure and metrics) separately from quantum. This would mean declaring up front how much would be paid as base salary, and how much could potentially be paid as STI, MTI and LTI.

Importantly, the LTI would be a true LTI. It would ensure that executives had a significant economic interest in building an enduring institution that enjoyed success over the long term, including the period beyond their own tenure as leaders.

Should Performance Related Remuneration be Discarded

There is also a somewhat radical third option to consider, which is to eliminate performance-related remuneration altogether. While we are still some way from the point where this is likely to occur, it is possible to mount an argument that executives should simply be paid a substantial and appropriate salary, augmented with a material but not excessive upfront award of shares which would align their economic interests with those of other shareholders.

It was mentioned at the end of Chapter 2 that in December 2015, I gave a talk at the Annual Conference of the Governance Institute of Australia entitled "Driving Long-term Value Creation".[3] *During this talk, I showed how the most common approach to executive reward plan design (and particularly LTI*

[3] At the time of writing, the presentation given to the *Governance Institute of Australia* Annual Conference in December 2015 was available from this link: https://www.kba.com.au/publications/driving-long-term-value-creation/.

design) used in Australia and the UK was inadvertently encouraging short-termism.

In the months that followed, we had several follow up discussions with directors of ASX-listed companies. A key part of each of these discussions involved explaining how to build a meaningful bridge linking the performance achieved by management in the market for their company's products and services, with the capital market outcomes experienced by shareholders.

Once they understood this mechanism, it became apparent to these board members that an approach to LTI plan design based on relative TSR and EPS growth (or another accounting metric like ROE or ROC) carried two potential risks. The first was the risk of a perverse outcome whereby the LTI would pay out at either a level above what shareholders would consider appropriate, or at a level below what executives would consider fair. The second was the risk that it would encourage short-termism, to the detriment of medium to longer-term shareholders and other stakeholders.

But they were still reluctant to move away from their traditional approach. The reason for this reluctance was their concern about the reaction of proxy advisors if they were to do anything new or different.

In one case, we were in discussions with the Chairman for many months. It was clear that he understood the situation. He openly acknowledged to us that by staying with relative TSR and EPS growth as the performance metrics in his company's LTI plan design, there was a chance that the board might not be acting in the long-term best interest of the company and its shareholders, because such a design had the potential to encourage short-termism. But ultimately, he and the members of the board's remuneration committee decided to stay with relative TSR plus EPS growth. He told us that the primary reason for this decision was the advice the board had received from a well-known remuneration consultant. This advice was that, unless the board could point to a fatal flaw with relative TSR and EPS growth, it was "far better and much

---

[4] The Two-Strikes Rule was introduced in Australia in July 2011. It is designed to hold directors accountable for executive salaries and bonuses. One of its consequences is that an entire company board can face re-election if shareholders disagree with how much executives are being paid. The "first strike" occurs when a company's remuneration report — which outlines the individual salary and bonus paid to each key management person — receives a "no" vote of 25 per cent or more by shareholders at the company's annual general meeting. The "second strike" occurs when a company's subsequent remuneration report also receives a "no" vote of 25 per cent or more. When a "second strike" occurs, the shareholders will vote at the same AGM to determine whether all the directors will need to stand for re-election. If this "spill" resolution passes with 50 per cent or more of eligible votes cast, then a "spill meeting" will take place within 90 days.

Shareholder say-on-pay rules have existed in many European countries for some time – being introduced in the UK in 2003, in the Netherlands in 2004, in Sweden in 2006, in Norway and Denmark in 2007, and in Belgium in 2012.

less risky to stick with the pack" and do what everyone else was doing, rather than adopt something new or different.

If the analysis presented in the Governance Institute of Australia presentation in December 2015, the research outcomes contained in Appendix 3 and summarised in Chapter 3, and the case of Sonic Healthcare described in this chapter, don't together constitute evidence of a fatal flaw, it's hard to imagine what would.

In our view, this situation has arisen in part (and perhaps in large part) as an unintended consequence of the introduction of the so-called Two Strikes Rule, which came into effect in Australia in 2011.[4]

Complexity in remuneration practices and a lack of standardisation in remuneration reporting mean that the introduction of the Two Strikes Rule inadvertently ceded a great deal of power to proxy advisors and other commentators who sit in judgement of listed companies on behalf of shareholders. It also placed the directors of listed companies under a great deal of additional pressure.

This might not have occurred if we had a clear consensus as to the best way to assess and measure the performance of listed companies. But at this stage we don't – as is evidenced by the widespread ongoing acceptance of the EPS Myth. Consequently, action taken by a company in an effort to avoid a strike by appeasing those who sit in judgement, might not always be in the long-term best interest of the company, its shareholders, or its other legitimate stakeholders.

The solution to this probably lies in boards becoming both familiar and comfortable with the concepts we have sought to present in this book. If all players involved were more familiar with these concepts, then there is every chance that a good deal of the tension around the topic of executive reward might be eased. Board members would also be in a much better position to resist calls from external parties for their companies to engage in short-termism, such as the use of stretch targets for EPS (or even EP) outcomes, or the pursuit of other short-term financial performance outcomes achieved at the expense of longer term-value creation.

Some Practical Considerations

Short of taking the radical step of setting aside the use of performance-based executive remuneration altogether, there are three fundamental impediments to progressing the executive reward debate towards a resolution that will be acceptable to all stakeholders.

The first is that there are many different stakeholder constituencies, and that each has a different perspective on the purpose of listed companies and the role played by executive reward in support of that purpose.

The second is that there are vastly different levels of understanding both between and within each of these stakeholder constituencies, in relation to how to measure the performance of listed companies; and what constitutes, good, mediocre or poor company performance.

The third is that executive reward has become a lightning rod for all forms of dissatisfaction with the actions or the behaviours of listed companies – particularly since the introduction of the Two Strikes Rule in Australia, and shareholder say-on-pay rules in the UK and Europe.

In this context, the first priority must be to get to a common understanding across all stakeholder groups as to the fundamental purpose of business in general and listed companies in particular, as well as how to measure and ultimately reward success (or respond to failure).

Perhaps the most fundamental understanding that must be achieved is agreement on exactly how the performance produced by management in the market for a company's products and services, translates into the capital market outcomes experienced by shareholders. Currently, there are multiple perspectives on this issue.

If the current impasse in relation to these matters is resolved (perhaps in part by adopting the thinking outlined in this book), then in order to implement an approach to executive reward consistent with the metrics and structures we have posited, there are a number of practical considerations that need to be taken into account. These include:

- Dealing with the possibility that the market capitalisation of the business at the *beginning* of the measurement period, may not be consistent with its underlying intrinsic value;
- Dealing with the possibility that the market capitalisation of the business at the *end* of the measurement period, may not be consistent with its underlying intrinsic value at that point in time; and
- Establishing a robust EP forecast for the first three-to-five years of any given measurement period, and in particular to avoid the possibility of EP forecasts being "low-balled".

All reward plans that incorporate metrics based on TSR are somewhat vulnerable to the first two issues. The approach we have outlined can mitigate these problems to some degree. *TSR Alpha* strips out the impact of underlying market movements, and a progression of *EP Bow Waves* can be used to point to the existence of company specific sentiment at either the beginning or the end of the measurement period.

Similarly, all reward plans that have a product and services market performance metric component (i.e. EPS, ROC, ROE or EP) need to establish forward-looking benchmarks at the beginning of the measurement period. If a company adopts the strategic planning framework that we have advocated in Part III, then the EP forecast for the next three-to-five years will be linked to the strategic position of the company, and the strategy that it is pursing (at both a segment level and a business unit level). It will also have at least two if not more layers of management commitment underpinning it, as described earlier in this chapter. In any event, even if the EP forecast were "low balled", the reward consequences would not be significant under the approach we advocate. This is because the focus of the reward plan is on the development and successful implementation of higher value strategies (the right-hand side of the *Pair of EP Bow Waves* in Fig. 3.4) not on exceeding expectations under the current strategy (the left-hand side of the *Pair Bow Waves*).

Synthesis and Concluding Remarks

This chapter has outlined the nature of the platform required to build an enduring institution. To summarise, there are five elements that make up this platform:

- *The right understanding*, recognising the importance of adopting customer value creation and shareholder wealth creation as joint and mutually reinforcing objectives, and accepting that if desired, they can be pursued in ways that either preserve or enhance the wellbeing of all stakeholders;
- *The right capabilities*, recognising that the way a company goes about developing the ability to create wealth for its shareholders has a major impact on its ability to do so on an ongoing basis;
- *The right business processes*, recognising that in a value-managed company, the core business processes must encourage the identification, development and successful implementation of series of higher value segment-level strategies, while at the same time encouraging the ongoing pursuit of even higher value strategies over time;

- *The right performance measures*, recognising firstly that the metrics embedded in reward plans employed in the majority of listed companies don't encourage the creation of shareholder wealth or the ongoing pursuit and successful implementation of higher value strategies; and secondly that a shift to more appropriate metrics can encourage behaviours that deliver significant value uplift (through an explicit focus on individual and organisational capability creation, rather than just short-term financial performance outcomes); and
- *The right executive reward plan design*, recognising that while there are many ways to progress an initiative of this nature, it will be difficult to succeed if the reward plan is not brought properly into alignment.

With these elements in place, a listed company will be in a good position to create customer value and build shareholder, and do so on an ongoing basis. It will also be well positioned to do this in a way that contributes to societal wellbeing and environmental sustainability – should its leadership team consider this an appropriate course of action.

Part IV

The Legacy

The legacy of good business leadership is an institution that not only outlives the tenure of the current board and its executive team, but which prospers well into the future as a result of the decisions taken and capabilities established during their tenure.

Such an institution must have the capability to create value for customers and wealth for shareholders on an ongoing basis. Because of this, it will also be well positioned to take the next step, which is to pursue these two joint goals in ways that at minimum preserve and wherever possible enhance the wellbeing of all its legitimate stakeholders, including the wider community and the environment.

11

An Organisation that Prospers Well into the Future

We made it clear at the outset that in our view, the legacy of good business leadership is an institution that not only outlives the tenure of the current board and executive leadership team, but which prospers well into the future as a result of the decisions taken and capabilities established during their tenure. We also indicated that we believed the most fundamental challenge facing every listed company board and executive team is to build such an institution – and to deliver significant benefits to both its customers and its shareholders along the way.

What does such an institution look like? What characterises it?

Characteristics of an Enduring Institution

An organisation that prospers well into the future and which is able to continually enhance the shape of its *EP Bow Wave* over an extended period, will have a number of important and in many ways defining characteristics.

- It will have developed the individual and organisational capabilities necessary to measure, create and manage both customer value and shareholder wealth – including having put in place an integrated strategic planning, resource allocation and performance management system focused on the ongoing development and successful implementation of higher value strategies.

D. Kilroy, M. Schneider, *Customer Value, Shareholder Wealth, Community Wellbeing*, DOI 10.1007/978-3-319-54774-9_11

- It will have a CEO and leadership team strong enough to rebuff external commentators calling for short-term measures to boost earnings, and instead maintain their focus on medium-term economic profit growth while building the internal capabilities necessary to deliver longer-term economic profit growth.
- It will have embraced customer value creation and shareholder wealth creation as joint and mutually reinforcing objectives, and will have established cycles of customer value and shareholder wealth creation in most of the needs based customer segments that it has chosen to serve.
- It will be producing products or delivering services that not only enable it to succeed in the market for those products and services, but also be seeing that success translate into success in the capital markets in the form of an improving *EP Bow Wave* and positive *TSR Alpha* outcomes.
- Where appropriate, it will have established value-creating networks, and be seeking to collaborate with other companies in its value chain so as to enhance value for both direct customers and end-consumers.
- Most if not all stakeholders in the company will be deriving a fair and appropriate amount of value or benefit from their interaction with the company.
- It will understand the importance of disciplined innovation centred on *Hybrid Thinking*, and it will honour and respect the nature of the creative process by encouraging its development within each individual employee.
- It will recognise that once in good shape economically, one of the best ways to create wealth for shareholders and continue to deliver a positive *TSR Alpha* outcome, will be by extending the length of its *EP Bow Wave* through investing in individual and organisational capability creation.
- It will be in a position to take the next step, which is to make a conscious choice as to whether the products or services it will produce in the future will seek to create a predominance of real value or artificial value for its customers.
- It will have the moral courage to be prepared to confront the question of whether it is in business to serve society, or instead to exploit it.
- It will have a long-term mindset, and in doing so behave as a *long-term value creator*, not a *short-term share price manager*.

The Imperative to Resist Short-Termism

In December 2015, Denis Kilroy gave a quite seminal presentation entitled *Driving Long-Term Value Creation* to the Annual Conference of the *Governance Institute of Australia.*[1] In that presentation, the change in the shape of the *EP Bow Wave* for a group of seven strong performing ASX-listed companies was used to demonstrate why it is so important to focus on the long term rather than the short term. Fig. 11.1 is a reproduction of the slide used at the time.

The four established companies all destroyed shareholder wealth by failing to meet expectations over the measurement period. But they all more than offset this as a result of the establishment of new EP expectations to be delivered beyond the measurement period.

The three relatively new companies all just made it over the line in terms of meeting expectations over the measurement period. But in all three cases, over 90 percent of the wealth created came from new EP expectations to be delivered beyond the measurement period. All seven companies grew their *EP Bow Wave* by 20 years or more.

Since then, we have conducted extensive research on this topic in the ASX, the NYSE and the LSE over the five years to 31 December 2015. The same picture evident in Fig. 11.1 can be seen in all three markets, as was clear from

	Total Shareholder Wealth Created (Billions of Dollars)	Impact of Meeting EP Expectations (Billions of Dollars)	Impact of Creating New Expectations (Billions of Dollars)	Increase in Bow Wave Length (Years)
Telstra	41.2	(3.7)	44.9	25
Amcor	8.4	(3.8)	12.2	25
Brambles	7.2	(0.9)	8.1	30
Wesfarmers	3.7	(3.6)	7.3	30
REA Group	3.0	0.1	2.9	30
Dominos	2.6	0.1	2.5	20
Carsales.com	1.0	0.1	0.9	20

Fig. 11.1 Sources of wealth creation – five years to 30 June 2015

[1] At the time of writing, the presentation given to the *Governance Institute of Australia* Annual Conference in December 2015 was available from this link: https://www.kba.com.au/publications/driving-long-term-value-creation/.

Figs. 3.11 to 3.13 at the end of Chapter 3 (and for which the underlying data is contained in Appendix 3).

This analysis demonstrates conclusively that successful companies generate far more wealth for shareholders by creating new EP expectations to be delivered beyond the measurement period, than by exceeding expectations over the measurement period.

Extending the length of the *EP Bow Wave* in this way is one of the main economic consequences of seeking to build an enduring institution. It means building the necessary capabilities we have spoken of throughout this book – both at an individual and at an organisational level.

If we boil it down, the fundamental message we want to convey is that it is more beneficial for everyone, and therefore more important for business leaders, to focus on the long term rather than the short term. The key to achieving better capital market outcomes over the short, the medium and the longer term, is to focus on achieving better product and service market outcomes over the long term (not the short term).

As we said at the end of *Chapter 3*, short-termism makes no sense at all. It serves neither the interests of medium to long term shareholders, nor those of the many other legitimate stakeholders of a listed company.

Listed company boards and executive leadership teams need to increase their understanding in relation to the principles that underpin these conclusions. Such an understanding is the best way for them to equip themselves to resist the calls from self-interested external parties, for their companies to engage in practices collectively referred to as short-termism.

They should also consider moving away from executive reward plan designs that use relative TSR and EPS growth (or another accounting-based metrics) in combination. This combination of metrics is widely used. But it is an approach that is grounded firmly in *The EPS Myth* and tends to encourage short-termism, largely because the lottery-like nature of relative TSR means the primary focus becomes earnings or EPS growth.

Ultimately, every listed company leadership team needs to be willing to consider how it might operate in the context of a new business paradigm under which its purpose is to build an organisation that prospers well into the future through serving society: by creating real or authentic value for customers; by building significant wealth for its shareholders; and by doing both in ways that quite deliberately seek to enhance the wellbeing of all its legitimate stakeholders (including its employees, its suppliers, the wider community and the environment).

While there is as yet no externally imposed requirement to move in the direction of creating customer value, shareholder wealth and societal well-being, in an environment where listed company ownership is increasingly in the hands of pension and superannuation funds with long investment horizons and a very real focus on ESG considerations, this seems to us to be the logical next step for the leaders of companies that are already focused on the ongoing and systematic creation of customer value and shareholder wealth.

12

Conclusion

In conclusion, we felt it appropriate to reflect on two questions.

1. Why hasn't the business community already made more progress towards embracing a more socially responsible business paradigm?
2. Where does the thinking presented in this book fit in the context of the other streams of thought that have emerged post the GFC in an effort to encourage more socially responsible business behaviour?

Why Hasn't More Progress Been Made?

The *EP Bow Wave* construct and the *Pair of EP Bow Waves* that together underpin the *EP Uplift + TSR Alpha Construct* are new. They were first described in *The Legacy of Good Leadership* which was released in Australia in late 2014, although the *EP Bow Wave* had been in development since 2006.

These new constructs make it much easier for companies to link the performance they achieve in the market for their products and services, with the capital market outcomes experienced by shareholders. This is important, because dissatisfaction with an existing framework is generally not enough to create change. There needs to be a better alternative available – and now there is one.

That said, while the potential new business paradigm that we have posited does represent a new way of thinking, many of the elements have been in

D. Kilroy, M. Schneider, *Customer Value, Shareholder Wealth, Community Wellbeing*, DOI 10.1007/978-3-319-54774-9_12

place for some time. For example, the notion of customer value creation and shareholder wealth creation serving as joint and mutually reinforcing objectives at the level of an individual needs-based customer segment, has existed for more than 20 years. We began working with it in 1994 and published a paper on the topic in the late 1990s.[1]

So, it is useful to explore why an approach to business centred on the adoption of customer value creation and shareholder wealth creation as joint and mutually reinforcing goals has not been more widely adopted. This is particularly important given the fact that embracing such an approach is an important stepping-stone to move towards the more socially responsible business paradigm we are proposing. In our view, there are three sets of reasons.

The first set contains reasons that are fundamentally backward looking in nature. They comprise the following:

- *A lack of holistic thinking in business education programs – both undergraduate and graduate.* Both authors have spent most of their careers in management consulting and have at times been closely involved with recruiting graduates and MBAs from leading universities and business schools into top-tier firms in Australia, the UK and to some extent in the USA. Our experience leads us to the perception that the understanding we have outlined is not taught in business schools. Management accounting, corporate finance, strategy and marketing are seen as separate and largely analytical disciplines. Softer disciplines like leadership and ethics, creativity, and more recently the integration of psychology and neuroscience to improve our understanding of human behaviour, are disconnected from the more analytical disciplines. They need to be brought together in an integrated fashion to embrace the thinking we have outlined.
- *Proprietary value-based performance metrics.* Many executives had difficult experiences with proprietary value-based performance metrics when they were introduced in the 1980s and 1990s. This resulted in an aversion towards economic performance measures. There is even a perception that economic profit is a complex notion – when clearly it is not. The difference between after tax earnings and economic profit is the charge for capital, in the same way that the difference between operating profit

[1] Kilroy, D., "Creating the Future: how creativity and innovation drive shareholder wealth", *Management Decision*, Vol. 37, No. 4 [1999], MCB University Press, pp. 363–371.

and earnings is the charge for debt and taxation. It is not a difficult or complex notion.

The proprietary metrics were discussed in Chapter 1 of this book, along with the economic engine approach to value creation that grew up around them. The metrics themselves were unnecessarily complicated, and we demonstrated in Chapter 1 that the economic engine approach could never successfully underpin or encourage the ongoing creation of both customer value and shareholder wealth. Perhaps the time has come to establish a proper standard for listed company performance measurement centred on *TSR-Ke, TSR Alpha* and the *Pair of EP Bow Waves.*

- *Implementation takes time and commitment.* The approach we have outlined takes time for any company to implement – roughly three years in fact. Not every organisation has the patience or the commitment to take this on, even if they appreciate the benefits that will flow. Short CEO tenure and the somewhat myopic focus on short-term earnings or EPS outcomes on the part of many commentators, hasn't helped either. In fact, they are major impediments. However, greater and more active investor engagement on the part of asset owning institutions like pension and superannuation funds is likely to change this. So are new and innovative approaches to executive reward plan design, such as the tax-effective 10 to 15-year vesting mechanism developed by a Sydney based remuneration consulting firm in 2015, or the alternatives we put forward in Chapter 10.[2]
- *Attachment to mythology around earnings, EPS and EPS growth.* This is an interesting challenge. Business schools need to take a stand here. So do professional bodies. But those best positioned to sort out this problem are probably corporate finance professionals, fund managers and listed company CFOs, many of whom already understand the nature of the *EPS Myth* and the potentially deleterious consequences that flow from adherence to it.

The second set of reasons is more forward looking. But it also has a backward-looking aspect since the reasons relate to the extent to which the current business paradigm is embedded in the consciousness of the business community. The current paradigm is centred on shareholder value

[2] The Godfrey Remuneration Group.

maximisation as a governing corporate objective, and is underpinned by a firm belief in the effectiveness of market forces working in tandem with rational, utility-maximising choice. But as is now being suggested, the notion of social capital, combined with the role that emotions play in market outcomes, calls this into question. The perceived supremacy of competition over collaboration also needs to be re-examined, as does the question of self-interest versus the common good. The attachment to the fundamental tenets of the current paradigm also lead business leaders to form the view that some of the choices we have posed – such as those pertaining to real versus artificial value – are not available to them. We would argue that this is not true, and dealing with these issues is the primary purpose of the second book in this series entitled *Noble Intent, Clear Purpose, Better Leader*.

The third set of reasons comprises issues that are primarily forward looking in nature and relate to the legal and regulatory milieu in which businesses operate. This includes the regulations surrounding many aspects of business including advertising, competition policy and accounting standards, together with taxation policy and corporate law. These rules have evolved around the current paradigm. However, they are not necessarily conductive to a new and more socially responsible business paradigm. Dealing with these is the primary purpose of the third book in this series entitled *Business Prosperity, Social Equity, Environmental Sustainability*.

Where Does the Thinking in This Book Fit?

There have been several attempts to change the business paradigm over the past 20 years. Two that emerged prior to the GFC were the notion of the *Triple Bottom Line* and *Corporate Social Responsibility*. Both had an impact but neither had the power to change the paradigm.

In addition to the approach we have outlined, two further streams of thought have emerged since the GFC. The first is *Conscious Capitalism*. The second is *Shared Value*. In parallel with both, the notion of *Benefit Corporations* has also emerged.

Our approach is quite different to *Shared Value*, which in our view is in large part an effort to make the current paradigm more palatable and more caring in a post-GFC world. But our approach shares a great deal with *Conscious Capitalism*. In fact, the advocates of *Conscious Capitalism* are in many respects focused on the same end state that we are advocating.

We differ from *Conscious Capitalism* only to the extent that we go somewhat further. For us the shift we are advocating requires all of the elements of *Conscious Capitalism*. But it also requires a new and more enlightened approach to corporate finance and business economics.

We also see our approach as very much aligned with the intent of groups like the *Purpose of the Corporation Project* and the *Modern Corporation Project*, as well as the *Coalition for Inclusive Capitalism*.

Changing the economic objective of a listed company from creating shareholder wealth *per se*, to building an enduring institution that can create value for customers and wealth for shareholders *on an ongoing basis*, might seem to some to be little more than a subtle shift in emphasis. But the inclusion of the words "on an ongoing basis" has profound consequences for both the business and the investment communities, together with all the other legitimate stakeholders in every listed company.

The Focus of the Other Two Books in The Series

Book 2. Noble Intent, Clear Purpose, Better Leader

The full title of Book 2 is *Noble Intent, Clear Purpose, Better Leader – A Roadmap for Company Directors and Senior Executives*. Its purpose is to guide business leaders in their most fundamental choices, both collectively and as individuals.

In *Customer Value, Shareholder Wealth, Community Wellbeing*, the reader has been given a destination and a roadmap.

The destination mirrors the belief that is not only possible, but also highly desirable, to build an enduring institution that that can create value for its customers and wealth for its shareholders on an ongoing basis – and at the same time, do so in ways that at minimum preserve and wherever possible enhance, societal wellbeing. The roadmap provides a clear path to follow in order to get there.

The role of the second book in the series, *Noble Intent, Clear Purpose, Better Leader*, is to provide a deeper philosophical underpinning for the material contained in *Customer Value, Shareholder Wealth, Community Wellbeing*. In a very simple sense, the message in the second book in the series is that the ends never justify the means. Instead the means qualify or condition the ends.

If we go a bit deeper, then the underlying purpose of the second book is to seek to raise management consciousness. Consciousness in this context means our awareness of ourselves and the world around us; together with the thoughts, feelings and attitudes we have or hold in relation to both. Raising consciousness means heightening our awareness through a better or more complete understanding – along a spectrum that potentially extends from ignorance to enlightenment.

We can use the term regressive consciousness to represent a world view that regards individuals, or individual companies, as free-standing entities that are able to act in whatever manner they deem appropriate in order to maximise their wealth, their power or their economic advantage over other entities (be they companies, individuals or groups of individuals) so long as it is within the law. Regressive consciousness leads to a dog-eat-dog existence where there is no real concern for others.

The term progressive consciousness can be used to represent a world view that regards individuals and companies as different entities that while separate in many respects and free to act independently, are nonetheless still all part of an integrated whole. The behaviour of one affects others in a positive or a negative way.

Progressive consciousness constitutes a much higher form of consciousness than regressive consciousness.

Fundamental to any attempt to raise management consciousness is a process of clarification of intent. Is it the intention of an individual executive, or the entire board and executive leadership team, to serve customers, end-consumers and ultimately the wider community – or is their intention to exploit them?

Every business must make this fundamental choice. Each can choose to act with the intention of truly serving its customers and the wider community. Or it can choose to act with the intention of exploiting them.

While a decision one way or the other is likely to lead to different outcomes, the real difference lies not in the outcomes, but in the underlying intention of the directors and the executives who control the business. For example, poor construction work may remain hidden in a building for many years and ownership of the building may pass through many hands before the faults reveal themselves. There is even the chance that the faults will never surface and the builder who cut corners to save costs will never be called to account. But that builder did make a clear and conscious choice to exploit the client. The underlying intention was unsound, regardless of the consequences.

The decision to act with the intention to serve, or to act with the intention to exploit, represents a conscious choice between two mutually exclusive alternatives. Outcomes arising from actions might be positive or negative to varying degrees – but not the intentions. With intentions, the choice is black or white. There are no shades of grey.

Regardless of how subtly it is done, or how well it is disguised, those who act with the intention to exploit do so out of a regressive consciousness that sees business as little more than a dog-eat-dog competition for advantage, wealth or power acquired at the expense of others.

It need not be so. When combined with the destination and the roadmap provided in *Customer Value, Shareholder Wealth, Community Wellbeing*, the second book in the series places a *beacon of noble intent* at the destination. This has the potential to illuminate the entire journey – should the leaders of a business choose to light it.

Book 3. Business Prosperity, Social Equity, Environmental Sustainability

The full title of Book 3 is *Business Prosperity, Social Equity, Environmental Sustainability – A Roadmap for Policymakers and Regulators.* Its purpose is to help shape the public policy and regulatory environment so that the business community is encouraged to create customer value, build shareholder wealth and at the same time, enhance both community wellbeing and environmental sustainability. This means creating the conditions under which a fairer, more noble, more inclusive, more sustainable and more socially responsible approach to business can flourish.

Specifically, it seeks to define the regulatory conditions and the regulatory and legislative mindset required to both encourage and sustain nobler or more virtuous business practices.

The destination outlined in *Customer Value, Shareholder Wealth, Community Wellbeing* mirrors the belief that is not only possible, but also highly desirable, to build an enduring institution that that can create value for customers and wealth for shareholders on an ongoing basis – and do so in a way that at minimum preserves and in wherever possible enhances societal wellbeing and environmental sustainability. The roadmap provides a clear way to get there.

But the reality is we need more than a destination, a roadmap and a conscious intent to serve. It is important to also have supportive conditions in which to operate – including the regulatory environment.

Why do some companies exploit their customers? Why do some employers exploit their employees? In the first instance, they do it because they choose to do so. It is their intention. But they also do it because the current paradigm encourages them to do so – at least to some extent. If the intention is to create wealth, and most of the key players with whom they interact (including government appointed regulators) believe that the only way to do so is at the expense of others, then exploitation will follow just as night follows day.

Here are some examples of beliefs held by law-makers and regulators that underpin the current paradigm. None is intrinsically true or even necessary for economic success as an individual, a business or a nation.

- In relation to some fast food, soft drink and OTC pharmaceutical segments…*Market integrity and a consumer's right to choose must be preserved at all costs* [even if consumers lack the information to make a wise choice and none of the options available to them if consumed serve their long-term best interest].
- In relation to taxation…*Companies should be taxed on the profit they generate* [even if their real objective is not to generate profits, but to create wealth, and any tax that they pay must be met from cash flow, which for a growing company is always less than profit, which in turn creates an incentive to look for ways to minimise taxation].
- In relation to advertising…*A successful advertising campaign is one that creates significant demand for the client's product* [regardless of whether consumption of the product serves the long-term best interest of the consumer].
- In relation to electricity distribution…*The best way to provide value for consumers is to ensure they get the lowest price* [even if it leads to under-investment in network infrastructure, an increased risk of outages, lower levels of safety or greater environmental degradation, or a reluctance to invest in renewable forms of energy].
- In relation to capital markets…*Market efficiency demands that short-selling be permitted* [even if it means selling something you don't own in the hope you can force down prices such that you can pay for what you have sold, but at lower price than you sold it]
- In relation to most fast-moving consumer goods markets…*Competition is the best protection for consumers* [regardless of the fact that consumers are only exploited when someone chooses to exploit them]

We have created an economic structure that gives primacy to the right of an individual or a company to act as they see fit so as to enhance their wealth, so long as it is within the law; and the maintenance of market efficiency almost regardless of the cost. In doing so, we have created a significant problem. Our narrow definition of economic benefit excludes large economic and social costs that arise either directly or indirectly from the activities of many industries. Examples include obesity and its link to the fast food and soft drink industries; attention deficit and hyperactivity disorder (ADHD) and its link to common preservatives used in factory-made bread; the many side effects associated with certain over-the-counter (OTC) and prescription pharmaceuticals; and of course the multitude of health consequences arising from tobacco use and alcohol consumption.

All of these industries are from time to time able to create wealth for their shareholders, but this may be a distorted reality because many of the costs they generate are not captured in the economic framework that we employ. These costs, which economists often refer to as externalities, are borne by individuals (often in the form of a negative impact on their health), or by the wider community through the taxation system.

Perhaps the greatest problem arises when a government itself becomes dependent upon taxation revenues from industries with high social costs. The gaming industry is a particularly interesting example of this phenomenon – with significant implications for Australia.

Ultimately, we need a different mindset at the level of our legislators and the regulators whom they appoint. And we must be prepared to let go of some of the ideas about the absolute primacy of free markets that have become articles of faith since the 1980s. Only then can we establish an economy that creates wealth by making the best use of available resources to generate products and services that serve the long-term best interests of individuals, the wider community and the environment.

Re-thinking the Interpretation of Director Duties

As what is essentially a *post-script*, we feel it is appropriate to propose a subtle rethink of director duties to the listed companies they serve. Directors have a fiduciary duty to act in the best interests of their company. In some jurisdictions, this has been interpreted somewhat simplistically as a responsibility to maximise returns for existing shareholders (which is then pursued erroneously by seeking to maximise short-term earnings or EPS).

This interpretation has the potential to constrain the behaviour of directors when confronted with ethical issues that affect the wellbeing of other stakeholders, including customers, suppliers, the wider community and the environment. Perversely, it could even force them to act inadvertently in a manner that is not in the long-term best interest of either their company or its shareholders – although this would not have been apparent without the breakthrough in applied corporate finance and business economic that gave rise to the *EP Bow Wave* and the *EP Uplift + TSR Alpha* construct.

The breakthrough in understanding arising from the *EP Bow Wave* and the *EP Uplift + TSR Alpha* construct provides an opportunity to embrace a more holistic interpretation of directors' fiduciary duties. A strong case can now be mounted to the effect that the responsibility of directors is to encourage the building of an enduring institution that creates value for customers and wealth for shareholders on an ongoing basis. The thinking we have presented also suggests that for most companies, directors can choose to do this in ways that lead to beneficial outcomes for all legitimate stakeholders, including the wider community and the environment.

Lawmakers and those who interpret the law in these matters need to appreciate that with the understanding that comes with the *EP Bow Wave* and the *EP Uplift + TSR Alpha* construct, maximising shareholder value **means** building an enduring institution that can create value for customer and wealth for shareholders on an ongoing basis.

The vast majority of directors of listed companies are intent on doing the right thing. So, it would be a pity if a narrow interpretation of the law based on an incomplete understanding of applied corporate finance and business economics, constrains them in moving in a direction that serves the best interest of all legitimate stakeholders in listed companies.

Appendix 1: Exploding the EPS Myth

The purpose of this Appendix is to demonstrate why the use of EPS growth does not normalise earnings growth to take account of the additional capital required to fund that growth.

Fig. A1.1 presents the same example used in Fig. 2.1. The three companies shown each grow their *earnings* by 15 percent per year over the measurement period. However, they each did it by employing different amounts of capital. As we pointed out in *Chapter 2*, this difference has enormous consequences for both *economic profit (EP)* and *value*.

Fig. A1.1 and the thinking presented in *Chapter 2* demonstrate quite clearly that earnings growth is clearly not a good indicator of management performance in creating shareholder wealth, because it fails to take account of the amount of capital required and so can be "purchased at any price". What about EPS?

EPS tends not to attract the same criticism as earnings due to what is really another widespread but nonetheless misguided belief. This is the belief that expressing earnings on a per share basis has the effect of normalising it for any additional capital requirements through the issuing of additional shares.

While it may seem counter intuitive, the normalising effect of expressing earnings on a per share basis is marginal at best. In the vast majority of cases, earnings growth and EPS growth will be virtually in lock-step, regardless of the amount of capital required. This is because new shares are issued at market value not at book value.

Figures A1.2, A1.3 and A1.4 contain summaries of the calculations that underpin each of the series of the numbers presented in Fig. A1.1. They also

D. Kilroy, M. Schneider, *Customer Value, Shareholder Wealth, Community Wellbeing*, DOI 10.1007/978-3-319-54774-9

	Base Year						Year 5			
	Equity Capital Employed	Earnings	Cost of Equity	Economic Profit	Earnings Growth	Growth in Equity	Equity Capital Employed	Earnings	Cost of Equity	Economic Profit
Company A	100	10	10%	0.0	15%	10%	161	20	10%	4.0
Company B	100	10	10%	0.0	15%	15%	201	20	10%	0.0
Company C	100	10	10%	0.0	15%	20%	249	20	10%	(4.8)

Fig. A1.1 Why earnings and EPS can be purchased at any price
Note: All figures are in millions of dollars except for percentages

Opening Equity Base	100	Growth in Earnings	15%
Opening Shares	100	Growth in Equity	15%
First Year Earnings	10	Cost of Equity	10%

	Base	1	2	3	4	5	6
Closing Equity ($m)	100.0	115.0	132.3	152.1	174.9	201.1	231.3
Earnings ($m)		10.0	11.5	13.2	15.2	17.5	20.1
Economic Profit ($m)		0.0	0.0	0.0	0.0	0.0	0.0
Operating Equity Cash Flow ($m)		(5.0)	(5.7)	(6.6)	(7.6)	(8.7)	(10.1)
Return of Capital ($m)		0.0	0.0	0.0	0.0	0.0	231.3
Total Equity Cash Flow ($m)		**(5.0)**	**(5.7)**	**(6.6)**	**(7.6)**	**(8.7)**	**221.2**
Present Value Factor		0.909	0.826	0.751	0.683	0.621	0.564
Discounted Cash Flow ($m)		(4.5)	(4.8)	(5.0)	(5.2)	(5.4)	124.9
Market Value ($m)	**100.0**	**115.0**	**132.3**	**152.1**	**174.9**	**201.1**	**0.0**
Number of Shares (m)	100.00	100.04	100.09	100.13	100.17	100.22	0.00
EPS (cents)		**10.0**	**11.5**	**13.2**	**15.2**	**17.5**	**20.1**

Fig. A1.2 Calculations for company B (base case)

show the value consequences in each case, on the extremely conservative assumption that capital is returned to investors at the end of the measurement period. The differences in the value consequences of the three strategies would be much greater if cash flows had been forecast over a longer time frame.

In the case of Company B (the base case) in Fig. A1.2, *earnings* grow at 15 percent per year so that they double over five years. EP is zero throughout, so the market value of equity is equal to the book value of equity ($100m).

In this case, even though there are insufficient earnings to fund all the capital requirements (so some shares do need to be issued), EPS rises from 10.0 cents to 20.1 cents over the measurement period.

Opening Equity Base	100	Growth in Earnings	15%
Opening Shares	100	Growth in Equity	10%
First Year Earnings	10	Cost of Equity	10%

	Base	1	2	3	4	5	6
Closing Equity ($m)	100.0	110.0	121.0	133.1	146.4	161.1	177.2
Earnings ($m)		10.0	11.5	13.2	15.2	17.5	20.1
Economic Profit ($m)		0.0	0.5	1.1	1.9	2.8	4.0
Operating Equity Cash Flow ($m)		(0.0)	0.5	1.1	1.9	2.8	4.0
Return of Capital ($m)		0.0	0.0	0.0	0.0	0.0	177.2
Total Equity Cash Flow ($m)		**(0.0)**	**0.5**	**1.1**	**1.9**	**2.8**	**181.2**
Present Value Factor		0.909	0.826	0.751	0.683	0.621	0.564
Discounted Cash Flow ($m)		(0.0)	0.4	0.8	1.3	1.8	102.3
Market Value ($m)	**106.6**	**117.2**	**128.5**	**140.2**	**152.3**	**164.7**	**0.0**
Number of Shares (m)	100.00	100.00	100.00	100.00	100.00	100.00	0.00
EPS (cents)		**10.0**	**11.5**	**13.2**	**15.2**	**17.5**	**20.1**

Fig. A1.3 Calculations for company A

Opening Equity Base	100	Growth in Earnings	15%
Opening Shares	100	Growth in Equity	20%
First Year Earnings	10	Cost of Equity	10%

	Base	1	2	3	4	5	6
Closing Equity ($m)	100.0	120.0	144.0	172.8	207.4	248.8	298.6
Earnings ($m)		10.0	11.5	13.2	15.2	17.5	20.1
Economic Profit ($m)		0.0	(0.5)	(1.2)	(2.1)	(3.2)	(4.8)
Operating Equity Cash Flow ($m)		(10.0)	(12.5)	(15.6)	(19.4)	(24.0)	(29.7)
Return of Capital ($m)		0.0	0.0	0.0	0.0	0.0	298.6
Total Equity Cash Flow ($m)		**(10.0)**	**(12.5)**	**(15.6)**	**(19.4)**	**(24.0)**	**268.9**
Present Value Factor		0.909	0.826	0.751	0.683	0.621	0.564
Discounted Cash Flow ($m)		(9.1)	(10.3)	(11.7)	(13.2)	(14.9)	151.8
Market Value ($m)	**92.6**	**111.8**	**135.5**	**164.7**	**200.5**	**244.5**	**0.0**
Number of Shares (m)	100.00	100.09	100.18	100.28	100.37	100.47	0.00
EPS (cents)		**10.0**	**11.5**	**13.2**	**15.2**	**17.4**	**20.0**

Fig. A1.4 Calculations for company C

In the case of Company A (which uses less capital) as shown in Fig. A1.3, earnings again double over the period. EP is positive from Year 2 and the market value of $106.6m is greater than the book value of $100m. In this case there is no need to issue additional shares. But once again, EPS rises from 10.0 cents to 20.1 cents over the period.

In the case of Company C (which uses more capital) as shown in Fig. A1.4, earnings double again yet EP is negative throughout and market value is $92.6m compared with a book value of $100m. In this case the need to issue new shares does impact EPS – but it is only a very marginal impact. EPS rises from 10.0 to 20.0 cents.

There are some important insights and conclusions that arise from this analysis.

- EPS grows at virtually the same rate as earnings in each case.
- EPS grows at virtually the same rate in all three cases, despite significant differences in the amount of equity capital employed by the end of the measurement period.
- EPS grows at virtually the same rate in all three cases, despite significant differences in the level of EP generated each year.
- EPS grows at virtually the same rate in all three cases, but the value of the business is quite different in each case – even under the most conservative assumptions.

These conclusions show that EPS is at best an incomplete indicator of management performance, and in many cases a relatively poor indicator. They also support the contention that total shareholder return (TSR) is much more closely aligned with growth in EP per share than it is with growth in earnings per share (EPS).

Appendix 2: Understanding TSR Alpha

TSR Alpha is the difference between the TSR delivered over a specified measurement period, and the TSR that would have been required by investors in order to match market performance over the same measurement period (after adjusting for company-specific risk). It is a variant of a concept known as Jensen's Alpha (which is used by portfolio managers) and constitutes the economic return on the market value of equity over the short to medium term. Over the long term, it is identical to TSR-Ke, the long-term economic return on market value.

The first step in calculating *TSR Alpha* is to determine the TSR required in order match market performance throughout the measurement period. We use the abbreviation TSRr for this in Fig. A2.1.

Under the capital asset pricing model (CAPM), the long-run Ke for a company is equal to the rate of return required on a risk free asset (Rf), plus a premium for taking an equity risk.

For the market as a whole, the equity risk premium (ERP) is the extent to which the return achieved in the market (Rm) exceeds Rf. In the case of the Australian Securities Exchange (ASX), Rm is the compound annual growth rate of the ASX All Ordinaries Accumulation Index. For a particular company, the premium for risk is the product of the ERP for the market as a whole; and Beta (β), which is a market-derived adjustment that captures the risk associated with the company in question, relative to the market as a whole.

The long run ERP is known to lie between 6 and 7 percent per year. We have assumed 6.5 percent in all of our analysis. However over the short term,

D. Kilroy, M. Schneider, *Customer Value, Shareholder Wealth, Community Wellbeing*, DOI 10.1007/978-3-319-54774-9

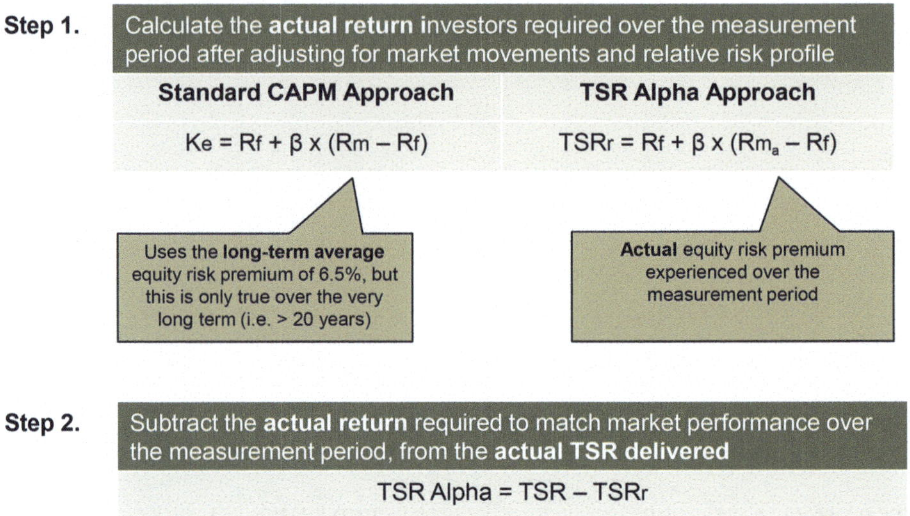

Step 1.
Calculate the actual return investors required over the measurement period after adjusting for market movements and relative risk profile
Standard CAPM Approach
TSR Alpha Approach
Ke = Rf + β x (Rm – Rf)
TSRr = Rf + β x (Rma – Rf)
Uses the long-term average equity risk premium of 6.5%, but this is only true over the very long term (i.e. > 20 years)
Actual equity risk premium experienced over the measurement period
Step 2.
Subtract the actual return required to match market performance over the measurement period, from the actual TSR delivered
TSR Alpha = TSR – TSRr

Fig. A2.1 TSR Alpha calculation methodology

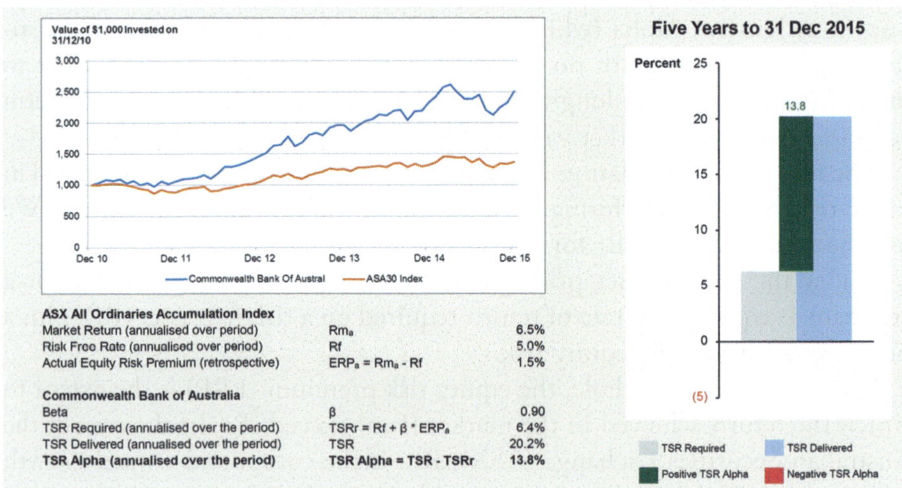

Fig. A2.2 Calculation of TSR Alpha for Commonwealth Bank

such as the three to five years often associated with the tenure of a CEO or the length of a typical long term incentive (LTI) plan, the actual return experienced in the market (Rm_a) and therefore the actual retrospectively derived ERP_a, can diverge significantly from the average.

Fig. A2.2 shows an example of the calculation of TSR required and *TSR Alpha* for the Commonwealth Bank for the five years to 30 June 2015.

Over the five-years ended 31 December 2015, Rm_a was 6.5 percent and Rf was 5.0 percent. So the ERP_a over that period was 1.5 percent, which is 5.0 percentage points lower than the long-run average of 6.5 percent.

If we apply the principles of CAPM and use the observed short-term ERP of 1.5 percent, rather than the long-run average ERP of 6.5 percent, we can calculate the TSR required over the five-year period from 31 December 2010 to 31 December 2015. *TSR Alpha* can then be determined by subtracting the TSR required from the TSR observed over the same period.

In the case of the Commonwealth Bank, the TSR required was made up of an Rf of 5.0 percent plus an ERP of 1.5 percent multiplied by the bank's β of 0.90 – giving a required TSR of 6.4 percent. The annualised TSR delivered for that five-year period was 20.2 percent, so *TSR Alpha* was 13.8 percent.

An annualised *TSR Alpha* of 13.8 percent represents outstanding performance relative to the market as a whole. It means that on average over the five years to 31 December 2015, shareholders in the Commonwealth Bank received a TSR that was 13.8 percentage points above that which they would have received had the bank matched the performance of the equities market as a whole over that period (after adjusting for company-specific risk).

The Commonwealth Bank was able to achieve a positive TSR Alpha in every year over the five years to 31 December 2015. This outcome is illustrated in Fig. A2.3.

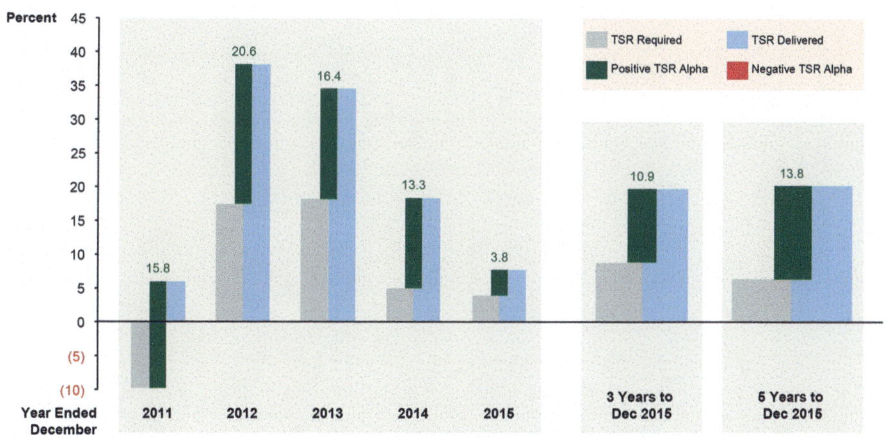

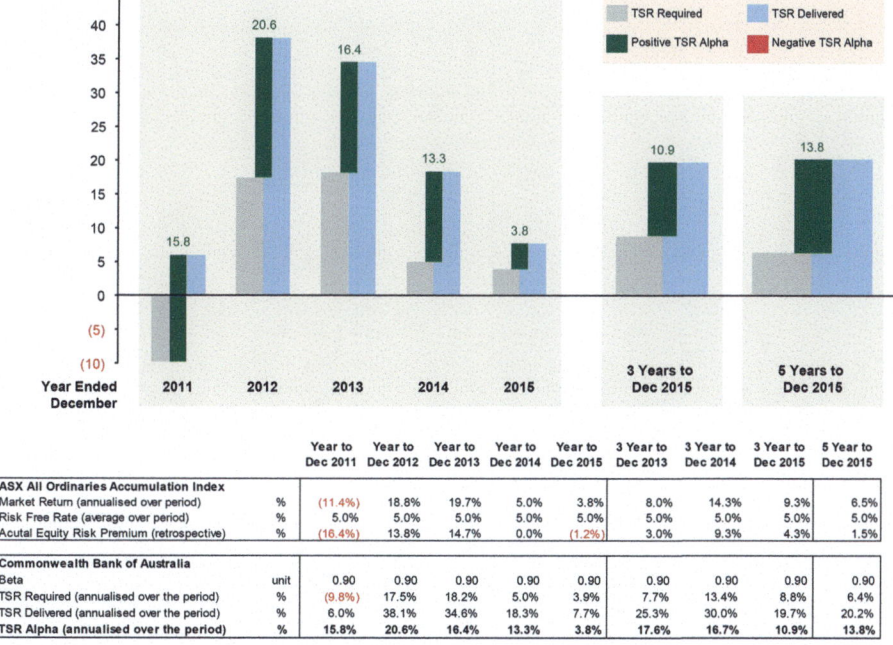

		Year to Dec 2011	Year to Dec 2012	Year to Dec 2013	Year to Dec 2014	Year to Dec 2015	3 Year to Dec 2013	3 Year to Dec 2014	3 Year to Dec 2015	5 Year to Dec 2015
ASX All Ordinaries Accumulation Index										
Market Return (annualised over period)	%	(11.4%)	18.8%	19.7%	5.0%	3.8%	8.0%	14.3%	9.3%	6.5%
Risk Free Rate (average over period)	%	5.0%	5.0%	5.0%	5.0%	5.0%	5.0%	5.0%	5.0%	5.0%
Acutal Equity Risk Premium (retrospective)	%	(16.4%)	13.8%	14.7%	0.0%	(1.2%)	3.0%	9.3%	4.3%	1.5%
Commonwealth Bank of Australia										
Beta	unit	0.90	0.90	0.90	0.90	0.90	0.90	0.90	0.90	0.90
TSR Required (annualised over the period)	%	(9.8%)	17.5%	18.2%	5.0%	3.9%	7.7%	13.4%	8.8%	6.4%
TSR Delivered (annualised over the period)	%	6.0%	38.1%	34.6%	18.3%	7.7%	25.3%	30.0%	19.7%	20.2%
TSR Alpha (annualised over the period)	**%**	**15.8%**	**20.6%**	**16.4%**	**13.3%**	**3.8%**	**17.6%**	**16.7%**	**10.9%**	**13.8%**

Fig. A2.3 Commonwealth Bank 5-year TSR Alpha performance

Appendix 3: Economic Performance Scorecards

The *EP Bow Wave* concept introduced in Chapter 3 makes it possible to express the market capitalisation of any listed company at any point in terms of its three primary dimensions. They are its height (economic profitability), its width (book equity) and its length (sustainability of a positive economic profit stream).

Our firm has invested heavily in the development of a database and analytical structure that makes it possible to quickly construct *EP Bow Waves* and *Pairs of EP Bow Waves* for the top 500 listed companies in any developed economy. We have drawn on this capability to underpin the empirical analysis contained in this book, particularly as it relates to the largest companies listed in Australia on the ASX, in the United States on the NYSE, and in the United Kingdom on the LSE.

For the purposes of this book, we have limited our empirical analysis to the top 100 companies listed on each of these stock exchanges – even though the capability exists to include many more.

There are a number of aspects that underpin the *Economic Performance Scorecard* and analytical structure supporting the concepts and empirical analysis contained within this book.

The first aspect is the construction of a database containing the source data and intermediate calculations required to assess historical economic profit performance, and to support the creation of *EP Bow Waves* for individual companies over the five years ending 31 December 2010, 2011, 2012, 2013, 2014 and 2015.

D. Kilroy, M. Schneider, *Customer Value, Shareholder Wealth, Community Wellbeing*, DOI 10.1007/978-3-319-54774-9

For this purpose, we derived the bulk of our source data from Bloomberg LLP. We cross-checked with company annual reports and where necessary inserted missing or replaced erroneous source data.
The data sourced from Bloomberg included historical income statement (P&L) and balance sheet metrics, TSR metrics, bond yield metrics, market capitalisation metrics, and earnings forecast metrics.
From this source data, we have conducted intermediate calculations to determine for each company:

- The cost of equity (Ke);
- A time series of historical equity cash flows;
- A time series of historical PAT and Book Equity consistent with the resultant equity cash flow;
- A time series of historical economic profit (EP) delivered;
- A time series of historical earnings per share (EPS);
- The TSR, *TSR-Ke* and *TSR Alpha* delivered over various time horizons;
- The forward-looking consensus analyst forecasts for the next five years as at 31 December 2010, 2011, 2012, 2013, 2014 and 2015.

The second aspect is the construction of the *EP Bow Wave* model itself in a way that makes it possible to quickly produce a progression of five *EP Bow Waves* for a large sample of companies listed on multiple stock exchanges for each of the years ending 31 December 2010, 2011, 2012, 2013, 2014 and 2015.
The third aspect is the construction of a *Pair of EP Bows* and the mechanism with which to calculate the extent to which wealth was created over a five-year measurement period as a result of exceeding EP expectations over the measurement period, versus the extent to which wealth was created over a five-year measurement period as a result of the establishment of higher EP expectations to be delivered beyond the measurement period. These two sources of wealth creation correspond to the red and green areas in Fig. 3.4.
The fourth aspect is the mechanism with which to calculate how much of the wealth creation came from higher returns and growth expectations versus how much of the wealth creation came from an extension in the length of the *EP Bow Wave.*
The fifth aspect is the mechanism with which to demonstrate the alignment between wealth creation outcomes drives from the *Pair of EP Bow Waves* with the wealth creation outcomes observed from the capital markets –

namely *TSR-Ke,* and the components of *TSR-Ke* that relate to market movements and from earning a positive *TSR Alpha.*

The creation of the database and analytical structures represents a significant break-through in terms of:

- Understanding the drivers of shareholder wealth creation and the requirement to create wealth on an ongoing basis;
- Linking performance in the market for a company's products and services with the wealth creation outcomes experienced by their shareholders;
- Demonstrating why it is imperative to focus on the long-term and why short-termism makes no sense at all;
- Understanding the performance required to be delivered over the next five years, as well as the length of time over which it is necessary to hold back the forces of competition beyond the next five years in order to at a minimum preserve shareholder wealth;
- Understanding the extent to which the current share price of a company may be influenced by either positive or negative sentiment;
- Understanding and quantifying the enormous wealth creation potential available as a result of investing in individual and organisational capabilities, in such a way as to extend the length of a company's *EP Bow Wave.*

The following tables contain *Economic Performance Scorecards* for the 100 largest companies listed on the ASX, the NYSE and the LSE over the five years to 31 December 2015. These scorecards reveal the dimensions of the *EP Bow Wave* for each company as at 31 December 2010 and 31 December 2015. They show how the change in shape of the *EP Bow Wave* can be used to determine the wealth created for shareholders over that five-year period. They also show how this wealth creation outcome can be derived directly from capital market performance using *TSR Alpha.*

The abbreviations used in the headings for each of the tables are explained below.

Capital market outcomes

TSR-Ke (%)	The economic return on the market value of equity, measured as total shareholder return (TSR) less the cost of equity capital (Ke)
Total WC ($m)	

(*continued*)

(continued)

	The total dollar amount of wealth that has been created over the five-year measurement period as a result of delivering a TSR greater than Ke
WC from MM ($m)	The component of the total wealth created as a result of positive or negative market movements.
WC from TSRA ($m)	The component of the total wealth created as a result of doing better than the market on a risk- adjusted basis (which we measure using TSR Alpha)
Bow wave as at 31 December 2010 (beginning of the measurement period)	
Book Equity ($m)	The book value of equity capital as at 31 December 2010
Average EPy (%)	The average forecast level of economic profitability (ROE-Ke) over the period from 2011 to 2015. This corresponds to the height of the *EP Bow Wave*
Average Growth (%)	The average forecast level of growth in the book value of equity over the period from 2011 to 2015. This corresponds to the change in the width of the *EP Bow Wave*.
BW Length (years)	The number of years of positive economic profits beyond 2015 required to justify the share price as at 31 December 2010, during which EPy is driven to zero and growth is driven to average economic growth of 2.5%
Market Value ($m)	The market value of equity as at 31 December 2010, being share price multiplied by number of shares
M:B Ratio (multiple)	The ratio of the market value of equity to the book value of equity. A high M:B ratio implies a strong *EP Bow Wave* (the combination of EPy, Growth and /or Length of the *EP Bow Wave*)
Bow wave as at 31 December 2015 (end of the measurement period)	
Book Equity ($m)	The book value of equity capital as at 31 December 2015
Average EPy (%)	The average forecast level of economic profitability (ROE-Ke) over the period from 2016 to 2020. This corresponds to the height of the *EP Bow Wave*
Average Growth (%)	The average forecast level of growth in the book value of equity over the period from 2016 to 2020. This corresponds to the change in the width of the *EP Bow Wave*.
BW Length (years)	The number of years of positive economic profits beyond 2020 required to justify the share price as at 31 December 2015, during which EPy is driven to zero and growth is driven to average economic growth of 2.5%

(continued)

(continued)

Market Value ($m)	The market value of equity as at 31 December 2015, being share price multiplied by number of shares
M:B Ratio (multiple)	The ratio of the market value of equity to the book value of equity. A high M:B ratio implies a strong *EP Bow Wave* (the combination of EPy, Growth and /or Length of the *EP Bow Wave*)

Results from pair of bow waves

Total WC ($m)	The total dollar amount of wealth that has been created over the five-year measurement period (sum of **red** and **green** areas in Fig. 3.4). This number is the same as that in the **Capital Market Outcomes**, but it is derived a different way
WC Meeting Expect ($m)	The component of the total wealth created arising as a consequence of meeting or exceeding the market's EP expectations over the measurement period (corresponding to the **red** area in Fig. 3.4)
WC New Expect ($m)	The component of the total wealth created arising as a consequence of creating new EP expectations to be delivered beyond the measurement period (corresponding to the **green** area in Fig. 3.4)
WC BW Length ($m)	The component of the wealth created from new expectations (the **green** area in Fig. 3.4) as a result of an increase in the length of the *EP Bow Wave* during the period between 2010 and 2015.
WC Returns /Growth ($m)	The component of the wealth created from new expectations (the **green** area in Fig. 3.4) as a result of an increase in expectations in relation to future returns and growth (or the underlying business economics) (Figs. A3.1, A3.2, and A3.3)

Num	Name	Ticker	Capital Market Outcomes				Bow Wave as at 31 December 2010						Bow Wave as at 31 December 2015						Results from Pair of Bow Waves				
			TSR-Ke (%)	Total WC ($m)	WC from MM ($m)	WC from TSRA ($m)	Book Equity ($m)	Average EPy (%)	Average Growth (%)	BW Length (years)	Market Value ($m)	M:B Ratio (multiple)	Book Equity ($m)	Average EPy (%)	Average Growth (%)	BW Length (years)	Market Value ($m)	M:B Ratio (multiple)	Total WC ($m)	WC Meeting Expect ($m)	WC New Expect ($m)	WC BW Length ($m)	WC Returns / Growth ($m)
1	Commonwealth Bank of Australia	CBA	7.8%	53,185	(24,342)	77,527	35,047	8.9%	4.9%	15	78,302	2.2	52,431	9.3%	5.0%	50	145,655	2.8	53,185	707	52,478	34,748	17,730
2	Westpac Banking Corporation	WBC	6.2%	35,354	(23,300)	58,654	38,189	5.0%	4.1%	10	66,453	1.7	53,098	5.5%	4.3%	50	111,948	2.1	35,354	3,157	32,198	23,034	9,164
3	BHP Billiton	BHP	(19.0%)	(252,352)	(92,026)	(160,326)	57,311	19.0%	12.5%	25	235,068	4.1	84,027	(3.4%)	4.0%	10	95,036	1.1	(252,352)	(61,628)	(190,723)	(1,081)	(189,643)
4	ANZ Banking Group	ANZ	(0.1%)	(337)	(21,253)	20,917	34,091	4.9%	8.2%	10	60,616	1.8	57,247	1.8%	6.6%	5	81,499	1.4	(337)	2,923	(3,260)	0	(3,260)
5	Rio Tinto	RIO	(18.9%)	(194,602)	(72,695)	(111,025)	56,932	14.3%	6.8%	30	167,698	2.9	51,233	1.1%	5.6%	20	80,398	1.6	(194,602)	(95,859)	(98,743)	(1,922)	(96,821)
6	National Australia Bank	NAB	3.4%	13,567	(17,214)	30,781	38,940	(0.6%)	2.7%	5	49,096	1.3	55,494	1.3%	3.2%	5	76,990	1.4	13,567	5,120	8,447	1,191	7,256
7	Telstra Corporation	TLS	13.8%	43,454	(6,877)	50,333	12,696	14.9%	6.0%	10	34,716	2.7	14,103	21.3%	7.5%	25	68,586	4.9	43,454	5,450	38,004	26,378	11,626
8	CSL	CSL	14.0%	26,151	(5,350)	31,501	4,215	17.1%	6.8%	40	19,652	4.7	3,564	43.5%	13.4%	35	48,739	13.7	26,151	(690)	26,841	0	26,841
9	Wesfarmers	WES	2.7%	7,198	(11,621)	18,818	24,694	0.1%	2.9%	10	33,143	1.3	24,781	3.5%	3.8%	50	46,759	1.9	7,198	(4,359)	11,556	8,410	3,146
10	Woolworths	WOW	(4.3%)	(9,439)	(7,714)	(1,724)	7,570	18.9%	7.1%	25	32,878	4.3	10,834	9.3%	4.7%	50	31,032	2.9	(9,439)	(2,899)	(6,539)	5,009	(11,548)
11	Macquarie Group	MQG	9.3%	11,186	(5,471)	16,657	11,232	(2.3%)	2.6%	5	12,620	1.1	13,909	5.1%	4.5%	50	28,167	2.0	11,186	767	10,419	6,601	3,818
12	Woodside Petroleum	WPL	(11.6%)	(25,486)	(14,453)	(11,033)	10,841	7.9%	10.4%	50	33,342	3.1	19,514	(1.7%)	5.5%	10	23,663	1.2	(25,486)	2,271	(27,757)	(323)	(27,434)
13	Brambles	BXB	6.4%	5,006	(2,560)	7,566	1,928	17.6%	6.9%	40	9,405	4.9	3,426	18.0%	7.1%	50	18,268	5.3	5,006	(831)	5,837	2,184	3,652
14	AMP	AMP	1.5%	1,386	(4,742)	6,128	2,938	17.9%	7.7%	25	10,940	3.7	8,519	6.4%	4.8%	50	17,244	2.0	1,386	1,945	(559)	1,207	(1,766)
15	QBE Insurance Group	QBE	(11.3%)	(13,210)	(5,913)	(7,297)	10,078	4.4%	12.2%	15	19,021	1.9	14,385	(1.5%)	7.5%	5	17,211	1.2	(13,210)	(5,263)	(7,947)	346	(8,293)
16	Suncorp Group	SUN	3.3%	2,958	(3,868)	6,827	13,933	(4.8%)	1.7%	40	11,033	0.8	13,483	(2.2%)	2.3%	5	15,619	1.2	2,958	(1,162)	4,120	1,546	2,574
17	Amcor	AMC	12.3%	8,010	(1,471)	9,482	4,068	6.9%	3.9%	5	7,427	1.8	1,902	37.2%	11.5%	20	15,565	8.2	8,010	(3,157)	11,168	8,652	2,515
18	Ramsay Health Care	RHC	23.9%	9,359	(713)	10,072	1,235	10.2%	4.8%	20	3,597	2.9	1,860	22.2%	7.8%	50	13,625	7.3	9,359	70	9,289	5,714	3,575
19	Insurance Australia Group	IAG	4.0%	2,570	(2,196)	4,766	4,486	4.7%	3.7%	15	8,067	1.8	6,817	4.4%	3.6%	50	13,516	2.0	2,570	(652)	3,222	2,043	1,179
20	AGL Energy	AGL	2.0%	1,031	(1,383)	2,414	5,800	(1.5%)	1.9%	5	6,979	1.2	8,806	0.3%	2.3%	15	12,199	1.4	1,031	(634)	1,665	623	1,041
21	Oil Search	OSH	(10.9%)	(6,234)	(2,873)	(3,361)	2,735	3.1%	11.2%	50	9,243	3.4	4,709	2.6%	10.7%	40	10,202	2.2	(6,234)	(1,593)	(4,641)	(375)	(4,266)
22	Caltex Australia	CTX	11.7%	4,442	(1,519)	5,961	3,071	(0.6%)	5.8%	5	3,880	1.3	2,776	10.2%	11.2%	50	10,179	3.7	4,442	(1,755)	6,197	4,959	1,238
23	Newcrest Mining	NCM	(29.5%)	(41,833)	(10,852)	(30,981)	4,954	17.0%	14.2%	35	30,950	6.2	8,918	(2.9%)	4.3%	5	9,935	1.1	(41,833)	(6,551)	(35,282)	1,115	(36,398)
24	Aurizon Holdings	AZJ	3.5%	1,806	(1,574)	3,380	2,684	5.6%	3.8%	35	6,710	2.5	6,506	0.4%	2.5%	30	9,169	1.4	1,806	4,002	(2,197)	0	(2,197)
25	Crown Resorts	CWN	0.5%	240	(2,712)	2,952	3,419	2.5%	7.7%	40	6,257	1.8	4,525	3.8%	8.3%	40	9,105	2.0	240	(341)	581	181	400
26	Asciano	AIO	1.2%	490	(2,225)	2,714	2,630	2.1%	7.8%	35	4,667	1.8	3,950	5.5%	9.5%	50	8,525	2.2	490	(1,085)	1,575	564	1,011
27	Qantas Airways	QAN	(5.0%)	(2,167)	(2,742)	575	5,939	(4.3%)	2.3%	20	5,753	1.0	3,442	10.7%	16.9%	25	8,422	2.4	(2,167)	(6,502)	4,335	601	3,734
28	CIMIC Group	CIM	(13.6%)	(8,794)	(5,366)	(3,428)	2,565	11.6%	13.2%	50	9,472	3.7	4,093	6.2%	10.5%	35	8,226	2.0	(8,794)	(2,565)	(6,229)	(215)	(6,014)
29	Origin Energy	ORG	(21.2%)	(15,324)	(3,459)	(11,866)	10,249	0.6%	2.5%	20	14,741	1.4	12,723	(5.7%)	1.0%	40	8,224	0.6	(15,324)	(5,501)	(9,824)	(1,982)	(7,842)
30	ASX	ASX	(1.9%)	(933)	(2,051)	1,118	2,921	6.1%	4.2%	50	6,599	2.3	3,760	5.9%	4.2%	50	8,220	2.2	(933)	(1,165)	232	93	139
31	TPG Telecom	TPM	30.3%	5,654	(768)	6,422	445	6.0%	14.9%	35	1,252	2.8	1,003	16.5%	22.3%	50	7,851	7.8	5,654	153	5,501	2,392	3,108
32	Sonic Healthcare	SHL	6.2%	2,199	(893)	3,092	2,556	3.2%	4.8%	20	4,506	1.8	3,274	4.3%	5.3%	50	7,387	2.3	2,199	195	2,003	1,388	615
33	REA Group	REA	24.4%	4,758	(627)	5,385	135	21.6%	20.3%	35	1,600	11.9	558	19.4%	18.9%	50	7,256	13.0	4,758	345	4,413	2,883	1,530
34	Coca-Cola Amatil	CCL	(6.2%)	(3,179)	(1,626)	(1,552)	1,833	19.1%	2.8%	45	8,210	4.5	2,086	14.8%	2.4%	35	7,101	3.4	(3,179)	(1,466)	(1,713)	(193)	(1,520)
35	Incitec Pivot	IPL	(7.4%)	(3,215)	(2,261)	(953)	3,609	3.0%	5.8%	45	6,450	1.8	4,685	0.6%	4.8%	30	6,681	1.4	(3,215)	(1,716)	(1,498)	(78)	(1,420)
36	Aristocrat Leisure	ALL	20.8%	3,712	(560)	4,272	190	12.3%	15.5%	50	1,597	8.4	917	13.2%	16.1%	50	6,505	7.1	3,712	317	3,395	526	2,869
37	Santos	STO	(29.5%)	(15,973)	(4,505)	(11,469)	7,605	(2.0%)	7.1%	35	11,506	1.5	10,202	(11.2%)	0.7%	5	6,500	0.6	(15,973)	(4,599)	(11,374)	3,816	(15,190)
38	Tatts Group	TTS	9.2%	2,567	(665)	3,232	2,468	0.9%	3.4%	25	3,356	1.4	2,971	4.3%	4.6%	50	6,429	2.2	2,567	1	2,565	853	1,712
39	Computershare	CPU	(6.5%)	(2,669)	(2,100)	(569)	1,254	13.8%	10.1%	50	5,990	4.8	1,510	12.9%	9.8%	50	6,379	4.2	(2,669)	(1,111)	(1,558)	228	(1,786)
40	Fortescue Metals Group	FMG	(32.0%)	(33,426)	(12,484)	(20,943)	1,744	16.0%	25.1%	50	20,357	11.7	9,761	(12.8%)	2.1%	5	5,823	0.6	(33,426)	5,318	(38,744)	3,920	(42,664)
41	Orica	ORI	(13.8%)	(7,693)	(3,530)	(4,163)	3,523	5.9%	9.0%	45	9,016	2.6	2,985	3.9%	8.0%	40	5,788	1.9	(7,693)	(2,995)	(4,698)	0	(4,698)
42	Bendigo and Adelaide Bank	BEN	(1.3%)	(351)	(1,127)	777	3,735	(5.4%)	1.4%	5	3,626	1.0	4,942	(2.4%)	2.1%	20	5,484	1.1	(351)	(71)	(280)	(322)	42
43	Cochlear	COH	(3.4%)	(1,092)	(1,417)	325	438	60.8%	3.6%	40	4,557	10.4	355	36.0%	14.0%	50	5,466	15.4	(1,092)	(1,625)	533	1,326	(793)
44	Seek	SEK	7.1%	1,514	(1,163)	2,676	353	13.4%	16.5%	50	2,232	6.3	1,134	10.8%	15.0%	50	5,292	4.7	1,514	470	1,044	273	771
45	AusNet Services	AST	12.4%	2,569	(392)	2,962	2,774	(6.4%)	0.5%	5	2,411	0.9	3,249	2.6%	2.7%	20	5,253	1.6	2,569	1,018	1,551	557	994
46	Bank of Queensland	BOQ	4.7%	899	(365)	1,763	2,405	(5.5%)	1.7%	10	2,209	0.9	3,469	1.4%	3.4%	50	5,239	1.5	899	(550)	1,449	400	1,049
47	Domino's Pizza Enterprises	DMP	53.8%	4,390	(117)	4,507	100	14.8%	6.2%	50	428	4.3	305	38.6%	12.2%	50	5,053	16.6	4,390	35	4,355	412	3,943
48	Challenger	CGF	6.1%	1,306	(1,186)	2,492	1,340	3.5%	4.4%	50	2,277	1.7	2,543	5.0%	4.8%	50	4,902	1.9	1,306	51	1,255	33	1,222
49	Platinum Asset Management	PTM	5.7%	1,303	(763)	2,066	225	55.4%	6.6%	50	2,801	12.4	349	59.9%	7.0%	50	4,740	13.6	1,303	(35)	1,338	191	1,147
50	Harvey Norman Holdings	HVN	0.5%	116	(1,354)	1,470	2,103	1.5%	3.6%	20	3,123	1.5	2,537	4.5%	4.3%	30	4,642	1.8	116	(777)	893	275	618

Fig. A3.1 Bow wave summary for the 100 largest ASX listed companies (Sorted by December 2015 market capitalisation)

Num	Name	Ticker	Capital Market Outcomes: TSR-Ke (%)	Capital Market Outcomes: Total WC ($m)	Capital Market Outcomes: WC from MM ($m)	Capital Market Outcomes: WC from TSRA ($m)	Bow Wave as at 31 December 2010: Book Equity ($m)	Bow Wave as at 31 December 2010: Average EPy (%)	Bow Wave as at 31 December 2010: Average Growth (%)	Bow Wave as at 31 December 2010: BW Length (years)	Bow Wave as at 31 December 2010: Market Value ($m)	Bow Wave as at 31 December 2010: M:B Ratio (multiple)
51	Boral	BLD	(9.5%)	(2,268)	(1,517)	(751)	2,624	(0.9%)	5.3%	15	3,499	1.3
52	Magellan Financial Group	MFG	66.7%	4,118	(115)	4,232	111	7.0%	8.2%	20	241	2.2
53	Washington H. Soul Pattinson & Company	SOL	2.0%	470	(819)	1,289	2,780	(2.1%)	2.0%	40	3,007	1.1
54	Flight Centre Travel Group	FLT	0.9%	182	(1,288)	1,470	711	15.4%	7.4%	50	2,473	3.5
55	Tabcorp Holdings	TAH	5.3%	953	(667)	1,621	3,455	(11.1%)	(0.1%)	5	2,147	0.6
56	BT Investment Management	BTT	48.1%	3,283	(171)	3,455	282	(0.9%)	6.3%	25	360	1.3
57	Blackmores	BKL	43.3%	3,166	(110)	3,276	72	21.3%	7.7%	50	469	6.5
58	Reece	REH	2.4%	394	(520)	913	595	8.6%	9.1%	50	2,215	3.7
59	Ansell	ANN	3.8%	511	(459)	970	651	8.0%	4.5%	45	1,687	2.6
60	Alumina	AWC	(27.0%)	(8,456)	(2,884)	(5,572)	3,002	2.2%	15.7%	35	6,052	2.0
61	Adelaide Brighton	ABC	(0.5%)	(86)	(821)	735	931	6.8%	4.7%	45	2,096	2.3
62	IOOF Holdings	IFL	3.6%	549	(705)	1,254	870	5.8%	4.5%	40	1,801	2.1
63	Carsales.com	CAR	13.0%	1,389	(386)	1,775	89	36.0%	11.9%	50	1,100	12.4
64	Event Hospitality and Entertainment	EVT	15.8%	1,529	(205)	1,734	760	0.5%	2.3%	20	1,033	1.4
65	Dulux Group	DLX	15.1%	1,412	(200)	1,612	85	19.5%	14.2%	50	1,011	11.9
66	Iluka Resources	ILU	(11.9%)	(2,828)	(1,331)	(1,497)	1,125	11.2%	5.7%	50	3,797	3.4
67	Qube Holdings	QUB	15.6%	1,030	(247)	1,278	444	0.9%	6.5%	25	632	1.4
68	BlueScope Steel	BSL	(28.6%)	(6,127)	(2,159)	(3,968)	5,661	(8.6%)	5.5%	10	4,145	0.7
69	Brickworks	BKW	1.7%	203	(388)	591	1,650	(3.3%)	1.9%	15	1,653	1.0
70	AP Eagers	APE	33.8%	1,832	(122)	1,954	360	(2.8%)	2.0%	10	393	1.1
71	Sirtex Medical	SRX	34.7%	1,709	(132)	1,841	52	12.2%	17.0%	50	337	6.5
72	Super Retail Group	SUL	11.1%	835	(304)	1,139	271	10.0%	5.5%	50	777	2.9
73	Premier Investments	PMV	11.3%	1,048	(376)	1,424	1,212	(7.2%)	1.2%	10	961	0.8
74	Nufarm	NUF	1.2%	120	(366)	486	1,749	(6.9%)	1.6%	10	1,346	0.8
75	Fairfax Media	FXJ	(13.4%)	(2,891)	(1,569)	(1,321)	5,298	(10.1%)	0.8%	10	3,293	0.6
76	Perpetual	PPT	3.6%	402	(603)	1,006	359	14.4%	7.0%	50	1,265	3.5
77	M2 Group	MTU	31.7%	1,551	(115)	1,665	77	11.5%	11.2%	50	368	4.8
78	Evolution Mining	EVN	23.4%	965	(124)	1,089	139	5.9%	13.9%	30	352	2.5
79	Graincorp	GNC	3.7%	380	(355)	735	1,283	(3.0%)	2.9%	20	1,304	1.0
80	JB Hi-Fi	JBH	(4.3%)	(621)	(765)	144	293	25.6%	9.4%	50	1,955	6.7
81	ALS	ALQ	22.2%	1,355	(237)	1,592	628	(8.9%)	1.1%	5	498	0.8
82	Navitas	NVT	(1.2%)	(121)	(387)	266	105	103.6%	0.0%	50	1,423	13.5
83	Northern Star Resources	NST	49.2%	1,254	(95)	1,349	5	65.0%	41.5%	50	116	22.9
84	Seven Group Holdings	SVW	(11.6%)	(2,110)	(1,281)	(829)	2,740	(5.0%)	2.1%	10	2,688	1.0
85	Virgin Australia Holdings	VAH	(10.4%)	(667)	(412)	(255)	933	(2.8%)	10.0%	30	950	1.0
86	Iress	IRE	(0.8%)	(68)	(342)	273	138	41.0%	5.2%	50	1,099	8.0
87	Downer Group	DOW	(13.5%)	(1,389)	(751)	(638)	1,243	(0.5%)	6.5%	15	1,575	1.3
88	Technology One	TNE	31.3%	1,203	(90)	1,293	63	16.2%	8.1%	50	291	4.6
89	nib Holdings	NHF	18.1%	1,139	(168)	1,306	391	2.4%	3.1%	20	616	1.6
90	New Hope Group	NHC	(17.6%)	(4,104)	(1,576)	(2,527)	2,340	3.1%	0.0%	50	4,027	1.7
91	Metcash	MTS	(13.5%)	(2,349)	(626)	(1,723)	1,318	7.5%	4.1%	30	3,159	2.4
92	Sims Metal Management	SGM	(28.6%)	(6,197)	(1,916)	(4,281)	3,279	(1.1%)	10.5%	20	4,420	1.3
93	CSR	CSR	(26.4%)	(10,034)	(2,995)	(7,039)	1,683	12.0%	9.7%	50	7,650	4.5
94	Automotive Holdings Group	AHG	8.0%	434	(289)	723	377	1.8%	4.0%	25	555	1.5
95	G8 Education	GEM	12.8%	199	(66)	265	84	3.0%	12.6%	20	153	1.8
96	Invocare	IVC	6.8%	407	(173)	581	96	23.5%	8.3%	50	738	7.7
97	Independence Group	IGO	(18.7%)	(1,327)	(677)	(650)	215	14.1%	20.6%	50	1,103	5.1
98	ARB Corporation	ARB	11.0%	537	(166)	703	111	10.5%	11.7%	50	533	4.8
99	Corporate Travel Management	CTD	43.1%	934	(68)	1,002	12	27.3%	16.8%	50	120	10.2
100	Vocus Communications	VOC	46.1%	569	(20)	590	10	10.5%	19.7%	40	74	7.5

Num	Ticker	Bow Wave as at 31 December 2015: Book Equity ($m)	Bow Wave as at 31 December 2015: Average EPy (%)	Bow Wave as at 31 December 2015: Average Growth (%)	Bow Wave as at 31 December 2015: BW Length (years)	Bow Wave as at 31 December 2015: Market Value ($m)	Bow Wave as at 31 December 2015: M:B Ratio (multiple)	Results from Pair of Bow Waves: Total WC ($m)	Results from Pair of Bow Waves: WC Meeting Expect ($m)	Results from Pair of Bow Waves: WC New Expect ($m)	Results from Pair of Bow Waves: WC BW Length ($m)	Results from Pair of Bow Waves: WC Returns / Growth ($m)
51	BLD	3,524	(1.3%)	5.2%	15	4,395	1.2	(2,268)	(1,673)	(594)	19	(613)
52	MFG	303	30.5%	17.6%	50	4,376	14.4	4,118	200	3,917	2,503	1,414
53	SOL	3,027	(0.6%)	2.4%	50	4,185	1.4	470	(255)	725	52	674
54	FLT	1,270	14.0%	7.0%	50	4,022	3.2	182	(340)	521	59	462
55	TAH	1,690	6.1%	4.2%	50	3,916	2.3	953	(1,059)	2,012	1,196	816
56	BTT	762	13.9%	13.7%	50	3,840	5.0	3,283	332	2,951	1,219	1,732
57	BKL	133	48.2%	14.4%	50	3,755	28.2	3,166	30	3,136	415	2,721
58	REH	926	8.4%	9.0%	50	3,405	3.7	394	(11)	405	141	264
59	ANN	1,494	6.0%	4.0%	40	3,242	2.2	511	(74)	584	0	584
60	AWC	2,715	(2.4%)	11.0%	20	3,241	1.2	(8,456)	(3,826)	(4,631)	(34)	(4,596)
61	ABC	1,205	9.0%	5.3%	45	3,082	2.6	(86)	(608)	522	48	474
62	IFL	1,363	6.1%	4.6%	40	2,850	2.1	549	129	420	39	381
63	CAR	227	37.3%	12.2%	50	2,813	12.4	1,389	224	1,165	174	991
64	EVT	963	7.6%	4.1%	50	2,610	2.7	1,529	179	1,350	540	810
65	DLX	350	15.6%	12.2%	50	2,588	7.4	1,412	434	977	194	783
66	ILU	1,409	4.5%	4.0%	30	2,559	1.8	(2,828)	(610)	(2,218)	(82)	(2,137)
67	QUB	1,398	2.5%	7.3%	40	2,536	1.8	1,030	134	896	202	694
68	BSL	4,276	(9.6%)	4.5%	10	2,531	0.6	(6,127)	(3,769)	(2,358)	(518)	(1,840)
69	BKW	1,824	(0.5%)	2.7%	20	2,334	1.3	203	(93)	295	7	288
70	APE	695	11.6%	5.6%	50	2,275	3.3	1,832	332	1,500	799	701
71	SRX	145	16.6%	20.1%	50	2,264	15.7	1,709	33	1,676	309	1,368
72	SUL	768	10.6%	5.7%	50	2,248	2.9	835	(30)	864	37	828
73	PMV	1,338	1.9%	3.5%	30	2,221	1.7	1,048	202	846	284	562
74	NUF	1,632	(0.3%)	4.9%	25	2,216	1.4	120	(404)	524	100	424
75	FXJ	1,946	(3.2%)	2.6%	20	2,116	1.1	(2,891)	(3,526)	635	(75)	710
76	PPT	584	15.3%	7.2%	50	2,104	3.6	402	42	361	40	321
77	MTU	366	13.9%	12.4%	50	2,098	5.7	1,551	220	1,331	121	1,209
78	EVN	1,125	2.3%	11.1%	30	2,034	1.8	965	347	619	62	556
79	GNC	1,822	(2.8%)	3.0%	20	1,973	1.1	380	405	(25)	(23)	(2)
80	JBH	343	23.8%	9.0%	50	1,930	5.6	(621)	(9)	(612)	59	(672)
81	ALQ	1,216	0.6%	3.5%	30	1,901	1.6	1,355	758	597	308	289
82	NVT	211	60.1%	0.0%	50	1,759	8.3	(121)	(404)	282	25	258
83	NST	323	19.2%	18.6%	50	1,668	5.2	1,254	107	1,147	62	1,085
84	SVW	2,797	(10.6%)	0.7%	10	1,638	0.6	(2,110)	(429)	(1,681)	(301)	(1,381)
85	VAH	1,077	(0.4%)	12.4%	35	1,603	1.5	(667)	(961)	294	62	232
86	IRE	339	24.7%	3.6%	50	1,580	4.7	(68)	(213)	145	28	117
87	DOW	2,035	(7.4%)	3.0%	10	1,551	0.8	(1,389)	(405)	(984)	0	(984)
88	TNE	118	32.7%	13.1%	50	1,541	13.1	1,203	60	1,142	115	1,027
89	NHF	345	16.5%	6.7%	50	1,541	4.5	1,139	176	963	453	510
90	NHC	1,853	(8.1%)	0.0%	5	1,533	0.8	(4,104)	(1,875)	(2,228)	533	(2,761)
91	MTS	1,149	0.0%	2.2%	10	1,499	1.3	(2,349)	(830)	(1,519)	(4)	(1,515)
92	SGM	2,113	(8.2%)	4.2%	10	1,476	0.7	(6,197)	(3,266)	(2,930)	165	(3,096)
93	CSR	1,146	(0.6%)	4.6%	10	1,462	1.3	(10,034)	(1,805)	(8,229)	(12)	(8,217)
94	AHG	672	6.3%	5.1%	50	1,386	2.1	434	(76)	510	106	404
95	GEM	603	4.4%	13.8%	30	1,331	2.2	199	(430)	629	189	440
96	IVC	202	22.5%	8.0%	50	1,316	6.5	407	97	310	56	254
97	IGO	665	1.7%	12.0%	20	1,299	2.0	(1,327)	(495)	(832)	(400)	(431)
98	ARB	226	13.0%	13.1%	50	1,278	5.6	537	77	461	78	383
99	CTD	223	20.3%	14.0%	50	1,274	5.7	934	62	872	51	821
100	VOC	196	7.1%	16.4%	30	793	4.0	569	67	502	(104)	606

Fig. A3.1 (Continued)

			Capital Market Outcomes				Bow Wave as at 31 December 2010						Bow Wave as at 31 December 2015						Results from Pair of Bow Waves				
Num	Name	Ticker	TSR-Ke (%)	Total WC ($m)	WC from MM ($m)	WC from TSRA ($m)	Book Equity ($m)	Average EPy (%)	Average Growth (%)	BW Length (years)	Market Value ($m)	M:B Ratio (multiple)	Book Equity ($m)	Average EPy (%)	Average Growth (%)	BW Length (years)	Market Value ($m)	M:B Ratio (multiple)	Total WC ($m)	WC Meeting Expect ($m)	WC New Expect ($m)	WC BW Length ($m)	WC Returns / Growth ($m)
1	Apple	AAPL	8.3%	220,070	73,532	146,538	47,791	21.1%	26.0%	25	297,089	6.2	119,355	33.1%	6.7%	35	583,613	4.9	220,070	80,616	139,454	95,967	43,487
2	Alphabet	GOOGL	11.5%	202,118	42,157	159,961	36,004	9.5%	18.1%	45	191,028	5.3	120,331	9.8%	18.4%	40	534,764	4.4	202,118	15,547	186,571	0	186,571
3	Microsoft	MSFT	7.2%	139,813	45,757	94,056	39,558	34.4%	15.5%	20	234,528	5.9	80,083	18.6%	10.0%	50	439,679	5.5	139,813	(16,905)	156,718	196,975	(40,257)
4	Berkshire Hathaway	BRK/A	(0.1%)	(1,468)	24,906	(26,376)	131,102	2.1%	7.1%	50	198,514	1.5	255,550	0.6%	6.1%	50	324,985	1.3	(1,468)	9,733	(11,201)	4,820	(16,022)
5	Exxon Mobil	XOM	(5.4%)	(123,327)	53,710	(177,036)	110,569	14.3%	3.4%	50	364,064	3.3	170,811	8.4%	2.6%	20	323,960	1.9	(123,327)	9,823	(133,150)	(62,668)	(70,482)
6	Amazon.com	AMZN	20.6%	182,106	17,915	164,191	5,257	22.9%	30.2%	25	81,180	15.4	13,384	20.8%	28.3%	35	318,344	23.8	182,106	(9,777)	191,883	196,643	(4,760)
7	General Electric	GE	1.2%	18,019	53,512	(35,493)	117,291	7.0%	3.8%	30	194,155	1.7	98,274	14.3%	5.2%	50	292,165	3.0	18,019	(95,225)	113,244	44,046	69,198
8	Johnson & Johnson	JNJ	7.0%	93,026	21,322	71,703	50,588	17.3%	5.1%	30	169,946	3.4	71,150	17.7%	5.2%	50	284,255	4.0	93,026	(548)	93,573	61,738	31,835
9	Wells Fargo	WFC	2.3%	29,356	35,989	(6,633)	111,786	5.9%	8.3%	10	163,078	1.5	192,998	3.6%	3.6%	50	276,808	1.4	29,356	(16,526)	45,881	46,759	(877)
10	JPMorgan Chase	JPM	(0.9%)	(10,731)	41,056	(51,786)	165,365	(0.2%)	4.4%	5	165,875	1.0	247,573	(0.5%)	4.3%	5	241,899	1.0	(10,731)	(82)	(10,649)	(904)	(9,745)
11	The Procter & Gamble Company	PG	0.8%	9,909	22,605	(12,695)	63,099	12.5%	4.1%	40	180,174	2.9	62,419	15.3%	4.7%	50	214,770	3.4	9,909	(19,797)	29,706	22,584	7,123
12	AT&T	T	2.0%	25,747	25,621	126	101,564	7.0%	4.7%	20	173,668	1.7	122,671	5.6%	4.3%	35	211,447	1.7	25,747	215	25,532	28,280	(2,748)
13	Pfizer	PFE	6.9%	77,322	20,697	56,626	90,014	8.5%	2.6%	10	140,290	1.6	64,720	14.5%	3.5%	50	199,329	3.1	77,322	(29,076)	106,398	81,617	24,780
14	Wal-Mart Stores	WMT	(0.3%)	(3,429)	16,348	(19,762)	65,285	12.0%	6.6%	30	193,231	3.0	81,394	11.2%	6.3%	25	196,773	2.4	(3,429)	7,686	(11,114)	0	(11,114)
15	Verizon Communications	VZ	10.3%	85,608	12,691	72,916	41,382	10.5%	5.6%	25	101,151	2.4	16,428	47.2%	16.6%	30	188,262	11.5	85,608	(26,314)	111,922	49,751	62,170
16	The Coca-Cola Company	KO	0.1%	1,412	18,913	(17,500)	24,799	29.2%	5.6%	50	150,745	6.1	25,554	33.3%	4.1%	50	185,759	7.3	1,412	(20,434)	21,846	7,854	13,993
17	Bank of America	BAC	(6.4%)	(61,549)	41,039	(102,588)	231,444	(5.8%)	4.1%	25	134,536	0.6	256,205	(5.7%)	2.8%	15	174,700	0.7	(61,549)	(61,273)	(276)	5,572	(5,848)
18	Chevron	CVX	(6.2%)	(72,563)	31,275	(103,838)	91,914	7.6%	2.5%	40	183,183	2.0	152,716	0.2%	1.4%	15	169,378	1.1	(72,563)	10,331	(82,894)	(12,099)	(70,795)
19	The Walt Disney Company	DIS	11.9%	78,719	15,702	63,016	33,734	9.8%	6.1%	30	71,153	2.1	44,525	13.8%	7.3%	50	168,128	3.8	78,719	(5,677)	84,396	39,178	45,218
20	Home Depot	HD	19.5%	114,192	9,829	104,364	17,777	17.5%	4.0%	35	57,569	3.2	9,322	55.9%	9.8%	50	167,693	18.0	114,192	(1,858)	116,050	54,317	61,733
21	Intel	INTC	2.3%	21,169	25,576	(4,407)	41,704	14.9%	7.7%	30	115,896	2.8	61,982	11.7%	6.7%	50	162,776	2.6	21,169	(802)	21,971	24,872	(2,901)
22	Oracle	ORCL	(7.3%)	(75,672)	34,889	(110,561)	25,090	36.6%	4.7%	50	158,096	6.3	48,663	20.1%	3.1%	40	153,718	3.2	(75,672)	(20,803)	(54,868)	(3,381)	(51,487)
23	Citigroup	C	(14.5%)	(126,941)	46,158	(173,099)	152,700	(2.3%)	6.0%	5	137,446	0.9	221,857	(5.3%)	4.4%	10	152,832	0.7	(126,941)	(59,178)	(67,763)	(24,731)	(43,032)
24	Merck & Co	MRK	4.3%	35,890	16,387	19,503	59,058	13.3%	1.1%	10	111,079	1.9	44,676	18.2%	1.3%	50	146,899	3.3	35,890	(34,686)	70,575	58,035	12,540
25	Pepsico	PEP	3.0%	22,615	12,959	9,656	16,804	32.4%	8.1%	30	103,287	6.1	11,923	49.2%	11.4%	35	144,684	12.1	22,615	(19,976)	42,591	31,801	10,790
26	Gilead Sciences	GILD	33.2%	120,651	3,647	117,002	6,367	32.1%	18.1%	10	29,064	4.6	18,534	42.5%	22.8%	15	143,892	7.8	120,651	11,829	108,822	58,143	50,678
27	Cisco Systems	CSCO	(3.2%)	(26,029)	27,925	(53,954)	38,647	13.6%	5.0%	50	112,823	2.9	59,698	11.2%	4.5%	50	138,002	2.3	(26,029)	(12,675)	(13,354)	2,205	(15,559)
28	Comcast Corporation	CMCSA	12.3%	68,490	11,901	56,589	42,721	5.3%	2.3%	10	61,000	1.4	52,269	13.0%	3.4%	50	137,825	2.6	68,490	(1,370)	69,860	48,939	20,921
29	IBM	IBM	(4.5%)	(52,641)	26,588	(79,228)	22,637	46.8%	16.6%	20	180,220	8.0	14,262	65.6%	22.3%	10	132,904	9.3	(52,641)	(18,897)	(33,744)	(43,817)	10,073
30	Allergan	AGN	69.3%	104,318	815	103,500	3,023	14.8%	3.4%	10	6,498	2.1	76,591	3.1%	3.3%	40	123,281	1.6	104,318	59,993	44,326	31,303	13,023
31	Amgen	AMGN	15.4%	71,321	6,420	64,901	22,667	15.0%	9.2%	10	51,167	2.3	28,083	19.8%	11.2%	25	122,397	4.4	71,321	(4,831)	76,153	56,037	20,116
32	Bristol-Myers Squibb	BMY	14.9%	61,290	6,637	54,652	14,843	17.7%	7.9%	25	44,990	3.0	14,266	21.7%	9.1%	50	114,260	8.0	61,290	(11,339)	72,629	52,492	20,138
33	Altria Group	MO	14.0%	63,554	6,452	57,102	4,069	89.9%	14.7%	15	51,425	12.6	2,880	145.8%	23.1%	20	114,095	39.6	63,554	(6,398)	69,953	52,947	17,005
34	UnitedHealth Group	UNH	17.7%	68,276	6,695	61,581	23,606	11.9%	4.2%	5	39,215	1.7	33,830	13.8%	4.6%	50	112,111	3.3	68,276	(3,846)	72,123	59,044	13,079
35	Medtronic	MDT	15.3%	57,453	6,798	50,655	13,182	20.1%	8.8%	15	39,815	3.0	53,230	4.8%	7.1%	50	108,161	2.0	57,453	25,297	32,156	32,880	(724)
36	CVS Health	CVS	13.4%	57,763	8,091	49,672	35,768	4.7%	2.1%	10	47,392	1.3	37,196	13.3%	3.4%	50	107,645	2.9	57,763	(4,818)	62,581	42,721	19,860
37	McDonald's	MCD	3.7%	21,989	10,147	11,842	14,034	28.4%	7.3%	40	80,874	5.8	7,088	52.0%	12.0%	45	107,129	15.1	21,989	(6,538)	28,527	19,528	8,999
38	Nike	NKE	14.4%	54,819	6,978	47,841	8,693	22.2%	7.9%	35	40,873	4.7	12,707	28.0%	9.3%	50	106,688	8.4	54,819	(2,212)	57,031	29,455	27,576
39	Boeing	BA	9.4%	39,936	10,589	29,347	2,128	106.5%	29.3%	15	47,983	22.5	6,335	62.6%	18.3%	30	96,387	15.2	39,936	1,914	38,022	49,857	(11,835)
40	Celgene	CELG	21.6%	62,300	4,104	58,196	4,395	34.9%	13.1%	15	27,819	6.3	5,919	73.2%	20.5%	15	94,203	15.9	62,300	(1,897)	64,198	27,243	36,955
41	Eli Lilly and Company	LLY	12.7%	45,088	5,961	39,127	9,524	19.7%	8.5%	35	40,407	4.2	14,571	21.1%	8.9%	40	93,130	6.4	45,088	235	44,854	16,159	28,695
42	Walgreens Boots Alliance	WBA	13.5%	45,465	7,011	38,453	14,376	8.7%	8.4%	45	35,937	2.5	30,861	10.8%	7.3%	50	92,449	3.0	45,465	9,754	35,711	6,606	29,105
43	3M	MMM	4.3%	20,553	10,490	10,062	12,764	27.4%	7.3%	30	61,444	4.8	11,708	32.6%	8.4%	50	91,789	7.8	20,553	(7,445)	27,997	27,601	396
44	Starbucks	SBUX	21.8%	56,297	4,655	51,642	3,046	35.2%	11.3%	35	23,860	7.8	5,818	41.6%	12.9%	50	89,181	15.3	56,297	(1,570)	57,866	31,368	26,498
45	Schlumberger	SLB	(15.3%)	(101,222)	28,128	(129,350)	19,120	20.3%	9.5%	50	113,644	5.9	35,633	8.3%	5.9%	40	87,606	2.5	(101,222)	(19,967)	(81,255)	(2,908)	(78,347)
46	United Parcel Service	UPS	(0.0%)	(17)	12,280	(12,297)	7,630	45.5%	11.0%	35	71,927	9.4	2,470	119.1%	25.7%	25	85,260	34.5	(17)	(7,968)	7,951	(20,157)	28,108
47	United Technologies	UTX	(2.6%)	(13,310)	14,149	(27,459)	20,066	11.7%	9.8%	50	72,522	3.6	27,358	10.9%	9.4%	40	80,540	2.9	(13,310)	893	(14,203)	(3,914)	(10,289)
48	Honeywell International	HON	5.2%	18,200	10,302	7,897	8,844	31.4%	10.7%	20	41,624	4.7	18,283	20.9%	8.1%	50	79,790	4.4	18,200	(8,401)	26,601	26,920	(318)
49	Goldman Sachs	GS	(9.4%)	(57,293)	25,347	(82,640)	70,714	3.3%	3.1%	30	91,967	1.3	86,728	(1.9%)	2.0%	35	75,603	0.9	(57,293)	(24,327)	(32,966)	(687)	(32,280)
50	Qualcomm	QCOM	(6.7%)	(35,823)	17,846	(53,669)	20,316	17.8%	7.1%	50	80,867	4.0	31,421	11.4%	5.5%	30	74,728	2.4	(35,823)	(3,861)	(31,963)	(7,796)	(24,167)

Fig. A3.2 Bow wave summary for the 100 largest NYSE listed companies (Sorted by December 2015 market capitalisation)

			Capital Market Outcomes				Bow Wave as at 31 December 2010						Bow Wave as at 31 December 2015						Results from Pair of Bow Waves				
Num	Name	Ticker	TSR-Ke (%)	Total WC ($m)	WC from MM ($m)	WC from TSRA ($m)	Book Equity ($m)	Average EPy (%)	Average Growth (%)	BW Length (years)	Market Value ($m)	M:B Ratio (multiple)	Book Equity ($m)	Average EPy (%)	Average Growth (%)	BW Length (years)	Market Value ($m)	M:B Ratio (multiple)	Total WC ($m)	WC Meeting Expect ($m)	WC New Expect ($m)	WC BW Length ($m)	WC Returns / Growth ($m)
51	U.S. Bancorp	USB	(0.1%)	(562)	10,108	(10,670)	25,963	6.5%	5.8%	50	51,807	2.0	46,131	4.7%	5.2%	40	74,467	1.6	(562)	1,468	(2,030)	(1,277)	(753)
52	American International Group	AIG	49.9%	65,770	2,277	63,493	69,824	(12.8%)	0.2%	50	6,780	0.1	89,658	(4.0%)	4.6%	5	73,987	0.8	65,770	22,243	43,527	7,663	35,864
53	Costco Wholesale	COST	11.9%	32,527	4,648	27,878	10,024	10.0%	10.3%	35	31,508	3.1	10,617	15.3%	13.2%	50	71,024	6.7	32,527	(2,466)	34,993	24,092	10,901
54	Mondelez International	MDLZ	6.7%	19,103	5,317	13,787	25,876	5.6%	1.4%	10	36,039	1.4	28,012	10.0%	1.9%	50	70,849	2.5	19,103	(16,897)	36,001	26,591	9,410
55	Lowe's	LOW	11.5%	36,132	6,821	29,310	18,055	8.2%	1.8%	35	34,962	1.9	9,968	39.1%	4.9%	50	69,729	7.0	36,132	(5,413)	41,544	11,432	30,112
56	Accenture	ACN	10.7%	31,553	5,765	25,787	2,887	68.4%	15.6%	20	33,769	11.7	6,134	42.9%	10.4%	50	67,769	11.0	31,553	2,223	29,330	33,586	(4,256)
57	American Express	AXP	0.4%	1,457	12,716	(11,259)	14,406	21.5%	6.6%	35	51,375	3.6	20,673	18.4%	5.9%	50	67,394	3.3	1,457	(3,937)	5,394	7,420	(2,026)
58	Biogen	BIIB	27.4%	50,912	2,379	48,533	6,222	14.3%	13.8%	15	16,128	2.6	9,373	27.9%	22.0%	20	66,968	7.1	50,912	1,455	49,457	25,359	24,098
59	Union Pacific	UNP	3.3%	11,877	10,052	1,826	16,801	16.0%	6.7%	20	45,548	2.7	20,702	18.2%	7.2%	30	66,408	3.2	11,877	(4,631)	16,509	12,621	3,887
60	Abbott Laboratories	ABT	11.1%	32,120	3,706	28,414	22,856	7.2%	2.9%	10	35,463	1.6	21,211	11.8%	3.8%	50	66,137	3.1	32,120	(4,832)	36,953	29,788	7,165
61	Reynolds American	RAI	24.2%	48,995	2,386	46,608	6,498	17.5%	5.1%	20	19,019	2.9	18,252	15.6%	5.9%	30	65,872	3.6	48,995	12,507	36,489	16,444	20,045
62	Lockheed Martin	LMT	19.4%	47,912	4,130	43,782	4,129	44.3%	5.4%	20	24,189	5.9	3,097	86.1%	9.5%	50	65,796	21.2	47,912	4,607	43,305	34,086	9,219
63	Danaher	DHR	4.1%	10,096	6,040	4,055	11,630	6.5%	13.2%	50	30,961	2.7	23,690	7.0%	13.6%	50	63,790	2.7	10,096	(4,745)	14,841	3,264	11,577
64	The Priceline Group	PCLN	16.8%	34,232	4,860	29,371	1,322	51.8%	37.9%	15	19,636	14.9	8,795	22.1%	20.0%	35	63,252	7.2	34,232	2,602	31,629	34,474	(2,845)
65	Morgan Stanley	MS	(8.8%)	(25,001)	12,550	(37,551)	46,688	(1.8%)	6.5%	20	41,142	0.9	75,182	(3.8%)	5.3%	5	61,076	0.8	(25,001)	(14,765)	(10,236)	5,043	(15,279)
66	Express Scripts	ESRX	11.6%	30,048	5,569	24,479	3,552	47.5%	11.5%	20	28,542	8.0	17,373	17.2%	5.4%	50	59,168	3.4	30,048	15,919	14,129	16,524	(2,395)
67	Du Pont	DD	(2.3%)	(7,586)	11,980	(19,565)	7,215	20.2%	19.3%	40	43,466	6.0	9,993	16.8%	17.3%	45	58,032	5.8	(7,586)	(5,044)	(2,541)	9,800	(12,341)
68	ConocoPhillips	COP	(5.6%)	(27,467)	14,492	(41,958)	62,023	2.3%	1.8%	15	74,277	1.2	39,762	2.4%	1.9%	20	57,709	1.5	(27,467)	(34,053)	6,586	6,510	77
69	The Dow Chemical Company	DOW	(1.4%)	(4,343)	13,382	(17,726)	20,555	7.8%	7.4%	30	39,849	1.9	25,374	9.2%	7.8%	35	57,500	2.3	(4,343)	(12,071)	7,728	4,629	3,099
70	Regeneron	REGN	69.6%	50,071	573	49,498	397	16.9%	25.6%	10	2,936	7.4	3,655	28.3%	36.4%	25	56,811	15.5	50,071	1,381	48,690	41,831	6,860
71	Thermo Fisher Scientific	TMO	12.1%	23,285	3,699	19,586	15,431	4.8%	9.2%	10	21,666	1.4	21,350	6.8%	10.5%	50	56,688	2.7	23,285	(7,614)	30,900	25,940	4,959
72	Ford Motor Company	F	(14.8%)	(56,597)	17,505	(74,102)	(7,820)	359.1%	216.9%	5	63,512	-8.1	28,642	12.0%	14.3%	10	55,930	2.0	(56,597)	(40,634)	(15,962)	11,173	(27,135)
73	BlackRock	BLK	11.2%	26,963	6,892	20,070	24,329	0.6%	12.6%	15	25,007	1.0	28,503	5.6%	7.9%	40	55,662	2.0	26,963	(207)	27,169	14,020	13,149
74	Texas Instruments	TXN	4.4%	12,667	5,598	7,070	9,722	21.7%	4.6%	30	37,942	3.9	9,946	26.2%	5.2%	50	55,428	5.6	12,667	(3,465)	16,132	13,203	2,929
75	Metlife	MET	(18.0%)	(47,202)	14,713	(61,915)	33,121	2.4%	12.5%	40	43,811	1.3	67,949	(3.0%)	8.2%	10	52,936	0.8	(47,202)	(18,631)	(28,571)	10,311	(38,883)
76	21st Century Fox	FOXA	4.5%	12,783	9,301	3,482	23,224	5.4%	2.6%	15	33,747	1.5	17,220	17.9%	4.5%	40	52,452	3.0	12,783	(11,662)	24,445	14,405	10,041
77	Salesforce.com	CRM	10.9%	18,362	5,291	13,071	672	22.7%	26.5%	40	17,345	25.8	3,975	9.1%	20.6%	50	52,058	13.1	18,362	(1,100)	19,461	23,322	(3,861)
78	Occidental Petroleum	OXY	(14.3%)	(63,293)	16,879	(80,172)	29,081	6.4%	9.4%	50	76,486	2.6	24,350	2.4%	7.2%	50	51,611	2.1	(63,293)	(25,396)	(37,897)	1,951	(39,848)
79	Time Warner	TWX	7.7%	22,863	8,389	14,473	33,396	0.2%	1.7%	5	33,895	1.0	23,619	10.6%	3.3%	40	51,413	2.2	22,863	(4,257)	27,119	18,290	8,829
80	EMC Corporation	EMC	(5.1%)	(16,662)	10,457	(27,120)	15,550	14.4%	3.8%	50	47,386	3.0	21,140	12.7%	3.5%	40	49,896	2.4	(16,662)	(6,971)	(9,692)	(946)	(8,746)
81	Duke Energy	DUK	13.3%	26,821	2,473	24,348	21,750	1.0%	1.3%	10	23,669	1.1	39,727	1.9%	1.4%	25	49,116	1.2	26,821	18,959	7,862	4,943	2,919
82	Netflix	NFLX	29.2%	33,492	1,809	31,682	199	59.2%	55.3%	15	9,274	46.6	2,223	21.7%	25.4%	25	48,948	22.0	33,492	(538)	34,030	36,323	(2,292)
83	PNC Financial Services	PNC	(0.4%)	(1,012)	7,048	(8,060)	29,942	0.4%	2.2%	50	31,939	1.1	44,710	0.4%	2.2%	50	48,036	1.1	(1,012)	(1,620)	608	96	512
84	Nextera Energy	NEE	9.6%	17,173	2,746	14,426	12,882	5.0%	7.8%	25	21,888	1.7	22,574	5.3%	8.0%	45	47,893	2.1	17,173	713	16,460	10,362	6,098
85	TJX Companies	TJX	17.7%	29,277	2,204	27,073	2,135	44.5%	7.9%	30	17,570	8.2	4,264	50.3%	5.8%	50	47,476	11.1	29,277	2,335	26,942	14,177	12,765
86	Adobe Systems	ADBE	14.2%	22,121	4,258	17,864	4,891	9.5%	15.0%	40	15,448	3.2	7,002	12.6%	17.2%	50	46,764	6.7	22,121	(2,932)	25,053	13,197	11,856
87	McKesson Corporation	MCK	14.4%	23,373	2,637	20,735	6,193	14.8%	5.9%	35	17,877	2.9	8,001	27.1%	8.9%	30	45,166	5.6	23,373	(2,169)	25,541	0	25,541
88	Target	TGT	(3.8%)	(10,862)	7,267	(18,129)	13,712	15.9%	5.1%	40	42,566	3.1	13,997	15.7%	5.0%	50	44,917	3.2	(10,862)	(11,113)	251	3,983	(3,732)
89	Bank of New York Mellon	BK	(4.9%)	(12,245)	7,315	(19,560)	28,977	1.6%	4.7%	50	37,494	1.3	38,037	1.0%	4.4%	50	44,738	1.2	(12,245)	(8,261)	(3,984)	256	(4,240)
90	Charles Schwab	SCHW	3.0%	5,078	5,670	(593)	5,073	10.5%	18.0%	35	20,573	4.1	13,402	6.1%	14.4%	50	43,479	3.2	5,078	(2,405)	7,483	11,259	(3,776)
91	Monsanto	MON	(0.8%)	(2,222)	7,289	(9,511)	10,056	13.8%	7.1%	50	37,359	3.7	6,990	26.2%	10.8%	40	43,375	6.2	(2,222)	(4,152)	1,930	(3,087)	5,017
92	Alexion Pharmaceuticals	ALXN	33.0%	30,941	1,087	29,853	688	17.4%	20.9%	25	7,370	10.7	8,259	11.7%	13.3%	40	43,042	5.2	30,941	5,257	25,684	17,366	8,317
93	General Dynamics	GD	5.2%	11,404	5,826	5,578	12,423	12.0%	3.4%	25	26,401	2.1	10,738	22.1%	4.9%	50	42,992	4.0	11,404	(7,380)	18,784	9,647	9,137
94	Southern Company	SO	2.0%	4,400	2,728	1,672	15,960	6.8%	3.4%	35	32,241	2.0	21,319	5.9%	3.8%	45	42,654	2.0	4,400	(924)	5,324	4,006	1,319
95	Carnival Corporation	CCL	(6.1%)	(15,236)	9,016	(24,252)	22,039	3.8%	5.3%	50	36,427	1.7	23,771	4.6%	5.6%	40	42,059	1.8	(15,236)	(14,478)	(758)	(925)	166
96	FedEx	FDX	(0.5%)	(1,174)	6,466	(7,640)	13,626	6.4%	6.8%	50	29,300	2.2	14,993	10.4%	8.4%	50	41,208	2.7	(1,174)	(7,353)	6,179	1,293	4,886
97	The Kroger Company	KR	19.7%	27,206	1,773	25,432	5,205	15.9%	4.8%	20	14,132	2.7	5,412	29.9%	7.6%	50	40,408	7.5	27,206	62	27,144	18,253	8,891
98	Dominion Resources	D	5.8%	10,752	2,594	8,157	11,442	8.4%	6.3%	25	24,820	2.2	12,664	10.8%	7.3%	40	40,313	3.2	10,752	(4,055)	14,806	10,163	4,643
99	Caterpillar	CAT	(15.0%)	(55,246)	18,251	(73,497)	8,740	40.5%	15.9%	15	59,832	6.8	14,809	12.0%	7.4%	30	39,575	2.7	(55,246)	(16,901)	(38,345)	10,671	(49,016)
100	Automatic Data Processing	ADP	9.7%	16,289	2,960	13,328	5,323	18.3%	5.4%	40	20,064	3.8	4,809	29.5%	7.6%	50	38,861	8.1	16,289	(1,767)	18,056	7,254	10,802

Fig. A3.2 (Continued)

Num	Name	Ticker	Capital Market Outcomes: TSR-Ke (%)	Total WC (£m)	WC from MM (£m)	WC from TSRA (£m)	Bow Wave as at 31 December 2010: Book Equity (£m)	Average EPy (%)	Average Growth (%)	BW Length (years)	Market Value (£m)	M:B Ratio (multiple)
1	HSBC Holdings	HSBA	(7.9%)	(57,552)	(36,792)	(20,760)	96,461	1.9%	6.6%	25	115,155	1.2
2	Royal Dutch Shell	RDSA	(9.3%)	(76,112)	(42,266)	(33,846)	94,935	7.2%	2.6%	5	132,287	1.4
3	Unilever	ULVR	4.0%	16,435	(13,666)	30,101	12,418	28.1%	1.8%	50	55,155	4.4
4	British American Tobacco	BATS	4.5%	16,812	(12,189)	29,001	9,206	38.2%	2.3%	35	49,191	5.3
5	GlaxoSmithKline	GSK	0.1%	452	(13,753)	14,205	8,887	51.1%	5.9%	25	64,434	7.3
6	SABMiller	SAB	4.6%	13,187	(11,422)	24,609	13,106	6.3%	10.6%	50	35,750	2.7
7	BP	BP	(9.4%)	(52,100)	(31,237)	(20,863)	60,924	8.8%	2.9%	5	87,516	1.4
8	Vodafone Group	VOD	1.9%	7,917	(14,655)	22,572	90,381	(4.7%)	0.6%	15	59,145	0.7
9	AstraZeneca	AZN	5.5%	16,969	(8,788)	25,757	14,889	20.2%	4.2%	20	41,171	2.8
10	Lloyds Banking Group	LLOY	(9.2%)	(28,162)	(21,304)	(6,859)	46,061	(0.8%)	1.8%	5	44,778	1.0
11	Diageo	DGE	4.5%	9,785	(6,330)	16,115	4,007	34.3%	16.9%	20	29,658	7.4
12	Reckitt Benckiser Group	RB	7.5%	14,764	(5,338)	20,102	5,058	26.0%	6.8%	30	25,008	4.9
13	BHP Billiton	BLT	(23.1%)	(163,333)	(62,924)	(100,409)	32,430	22.7%	21.2%	50	132,259	4.1
14	BT Group	BT	15.2%	20,616	(4,483)	25,099	(2,650)	143.9%	53.5%	10	14,031	-5.3
15	Prudential	PRU	8.5%	13,463	(8,090)	21,553	8,031	7.7%	13.2%	35	17,005	2.1
16	Barclays	BARC	(9.4%)	(20,418)	(15,165)	(5,253)	50,858	(2.9%)	6.3%	50	31,874	0.6
17	Rio Tinto	RIO	(20.4%)	(98,278)	(38,296)	(59,982)	37,359	13.9%	6.5%	50	88,028	2.4
18	Royal Bank of Scotland	RBS	(14.2%)	(36,139)	(16,911)	(19,228)	75,132	(5.6%)	2.3%	40	42,765	0.6
19	National Grid	NG	6.3%	9,192	(3,482)	12,672	4,199	18.8%	10.5%	30	19,332	4.6
20	Imperial Brands	IMB	8.1%	12,916	(4,273)	17,193	7,029	20.3%	4.3%	15	20,042	2.9
21	Carnival	CCL	(2.5%)	(4,130)	(7,527)	3,397	14,781	4.2%	3.5%	40	23,558	1.6
22	Shire	SHP	17.4%	15,091	(2,772)	17,862	1,572	26.0%	25.2%	15	8,675	5.5
23	Associated British Foods	ABF	15.7%	13,679	(2,317)	15,995	5,293	4.9%	8.2%	25	9,350	1.8
24	RELX Group	REL	11.0%	11,589	(3,039)	14,628	1,943	38.7%	18.9%	15	12,265	6.3
25	Aviva	AV	4.6%	4,322	(4,807)	9,130	13,984	(2.7%)	5.5%	10	11,050	0.8
26	WPP Group	WPP	8.7%	7,767	(3,947)	11,715	6,447	5.6%	8.4%	20	9,982	1.5
27	Compass Group	CPG	6.3%	5,720	(2,885)	8,604	3,068	20.6%	2.9%	35	11,642	3.8
28	Sky	SKY	3.8%	3,564	(2,754)	6,318	560	35.6%	30.5%	30	12,901	23.0
29	Standard Chartered	STAN	(24.4%)	(50,412)	(17,622)	(32,790)	24,509	3.1%	8.3%	50	40,507	1.7
30	Legal & General Group	LGEN	14.7%	8,656	(2,684)	11,340	4,827	3.5%	6.4%	5	5,641	1.2
31	BAE Systems	BA	2.7%	2,412	(3,351)	5,763	5,332	14.3%	10.6%	10	11,837	2.2
32	SSE	SSE	1.1%	853	(2,053)	2,906	3,125	22.7%	9.0%	15	11,400	3.6
33	ARM Holdings	ARM	11.1%	5,781	(2,031)	7,811	895	13.3%	17.9%	40	5,689	6.4
34	International Airline Group	IAG	20.2%	7,157	(1,368)	8,525	2,165	5.2%	15.4%	10	3,144	1.5
35	Tesco	TSCO	(20.4%)	(34,349)	(9,650)	(24,699)	14,596	6.5%	9.5%	50	34,085	2.3
36	ITV	ITV	24.3%	7,844	(1,078)	8,922	661	33.2%	13.3%	15	2,726	4.1
37	Centrica	CNA	(8.9%)	(8,811)	(3,648)	(5,163)	5,819	16.6%	7.4%	20	17,091	2.9
38	Smith & Nephew	SN	4.7%	2,256	(1,375)	3,631	1,779	11.3%	11.6%	40	6,446	3.6
39	Next	NXT	22.2%	8,295	(884)	9,179	134	113.5%	36.7%	15	3,569	26.7
40	Rolls-Royce Holdings	RR	(8.4%)	(6,450)	(4,612)	(1,838)	3,975	10.7%	14.1%	30	11,663	2.9
41	London Stock Exchange	LSE	21.0%	5,219	(811)	6,030	928	9.0%	12.8%	25	2,272	2.4
42	Wolseley	WOS	1.6%	787	(2,486)	3,273	3,059	10.4%	13.0%	15	6,286	2.1
43	Schroders	SDR	2.3%	950	(2,192)	3,142	1,797	10.4%	11.2%	40	5,038	2.8
44	Old Mutual	OML	(3.7%)	(1,978)	(3,629)	1,651	9,711	(3.6%)	5.3%	50	7,011	0.7
45	Capita	CPI	6.5%	2,191	(933)	3,124	496	47.0%	16.5%	15	4,371	8.8
46	Whitbread	WTB	12.0%	3,436	(1,009)	4,446	1,107	10.8%	13.5%	25	3,159	2.9
47	Kingfisher	KGF	(1.3%)	(562)	(1,761)	1,200	4,945	1.9%	1.7%	35	6,221	1.3
48	Marks & Spencer	MKS	(0.5%)	(226)	(1,654)	1,428	2,169	9.9%	8.7%	40	5,841	2.7
49	easyJet	EZJ	19.3%	4,396	(898)	5,294	1,501	6.0%	10.8%	5	2,064	1.4
50	Sage	SGE	7.6%	2,405	(1,211)	3,616	1,649	14.4%	7.3%	15	3,789	2.3

Num	Name	Ticker	Bow Wave as at 31 December 2015: Book Equity (£m)	Average EPy (%)	Average Growth (%)	BW Length (years)	Market Value (£m)	M:B Ratio (multiple)	Results from Pair of Bow Waves: Total WC (£m)	WC Meeting Expect (£m)	WC New Expect (£m)	WC BW Length (£m)	WC Returns / Growth (£m)
1	HSBC Holdings	HSBA	129,318	(1.9%)	4.5%	30	105,551	0.8	(57,552)	(16,655)	(40,897)	(3,307)	(37,590)
2	Royal Dutch Shell	RDSA	110,544	(2.1%)	1.2%	20	97,813	0.9	(76,112)	(46,035)	(30,077)	(3,184)	(26,893)
3	Unilever	ULVR	11,386	47.9%	2.8%	50	83,079	7.3	16,435	(11,639)	28,074	2,329	25,745
4	British American Tobacco	BATS	4,894	86.8%	4.8%	50	70,300	14.4	16,812	(9,522)	26,335	13,025	13,309
5	GlaxoSmithKline	GSK	5,114	70.2%	15.6%	20	66,862	13.1	452	(9,292)	9,744	0	9,744
6	SABMiller	SAB	15,611	11.4%	13.9%	50	65,438	4.2	13,187	(6,219)	19,406	4,394	15,012
7	BP	BP	65,981	(0.1%)	1.6%	0	65,069	1.0	(52,100)	(42,861)	(9,240)	0	(9,240)
8	Vodafone Group	VOD	66,145	(2.5%)	0.9%	10	58,670	0.9	7,917	(6,626)	14,543	0	14,543
9	AstraZeneca	AZN	12,549	22.7%	3.1%	45	58,358	4.7	16,969	(9,609)	26,578	18,593	7,985
10	Lloyds Banking Group	LLOY	46,589	2.0%	2.2%	10	52,233	1.1	(28,162)	(33,280)	5,118	2,174	2,944
11	Diageo	DGE	7,771	18.8%	10.7%	45	46,698	6.0	9,785	(2,469)	12,254	21,907	(9,653)
12	Reckitt Benckiser Group	RB	6,904	28.3%	5.4%	50	44,474	6.4	14,764	(2,164)	16,929	11,863	5,066
13	BHP Billiton	BLT	41,188	(1.9%)	6.4%	10	40,453	1.0	(163,333)	(51,872)	(111,460)	(6,639)	(104,821)
14	BT Group	BT	808	139.7%	59.9%	15	39,464	48.8	20,616	(677)	21,293	21,827	(534)
15	Prudential	PRU	12,955	11.6%	15.7%	30	39,384	3.0	13,463	(1,768)	15,231	0	15,231
16	Barclays	BARC	59,810	(4.3%)	5.4%	30	36,786	0.6	(20,418)	(21,070)	652	2,777	(2,125)
17	Rio Tinto	RIO	25,349	3.2%	3.8%	40	35,803	1.4	(98,278)	(57,701)	(40,577)	(377)	(40,200)
18	Royal Bank of Scotland	RBS	53,431	(5.8%)	2.2%	10	35,108	0.7	(36,139)	(44,684)	8,545	8,111	434
19	National Grid	NG	11,962	10.0%	6.9%	50	35,095	2.9	9,192	2,102	7,089	7,798	(709)
20	Imperial Brands	IMB	5,327	32.7%	6.1%	40	34,326	6.4	12,916	(5,967)	18,883	15,050	3,832
21	Carnival	CCL	15,810	5.8%	4.0%	50	29,846	1.9	(4,130)	(7,867)	3,737	1,720	2,017
22	Shire	SHP	6,671	12.1%	17.7%	35	28,240	4.2	15,091	1,008	14,082	13,496	587
23	Associated British Foods	ABF	6,336	9.6%	11.0%	50	26,458	4.2	13,679	(2,084)	15,763	10,831	4,931
24	RELX Group	REL	2,144	38.6%	18.9%	35	25,040	11.7	11,589	(2,032)	13,621	14,301	(680)
25	Aviva	AV	17,087	1.5%	8.1%	30	20,853	1.2	4,322	(1,986)	6,308	2,185	4,122
26	WPP Group	WPP	7,637	9.5%	10.4%	50	20,778	2.7	7,767	(1,957)	9,724	6,273	3,452
27	Compass Group	CPG	1,937	38.1%	9.4%	45	19,466	10.0	5,720	(2,699)	8,418	4,492	3,926
28	Sky	SKY	3,165	21.7%	13.4%	30	19,115	6.0	3,564	3,739	(176)	2,444	(2,620)
29	Standard Chartered	STAN	32,707	(5.9%)	3.3%	35	18,460	0.6	(50,412)	(13,544)	(36,868)	776	(37,644)
30	Legal & General Group	LGEN	6,404	10.1%	9.1%	50	15,871	2.5	8,656	(592)	9,248	6,777	2,471
31	BAE Systems	BA	2,989	27.1%	9.1%	30	15,813	5.3	2,412	(5,864)	8,276	7,691	584
32	SSE	SSE	6,081	10.2%	7.9%	25	15,338	2.5	853	(1,450)	2,303	3,858	(1,556)
33	ARM Holdings	ARM	1,798	16.2%	20.1%	50	14,675	8.2	5,781	(159)	5,940	4,476	1,463
34	International Airline Group	IAG	3,854	12.9%	22.4%	20	12,365	3.2	7,157	(571)	7,728	4,765	2,963
35	Tesco	TSCO	7,071	5.5%	8.9%	30	12,165	1.7	(34,349)	(15,773)	(18,577)	(1,275)	(17,301)
36	ITV	ITV	1,114	39.9%	15.4%	50	11,134	10.0	7,844	(425)	8,270	6,233	2,037
37	Centrica	CNA	1,178	45.7%	37.7%	10	11,044	9.4	(8,811)	(8,609)	(202)	(4,886)	4,684
38	Smith & Nephew	SN	2,692	11.3%	11.6%	40	10,830	4.0	2,256	(480)	2,736	933	1,803
39	Next	NXT	322	116.3%	37.5%	20	10,806	33.6	8,295	1,278	7,017	4,760	2,258
40	Rolls-Royce Holdings	RR	5,014	7.3%	13.7%	20	10,569	2.1	(6,450)	(2,313)	(4,137)	(1,030)	(3,107)
41	London Stock Exchange	LSE	2,744	9.2%	12.9%	50	9,557	3.5	5,219	(14)	5,233	3,384	1,849
42	Wolseley	WOS	2,600	16.6%	8.4%	40	9,503	3.7	787	(3,133)	3,920	3,510	410
43	Schroders	SDR	2,796	11.8%	11.9%	50	8,407	3.0	950	(399)	1,349	966	383
44	Old Mutual	OML	6,952	1.4%	8.0%	50	8,312	1.2	(1,978)	(5,791)	3,813	49	3,764
45	Capita	CPI	679	44.2%	15.7%	30	8,094	11.9	2,191	(1,375)	3,566	4,266	(700)
46	Whitbread	WTB	1,972	11.2%	13.8%	35	8,030	4.1	3,436	(252)	3,688	2,376	1,312
47	Kingfisher	KGF	6,229	1.3%	1.6%	50	7,639	1.2	(562)	(536)	(26)	226	(252)
48	Marks & Spencer	MKS	3,200	9.4%	7.5%	35	7,426	2.3	(226)	(234)	8	0	8
49	easyJet	EZJ	2,249	11.9%	14.3%	30	6,908	3.1	4,396	40	4,356	3,413	943
50	Sage	SGE	862	26.7%	11.0%	50	6,749	7.8	2,405	(1,701)	4,107	3,849	258

Fig. A3.3 Bow wave summary for the 100 largest LSE listed companies (Sorted by December 2015 market capitalisation)

			Capital Market Outcomes				Bow Wave as at 31 December 2010						Bow Wave as at 31 December 2015						Results from Pair of Bow Waves				
Num	Name	Ticker	TSR-Ke (%)	Total WC (£m)	WC from MM (£m)	WC from TSRA (£m)	Book Equity (£m)	Average EPy (%)	Average Growth (%)	BW Length (years)	Market Value (£m)	M:B Ratio (multiple)	Book Equity (£m)	Average EPy (%)	Average Growth (%)	BW Length (years)	Market Value (£m)	M:B Ratio (multiple)	Total WC (£m)	WC Meeting Expect (£m)	WC New Expect (£m)	WC BW Length (£m)	WC Returns / Growth (£m)
51	Taylor Wimpey	TW	36.4%	5,363	(398)	5,761	1,822	(5.6%)	2.6%	50	1,007	0.6	2,723	9.0%	9.2%	50	6,618	2.4	5,363	759	4,604	183	4,420
52	InterContinental Hotels Group	IHG	5.7%	2,013	(1,649)	3,662	182	81.9%	46.6%	15	4,170	22.9	210	72.5%	33.5%	30	6,592	31.4	2,013	352	1,661	4,252	(2,591)
53	United Utilities Group	UU	6.4%	1,934	(727)	2,661	1,508	12.9%	3.0%	35	4,035	2.7	2,434	11.2%	5.6%	30	6,379	2.6	1,934	418	1,516	0	1,516
54	Bunzl	BNZL	13.7%	3,128	(631)	3,759	796	18.5%	13.6%	15	2,545	3.2	1,016	18.7%	13.7%	50	6,318	6.2	3,128	(657)	3,785	3,589	195
55	Barratt Developments	BDEV	37.7%	4,931	(372)	5,303	2,900	(9.8%)	0.3%	50	856	0.3	3,702	8.4%	3.1%	50	6,274	1.7	4,931	609	4,322	45	4,277
56	Persimmon	PSN	31.2%	5,052	(403)	5,455	1,744	(5.6%)	2.4%	5	1,261	0.7	2,456	9.7%	10.8%	45	6,215	2.5	5,052	1,151	3,901	2,645	1,256
57	Pearson	PSON	(8.4%)	(4,117)	(2,030)	(2,087)	5,538	6.6%	2.3%	10	8,192	1.5	6,414	(1.3%)	1.1%	5	6,043	0.9	(4,117)	(1,934)	(2,183)	0	(2,183)
58	Johnson Matthey	JMAT	(4.6%)	(1,581)	(1,919)	338	1,249	14.4%	14.1%	35	4,853	3.9	1,811	14.2%	14.0%	25	5,765	3.2	(1,581)	(836)	(745)	(548)	(196)
59	Ashtead Group	AHT	34.1%	4,296	(409)	4,706	500	8.6%	3.2%	10	860	1.7	1,112	38.7%	7.7%	30	5,611	5.0	4,296	218	4,078	2,189	1,889
60	GKN	GKN	(2.7%)	(743)	(1,681)	938	1,313	11.8%	14.6%	25	3,534	2.7	1,863	12.8%	15.2%	30	5,323	2.9	(743)	(1,473)	730	743	(13)
61	Burberry Group	BRBY	(6.6%)	(2,187)	(1,935)	(251)	590	22.8%	17.0%	50	4,893	8.3	1,401	15.5%	13.4%	30	5,317	3.8	(2,187)	99	(2,285)	(1,420)	(865)
62	St. James's Place	STJ	24.4%	3,587	(413)	4,000	586	15.9%	6.5%	10	1,292	2.2	1,096	17.6%	6.9%	45	5,289	4.8	3,587	(99)	3,686	2,977	709
63	Severn Trent	SVT	5.4%	1,393	(631)	2,024	941	20.7%	4.2%	30	3,504	3.7	810	24.1%	9.5%	50	5,210	6.4	1,393	(559)	1,953	1,665	288
64	Babcock International Group	BAB	7.9%	1,330	(580)	1,910	81	87.4%	62.9%	10	2,047	25.4	2,180	9.5%	12.2%	20	5,123	2.3	1,330	276	1,055	1,539	(485)
65	Inmarsat	ISAT	5.8%	1,362	(662)	2,024	698	37.6%	0.0%	35	3,102	4.4	848	44.2%	0.0%	50	5,112	6.0	1,362	(916)	2,278	544	1,734
66	Berkeley Group	BKG	27.9%	3,787	(290)	4,077	859	6.3%	4.5%	5	1,168	1.4	1,638	14.0%	6.8%	50	5,040	3.1	3,787	510	3,277	2,377	899
67	DCC	DCC	14.7%	2,483	(566)	3,049	743	15.2%	16.4%	10	1,772	2.4	983	16.3%	17.1%	50	5,006	5.1	2,483	(820)	3,303	2,943	361
68	Sainsbury's	SBRY	(9.7%)	(3,971)	(1,739)	(2,233)	4,966	2.9%	2.3%	35	7,017	1.4	5,539	(2.3%)	1.3%	5	4,978	0.9	(3,971)	(1,154)	(2,817)	167	(2,984)
69	Provident Financial	PFG	28.3%	3,764	(214)	3,978	309	18.3%	9.0%	25	1,186	3.8	708	19.2%	9.3%	50	4,956	7.0	3,764	379	3,385	2,243	1,142
70	Travis Perkins	TPK	2.9%	636	(1,217)	1,853	1,952	3.3%	10.3%	10	2,557	1.3	2,790	3.9%	10.7%	50	4,929	1.8	636	(894)	1,530	1,472	58
71	Admiral Group	ADM	(0.2%)	(70)	(1,008)	938	350	46.0%	8.2%	50	4,069	11.6	616	39.0%	7.1%	40	4,672	7.6	(70)	412	(482)	(275)	(206)
72	Antofagasta	ANTO	(22.7%)	(16,648)	(3,938)	(12,710)	3,958	12.2%	8.4%	50	15,892	4.0	4,511	(0.8%)	3.2%	5	4,627	1.0	(16,648)	(1,992)	(14,656)	(1,991)	(12,665)
73	3i Group	III	(1.3%)	(318)	(1,359)	1,041	3,068	0.3%	6.7%	5	3,124	1.0	3,806	1.5%	7.4%	40	4,606	1.2	(318)	(1,074)	756	568	188
74	Hikma Pharmaceuticals	HIK	16.1%	2,368	(389)	2,757	477	11.7%	15.3%	20	1,570	3.3	907	11.6%	15.2%	50	4,602	5.1	2,368	(108)	2,476	2,412	64
75	Intertek Group	ITRK	3.0%	617	(702)	1,318	459	19.7%	17.0%	25	2,832	6.2	312	19.5%	16.9%	50	4,481	14.4	617	(686)	1,303	2,884	(1,581)
76	RSA Insurance Group	RSA	(8.0%)	(2,117)	(1,085)	(1,033)	3,766	1.8%	7.9%	10	4,377	1.2	3,642	1.4%	7.5%	20	4,338	1.2	(2,117)	(2,360)	243	363	(121)
77	Rexam	REX	(2.6%)	(648)	(1,033)	384	2,322	8.9%	9.1%	5	3,647	1.6	1,405	8.9%	9.1%	50	4,264	3.0	(648)	(2,914)	2,266	2,289	(23)
78	Croda International	CRDA	6.6%	1,173	(624)	1,797	273	24.3%	16.8%	35	2,204	8.1	601	24.7%	17.0%	25	4,135	6.9	1,173	108	1,065	(764)	1,828
79	Informa	INF	0.0%	8	(1,165)	1,173	1,401	7.8%	10.2%	20	2,449	1.7	1,266	15.3%	8.4%	50	3,978	3.1	8	(1,659)	1,667	1,080	587
80	Paddy Power Betfair	PPB	17.1%	2,237	(339)	2,576	196	24.2%	13.2%	35	1,368	7.0	51	138.0%	29.3%	35	3,928	76.9	2,237	(224)	2,461	809	1,652
81	Randgold Resources	RRS	(11.8%)	(3,746)	(1,026)	(2,085)	1,149	12.3%	16.3%	50	4,805	4.2	2,222	1.1%	7.3%	50	3,863	1.7	(3,746)	(486)	(3,260)	80	(3,340)
82	Anglo American	AAL	(39.8%)	(66,408)	(20,852)	(45,556)	21,961	9.2%	6.7%	50	40,285	1.8	11,245	(9.8%)	1.0%	45	3,847	0.3	(66,408)	(40,251)	(26,157)	0	(26,157)
83	Aberdeen Asset Management	ADN	6.6%	377	(919)	2,252	1,171	19.6%	3.1%	5	2,323	2.0	2,158	3.5%	1.5%	50	3,809	1.8	377	152	225	411	(186)
84	DS Smith	SMDS	18.8%	1,807	(381)	2,187	475	10.2%	12.2%	10	875	1.8	1,019	11.2%	12.8%	50	3,747	3.7	1,807	(600)	2,407	1,994	413
85	Smiths Group	SMIN	(9.8%)	(2,852)	(1,377)	(1,475)	1,095	14.2%	9.4%	50	4,865	4.4	1,419	14.0%	9.3%	20	3,710	2.6	(2,852)	(360)	(2,492)	(1,408)	(1,083)
86	Pennon Group	PNN	4.2%	691	(408)	1,099	663	10.4%	8.9%	35	2,267	3.4	1,354	6.9%	7.1%	40	3,549	2.6	691	320	371	420	(49)
87	Henderson Group	HGG	18.6%	2,246	(447)	2,693	354	15.7%	12.1%	30	1,130	3.2	1,037	18.8%	4.5%	50	3,504	3.4	2,246	667	1,579	521	1,058
88	William Hill	WMH	14.2%	1,610	(383)	1,992	843	7.5%	7.9%	5	1,197	1.4	1,216	12.3%	10.0%	30	3,502	2.9	1,610	(557)	2,167	1,609	558
89	G4S	GFS	(6.5%)	(1,413)	(767)	(646)	1,577	10.4%	2.8%	35	3,591	2.3	673	17.5%	8.9%	50	3,499	5.2	(1,413)	(2,276)	863	858	5
90	Bellway	BWY	25.4%	2,386	(259)	2,645	1,035	(4.3%)	4.3%	5	810	0.8	1,576	6.2%	12.2%	30	3,475	2.2	2,386	422	1,965	1,433	531
91	Wm Morrison Supermarkets	MRW	(10.8%)	(4,296)	(1,517)	(2,779)	4,949	5.9%	2.1%	10	7,109	1.4	3,594	(0.7%)	1.1%	5	3,460	1.0	(4,296)	(2,738)	(1,559)	0	(1,559)
92	Cobham	COB	2.6%	465	(665)	1,130	1,076	12.4%	6.5%	15	2,349	2.2	909	15.7%	6.3%	50	3,440	3.8	465	(967)	1,432	1,407	25
93	Inchcape	INCH	8.1%	1,211	(719)	1,929	1,263	5.0%	3.4%	10	1,652	1.3	1,219	16.3%	5.6%	50	3,429	2.8	1,211	(740)	1,951	1,178	773
94	Howden Joinery Group	HWDN	29.3%	2,450	(256)	2,706	23	38.2%	78.8%	15	648	28.0	422	39.0%	10.1%	35	3,384	8.0	2,450	245	2,205	1,561	644
95	ICAP	IAP	(6.9%)	(1,577)	(1,135)	(442)	1,198	17.9%	1.4%	45	3,552	3.0	972	19.8%	4.5%	40	3,317	3.4	(1,577)	(1,440)	(137)	0	(137)
96	Halma	HLMA	12.5%	1,477	(335)	1,812	322	13.7%	11.2%	40	1,352	4.2	549	14.2%	11.5%	45	3,276	6.0	1,477	(12)	1,489	603	886
97	Booker Group	BOK	22.8%	2,132	(193)	2,325	277	14.0%	11.0%	25	905	3.3	598	15.0%	11.5%	40	3,206	5.4	2,132	168	1,965	1,186	778
98	Regus	RGU	21.0%	1,967	(357)	2,324	486	11.4%	10.5%	5	821	1.7	584	17.0%	13.0%	50	3,169	5.4	1,967	(430)	2,397	2,135	262
99	Hiscox	HSX	4.9%	762	(445)	1,206	1,266	5.9%	2.8%	20	2,084	1.6	1,528	5.9%	2.8%	50	3,001	2.0	762	44	718	616	102
100	Investec	INVP	(13.9%)	(3,813)	(2,210)	(1,603)	2,955	3.7%	4.2%	35	4,269	1.4	3,531	(2.3%)	1.6%	30	2,960	0.8	(3,813)	(1,497)	(2,316)	0	(2,316)

Fig. A3.3 (Continued)

Appendix 4: A Holistic Re-Think of Long-Term Incentive Plan Design

While intended to illustrate one potential way to better align executive reward plan design with the goal of building an enduring institution that can create value for customers and wealth for shareholders on an ongoing basis, the potential refinements proposed below could also achieve two further outcomes. They could simplify executive reward plan design; and they could make the entire plan much more transparent, both at the beginning when it is adopted and at the end when its outcome becomes apparent.

The approach described (for the purposes of illustration) would avoid open-ended arrangements by approaching quantum and structure as separate considerations. It would have three distinct components.

- There could be a small STI paid annually and based on performance on a series of non-financial measures.
- There could be a larger medium-term incentive (MTI) based on financial performance achieved in the product and service market over a three-year period. This relates to the left-hand side of the *Pair of EP Bow Waves.*
- There could be an even larger LTI that would be truly long-term in nature that would encourage the building of an enduring institution by focussing on the right-hand side of the *Pair of EP Bow Waves.*

By way of illustration, if this approach were adopted, there could be 11 steps involved in the design process.

D. Kilroy, M. Schneider, *Customer Value, Shareholder Wealth, Community Wellbeing*, DOI 10.1007/978-3-319-54774-9

Step 1. Break the plan design into its two fundamental components of quantum and structure.

Step 2. Declare upfront the maximum quantum payable as base salary, as a STI, as a MTI and as an LTI; having regard to the standards and the expectations of all the company's legitimate stakeholder groups, as well as the wider community.

Step 3. Structure the MTI and the LTI based on performance over a series of rolling three-year periods, with no MTI or LTI payable until the end of the first three-year period. STI awards paid annually would be based entirely on non-financial measures.

Step 4. Make 10–20 percent of the at-risk component of reward payable on STI performance, 15–25 percent on MTI performance and 55–75 percent on LTI performance.

Step 5. Structure the MTI based on the left-hand side of the *Pair of EP Bow Waves* in Fig. 3.4. This could be achieved either by measuring the EP delivered versus the expectations in place at the beginning of the measurement period, or by measuring the wealth created as a consequence of EP performance delivered versus expectations over the measurement period.

Step 6. Structure the LTI based on wealth created as a consequence of establishing new EP expectations during the measurement period, that will be delivered beyond the measurement period; using either *Residual TSR Alpha or Residual TSR-Ke.*

Both measures capture the value consequences of establishing new EP expectations to be delivered beyond the measurement period (i.e. the value consequences associated with the right-hand side of the *Pair of EP Bow Waves* illustrated in Fig. 3.4). *Residual TSR Alpha* strips out the effect of market movements. *Residual TSR-Ke* does not.

Step 7. Make the maximum MTI and LTI payable upon the achievement of excellent performance in each case.

Step 8. Pay MTI awards in cash, commencing at the end of the first three-year period.

Step 9. Issue shares for the cash value of the LTI award, at the volume weighted average share price for either the month or the three months leading up to the end of the relevant measurement period.

Step 10. Permit executives to sell a proportion of the shares awarded within one year of the award being made, to meet the consequential income tax obligations.

Step 11. Hold the remainder of shares issued as part of the LTI award in escrow for a period of up to five years – with shares either being released from escrow at the end of the period, or in equal instalments at the end of each year throughout the period. This would also apply to all awards, including those made towards the end of the executive's tenure at the company, which would mean some shares would remain in escrow after the executive's departure.

When considering quantum, it might be appropriate for a board to set an expectation that the total remuneration of the CEO would be capped at an acceptable multiple of the average income across the group, or the average income across the wider community.

While the wealth creation outcomes experienced by shareholders are determined by *TSR-Ke,* such outcomes include the effect of market movements. It can be relatively easy to achieve a positive *TSR-Ke* outcome in a rising market, but very difficult in a falling market. *TSR Alpha* strips out the effect of market movements, and this is almost certainly fairer for executives. However, the use of *TSR Alpha* can in principle result in an LTI payment for executives when wealth was destroyed for shareholders, because of an unfavourable movement in the market as a whole. This may be unacceptable to some boards. Ultimately, each board would need to make a policy decision about this, and having done so, adopt either *Residual TSR Alpha* or *Residual TSR-Ke* as the LTI performance metric.

Because the maximum quantum has already been defined in each case, neither the MTI or LTI mechanism would produce an open-ended outcome.

The maximum MTI would be payable in the event of a small positive EP increment above expectations over the three-year period (say 105 percent of expectations), with a sliding scale down to a zero in the event of a small negative EP increment below expectations (say 95 percent of expectations).

Assuming the board adopts *Residual TSR Alpha* rather than *Residual TSR-Ke* as the LTI performance metric, the maximum LTI would be payable for an annualised *Residual TSR Alpha* outcome in the order of 10 percent over the three-year period, with a sliding scale down to zero in the event of a *Residual TSR Alpha* outcome of zero. There would be no additional benefit to executives for producing a *Residual TSR Alpha* outcome greater than 10 percent per year.

The boards of some high growth companies may choose to make the maximum LTI payable only in the event of a *Residual TSR Alpha* outcome of 12 or even 15 percent per year. But in general, an outcome of 10 percent per annum constitutes excellent performance.

Issuing shares for the cash value of the LTI award at the end of the measurement period creates an incentive to keep the market value and the intrinsic value of the business in line. If the share price is pumped up by management actions aimed at evoking positive sentiment, less shares would be issued and the executive would be worse off in the longer term. Conversely, if the share price is artificially depressed, management would risk failing to achieve a positive *TSR Alpha* outcome.

Holding the bulk of the shares awarded as the LTI in escrow for up to five years would create an incentive to ensure sound succession planning. Awards made towards the end of the executive's tenure would result in them having a strong economic interest in the performance of the company under the leadership of those whose development they had overseen.

Some boards may choose to hold some or all the shares in escrow for longer – depending upon the situation and the age of the executive.

Appendix 5: Linking Value with Sustainable Returns and Growth

In Chapter 2, we used a perpetuity construct to demonstrate the fundamental relationship that exists between EP and value. A perpetuity construct relies on two simplifying assumptions: a zero-growth assumption; and the assumption that economic profitability remains constant in perpetuity.

In Chapter 3, we introduced the *EP Bow Wave* – a construct that is far more representative of what happens in the real world than a perpetuity construct. With the *EP Bow Wave*, we can express value in terms of expected returns (economic profitability), growth and the sustainability of both.

For many years, until the *EP Bow Wave* emerged, those familiar with the principles of Managing for Value (MFV) tended express value in terms of sustainable returns (economic profitability) and sustainable growth. Effectively this meant relaxing the zero-growth assumption in the perpetuity construct, but maintaining the assumption that economic profitability remains constant in perpetuity. Brian Hartzer referred to this way of thinking in his foreword.

If we take the perpetuity construct used in Chapter 2, and relax just the zero-growth assumption, we find that it is possible to establish a relationship between a company's sustainable economic profitability, the sustainable growth (g) in the equity capital base on which the economically profitable return is earned, and the company's market to book (M:B) ratio. There are two ways to express this relationship. The first is as the PV of an expected cash flow stream. The second is in terms of an expected EP stream.

The cash flow formulation is as follows:

$M = B * (ROE - g)/(Ke - g)$, *or* $M{:}B = (ROE - g)/(Ke - g)$;

where M refers to market value and B refers to book value.

D. Kilroy, M. Schneider, *Customer Value, Shareholder Wealth, Community Wellbeing*, DOI 10.1007/978-3-319-54774-9

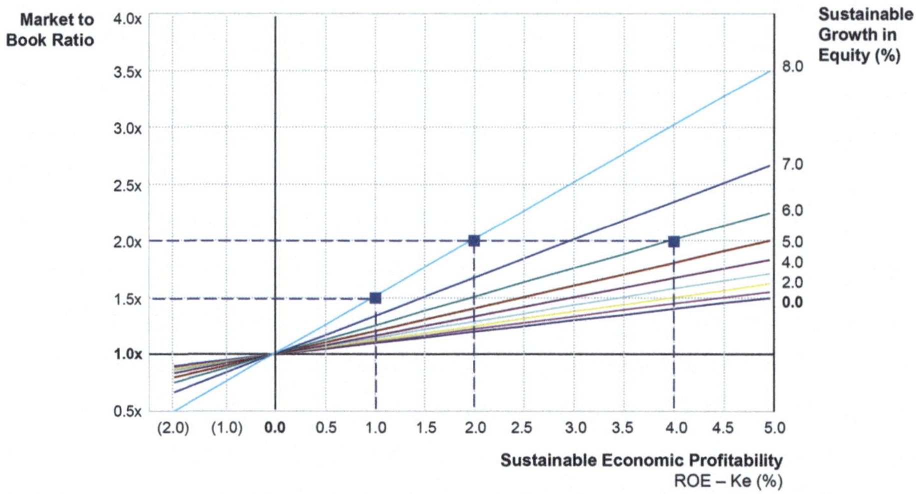

Fig. A5.1 Linking M:B Ratio with Economic Profitability and Growth

It can also be expressed as:

*M = B * [1 + (ROE – Ke)/(Ke – g), or M:B = 1 + (ROE – Ke)/(Ke – g); where M refers to market value and B refers to book value.*

Although a derivation of both relationships is provided later, it is not necessary to understand these derivations in order to make use of the principles. What is important, is to understand that M:B is a function of sustainable economic profitability (ROE - Ke) and sustainable growth (g).

Fig. A5.1 illustrates these relationships by plotting M:B on the Y-axis against sustainable economic profitability (or ROE-Ke) on the X-axis. The coloured lines passing through the origin represent lines of constant growth in the capital base.

An important observation from Fig. A5.1 is that different combinations of economic profitability and growth can deliver the same M:B ratio and therefore the same intrinsic and ultimately market value outcomes. Another is that when economic profitability is zero, the M:B ratio is 1.0x irrespective of the growth rate that can be sustained.

The points denoted by the blue markers in Fig. A5.1 illustrate that with a sustainable economic profitability of 1.0 percent and a sustainable growth rate of 8.0 percent, the M:B ratio is 1.5x. If the sustainable economic profitability is increased to 2.0 percent at the same growth rate, the M:B ratio becomes 2.0x. If the sustainable growth rate drops to 6.0 percent, sustainable economic profitability needs to increase to 4.0 percent to achieve a M:B ratio of 2.0x.

Clearly there is a trade-off between returns and growth, the nature of which varies depending upon the level of economic profitability. For example, in high return businesses, it will typically be more value creating to pursue higher growth than to seek to enhance returns. The opposite applies in the case of a low return business.

To illustrate this point, consider a business with a sustainable economic profitability of 4.0 percent and a sustainable growth rate of 6.0 percent. If sustainable growth can be increased to 8.0 percent, the M:B ratio will increase from 2.0x to 3.0x and market value will increase by 50 percent.

In contrast, for a lower return business with a sustainable economic profitability of 2.0 percent and a sustainable growth rate of 6.0 percent, increasing growth from 6.0 to 8.0 percent will only increase the M:B ratio from 1.5x to 2.0x, which represents an increase in market value of 33 percent.

While the construct presented in Fig. A5.1 is closer to reality than the perpetuity framework used for demonstration purposes in Chapter 2, it is still some distance from what happens in the real world. The *EP Bow Wave* provides a more complete approach.

Derivation of Perpetuity Formulae

The purpose of this section is provide the mathematical derivation of the two forms of the M:B formulae shown above.

Starting from the Discounted Cash Flow Model

The intrinsic value of a business under a given strategy is equal to the present value (PV) of future cash flows to be delivered under the current strategy. This notion is commonly referred to as the discounted cash flow (DCF) model. Having determined the appropriate cost of equity (Ke), the DCF model is expressed as the sum of a series of cash flows discounted to the present value as follows:

$$MarketValue = CF_1/(1+Ke)^1 + CF_2/(1+Ke)^2 + CF_3/(1+Ke)^3 + \ldots\ldots$$

In this formulation of the DCF model, the numerator of the terms [CF_1, CF_2, CF_3 and so on] represents the cash flows to be delivered in year 1, 2, 3, and so on, into perpetuity. The denominator of the terms [$(1+Ke)^1$, $(1+Ke)^2$, $(1+Ke)^3$ and so on] represents the mechanism of discounting those cash flows to the present day to reflect the present value of those cash flows.

When assessing the market value of equity, the cash flows that are required to be discounted are equity cash flows (ECF). Equity cash flows are primarily made available to shareholders in the form of dividends and other capital distributions (such as though share buy-backs).

However, at times, a company may raise additional equity capital (such as through the issue of new shares), and such capital raisings represent a form of negative equity cash flow.

With this in mind, equity cash flow can be defined as:

$$ECF = Dividends + Capital\ Distributions - Share\ Issues$$

With a proper flow-through achieved between the income statement (P&L) and balance sheet, such equity cash flows can also be defined as:

$$ECF = PAT - \Delta\ Book\ Equity$$

Simplification of a Geometric Series

When making the simplifying assumption of constant growth in the equity cash flow stream, the discounted cash flow model of value (being an infinite sum of terms whose values are derived from a single point) is known as a geometric series. The sum of a series of this nature can be expressed as:

$$MarketValue = ECF_1/(Ke - g)$$

Derivation of the M:B = (ROE – g) / (Ke – g) Formula

Starting from the simplified formula, and substituting the P&L and balance sheet calculation of equity cash flows, we get:

$$MarketValue = (PAT - \Delta Book\ Equity)/(Ke - g)$$

Dividing throughout by the opening value of Book Equity (B), and recognising that growth in PAT and growth in B are the same when ROE is constant, we get:

$$M : B = (ROE - g)/(Ke - g)\ noting\ that\ ROE = PAT/B\ and\ g = \Delta B/B$$

This relationship can also be expressed as:

$$M = B \times [(ROE - g)/(Ke - g)]$$

Derivation of the M:B = 1 + (ROE-Ke) /(Ke-g) Formula

We know that:

$$EP = B \times (ROE - Ke)$$

We also know from the previous derivation that:

$$M = B \times [(ROE - g)/(Ke - g)]$$

If we insert 0 = Ke – Ke, we can rearrange the previous result to give:

$$M = B \times [(ROE - (Ke - Ke) - g)/(Ke - g)]$$

$$M = B \times [((ROE - Ke) + (Ke - g))/(Ke - g)]$$

$$M = B \times (ROE - Ke)/(Ke - g) + Bx(Ke - g)/(Ke - g)$$

$$M : B = (ROE - Ke)/(Ke - g) + (Ke - g)/(Ke - g)$$

$$M : B = 1 + (ROE - Ke)/(Ke - g)$$

Glossary of Terms

Term		Description
Beta	β	A measure of relative risk of a company compared with the market as a whole. It is an important input parameter in the capital asset pricing model used to calculate the cost of equity capital (Ke)
Capital Asset Pricing Model	CAPM	A fundamental principle of corporate finance that defines the means with which to calculate the risk-adjusted cost of equity capital (Ke). The inputs to the CAPM are the risk free rate of return (Rf), beta (β) and the equity risk premium (ERP)
Choice Modelling		A statistical technique used in market research and elsewhere that attempts to model the decision process of an individual or segment in a particular context. It can be used to obtain similar information to conjoint analysis.
Conjoint Analysis		A statistical technique used in market research to determine how people value different features that make up an individual product or service. It is used to measure preferences for product features, to learn how changes to price affect demand for products or service, and to forecast the likely acceptance of a product if brought to market
Company-specific Sentiment		The extent to which the market capitalisation of a company differs from its underlying intrinsic value by virtue of investor attitudes specific to the company at a specific point in time

(*continued*)

D. Kilroy, M. Schneider, *Customer Value, Shareholder Wealth, Community Wellbeing*, DOI 10.1007/978-3-319-54774-9

(continued)

Term		Description
Cost of Equity Capital	Ke	The minimum return on equity capital required by shareholders in order to preserve the value of their investment. It is calculated using the capital asset pricing model such that Ke = Rf + ⊠ x ERP
Customer Value – Real or Authentic		Value derived from a product or service, the consumption or use of which enhances the long-term wellbeing of customers and /or end consumers
Customer Value – Artificial		Value derived from a product or service by satisfying a desire (which may have been created through a clever marketing campaign) with no thought given to the long-term wellbeing of the customer or end consumer
Earnings Before Interest and Tax	EBIT	An accounting measure representing the pre-tax profit available to the providers of both debt and equity capital
Earnings per Share	EPS	An accounting measure representing the after-tax profit (PAT) available to the providers of equity capital (shareholders) divided by the weighted average number of shares on issue over the measurement period
Economic Profit	EP	An economic metric representing the after-tax profit available to the providers of capital after subtracting a charge for capital commensurate with their opportunity cost of capital. It is also equivalent to economic profitability (EPy) multiplied by opening equity capital. The benchmark level of EP is zero, which when achieved, preserves the book value of capital
Economic Profitability	EPy	An economic measure representing the percentage by which the return on equity (ROE) exceeds the cost of equity capital (Ke). It is also equivalent to economic profit (EP) divided by opening equity capital and can be considered the economic return on the book value of capital
Equity Risk Premium	ERP	The excess return achieved in the equity market over and above the return achieved on a risk free asset (Rm-Rf). Over the long run (> 20 years), this has been and is expected to remain approximately six percent, but can vary significantly over shorter periods
Growth	g	When applied to economic metrics, growth specifically refers to the growth in the equity capital base upon which returns are earned over a specific measurement period

(continued)

Term		Description
Intrinsic Value		The theoretical value of a company under a particular strategy based on the present value of expected future cash flows or the sum of book equity and the present value of expected future economic profits (EP)
Intrinsic Value Uplift		The change in intrinsic value over a specified measurement period. It can be calculated from an internal perspective as the present value (PV) of the expected increase in either economic profit (EP) or cash flow, or from an external perspective using TSR Alpha
Managing for Value	MFV	A management philosophy as well as a structured and replicable process by which a management team can systematically enhance the value of the business or businesses for which it is responsible. Also referred to as VBM.
Market Capitalisation		The stock market's view of the value of the shareholders' equity in a company under a given strategy (and equal to share price multiplied by shares on issue). It may be higher or lower than intrinsic value depending upon the existence and nature of either positive or negative sentiment
Market Return	Rm	The return achieved by investors across the equities market as a whole. In Australia, this is the compound annual growth rate of the All Ordinaries Accumulation Index
Market Sentiment		The extent to which the market capitalisation of a company differs from its underlying intrinsic value by virtue of investor attitudes to the equity market as a whole at a specific point in time. It can also be thought of as the extent to which overall investor attitudes push the total shareholder return (TSR) achieved in the market as a whole above or below the long-run expectations embedded in the equity risk premium (ERP)
Market to Book Ratio	M:B	The ratio of the market value of equity capital to the underlying book value of equity capital. It is also a measure of the extent to which a management team has succeeded in putting in place a strategy capable of delivering and sustaining a positive economic profit (EP) stream. The M:B ratio has a benchmark of 1x which occurs when EP is expected to be zero in the future

(*continued*)

(continued)

Term		Description
Present Value	PV	The process of converting a monetary amount or a monetary stream into a single value today – taking into account the time value of money. The time value of money reflects the fact that a dollar received in the future time is worth less than a dollar received today
Profit after Tax	PAT	An accounting measure that represents the after-tax profit available to the providers of equity capital (shareholders)
Relative TSR	rTSR	The total shareholder returns of a company over a specified period measured relative to those of either a defined peer group or an index. It is currently used widely for vesting purposes in long-term incentive plans
Residual TSR-Ke		The wealth creation associated with the right hand side of the *Pair of EP Bow Waves* – expressed as a percentage on an annualised basis. The right hand side of the *Pair of EP Bow Waves* relates to the value consequences of establishing new EP expectations to be delivered beyond the measurement period.
Residual TSR Alpha		The wealth creation associated with the right hand side of the *Pair of EP Bow Waves* after adjusting for movements in the market as a whole – and expressed on an annualised basis. It is calculated by subtracting from *TSR Alpha*, the value consequences of meeting or exceeding EP expectations over a specified measurement period, and expressing the result on an annualised basis.
Return on Equity	ROE	Profit after tax (PAT) divided by the equity capital employed at the beginning of the measurement period
Risk Free Rate	Rf	The return required on an investment in a risk free asset. Rf is typically measured using the yield on Australian Government (treasury) bonds. The term structure of the investment will dictate whether it is appropriate to adopt a 10-year, 5-year or 1-year risk free rate
Shareholders' Equity		The value of the shareholders' investment in the company. The book value of shareholders' equity is that component of the capital invested in the company that is owned by shareholders. It is also referred to as equity capital. The market value of

(continued)

Term		Description
		shareholders' equity is the market value of that capital – or market capitalisation
Total Shareholder Return	TSR	A market-based metric that captures the return derived by shareholders in the form of dividends plus share price appreciation. It is defined as dividends plus change in share price over a given measurement period, divided by the share price at the beginning of the period
TSR Alpha		An economic metric representing the extent to which the total shareholder return delivered (TSR) over a particular measurement period exceeds that required by shareholders in order to match market performance after adjusting for company-specific risk. Whereas economic profitability (EPy) is the economic return on the book value of capital, TSR Alpha™ is the economic return on the market value of capital over the short to medium term. TSR-Ke is the economic return on market value over the long term.
TSR Required	TSRr	The total shareholder return (TSR) required by investors in order to match market performance after adjusting for company-specific risk.
Value Based Management	VBM	A management philosophy as well as a structured and replicable process by which a management team can systematically enhance the value of the business or businesses for which it is responsible. Also referred to as MFV.
Wealth Creation		In the absence of any material movements in either market or company-specific sentiment, wealth creation occurs for shareholders when management action causes an uplift in intrinsic value. It can also be considered the value uplift arising from delivery of a TSR greater than Ke

Index

A
Airline industry, 172
ANZ Banking Group (listed on ASX), xii, 55–56, 59
Artificial customer value, *see* Real and artificial customer value
Aspen Institute (USA), xxi
ASX (Australian Securities Exchange), xxi, xxii, 45, 63–68
  ANZ Banking Group, xii, 55–56, 59
  Bank of Queensland, 55–56, 59
  Bendigo and Adelaide Bank, 55–56, 59
  Brambles Limited, 112–114, 115
  cloud technology company, 118
  Commonwealth Bank of Australia, 55–60
  National Australia Bank, 55–56, 59
  Ramsay Health Care, 116–117
  Sonic Healthcare Limited, 209–212
  Wesfarmers Limited, 111–112
  Westpac Banking Corporation, ix, x, xii, 55–56, 59
  Woolworths Limited, 118–119
Authentic and inauthentic customer value, xxv, xxxviii, 103, 185, 228

B
Bank of America (listed on NYSE), 55–56, 59
Bank of New York Mellon (listed on NYSE), 55–56, 59
Bank of Queensland (listed on ASX), 55–56, 59
Banks and shareholder wealth creation, 55–57
Barclays Bank (listed on LSE), xii, 55–56, 57, 59
Bendigo and Adelaide Bank (listed on ASX), 56–57, 59
Benefit corporations, 103, 234
BlackRock (Investment management company), 29
Book value of a listed company, 7
Boulos, Fares, 13, 15
Bow Wave of Expected Economic Profits, xi, xiii, xviii, 45, 71
  aligning internal and external wealth creation perspectives, 63
  change of shape in, 69
  continually producing a positive TSR Alpha, 60–62
  economic performance in three exchanges, 63–68

D. Kilroy, M. Schneider, *Customer Value, Shareholder Wealth, Community Wellbeing*, DOI 10.1007/978-3-319-54774-9

Bow Wave of Expected Economic Profits (*cont.*)
managing the link between product and capital markets, 47–52
measuring wealth creation, external perspective, 58–59
measuring wealth creation, internal perspective, 52–58
Brambles Limited (listed on ASX), 112–114
Building an enduring institution, xxvi, 68, 108, 193–222, 235, 240, 261
characteristics of an enduring institution, 225–226
ensuring the right executive reward plan design, 203–221, 222
establishing the right business processes, 197–201, 221
establishing the right capabilities, 196–197, 221
establishing the right performance measures, 201–203, 222
establishing the right understanding, 193–196, 221 (*see also* Executive rewards; Performance measurement of listed companies)
Building products manufacturing (Australia), 165–166, 167–168, 173
Building products (USA), 148
Business paradigm
shareholder primacy, xix, xxiv, xxv, xxxv, 3
socially responsible, xxxvi, 231–235
Business Prosperity, Social Equity, Environmental Sustainability - A Roadmap for Policymakers and Regulators (Denis Kilroy and Marvin Schneider), forthcoming, 237–240

C
Capital intensive manufacturing business, 136–137, 140
Capital market outcomes, xvii, xxii, xxix, xl, 7, 23, 24, 29, 30, 32, 44, 45, 58, 68, 71, 100, 194, 203, 205–208, 210, 212, 220, 228, 231, *see* Performance measurement of listed companies
Cash flow return on investment (CFROI) [HOLT Value Associates], 9–10
Cass Business School (Modern Corporation Project), xvi, xxi, xxiv
The CEO, Strategy and Shareholder Value (Peter Kontes), 24
The Chief Shows Them How at Indian Head (article), 5
Citigroup (listed on NYSE), 55–56, 59
Cloud technology company (listed on ASX), 118
Coalition for Inclusive Capitalism, 235
Commonwealth Bank of Australia (listed on ASX), 55–60
Conscious Capitalism movement, xxi, xxiii, 17, 182, 234–235
Core ideas summary, xxxv–xxxviii
Corporate governance, xv, xvi, xvii, xxiv
governing corporate objective, xvi, xix, 4, 5, 6, 16, 180, 189, 234
Corporate Governance for a Changing World (Filip Gregor et al), xv
Corporate Governance for a Changing World: Report of a Global Roundtable Series, xvi, xxiv
Creating Sustainable Companies Summit, xxiv
Creative thinking and value creation mindset, *see* Mindset of creative thinking and value creation

Current strategy valuation for a business, 90, 105, 106, 109–110, 118, 120–121, 124, 132, 134, 137–139, 141
completing the current strategy valuation, 120–140
five process steps, 109
identifying opportunities for immediate value uplift, 134–140
understanding embedded expectations, 109–121
Customer segmentation
and current strategy valuation, 141
and hybrid thinking, 144, 176
needs-based, 75–77, 144, 176
Customer value and shareholder wealth creation, xvi, xxv, xxxviii, 3–20
on an ongoing basis, xvii, xviii, xx, xxv, xxxvi, 14–16, 17–18, 81–95, 235
authentic and inauthentic customer value, xxv, xxvi, xxxiv, 103, 185, 229
creative thinking and value creation mindset in order to succeed, 81–95
customer segmentation, 75–77, 144, 176
linking customer value and shareholder wealth, xxiv, 74–75
mutually reinforcing objectives, 71–79
real and artificial customer value, xvi, xxv, xxvi, xxxiv, 103, 185, 186, 188, 195, 226
role of innovation, 77–78
shareholder wealth creation, 52–59, 64
See also Organisational response to creating value for customers and wealth for shareholders on an ongoing basis

D

Drucker, Peter, xviii

E

Economic performance measures, *see* Performance measurement of listed companies
Economic profitability
analysis, 125–131
definition, 9
investing in economically profitable segments, 135–138
See also Bow Wave of Expected Economic Profits; Performance measurement of listed companies
Economic Profit Bow Wave, *see* Bow Wave of Expected Economic Profits
Economic profit definition, 9
Economic rationalism, xx, xxiv, 158
Economic value added (EVA) [Stern Stewart & Co], 9, 11–12
Electricity distribution infrastructure (Australia), 156–159
Electricity retailing (Australia), 163–165
Electricity supply (Australia), 145–147
End consumers, 144–152, 176, 185–188, 196
Enduring institution, *see* Building an enduring institution
Environmental, social and governance (ESG) responsibilities, 16–17
Environmental sustainability and societal wellbeing, xvi, xxii, 6, 222
See also Stakeholder wellbeing
EPS (earnings per share) myth, xxiii, 24–31, 32, 43, 45, 69, 241–244
EP Uplift + TSR Alpha Construct, 62, 63, 69
ESG (environmental, social and governance) movement, 16–17

EVA Bonus Bank, 10
Executive incentive plans, *see* Executive rewards
Executive rewards, xxii, xxiv, xxvi, 13, 105, 107, 183, 193, 199, 204, 205, 206, 207, 209, 212, 216, 219, 220, 228, 233, 261
  plans, 13, 30, 183, 193, 197–200, 203–220, 228, 261–264
  rethink of, xxi, xxii

F

Financial planning (Australia), 149
Fink, Larry, 29
Fire protection business, 132–133, 135–136, 139–140
Firms of Endearment (Raj Sisodia et al), xxi, 193
First Manhattan Consulting Group, xi
Fortune magazine, 5
Frank Bold Lawyers, xiv, xv, xxi
Freeman, R Edward, 4

G

Getting Started with Conjoint Analysis - Strategies for Product Design and Pricing Research (Brian Orme), 169
Global Financial Crisis (GFC), xii, xiii, xviii, xix, xx, 30
Glossary, 269–274
Governing corporate objective, 4, 16
Gregor, Filip, xv

H

Hartzer, Brian, ix
Harvard Business Review, 4
Haspeslagh, Philippe, 13, 15
Heskett, James, xii
Hester, Stephen, xii
Higher value strategies for a business, 72–74, 79
  alternative strategy development, 170–173
  applying disciplined innovation, 160–162
  backing new ideas with analysis as a proving mechanism, 159–160
  bias towards value pricing, 154–159
  building management commitment, 175–176
  focus on end consumer needs, 145–152
  four aspects to value creation mindset, 144, 176–177
  possibility thinking, 162–166
  preparedness to build value creating networks, 151–154
  valuation and strategy selection, 174–175
  value proposition development, 167–168
HOLT Value Associates, 9
Home Depot Inc (listed on NYSE), 116–117
HSBC Bank (listed on LSE), 55, 57, 59
Hybrid thinking, xxxvii, 88–93, 95, 195
  applying hybrid thinking, 106, 144, 151, 154, 159–162, 175, 176
  and strategy development process, 175
  and value proposition enhancement, 171–172

I

Inauthentic customer value, *see* Authentic and inauthentic customer value
Incentive plans, *see* Executive rewards
Inclusive capitalism, xxi

Indian Head Mills (US textiles company), 5
Innovation
  disciplined innovation, 83–88, 160–161, 176, 195
  role of, 77–78
INSEAD (Business School), 13, 15
Intrinsic value of a listed company, 7–8, 35–38, 43

J

Jensen's Alpha, 58
Jones, Thomas, xii
Joss, Bob, xii
Journal of Business Ethics, 5
JPMorgan Chase (listed on NYSE), 55–56, 59

K

Kelly, Gail, xii
Kontes, Peter, 13, 14, 24, 27, 28

L

The Legacy of Good Leadership (Denis Kilroy and Marvin Schneider), x, xxi
Levitt, Theodore, 4
Listed companies
  book value, 7
  economic performance, 43, 249–259
  intrinsic value, 7–8, 35–39, 43
  market value, 7
  See also Performance measurement of listed companies; Products and services; Shareholder capital
Lloyd's Bank (listed on LSE), xi, 4, 55, 57, 59
Loveman, Gary, xii
LSE (London Stock Exchange), xxii, 45, 59, 60, 61, 63–66
  Barclays Bank, xi, 55, 57, 59
  HSBC Holdings, 55, 57, 59
  Lloyds Banking Group, xi, 4, 55, 57, 59
  Rolls Royce Plc, 118–119
  Royal Bank of Scotland, xii, 55, 57, 59
  Standard Chartered, 55, 57, 59
  Unilever Plc, 114–118

M

Mackey, John, xxiii
Management commitment, 107, 161, 174–175, 202, 221
Managing for value (MFV), 3–16
  on an ongoing basis, 14–16
  governing objective debate, 4–7
  metric-based economic engine approach, 8–12
  needs-based customer segmentation, 75–77, 144, 176
  plan-based approach, 12–14
  three perspectives on value, 7–8
Mankins, Michael, 13, 14
Marakon Associates, 13, 24
Market segmentation, 121–125
Market sentiment, 115–120
Market value of a listed company, 7
McFarlane, John, xii
McTaggart, James, 13, 14
MFV, *see* Managing for value (MFV)
Mindset of creative thinking and value creation, 81–95
  avoiding a cost reduction mindset, 82–83
  disciplined innovation
    and the creative process, 83–88, 160–162
  establishing a mindset for success, 94
  hybrid thinking, 88–95

Modern Corporation Project (Cass Business School), xvi, xxi, xxiv, 235
Morgan, David, xii
Motor vehicle industry, 172

N

National Australia Bank (listed on ASX), 55, 59
Noble Intent, Clear Purpose, Better Leader - A Roadmap for Company Directors and Senior Executives (Denis Kilroy and Marvin Schneider), forthcoming, 235–237
Noda, Tomo, 13, 15
NYSE (New York Stock Exchange), xxii, 45, 63–66
  Bank of America, 55, 59
  Bank of New York Mellon, 55, 59
  Citigroup, 55, 59
  Home Depot Inc, 116–117
  JPMorgan Chase, 55, 59
  Oracle Inc, 118–119
  PNC Financial Services, 55, 59
  U.S. Bancorp, 55, 59
  Wells Fargo, 55–56, 59

O

Oracle Inc (listed on NYSE), 118–119
Organisational response to creating value for customers and wealth for shareholders on an ongoing basis, xviii, xx, xxvi, 81, 176, 189
  establishing necessary mindset, 100–104
  establishing necessary skillset, 104–108
  six steps to the journey, 99–100
Orme, Brian, 169

P

Packaging industry, 150–151
Pair of Intersecting EP Bow Waves, 56–57, 69, 71
Payments to suppliers, 11
Performance measurement of listed companies, xxii, 23, 32, 212, 233
  applying truths to a hypothetical situation, 39–42
  economic performance measures, 8–12, 45, 249–259
  EPS myth, xxiii, 24–30, 241–244
  fundamental truth, 23–24
  linking intrinsic value to expected economic profit, 35–37
  linking intrinsic value uplift to change in expected EP, 37–38
  linking product and capital market performance, xxiii, 32–33, 47–52
  management compared with investors, 45, 69
  shareholders and high dividend yields, 30–32
  success in the market for products and services, 33–34, 42
  success in the market for shareholder capital, 35, 43
  summarising the truths, 43–44
  total shareholder return (TSR), 22, 71–72
Pittman, Brian, xi, 4
PNC Financial Services (listed on NYSE), 55, 59
Products and services, xvii, xx, xxii, xxix, xl, 7, 23, 24, 29, 30, 32, 33, 35, 38, 40, 43, 44, 45, 47, 50, 54, 68, 71, 74, 75, 76, 82, 100, 101, 103, 122, 124, 146, 149, 168, 184, 185, 187, 194, 198, 201, 209, 211, 212, 220, 226, 231, 239, 251

performance measurement in market for, 44, 69
primary factors in market for, 75
relationship between market for products and services and capital market outcomes, xxii, xxxvi, 23, 24, 29, 30, 32–33, 40, 47–52
success in the market for, 33–34, 43
true costs associated with, 23
Purpose of the Corporation Project (Frank Bold Lawyers), xv, xvi, xxi, xxiv, 235

R

Ramsay Health Care (listed on ASX), 116–117
Real and artificial customer value, xvii, xxv, xxxviii, 103, 185, 188, 196, 226
Remuneration, executive, *see* Executive rewards
Restoring Customer Faith initiative, xii
Rolls Royce Plc (listed on LSE), 118–119
Royal Bank of Scotland (listed on LSE), xi, 55, 57, 59

S

Service-Profit Chain concept, xii
Shared Value movement, xxi, 17, 152, 234
Shareholder capital, 23, 32, 35, 43, 74–75, 194, 211
market for, 75
Shareholder primacy paradigm, xix, xxiii, xxiv, xxv, xxxv, 3
The Shareholder Value Myth (Lynn Stout), xxi, xxiii
Shareholder wealth and customer value creation, *see* Customer value and shareholder wealth creation
Short-termism, xvi, xvii, xxii, 30, 45, 67–68, 227–229
Sisodia, Raj, xxiii, 17, 193
Smith, Adam, xvii
Social and environmental costs of business, xx
Socially responsible business paradigm, xxi, xxxviii
encouraging more socially responsible business behaviour, 234–239
why hasn't more progress been made, 231–234
Sonic Healthcare Limited (listed on ASX), 209–212, 219
Stakeholder wellbeing, 179–192, 193
elements of a new business paradigm, 189–192
explicit focus on societal wellbeing, 182–188
shift in thinking, 180–182
Standard Chartered Bank (listed on LSE), 55, 57, 59
Steel industry (Australia), 151
Stern Stewart & Co, 9
Stout, Lynn, xxiii
Strategy valuation for a business, *see* Current strategy valuation for a business
Sustainable returns and growth, 265–269

T

Total shareholder return (TSR), 22, 71–72
Triple bottom line, 234
TSR Alpha, 58, 60–62, 71, 245–247

U

Unilever Plc (listed on LSE), 114–115, 116–118
University of Oslo, Faculty of Law, xxi
Unsustainable Dividend Yield Chasers, 31
U.S. Bancorp (listed on NYSE), 55, 59

V

Value, *see* Customer value and shareholder wealth creation; Managing for value
  Value creation and creative thinking mindset, *see* Mindset of creative thinking and value creation
The Value Imperative (McTaggart, Kontes and Mankins), 13
Value pricing, 154–159
Value strategies for a business, *see* Higher value strategies for a business
VBM (value-based management), 7

W

Wall St (USA), 27
Wealth creation, *see* Customer value and shareholder wealth creation
Wellbeing
  community wellbeing, xxxvii–xxxviii
  environmental sustainability and societal wellbeing, xvi, xxiv, 6, 222
  See also Stakeholder wellbeing
Wells Fargo Bank (listed on NYSE), 55–56, 59
Wesfarmers Limited (listed on ASX), 111–112
Westpac Banking Corporation (listed on ASX), ix, x, xii, 55–57, 59
Wine producer, 137–138
Woolworths Limited (listed on ASX), 118–119

Y

Yale School of Management, 28

The manufacturer's authorised representative in the EU is Springer
Nature Customer Service Centre GmbH, Europaplatz 3, 69115 Heidelberg,
Germany. If you have any concerns regarding our products, please
contact ProductSafety@springernature.com

Printed and bound by CPI Group (UK) Ltd, Croydon, CR0 4YY
27/04/2026
02097560-0008